Rick Steves' ®

IRELAND
2006

Rick Steves & Pat O'Connor

LEGEND

==M4== Freeway/Motorway		**Dingle**	Recommended location*
—— Major Rail Line		Sligo	Just passing through**
✈ Airport		▪	Ruin, Museum, other Point of Interest
🌲 National Park or Natural Wonder		♜	Castle/Monument/Palace
Gaeltacht Regions			

* Black locations are places of interest to tourists, sized by importance. Many are covered in this guidebook.

** Gray locations are places of little or no interest to tourists and are sized by population.

0 km   50 kilometers

0 miles   50 miles

Bun B

Dunglo

Don

MAYO

N59

Drumcliff ▪

Sligo

Lough Gill

Achill Island

Ballina

N17

N5

Clare Island

Carrick-on-Shannon

Westport

Croagh Patrick

Knock

Strokestown •

Leenane

Kylemore Abbey ♜

Clifden

CONNEMARA

Cong

N17

Long

Ashford Castle ♜

Lough Corrib

Roscommon •

L

N59

N84

Rossaveel •

Salthill •

Galway

N6

Athlone

Dún Aenghus ▪

Kilronan

Dunguaire

River Shan

Aran Islands

Ballyvaughan

Kinvarra

Doolin •

THE BURREN

CLIFFS OF MOHER

Lisdoonvarna

IRE

Lahinch

N18

Lough Derg

Kilkee •

CLARE

Ennis

N7

N67

N68

Bunratty Castle & Folk Park

Killimer

Shannon ✈

N69

Tarbert

Limerick

AN DAINGEAN PEN.

Gallaras Oratory

N86

Tralee

N21

Limerick Junction

Rock of Cashel ♜

Cashel

Ceann Sleibhe

An Blascaod Mór

An Daingean

Minard Castle ♜

Inch Strand

Kerry Airport ✈

KERRY

Tipperary

N8

N70

N72

Killarney

Mallow

N20

Caher

Clonm

RING OF KERRY

Muckross House ♜

N72

N72

Port-magee

Sneem

Kenmare

Macroom

Blarney

N8

Dungarvan •

Skellig Michael

Derrynane House ♜

N71

N22

Midleton

Youghal

Glengarriff

Cork ♜

N25

BEARA

Bantry

Kinsale

Cobh

Ardmore

Bantry Bay

N71

R600

Skibbereen

Drombeg Stone Circle

To Roscoff, France

Rick Steves'

IRELAND
2006

AVALON
TRAVEL

CONTENTS

Top Destinations in Ireland

INTRODUCTION

Flung onto the foggy fringe of the Atlantic pond like a mossy millstone, Ireland drips with mystery, drawing you in for a closer look and then surprising you. An old farmer cuts turf from the bog, while his son staffs the tech help-line for an international software firm. Buy them both a pint in a pub that's whirling with playful conversation and exhilarating traditional music. Pious, earthy, witty, brooding, proud, and unpretentious, Irish culture is an intoxicating potion to sip or slurp as the mood strikes you.

This book breaks Ireland into its top big-city, small-town, and rural destinations. It gives you all the information and opinions necessary to wring the maximum value out of your limited time and money. If you plan three weeks or less for Ireland and have a normal appetite for information, this lean and mean book is all you need. If you're a travel-info fiend, this book sorts through all the superlatives and provides a handy rack upon which to hang your supplemental information.

Experiencing Irish culture, people, and natural wonders economically and hassle-free has been my goal for three decades of traveling, tour guiding, and travel writing. With this new edition, I pass on to you the lessons I've learned, updated for your trip in 2006.

The places I cover are balanced to include a comfortable mix of exciting big cities and great-to-be-alive-in small towns. Note that this book covers the highlights of the entire island, including Northern Ireland. While you'll find the predictable biggies (such as the Book of Kells, Brú na Bóinne, and the Cliffs of Moher), I also mix in a healthy dose of Back Door intimacy (rope-bridge hikes, holy wells, and pubs with traditional Irish music). I've been selective. On a short trip, visiting both the monastic ruins of Glendalough and Clonmacnoise is redundant; I cover only the best

(Glendalough). There are plenty of great manor-house gardens; again, I recommend just the top one (Gardens of Powerscourt).

The best is, of course, only my opinion. But after spending half my adult life researching Europe, I've developed a sixth sense for what travelers enjoy. The places featured in this book will give anyone the "gift of gab."

This Information Is Accurate and Up-to-Date

This book is updated every year. Most publishers of guidebooks that cover a country from top to bottom can afford an update only every two or three years (and even then, it's often by e-mail or fax). Since this book is selective, covering only the sights that make the top three weeks of sightseeing in Ireland, I can research it every summer in person. The telephone numbers, hours, and prices of the places listed in this book are accurate as of mid-2005. Even with annual updates, things change. Still, if you're traveling with the current edition of this book, I guarantee you're using the most up-to-date information available in print. For the latest, visit www .ricksteves.com/update. Also at my Web site, you'll find a valuable list of reports and experiences—good and bad—from fellow travelers who have used this book (www.ricksteves.com/feedback).

Use this year's edition. People who try to save a few bucks by traveling with an old book are not smart. They learn the seriousness of their mistake...in Ireland. Your trip costs about $10 per waking hour. Your time is valuable. This guidebook saves lots of time.

About This Book

Rick Steves' Ireland is a personal tour guide in your pocket. Better yet, it's actually two tour guides in your pocket: The co-author of this guidebook is Pat O'Connor. Pat is the Ireland specialist and senior Ireland tour guide at Rick Steves' Europe Through the Back Door. Rick has enjoyed traveling in Ireland for many years, but nobody has a more Irish name than Pat—whose travel passion has long been the Emerald Isle. Together, Pat and I will keep this book up-to-date and accurate. For simplicity, from this point, "we" will shed our respective egos and become "I."

This book is organized by destination, each one a mini-vacation on its own, filled with exciting sights and homey, affordable places to stay. In the following chapters, you'll find:

Planning Your Time, a suggested schedule with thoughts on how to best use your limited time.

Orientation, including tourist information, city transportation, and an easy-to-read map designed to make the text clear and your arrival smooth.

Self-Guided Walks, taking you through interesting neighborhoods with a personal tour guide in hand.

Sights, a succinct overview of Ireland's most important attractions, arranged by neighborhood, with ratings: ▲▲▲—Don't miss; ▲▲—Try hard to see; ▲—Worthwhile if you can make it; No rating—Worth knowing about.

Sleeping and **Eating,** with addresses, phone numbers, and Web sites of my favorite good-value hotels and restaurants.

Transportation Connections to nearby destinations by train or bus and route tips for drivers.

The chapter **Ireland: Past and Present** gives you an overview of Irish history, a look at contemporary Ireland, and a taste of the Irish language.

The **appendix** is a traveler's tool kit, with helpful information on telephones, festivals and holidays, climate, metric conversion, and an Irish-Yankee vocabulary list.

Browse through this book, choose your favorite destinations, and link them up. Then have a great trip! Traveling like a temporary local, you'll get the absolute most out of every mile, minute, and dollar. And as you travel the route I know and love, I'm happy you'll be meeting some of my favorite Irish people.

PLANNING

Trip Costs

Five components make up your trip costs: airfare, surface transportation, room and board, sightseeing/entertainment, and shopping/miscellany.

Airfare: Don't try to sort through the mess. Find a good travel agent. A round-trip U.S.-to-Dublin flight costs $400–1,000 (even cheaper in winter), depending on where you fly from and when. If your travels take you beyond Ireland, consider saving time and money by flying "open-jaw" (into one city and out of another; for instance, into Dublin and out of Paris).

Surface Transportation: For a three-week whirlwind trip of all my recommended Irish destinations, allow $250 per person for public transportation (train tickets and key buses), or $750 per person for car rental (based on 2 people sharing a 3-week rental), including gas and insurance. Car rental is cheapest if arranged from the U.S. Since Ireland's train system has gaps, you'll usually save money by simply buying train and bus tickets as you go, rather than buying a railpass (see "Transportation," page 18).

Room and Board: You can manage just fine in Ireland on an average of $115 a day per person for room and board (allow less for villages and more for Dublin). A $115-per-day budget allows $15 for lunch, $25 for dinner, $5 for snacks or a Guinness, and $70 for lodging (based on 2 people splitting a $140 double room that includes breakfast). That's doable, particularly outside Dublin.

Irish Sightseeing Deals

Ireland offers two different passes (each covering a different set of sights) that can save you money. The first is smart for anyone, and the second works best for two people traveling together. Couples who love to sightsee should get both passes.

The **Heritage Card** gets you into 99 historical monuments, gardens, and parks maintained by the OPW (Office of Public Works) in the Republic of Ireland. It will pay off if you plan on visiting half a dozen or more included sights over the course of your trip (€20, seniors age 60 and older-€15, students-€7.50, families-€50, covers free entry to all Heritage sights for 1 year, card comes with handy map and list of sights' hours and prices, purchase at any Heritage sight or Dublin's tourist information office on Suffolk Street, tel. 01/605-7700, www.heritageireland.ie). People traveling by car are most likely to get their money's worth out of the card.

If, instead of getting the Heritage Card, you pay for the sights individually, your costs will add up fast. Adult entry prices range from €1.50 to €9.75. An energetic sightseer with three weeks in Ireland will probably pay to see nearly all 20 of the following sights (covered in this book): Dublin Castle-€5, Kilmainham Gaol-€5 (Dublin); Brú na Bóinne (Knowth and Newgrange tombs and Visitors Centre)-€9.75, Hill of Tara-€2, Old Mellifont Abbey-€2, Trim Castle-€3.75 (Valley of the Boyne); Glendalough Visitors Centre-€2.75 (Wicklow Mountains); Kilkenny Castle-€5 (Kilkenny); Rock of Cashel-€5 (Cashel); Reginald's Tower-€2 (Waterford); Charles Fort-€3.50, Desmond Castle-€2.75 (Kinsale); Muckross House and Farm-€8.25 (near Killarney); Derrynane House-€2.75 (Ring of Kerry); Ionad An Blascaod Mór (Great Blasket Centre)-€3.50 (near An Daingean); Ennis Friary-€1.50 (Ennis); Dún Aenghus-€2 (Inishmore, Aran Islands); Connemara National Park-€2.75 (near Galway); Newmills Corn and Flax Mill-€3, Glenveagh Castle and National Park-€3 (Donegal). This totals over €75.25; a pass saves you €55.25 (about $65) per person over paying individual entrance fees. Note that scheduled tours given by OPW guides at

---

Students and tightwads can do it on $40 ($20 for a bed in a hostel, $20 a day for meals—mostly picnics—and snacks).

Sightseeing and Entertainment: In big cities, figure $7–10 per major sight (e.g., the Book of Kells at Trinity College-$9), $3 for minor ones (climbing church towers), $12 for guided walks, $30–40 for day-trip bus tours, and up to $60 for splurge experiences (such as the Dunguaire Castle medieval banquet). An overall average of $25 a day works for most. Buying a discount pass can save you money (see "Irish Sightseeing Deals" sidebar above). Don't skimp here. After all, this category is the driving force behind your trip—you came to sightsee, enjoy, and experience Ireland.

any of these sites are included in the price of admission—regardless of whether you have the Heritage Card—and that the card covers no sights in Northern Ireland.

Ambitious travelers covering more ground should seriously consider the **Heritage Island Explorer Touring Guide** (€5), which does not overlap with the above Heritage sights and gives a variety of discounts (usually 2-for-the-price-of-1 entries, but occasionally 20 percent off) at sights in both the Republic and Northern Ireland. This is a no-brainer great deal for two people traveling together (just buy one Touring Guide for both of you); you save the cost of the guide after only a couple stops. Solo travelers might have to go to half a dozen sights before the discounts recoup the initial €4.50. The guide can be bought at TIs and participating sights, but study the full list of sights first (tel. 01/236-6890, www.heritageisland.com). Sights mentioned in this guidebook include: Trinity College Library (Book of Kells and *Dublin Experience*), Dublin City Hall, Dublinia, James Joyce Cultural Centre, Hugh Lane Art Gallery, Old Jameson Distillery, Jameson Distillery Chimney Viewing Tower, Guinness Storehouse, Gaelic Athletic Association Museum (Dublin); Gardens of Powerscourt (Enniskerry); Bru Boru Cultural Centre (Rock of Cashel); Waterford Museum of Treasures, Waterford Crystal Factory, Hook Head Lighthouse (Waterford); *Dunbrody* Famine Ship (New Ross); Irish National Heritage Park (Wexford); Kinsale Regional Museum (Kinsale); Queenstown Story (Cobh); Old Midleton Distillery (Midleton); Blarney Castle (County Cork); Kerry the Kingdom Museum, Siamsa Tire Theatre (Tralee); Galway Irish Crystal Heritage Centre (Galway); Clare Museum, Glór Irish Music Centre (Ennis); Kylemore Abbey (Letterfrack); Ulster Museum, W5 Science Centre (Belfast); Ulster Folk and Transport Museum (Cultra); Giant's Causeway (Portrush); Belleek Pottery Visitors Centre (Belleek); and Ulster American Folk Park (Omagh).

Shopping and Miscellany: Figure $2 per postcard, tea, or ice-cream cone, and $5 per pint of beer. Shopping can vary in cost from nearly nothing to a small fortune. Good budget travelers find that this category has little to do with assembling a trip full of lifelong and wonderful memories.

When to Go

July and August are peak season—my favorite time—with long days, the best weather, and the busiest schedule of tourist fun.

Prices and crowds don't go up as dramatically in Ireland as they do in much of Europe. Still, travel during "shoulder season"

Ireland's Best Three-Week Trip by Car

Day	Plan	Sleep in
1	Fly into Dublin, rent car, Glendalough	Kilkenny
2	Kilkenny with side-trip to Cashel	Kilkenny
3	Waterford	Waterford
4	Explore Wexford	Waterford
5	Cobh	Kinsale
6	Kinsale	Kinsale
7	Muckross House and Farms	Kenmare
8	Ring of Kerry	An Daingean
9	An Daingean Peninsula loop	An Daingean
10	Blaskets, An Daingean town (laundry and rest)	An Daingean
11	Cliffs of Moher, Burren, Dunguaire banquet	Galway
12	Galway	Galway
13	Aran Islands	Aran Islands
14	Tour Connemara and County Mayo	Westport
15	Drive to Northern Ireland	Derry
16	Side-trip to Donegal	Derry
17	Explore Derry, then drive to Portrush	Portrush
18	Explore Antrim Coast	Portrush
19	Belfast	Belfast
20	Drive to Valley of the Boyne sights, return car	Dublin
21	Dublin	Dublin
22	Dublin	Dublin
23	Fly home	

While this three-week itinerary (stretched to 23 days by using weekends at each end) is designed to be done by car, most of it can be done by train and bus. For three weeks without a car, spend your first three nights in Dublin, using buses and taxis. Cut back on the recommended sights with the most frustrating public transportation (Ring of Kerry, Valley of the Boyne, Connemara,

(May, early June, Sept, and early Oct) is easier and a bit less expensive. Shoulder-season travelers get smaller crowds, decent weather, the full range of sights and tourist fun spots, and the joy of being able to just grab a room almost whenever and wherever they like—often at a flexible price.

Winter travelers find absolutely no crowds and soft room prices, but shorter sightseeing hours and fewer activities. Some attractions are open only on weekends or are closed entirely in the

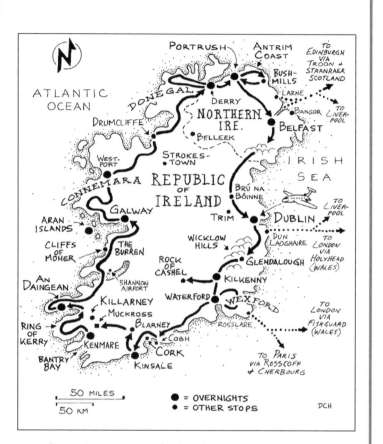

and counties Mayo, Wexford, and Donegal). You can book day tours by bus for some of these areas at local tourist offices. For at least two people traveling together, taxis—though expensive—can work in a pinch if bus schedules don't fit your plans (i.e., Cork to Kinsale, Waterford to New Ross, Dublin to Trim).

winter (Nov–Feb). Confirm your sightseeing plans locally, especially when traveling outside of peak season. The weather can be cold and dreary, and nightfall draws the shades on sightseeing well before dinnertime. While Ireland's rural charm falls with the leaves, city sightseeing is fine in the winter.

Plan for rain no matter when you go. Just keep traveling and take full advantage of "bright spells." Conditions can change several times in a day, but rarely is the weather extreme. As the locals say, "There is no bad weather, only inappropriate clothing." Daily averages throughout the year range between 42°F and 70°F. Temperatures below 32° or over 80° are cause for headlines (see the climate chart in the appendix). While sunshine may be rare, summer days are very long. Dublin is as far north as Edmonton, Canada, and Portrush is as far north as Ketchikan on the Alaskan panhandle. The summer sun is up from 5:00 until 22:00. It's not uncommon to have a gray day, eat dinner, and enjoy hours of sunshine afterward.

Sightseeing Priorities

Depending on the length of your trip, here are my recommended priorities:

3 days:	Dublin
5 days:	Dublin, An Daingean Peninsula
7 days, add:	Galway, a day in Belfast
9 days, add:	County Clare/Burren
11 days, add:	Northern Ireland's Antrim Coast
15 days, add:	Aran Islands, Wicklow Mountains
19 days, add:	Kinsale, Waterford, Valley of the Boyne
23 days, add:	Ring of Kerry, Connemara, Derry, Donegal

(This includes virtually everything on the "Ireland's Best Three-Week Trip by Car" map and itinerary on pages 6 and 7.)

Itinerary Specifics

Most people fly into Dublin and remain there for a few days. If you're picking up a car at Dublin Airport, consider a gentler small-town start in Trim or Kilkenny, and let Dublin be your trip finale.

To give yourself a little rootedness, minimize one-night stays. It's worth a long drive after dinner to be settled into a town for two nights. B&Bs are also more likely to give a good price to someone staying more than one night.

Consider making the following arrangements before you go:
- Reserve a room for your first night.
- If you'll be traveling in late June, July, or August and want to sleep in my lead listings, book your B&Bs (and the Dunguaire Castle medieval banquet) as soon as you're ready to commit to a date.
- Confirm car-rental and pick-up plans with your rental agency (picking up a car on Sat afternoon or Sun can be difficult).

Travel Smart

Your trip to Ireland is like a complex play—easier to follow and to really appreciate on a second viewing. While no one does the same trip twice to gain that advantage, reading this book in its entirety before your trip accomplishes much the same thing.

Reread entire chapters as you travel, and visit local tourist information offices. Upon arrival in a new town, lay the groundwork for a smooth departure. Buy a phone card and use it for reservations and confirmations. You speak the language—use it! Enjoy the friendliness of the local people. Ask questions. Most locals are eager to point you in their idea of the right direction. Those who expect to travel smart, do. Bring along a pocket-size notebook to organize your thoughts. Plan ahead for laundry, Internet stops, and picnics. Mix intense and relaxed periods. Every trip (and every traveler) needs at least a few slack days. Pace yourself. Assume you will return.

Design an itinerary that enables you to hit the various sights at the best possible times. As you read this book, make note of festivals, colorful market days, and days when sights are closed. Sundays have pros and cons, as they do for travelers in the U.S. (special events, limited hours, closed shops and banks, limited public transportation, no rush hours). Saturdays are virtually weekdays. Popular places are even more popular on weekends—especially sunny weekends, which are sufficient cause for an impromptu holiday in this soggy corner of Europe. Be aware of upcoming holidays that could affect your trip (see page 14) and book your rooms in advance.

RESOURCES

Tourist Information Offices

In the U.S.

Ireland's national tourist office in the U.S.—called **Tourism Ireland**—offers a wealth of information on both the Republic of Ireland and Northern Ireland. You can contact them at: 345 Park Ave., 17th floor, New York, NY 10154, tel. 800-223-6470 or 212/418-0800, fax 212/371-9052, www.tourismireland.com, info .us@tourismireland.com. Tourism Ireland also provides information to travelers who wish to visit Northern Ireland. Learn more about sightseeing opportunities and ask about a vacation-planner packet, maps, walking routes, and horseback riding.

In Ireland

Virtually every town in Ireland has a tourist information center (abbreviated **TI** in this book). Take full advantage of this service. Arrive (or telephone) with a list of questions and a proposed sightseeing plan. Pick up maps, brochures, and walking-tour information. In Dublin, try to get everything you'll need for Ireland in one stop at the TI in the old church on Suffolk Street. The general nationwide tourist information phone number for travelers calling from within Ireland is 1-850-230-330.

For all the help TIs offer, steer clear of their room-finding services (bloated prices, €5 booking fee, no opinions, and they take a 10 percent cut from your B&B host). If you're desperate, their nationwide room-booking phone number for travelers calling from within Ireland is 1-800-363-626 (Mon–Sat 9:00–20:00, closed Sun).

Rick Steves' Guidebooks, Public Television Show, and Radio Show

Rick Steves' Europe Through the Back Door gives you budget-travel skills, such as minimizing jet lag, packing light, planning your itinerary, traveling by car or train, finding rooms, changing money, avoiding rip-offs, buying a mobile phone, hurdling the language barrier, staying healthy, taking great photographs, using a bidet, and much more. The book also includes chapters on 38 of my favorite "Back Doors," two of which are in Ireland.

Country Guides: These annually updated books offer you the latest on the top sights and destinations, with tips on how to make your trip efficient and fun. Here are the titles:

Rick Steves' Best of Europe
Rick Steves' Best of Eastern Europe
Rick Steves' England (new in 2006)
Rick Steves' France
Rick Steves' Germany & Austria

Rick Steves' Great Britain
Rick Steves' Ireland
Rick Steves' Italy
Rick Steves' Portugal
Rick Steves' Scandinavia
Rick Steves' Spain
Rick Steves' Switzerland

City and Regional Guides: Updated every year, these focus on Europe's most compelling destinations. Along with specifics on sights, restaurants, hotels, and nightlife, you'll get self-guided, illustrated tours of the outstanding museums and most characteristic neighborhoods.

Rick Steves' Amsterdam, Bruges & Brussels
Rick Steves' Florence & Tuscany
Rick Steves' London
Rick Steves' Paris

Rick Steves' Prague & the Czech Republic
Rick Steves' Provence & the French Riviera
Rick Steves' Rome
Rick Steves' Venice

Rick Steves' Phrase Books: In much of Europe, a phrase book is as fun as it is necessary. This practical and budget-oriented series covers French, German, Italian, Spanish, Portuguese, and French/Italian/German. You'll be able to make hotel reservations over the phone, chat with your cabbie, and bargain at street markets.

Begin Your Trip at www.ricksteves.com

At www.ricksteves.com you'll find a wealth of **free information** on destinations covered in this book, including fresh European travel and tour news every month and helpful "Graffiti Wall" tips from thousands of fellow travelers.

While you're there, the **online Travel Store** is a great place to save money on travel bags and accessories designed by Rick Steves to help you travel smarter and lighter, plus a wide selection of guidebooks, planning maps, and DVDs.

Traveling through Europe by rail is a breeze, but choosing the right railpass for your trip—amidst hundreds of options—can drive you nutty. At www.ricksteves.com, you'll find **Rick Steves' Annual Guide to European Railpasses**—your best way to convert chaos into pure travel energy. Buy your railpass from Rick, and you'll get a bunch of free extras to boot.

Travel agents will tell you about mainstream tours of Europe, but they won't tell you about **Rick Steves' tours.** Rick Steves' Europe Through the Back Door travel company offers more than two dozen itineraries and 300 departures reaching the best destinations in this book...and beyond. You'll enjoy the services of a great guide, a fun bunch of travel partners (with small groups of around 25), and plenty of room to spread out in a big, comfy bus. You'll find trips to fit every vacation size, from week-long city getaways to longer cross-country adventures. For details, visit www.ricksteves.com or call 425/771-8303 ext. 217.

And More Books: *Rick Steves' Europe 101: History and Art for the Traveler* (with Gene Openshaw) gives you the story of Europe's people, history, and art. Written for smart people who were sleeping in their history and art classes before they knew they were going to Europe, *101* helps Europe's sights come alive. However, this book has far more coverage of the European continent than of Ireland.

Rick Steves' Easy Access Europe, geared for travelers with limited mobility, covers London, Paris, Bruges, Amsterdam, and the Rhine River Valley.

Rick Steves' Postcards from Europe, my autobiographical book, packs 25 years of travel anecdotes and insights into the ultimate 2,000-mile European adventure.

My latest book, *Rick Steves' European Christmas,* covers the joys, history, and quirky traditions of the holiday season in seven European countries.

Public Television Show: My series, *Rick Steves' Europe,* keeps churning out shows (60 at last count), including several featuring the sights in this book.

Public Radio Show: My new weekly radio show, which combines call-in questions (à la *Car Talk*) and interviews with travel experts, airs on public radio stations. For a schedule of upcoming topics and an archive of past programs (just click on a topic of your choice to listen), see www.ricksteves.com/radio.

Other Guidebooks

You may want some supplemental travel guidebooks, especially if you're traveling beyond my recommended destinations. I know it hurts to spend $30 on extra books and maps, but when you consider the money they'll save you and the improvements they'll make in your $3,000 vacation, not buying them would be penny-wise and pound-foolish.

While this book offers everything you'll need for the structure of your trip, each place you will visit has plenty of great little guidebooks to fill you in on local history. For cultural and sightseeing background in bigger chunks, Michelin and Cadogan guides to Ireland are good. The best budget travel guides to Ireland are the *Lonely Planet* and *Let's Go* guidebooks. *Lonely Planet*'s guidebook is more thorough and informative, but it's not annually updated. *Let's Go Ireland* is annually updated and youth-oriented, with good coverage of nightlife, hostels, and cheap transportation deals.

More Recommended Reading and Movies

For information on Ireland past and present, consider these books and films:

Non-Fiction: *A Short History of Ireland* (Richard Killeen), *How the Irish Saved Civilization* (Thomas Cahill), *Ireland: A Concise History* (Maire MacEntee O'Brien), *Traveller's History of Ireland* (Peter Neville), *Angela's Ashes* (Frank McCourt), *O Come Ye Back to Ireland: Our First Year in County Clare* (first in series of 4 by Niall Williams and Christine Breen), *Are You Somebody? The Accidental Memoir of a Dublin Woman* (Nuala O'Faolain), *To School Through the Fields: An Irish Country Childhood* (Alice Taylor), *Round Ireland with a Fridge* (Tony Hawks), *The Back of Beyond: A Search for the Soul of Ireland* (James Charles Roy), *Culture Shock: Ireland* (Patricia Levy), and *Adapter Kit Ireland* (Steenie Harvey).

Fiction: *Trinity* (Leon Uris); *The Bódhran Makers* (J.B. Keane); Morgan Llewelyn's historical epics; Roddy Doyle's gritty portraits of working-class Dubliners; *Finbar's Hotel* (anthology of short stories by Irish writers); *Ladies' Night at Finbar's Hotel* (anthology of short stories by Irish women writers); and the works of masters such as James Joyce, Oscar Wilde, Jonathan Swift, W. B. Yeats, G. B. Shaw, Samuel Beckett, Alexander Pope, Michael Comyn, Brendan Behan, Oliver Goldsmith, Thomas Kinsella, and Seamus Heaney.

Films: Classics include *The Quiet Man* (1952, John Wayne returns to his native Ireland) and *Odd Man Out* (1947, film noir about the early IRA, with a great scene filmed in the Crown Bar in Belfast). Fans of biographies will like *Michael Collins* and the thriller, *Veronica Guerin.* Upbeat crowd-pleasers include *Far and Away, Circle of Friends, Evelyn, Into the West, The Matchmaker, Widow's Peak, Laws of Attraction,* and *Waking Ned Devine.* For humor, check out *The Commitments, The Snapper, The Van,* and *Hear My Song.* For hard-hitting drama, look for *In the Name of the Father, The Boxer, The Field, My Left Foot, Some Mother's Son, The Magdalene Sisters,* and *Angela's Ashes.* The *Secret of Roan Inish* takes place in Donegal, and *Ryan's Daughter* was filmed on the An Daingean peninsula. Other Irish-themed films are *Agnes Browne, Cal, The Dead, The Playboys, The Run of the Country* (romance), *Dancing at Lughnasa,* and *This Is My Father.*

Maps

The black-and-white maps in this book, drawn by Dave Hoerlein, are concise and simple. Dave, who is well-traveled in Ireland, has designed the maps to help you locate recommended places and get to the TI, where you'll find more in-depth, cheap (or free) maps. Better maps are sold at newsstands—take a look before you buy to be sure the map has the level of detail you want.

Train travelers can do fine with a simple rail map (available as part of the free Intercity Timetable found at Irish train stations) and city maps from TIs. (Get free maps of Dublin and Ireland from the Irish Tourism before you go; see "Tourist Information Offices," above.) If you're driving, get a road atlas covering all of Ireland. Ordnance Survey, AA, and Bartholomew editions are available for about €12.50 in TIs, gas stations, and bookstores. Drivers, hikers, and bikers may want more detailed maps for An Daingean, Connemara, Donegal, Wexford, the Antrim Coast, the Ring of Kerry, and the Valley of the Boyne (easy to buy locally at TIs).

PRACTICALITIES

Red Tape: You need a passport, but no visa or shots, to travel in Ireland.

Time: In Ireland—and in this book—you'll be using the 24-hour clock. After 12:00 noon, keep going—13:00, 14:00, and so on. For anything over 12, subtract 12 and add p.m. (14:00 is 2 p.m.).

Like Great Britain, Ireland's time zone is five/eight hours ahead of the East/West Coasts of the U.S., and one hour behind the rest of Europe.

Business Hours: Most shops are open Monday through Saturday from roughly 10:00–17:30, with a late night on Wednesday or Thursday (until 19:00 or 20:00), depending on the neighborhood. On Sunday, when some stores are closed, street markets are lively with shoppers.

Holidays: Holidays bring most businesses to a grinding halt on Good Friday through Easter Monday (April 14–17 in 2006); the first Mondays in May, June, and August; and Christmas, December 26, and New Year's Day. For a list of events and festivals—which can also enhance or complicate sightseeing plans—see page 366.

Discounts: While discounts (called "concessions" in Ireland) are not listed in this book, many Irish sights are discounted for seniors (loosely defined as anyone retired or willing to call themselves a senior), youths (ages 8–18), students, groups of 10 or more, and families.

Watt's Up? If you're bringing electrical gear, you'll need an adapter plug. Ireland's plugs have three square-shaped prongs (not the 2 round prongs used in continental Europe). You may also need a converter to deal with the increased voltage. Travel appliances often have convenient, built-in converters; look for a voltage switch marked 120V (U.S.) and 240V (Europe).

News: Americans keep in touch in Europe with the *International Herald Tribune* (published almost daily via satellite). Every Tuesday, the European editions of *Time* and *Newsweek* hit the stands with articles of particular interest to travelers in Europe. Sports addicts can get their fix from *USA Today*. Good Web sites include www.europeantimes.com and http://news.bbc.co.uk.

MONEY

Banking

Bring plastic (ATM, credit, or debit cards) along with a few hundred dollars as a backup (but bring smaller bills—banks in Ireland have had problems with phony $100 bills, and will not accept them). Traveler's checks are a waste of time and money.

Before you go, verify with your bank that your card will work, inquire about fees (can be up to $5 per transaction), and alert them that you'll be making withdrawals in Europe; otherwise, the bank

may not approve transactions if it perceives unusual spending patterns. Bring an extra card in case one gets demagnetized or gobbled up by a machine. Since fees are charged per exchange, and most ATM screens top out at a couple hundred euros or pounds, save money by pushing the "other amount" button and asking for a higher amount.

Exchange Rates

I've priced things throughout this book in local currencies. The Republic of Ireland uses the euro currency. Northern Ireland, which is part of the United Kingdom, has retained its traditional currency, the British pound sterling.

1 euro (€) = about $1.20
1 British pound (£1) = about $1.80

Republic of Ireland: Like dollars, one euro (€) is broken down into 100 cents. You'll find coins ranging from 1 cent to 2 euros and bills ranging from 5 euros to 500 euros. To roughly convert prices in euros to dollars, add 20 percent to Irish prices: €20 is about $24, €45 is about $55, and so on.

Northern Ireland: The British pound sterling (£), also called a "quid," is broken into 100 pence (p). Pence means "cents." You'll find coins ranging from 1p to £2 and bills from £5 to £50. Some travelers try to kid themselves that pounds are dollars. But when they get home, that £1,000-pound Visa bill isn't asking for $1,000...it wants $1,800. To avoid this shock, double British prices to estimate dollars. By overshooting it, you'll spend less...maybe even less than you budgeted (good luck).

Northern Ireland issues its own currency worth the same as an English pound. If you'll be traveling in Great Britain, note that English and Northern Ireland's Ulster pounds are technically interchangeable in both regions, although Ulster pounds are "undesirable" in Britain. Banks in either region will convert your Ulster pounds into English pounds at no charge. Don't worry about the coins, which are accepted throughout Great Britain and Northern Island.

Credit (or debit) cards are handy for booking rooms and transportation tickets over the phone, and necessary for renting a car. In general, Visa and MasterCard are far more widely accepted than American Express.

Even in mist-kissed Ireland, you should use a money belt (a pouch with a strap that you buckle around your waist like a belt, and wear under your clothes). Thieves target tourists, especially Americans. A money belt provides peace of mind. You can carry lots of cash safely in a money belt, and given the bank and ATM fees, you should.

Don't be petty about changing money; it's not efficient to visit ATMs and banks frequently to withdraw a minimum amount of cash each time. Change a week's worth of money, get big bills, stuff them in your money belt, and travel!

Damage Control for Lost or Stolen Cards

If you lose your credit, debit, or ATM card, you can stop people from using your card by reporting the loss immediately to the respective global customer-assistance centers. Call these 24-hour U.S. numbers collect: Visa (tel. 410/581-9994), MasterCard (tel. 636/722-7111), and American Express (tel. 336/393-1111).

Have, at a minimum, the following information ready: the name of the financial institution that issued you the card, along with the type of card (classic, platinum, or whatever). Ideally, plan ahead and pack photocopies of your cards—front and back—to expedite their replacement. Providing the following information will allow for a quicker cancellation of your missing card: full card number, whether you are the primary or secondary cardholder, the cardholder's name exactly as printed on the card, billing address, home phone number, circumstances of the loss or theft, and identification verification (your birthdate, your mother's maiden name, or your Social Security number—memorize this, don't carry a copy). If you are the secondary cardholder, you'll also need to provide the primary cardholder's identification verification details. You can generally receive a temporary card within two or three business days in Europe.

If you promptly report your card lost or stolen, you typically won't be responsible for any unauthorized transactions on your account, although many banks charge a liability fee of $50.

Tips on Tipping

Tipping in Ireland isn't as automatic and generous as it is in the U.S., but for special service, tips are appreciated, if not expected. As in the U.S., the proper amount depends on your resources, tipping philosophy, and the circumstance, but some guidelines apply.

Restaurants: At pubs where you order at the counter, don't tip. At a pub or restaurant with wait staff, check the menu or your bill to see if the service is included; if not, tip around 10 percent.

Taxis: To tip the cabbie, round up. For a typical ride, round up to a maximum of 10 percent (to pay a €4.50 fare, give €5; for a €28 fare, give €30). If the cabbie hauls your bags and zips you to the airport to help you catch your flight, you might want to toss in a little more. But if you feel like you're being driven in circles or otherwise ripped off, skip the tip.

Special Services: Tour guides at public sites might hold out their hands for tips after they give their spiel. If I've already paid for the tour, I don't tip extra, though some tourists do give a euro, particularly for a job well done. I don't tip at hotels (whether or not a service charge has been tacked on), but if you're a tipper, give the porter about a euro for carrying bags and leave a couple euros in your room at the end of your stay for the maid, if the room was kept clean. In general, if someone in the service industry does a super job for you, a tip of a euro or two is appropriate...but not required.

When in doubt, ask. If you're not sure whether (or how much) to tip for a service, ask your hotelier or the tourist information office; they'll fill you in on how it's done on their turf.

VAT Refunds for Shoppers

Wrapped into the purchase price of your Irish souvenirs is a 21 percent Value Added Tax (VAT). If you make a purchase at a store that participates in the VAT refund scheme, you're entitled to get most of that tax back. Personally, I've never felt that VAT refunds are worth the hassle, but if you do, here's the scoop.

If you're lucky, the merchant will subtract the tax when you make your purchase (this is more likely to occur if the store ships the goods to your home). Otherwise, here's what you'll need to do:

Get the paperwork. Have the merchant completely fill out the necessary refund document, called a "Tax-Free Shopping Cheque." You'll have to present your passport at the store.

Get your stamp at the border. Have your cheque(s) stamped at your last stop in the European Union (e.g., the airport) by the customs agent who deals with VAT refunds. It's best to keep your purchases in your carry-on for viewing, but if they're too large or dangerous to carry on, then track down the proper customs agent to inspect them before you check your bag. You're not supposed to use your purchased goods before you leave. If you show up at customs wearing your new Irish sweater, officials might look the other way—or deny you a refund.

Collect your refund. You'll need to return your stamped documents to the retailer or its representative. Many merchants work with a service, such as Global Refund or Premier Tax Free, which have offices at major airports, ports, and border crossings. These services, which extract a 4 percent fee, can refund your money immediately in your currency of choice or credit your card (within 2 billing cycles). If you have to deal directly with the retailer, mail the store your stamped documents and then wait. It could take months.

Customs Regulations

You can take home $800 in souvenirs per person duty-free. The next $1,000 is taxed at a flat 3 percent. After that, you pay the individual item's duty rate. You can also bring in duty-free a liter of alcohol (slightly more than a standard-sized bottle of wine), a carton of cigarettes, and up to 100 cigars. As for food, anything in cans or sealed jars is acceptable. Skip dried meat, cheeses, and fresh fruits and veggies. To check customs rules and duty rates, visit www.customs.gov.

TRANSPORTATION

By Car or Train?

To see all of Ireland, especially the sights with far-flung rural charm, I prefer the freedom of a rental car. Connemara, the Ring of Kerry, the Antrim Coast, Donegal, Wexford, and the Valley of the Boyne are really only worth it if you have wheels. Cars are best for three or more traveling together (especially families with small kids), those packing heavy, and those scouring the countryside. Trains and buses are best for solo travelers, blitz tourists, and city-to-city travelers.

Travelers who don't want (or can't afford) to drive a rental car find they still enjoy their travels using public transportation. Most rail lines spoke outward from Dublin, so you'll need to mix in bus transportation to bridge the gaps. Ireland has a good train-and-bus system, though departures are not as frequent as the European norm. Buses pick you up when the trains let you down.

Rails, Wheels, and Wings in Ireland

Schedules: The best overall source of schedules for public transportation in the Republic as well as Northern Ireland—including rail, cross-country and city buses, and Dublin's DART and LUAS transit—is the Discover Ireland Web site: www.iol.ie/~discover/rail.htm.

Trains: Ireland's various passes offer a better value than BritRail's pricey "BritRail plus Ireland" pass (see chart on page 19). Irish railpasses can be purchased easily and cheaply in Ireland at major stations (Dublin info tel. 01/836-6222).

If you'd rather use point-to-point tickets, just buy your tickets in Ireland as you go. Fares are often higher for peak travel on Fridays and Sundays. To avoid long station lines in Dublin, you can book train tickets in advance in person or by phone with your credit card at the Iarnrod Éireann Travel Centre (35 Lower Abbey St., Mon–Fri 9:00–17:00, closed Sat–Sun, tel. 01/703-4070).

Research options in advance by studying Irish train schedules at www.irishrail.ie or listening to a talking timetable at 01/805-4222.

Students are eligible for an **Irish Rail Student Travelcard** (which offers varying discounts per ride), but you have to plan a couple months ahead: Go to www.irishrail.ie, print the application form, get it stamped at your university student-travel office, and mail it to Ireland (include 2 passport photos and €12, payable by

Railpasses

Prices listed are for 2005. My free *Rick Steves' Guide to European Railpasses* has the latest prices and details (and easy online ordering) at www.ricksteves.com/rail.

BRITRAIL PLUS IRELAND PASS

	1st Class	2nd Class
5 days out of 1 month	$579	$419
10 days out of 1 month	959	669

This pass covers the entire British Isles (England, Wales, Scotland, Northern Ireland, and the Republic of Ireland), including a round-trip Stena Line ferry crossing between Wales or Scotland and the Emerald Isle during the validity of the pass (okay to leave via one port and return via another). Reserve boat crossings a day or so in advance—sooner for holidays. One child (5-15) travels along free with each pass. Extra kiddies pay half fare; under 5 free.

DEALS ONCE YOU GET TO IRELAND:

These local specials are sold at major train stations in Ireland. €1.20 = about $1 U.S.

Ireland:
Approximate point-to-point one-way 2nd class fares in $US by rail (solid line), bus (dashed line), and ferry (dotted line). First class costs 50% more. Add up fares for your itinerary to see whether a rail and/or bus pass will save you money.

Pass Name	Version	Area	Duration	Price
Emerald Card	Rail & Bus	Republic & North	Any 8 days in 15	€218
			Any 15 days in 30	€375
Irish Explorer	Rail & Bus	Republic only	Any 8 days in 15	€194
Irish Rover	Rail only	Republic & North	Any 5 days in 15	€157
Irish Explorer	Rail only	Republic only	Any 5 days in 15	€127
Irish Rover	Bus only	Republic & North	Any 3 days in 8	€68
			Any 8 days in 15	€152
			Any 15 days in 30	€226
Irish Rambler	Bus only	Republic only	Any 3 days in 8	€53
			Any 8 days in 15	€116
			Any 15 days in 30	€168

SEALINK FERRIES AND CATAMARANS CONNECTING BRITAIN AND IRELAND

British port to...	Irish port	crossings daily	ferry/cat. hrs	ferry/cat. cost
Holyhead	Dun Laoghaire	3	3.5 / 1.5	$35 / $50
Fishguard	Rosslare	6	3.5 / 1.5	$30 / $40
Stranraer	Belfast	6	3.5 / 1.5	$35 / $40

See also www.seaview.co.uk. Dun Laoghaire is a 30-minute bus or train ride from Dublin. Travelers from London to Dublin may find it worthwhile to catch a quick $80 shuttle flight (see www.cheapflights.com).

Public Transportation in Ireland

credit card; they'll mail you the card in 4–6 weeks).

Buses: Buses are about a third slower than trains, but they're also a lot cheaper. Round-trip bus tickets usually cost less than two one-way fares (i.e., Tralee to An Daingean costs €9 one-way and €15 round-trip). The Irish distinguish between "buses" (for local runs with lots of stops) and "coaches" (long-distance express runs). On many Irish buses, pop music or sports games are piped throughout the bus; have earplugs handy if you prefer silence.

From Dublin to An Daingean without a car, you'll need to take a train to Tralee and then catch a bus from there. From Dublin to Kinsale without a car, you'll need to take a train to Cork and then a bus from there.

· If you're traveling up and down Ireland's west coast, buses are best (or a combination of buses and trains); relying on rail-only here is too time-consuming.

Bus stations are normally at or near train stations. The Bus Éireann Expressway Bus Timetable comes in handy (free, available at some bus stations or online at www.buseireann.ie, bus info tel. 01/836-6111).

Some companies offer **backpacker's bus circuits.** These hop-on, hop-off bus circuits take mostly youth hostelers around the country super-cheap and easy with the assumption that they'll be sleeping in hostels along the way. For instance, Paddy Wagon cuts Ireland in half and offers three- or six-day "tours" of each half (north and south) that can be combined into one whole tour connecting Dublin, Cork, Killarney, An Daingean, Galway, Westport, Donegal, Derry, and Belfast (May–Oct, 3 days/€139, 6 days/€269, 5 Beresford Palace, Dublin, tel. 01/823-0822, toll-free from UK tel. 0800-783-4191, www.paddywagontours.com). They also run one-day tours of Belfast from Dublin (€40, Sat, Sun, and Wed).

Students can use their ISIC (student card, www.isic.org) to get discounts on cross-country coaches (up to 50 percent). Children 5–15 pay half-price on trains, and wee ones under age 5 go free.

Flights: If you're connecting Ireland with Britain or the Continent, look into cheap flights offered by Ryanair (Irish tel. 01/609-7878, www.ryanair.com), bmi (British Midland, Irish tel. 01/407-3036, U.S. tel. 800-788-0555, www.flybmi.com), and easyJet (flies in and out of Belfast only, Irish tel. 04894-484-929, British tel. 0870-600-0000, www.easyjet.com). Also consider www.cheapflights.co.uk and www.skyscanner.com.

Round-trip can be cheaper than one-way—ask. To get the best prices, book in advance, as soon as you have a date set (the best fares are generally available online, not by phone). Each flight has an allotment of cheap seats; these sell fast, leaving the higher-priced seats for latecomers. Ryanair is the exception, offering promotional deals throughout the year.

If you're flying within Ireland, try Aer Arann (Irish tel. 01/814-1058, British tel. 0800-587-2324, tel. from U.S. 011-353-61-704-428, www.aerarann.com). They fly from Dublin to Cork, Kerry, Galway, Knock, Sligo, and Donegal. Be aware that some of these smaller regional airports may not have car-rental offices.

Car Rental and Leasing

To save money, arrange your rental car in advance from the U.S. (either on your own or through your travel agent) rather than in Ireland. The best rental rates are weekly, with unlimited mileage. Expect to pay about $500 per week, including gas and insurance, for a basic rental. As long as you're age 75 or younger, you can pick up and drop off just about anywhere, anytime. For a trip covering both Ireland and Britain, you're better off with two separate car rentals. You can drive your rental car from the Republic of Ireland into Northern Ireland, but be aware of drop-off charges ($75–150) if you drop it off in the North. You'll pay a smaller drop-off charge ($25–50) for picking up the car at one place and dropping it off at another within the same country (even picking up in downtown

Dublin and dropping off at Dublin Airport). If you pick up the car in a smaller city, you'll more likely survive your first day on the Irish roads. If you drop the car off early or keep it longer, you'll be credited or charged at a fair, pro-rated price. Big companies have offices in most cities. (Ask to be picked up at your hotel.) Small local rental companies can be cheaper but aren't as flexible.

The Ford 1.3-liter Escort-category car costs about $50 more per week than the smallest cars, but feels better on the motorways and safer on the small roads. Remember, minibuses are a great budget way to go for five to nine people. An automatic transmission is going to add at least 25 percent to the car-rental cost over a manual transmission. Weigh this against the fact that in Ireland you'll be sitting on the right side of the car, and shifting with your left hand...while driving on the left side of the road.

In recent years, Ireland has run neck-and-neck with Portugal for the most traffic accidents in Western Europe. For peace of mind, I spring for the Collision Damage Waiver insurance (CDW, about $15–25 per day), which limits my financial responsibility in case of an accident. Unfortunately, CDW now has a high deductible hovering around $1,200. When you pick up your car, many car-rental companies will try to sell you "super CDW" at an additional cost of $7–15 per day to lower the deductible to zero.

Some credit cards offer CDW-type coverage for no charge to their customers. Quiz your credit-card company on the worst-case scenario. You have to choose either the coverage offered by your car-rental company or by your credit-card company. This means that if you go with the credit-card coverage, you'll have to decline the CDW offered by the car-rental company. In this situation, some car-rental companies put a hold on your credit card for the amount of the full deductible (which can equal the value of the car). This is bad news if your credit limit is low—particularly if you plan on using that card for other purchases during your trip.

Buying CDW—and the supplemental insurance to buy down

Driving in Ireland: Distance and Time

Aran Islands · Doolin — 30m · 1.25h
Kilrush · Killimer · Tarbert — .75h
Tarbert · Tralee — 30m · .75h

Bunbeg — Loop: 75m · 4h
40m · .75h · Portrush
Derry
Donegal — 40m · 1h
35m · .75h · Omagh
60m · 1.75h · Bangor
Sligo — 40m · .75h
NORTHERN IRELAND
Belfast — 15m · .25h
Westport — 60m · 1.5h
130m · 2.5h
80m · 1.75h
100m · 2.5h
25m · .75h · Cong
30m · .5h
Trim — 20m · .5h · Brú na Bóinne (Newgrange)
Galway — 140m · 2.5h
30m · .5h
30m · .75h
IRELAND
30m · .5h · Dublin
Cliffs of Moher/Burren/Doolin — 40m · 1h
40m · 1h
See map detail above.
15m · .25h
120m · 2h
An Daingean — Loop: 30m · 2h
30m · 1.25h
Tralee
20m · .25h
Shannon · Limerick · Kilkenny · Glendalough
60m · 1h
130m · 2.75h
Cashel — 35m · .5h
70m · 1.25h
30m · 1.25h
40m · 1.5h
Killarney — 65m · 1h
45m · .75h
65m · 1.25h
Loop: 100m · 4.5h
20m · 1h
Blarney — 30m · .5h
35m · .5h · Wexford
Kenmare — 75m · 2.5h
75m · 1.5h · Waterford
Cork · Cobh
Kinsale — 15m · .5h

m = miles
h = hours

Note: Your times may vary based on traffic, construction, and sheep on road.

the deductible, if you choose—is the easiest but priciest option. Using the coverage that comes with your credit card is cheaper, but can involve more hassle. For longer trips, look into leasing.

Leasing: For trips of two and a half weeks or more, leasing (which automatically includes CDW insurance with no deductible) is the best way to go. By technically buying and then selling back the car, you save lots of money on tax and insurance. Leasing provides you a brand-new car with unlimited mileage and a 24-hour emergency assistance program. You can lease for as little as 17 days to as long as six months. Car leases must be arranged from the U.S. A reliable company offering 17-day lease packages for about $750–800 is Europe by Car (U.S. tel. 800/223-1516, www.europebycar.com).

Driving

Your U.S. driver's license is all you need to drive in Ireland. Driving in Ireland is basically wonderful—once you remember to stay on the left and after you've mastered the roundabouts. Traffic

Tips on Driving

Driving gives you access to the most rural sights and is my favorite mode of transportation in Ireland. Here's what I've learned in the school of hard brakes and adrenaline rushes:

- The *Complete Road Atlas of Ireland* by Ordnance Survey (€12.50, handy ring-binder style, 1:210,000 scale) is the best Irish road map, and includes translations of Irish place names on last pages. It covers every road your car can wedge onto. Flipping to the next page  of an atlas is easier to manage in a cramped front seat than wrestling with a large, ungainly folding map. Buy the atlas at the first TI or gas station you come to.
- Study your map before taking off. Know the areas you'll be lacing together, as road numbers are inconsistent.
- Road signs can be confusing, too little, and too late. There are three main kinds of signs: (1) Those with white lettering on a green background are found on major routes and give distances in kilometers. (2) Signs with black lettering on a white background are older and trickier: Distances shown with a "km" following it are in kilometers, while distances with nothing following it are in miles (slowly being phased out). (3) Brown signs with white lettering alert drivers to sights, lodging, and tourist offices.
- Figure out your lights, wipers, and radio before you're on the road.
- Adjust your side-view mirrors and get in the habit of using them. Many are spring-loaded to snap back into place (a pragmatic solution on narrow roads). Get comfortable with the sound of vegetation whisking the side of your car (it rarely scratches).
- Drive with your lights on to make your vehicle more visible.
- You'll get used to shifting with your left hand. Find reverse... before you need it. (I love the smell of burnt clutch in the morning.)
- Car travel in Ireland isn't fast. Plan your itinerary estimating your average speed at 40 miles per hour (roughly 1 km per minute). Give your itinerary a reality check by finding distances and driving times between destinations on the driving map (page 23) or online (www.viamichelin.com).
- The shortest distance between any two points is usually the motorway (highway). Miss a motorway exit and you can lose 30 minutes.

- Avoid driving in big cities if possible; use ring roads to skirt the congestion. Dublin traffic has gotten clogged over the years, and you'll find sightseeing easier on foot, by bus (particularly the hop-on, hop-off tours), or by taxi. Spare yourself the traffic stress and parking expense (€3/hr) of trying to drive in Dublin.
- When it comes to narrow rural roads, adjust your perceptions of personal space. It's not "my side of the road" or "your side of the road." It's just "the road"—and it's shared as a cooperative adventure. Locals are usually courteous, pulling over against a hedgerow and blinking their headlights for you to pass while they wait. Return the favor when you are closer to a wide spot in the road than they are. Pull over frequently—to let faster locals pass and to check the map.
- Watch the road ahead and always expect that a slow tractor, a flock of sheep, a one-lane bridge, and a baby stroller are lurking around the next turn. Honk when approaching blind corners to alert approaching drivers.
- Tune in RTE One, the national radio station (89 FM), for long drives. Its interviews/music are an education in Irish culture and good company.
- Make your road trip fun. Establish a cardboard-box pantry of munchies. Keep a rack of liter boxes of juice in the trunk. Buy some Windex and a roll of paper towels for cleaner sightseeing.
- Be very careful with alcohol...the Garda (police) set up random checkpoints, and if you drink more than one pint, you're legally drunk in Ireland.
- The most common mistake is getting a late start, which causes you to rush, which makes you miss turns, which causes you stress, which decreases your enjoyment, which makes it feel less like a vacation.
- If you're driving between the Republic and Northern Ireland, keep these basic differences in mind: In the Republic, the speed limit is in kilometers per hour, unleaded costs €1 per liter ($6 per gallon), and the roads can be bumpy, narrow, and winding. In Northern Ireland, the speed limit is in miles per hour, unleaded costs £.80 per liter ($7 per gallon), and roads are better maintained.
- Travelers who want to use designated disabled parking spaces in Ireland can bring their Disabled Persons Parking Card from the U.S. (even though the Irish have a different card that they set on their dashboard). For more information, call the Irish Wheelchair Association at tel. 045/893-094 (from the U.S., dial 011-353-45-893-094).

in roundabouts has the right-of-way; entering traffic yields (look to your right as you merge). It helps to remember that the driver is always in the center of the road. But be warned: Every year I get a few cards from traveling readers advising me that, for them, trying to drive Ireland was a nerve-racking and regrettable mistake.

If you want to get a little slack on the roads, drop by a gas  station or auto shop and buy a red "L" (new driver with license) sign to put in your window.

An Irish Automobile Association membership comes with most rentals (www.aaireland .ie). Understand its towing and emergency-road-service benefits. Seat belts are required by law. Speed limits are 50 kilometers per hour (roughly 30 miles per hour) in towns, 80 kph (approximately 50 mph) on rural roads (such as R-257, R-600, etc.), 100 kph (about 60 mph) on national roads (N-8, N-30, and so on), and 120 kph (roughly 75 mph) on motorways (M-1, M-50, etc.). Some sections of the motorways near Dublin may charge tolls of as much as €1.80.

Note that road-surveillance cameras strictly enforce speed limits. Any driver (including foreigners renting cars) photographed speeding will get a nasty bill in the mail. (Cameras—you'll see the foreboding gray boxes—flash on your rear license plate in order not to invade the privacy of anyone sharing the front seat with someone they shouldn't be with.)

Parking is confusing. One yellow line marked on the pavement means no parking Monday through Saturday during business hours. Double yellow lines mean no parking at any time. Broken yellow lines mean short stops are OK, but you should always look for explicit signs or ask a passerby.

Even in small towns, rather than fight it, I just pull into the most central "disk" or pay-and-display lot I can find. Disks can be bought at nearby shops. You buy one disk for each hour you want to stay. Scratch off the time you arrived on the disk and put it on your dashboard. I keep a bag of coins in the ashtray for meter/voucher machines (no change given for large coins). These modern pay-and-display machines are solar-powered and placed regularly along the street (about 6 feet tall, look for blue circle with white letter "P"). Signs along the street will state whether parking disc or pay-and-display laws are in effect for that area.

COMMUNICATING

Telephones

Smart travelers learn the phone system and use it daily for making hotel/restaurant reservations, verifying hours at sights, and phoning home. If you call before heading out, you'll travel more smoothly.

Types of Phones

You'll encounter various kinds of phones in Ireland:

• Irish **public pay phones** are great, easy-to-use, and everywhere. Phones are either coin- or card-operated. They clearly list which coins they'll take, and a display shows how your money supply's doing. Only completely unused coins will be returned, so put in biggies with caution. (If money's left over, rather than hanging up, push the "make another call" button.)

• **Hotel room phones** are fairly cheap for local calls, but pricey for international calls, unless you use an international calling card (see below).

• **American mobile phones** work in Europe if they're GSM-enabled, tri-band (or quad-band), and on a calling plan that includes international calls. With a T-Mobile phone, you can roam using your home number, and pay $1–2 per minute for making or receiving calls.

• Some travelers buy a **European mobile phone** in Europe. For about $125, you can get a phone that will work in most countries once you pick up the necessary chip (about $30) per country. Or you can buy a cheaper, "locked" phone that only works in the country where you purchased it (about $100, includes $20 worth of calls). If you're interested, stop by any European shop that sells mobile phones (such as Vodafone, O2, and Orange); you'll see prominent store-window displays. You aren't required to (and shouldn't) buy a monthly contract—buy prepaid calling time instead (as you use it up, buy additional minutes at newsstands or mobile-phone shops). If you're on a budget, skip mobile phones and use phone cards instead.

Paying for Calls

You can spend a fortune making phone calls in Ireland...but why would you? Here's the skinny on different ways to pay, including the best deals.

Buy a Telecom Éireann **phone card** (€4, €7, or €15 at newsstands, TIs, and post offices). Insert the card into the phone and dial away.

Prepaid **international calling cards** are the cheapest way to make international calls from Ireland (usually figure on 5 minutes per dollar to the U.S. at most). These are sold at most newsstands, mini-marts, post offices, and exchange bureaus in denominations of €5, €10, and €20 in the Republic of Ireland, and £5, £10, and £20 in Northern Ireland.

There are many different brands, so ask the clerk which one has the best rates to wherever you're calling. Because cards are occasionally duds, avoid the high denominations.

Since you don't insert these cards into the phone, you can use them from anywhere, including your hotel room, avoiding pricey hotel rates. You'll actually get more minutes per card if you call from your hotel rather than phone booths, which come with a hefty surcharge. Make sure, however, that your hotel isn't overcharging you to dial the access number (it's free to dial from phone booths).

To use a card, scratch off the back to reveal your code. After you dial the access phone number, the message tells you to enter your code and then dial the phone number you want to call. To call the U.S., see "Dialing International Calls," below. To make calls within Ireland, dial the area code plus the local number; when using an international calling card, the area code must be dialed even if you're calling across the street. International calling cards work only within the country of purchase, with the exception of some of the Spirit brand cards, usable in both the Republic of Ireland and the United Kingdom (confirm before buying).

To make numerous, successive calls with an international calling card without having to redial the long access number each time, press the keys (see instructions on card) that allow you to launch directly into your next call.

Dialing direct from your hotel room without using an international calling card is usually quite expensive for international calls. I always ask first how much I'll be charged. Keep in mind that you might have to pay for local and occasionally even toll-free calls.

Receiving calls in your hotel room is often the cheapest way to keep in touch with the folks back home—especially if your family has an inexpensive way to call you (either a good deal on their long-distance plan, a prepaid calling card with good rates to Europe, or access to an Internet phone service such as Skype, www.skype.com). Give them a list of your hotels' phone numbers before you go. As you travel, send your family an e-mail or make a quick payphone call to set up a time for them to call you, and then wait for the ring.

U.S. calling cards (such as the ones offered by AT&T, MCI, or Sprint) are the worst option. You'll nearly always save a lot of money by paying with an international calling card.

How to Dial

Calling from the U.S. to Ireland, or vice versa, is simple—once you break the code. The European calling chart on page 362 will walk you through it. Remember that Irish time is five/eight hours ahead of the East/West Coasts of the U.S. and one hour behind the rest of Europe.

Dialing Long Distance within the Republic of Ireland or Northern Ireland: Ireland, like much of the U.S., uses an area-code dialing system. If you're dialing within an area code, you just dial the local number to be connected; but if you're calling outside your area code, you have to dial both the area code (which starts with a 0) and the local number.

You'll find area codes listed throughout this book, or you can get them from directory assistance (dial 11811 in the Republic, 192 in Northern Ireland).

Dialing International Calls: For a listing of country codes, see the appendix. When making an international call to the Republic of Ireland, first dial the international access code of the country you're in (011 from the U.S. or Canada, 00 if you're calling from Europe), then Ireland's country code (353), then the area code (without its initial 0) and the local number. For example, Dublin's area code is 01. To call one of my recommended Dublin hotels from the U.S., dial 011 (U.S. international access code), 353 (Ireland's country code), 1 (Dublin's area code without its initial 0), then 679-6500 (the hotel's number).

To call Northern Ireland from the U.S., dial 011, 44 (the U.K. country code), 28 (Northern Ireland's area code without its initial 0), then the local number. To call Northern Ireland from the Republic of Ireland, dial 048, then the local number without any area code at all. To call the Republic of Ireland from Northern Ireland, dial 00, 353 (Ireland's country code), the area code without its initial zero, then the local number.

To dial out of Ireland, start your call with its international code (00), then dial the country code of the country you're calling, then the number you're calling. To call my office from anywhere in Ireland, I dial 00 (Europe's international access code), 1 (U.S. country code), 425 (Edmonds' area code), then 771-8303.

E-mail and Mail

E-mail: Internet cafés are easy to find in big cities such as Dublin. Many libraries offer free access, but they also tend to have limited opening hours and may require reservations. Look for the places listed in this book, or ask the local TI, computer store, or your B&B host. Some hotels have a dedicated computer for guests' e-mail needs. Small places are accustomed to letting clients sit at their desk for a few minutes just to check their e-mail, if you ask politely.

Mail: Get stamps at the neighborhood post office, news-stands within fancy hotels, and some mini-marts and card shops. To arrange for mail delivery, reserve a few hotels along your route in advance, and give their addresses to friends. Allow 10 days for a letter to arrive. Phoning and e-mailing is so easy that I've dispensed with mail stops altogether.

SLEEPING

In the interest of the smart use of your time, I favor accommodations (and restaurants) handy to your sightseeing activities. Rather than list hotels scattered throughout a city, I choose two or three favorite neighborhoods and recommend the best accommodation values in each, from $20 bunk beds to fancy-for-my-book $200 doubles. Outside of Dublin, you can expect to find good doubles for $80–130, including tax and a cooked breakfast.

I've described my recommended hotels and B&Bs with a standard code. Prices listed are for one-night stays in peak season, include a hearty breakfast (unless otherwise noted), and assume you're booking direct and not through a TI. Prices can soften off-season, for stays of two nights or longer, or for payment in cash (rather than by credit card). Teenagers are generally charged as adults. Little kids sleep almost free.

When establishing prices with a hotelier or B&B owner, confirm whether the charge is per person or per room (if a price is too good to be true, it's probably per person). Because many places in Ireland charge per person, small groups often pay the same for a single and a double as they would for a triple. Note: In this book, room prices are listed per room, not per person.

Most places I list have three floors of rooms, steep stairs, and no elevator. If you're concerned about stairs, call and ask about ground-floor rooms. Remember that in Europe, the "first floor" is one floor above street level (what we would call the "second floor" back home).

"Twin" means two single beds, and "double" means one double bed. If you'll take either one, let them know or you might be needlessly turned away. Virtually all rooms have sinks. Rooms with a private bathroom (toilet plus shower and/or tub) are called "en suite"; rooms that lack private plumbing are "standard" (many places have standard rooms that they don't even advertise). As more rooms go en suite, the hallway bathroom is shared with fewer standard rooms. (B&B owners sometimes use the term "private bathroom" for a bathroom down the hall that only your room has the key for.) If money's tight, ask for standard rooms.

Ireland has a rating system for hotels and B&Bs. These stars and shamrocks are supposed to imply quality, but I find that they

Sleep Code

To help you easily sort through the accommodations listed, I've divided the rooms into three categories based on the price for a standard double room with bath.

$$$ **Higher Priced**
$$ **Moderately Priced**
$ **Lower Priced**

To give maximum information with a minimum of space, I use this code to describe accommodations listed in this book. Prices are listed per room, not per person. Breakfast is included.

S = Single room, or price for one person in a double.

D = Double or twin room. (I specify double- and twin-bed rooms only if they are priced differently, or if a place has only one or the other. When reserving, you should specify.)

T = Three-person room (often a double bed with a single).

Q = Four-person room (adding an extra child's bed to a triple is usually cheaper).

b = Private bathroom with toilet and shower or tub.

s = Private shower or tub only. (The toilet is down the hall.)

Non-smoking—With this edition, about 80 percent of my recommended B&Bs prohibit smoking. While some places allow smoking in the sleeping rooms, breakfast rooms are nearly always smoke-free.

Family deal—Indicates that parents with young children can easily get a room with an extra child's bed, or a discount for larger rooms. Call to negotiate the price. Teenage kids are generally charged as adults. Little kids sleep almost free.

According to this code, a couple staying at a "Db-€90" hotel would pay a total of €90 (about $110) per night for a room with a private toilet and shower (or tub). The hotel accepts credit cards or cash. You can assume credit cards are accepted unless otherwise noted.

mean only that the place sporting symbols is paying dues to the tourist board. Rating systems often have little to do with value.

The places I've chosen are generally rooms in B&Bs and hotels, rather than stand-alone cottages. If you're looking to settle down in base and rent a place (a cottage or apartment with a kitchen and living space) for a week or more, you'll find a list of these self-catering options under accommodation on www.tourismireland.com.

Bed-and-Breakfasts (B&Bs)

Compared to hotels, bed-and-breakfast places give you double the cultural intimacy for half the price. In 2006, you'll generally pay €40–55 (about $50–65) per person for a double room in a B&B in Ireland. Prices include a big cooked breakfast. The amounts of coziness, teddies, tea, and biscuits tossed in varies tremendously.

If you have a reasonable but limited budget, skip hotels. Go the B&B way. If you can use a telephone and speak English, you'll enjoy homey, friendly, clean rooms at a great price by sticking to my listings. Always call first.

If you're traveling beyond my recommended destinations, you'll find B&Bs where you need them. Any town with tourists has a TI that books rooms or can give you a list and point you in the right direction. In the absence of a TI, ask people on the street for help.

B&Bs range from large guest houses with 15–20 rooms to small homes renting out a spare bedroom. The philosophy of the management determines the character of a place more than its size and the facilities offered. Avoid places run as a business by absentee owners. My top listings are run by couples who enjoy welcoming the world to their breakfast table.

The B&Bs I've recommended are nearly all stocking-feet comfortable. I look for a place that is friendly (i.e., enjoys Americans); located in a central, safe, quiet neighborhood; has clean rooms with firm beds; is a good value; is not mentioned in other guidebooks (and is therefore filled mostly by Irish travelers); and is willing to hold a room until 16:00 or so without a deposit (though more and more places are requiring a deposit or credit card number). In certain cases, my recommendations don't meet all of these prerequisites. I'm more impressed by a handy location and a fun-loving philosophy than hair dryers and shoe-shine machines.

A few tips: B&B proprietors are selective as to whom they invite in for the night. At some B&Bs, children are not welcome. Risky-looking people (2 or more single men are often assumed to be troublemakers) find many places suddenly full. If you'll be staying for more than one night you are a "desirable." Sometimes staying several nights earns you a better price—ask about it. If you book through a TI, it takes a 10 percent commission and may charge you an extra euro or two. If you book direct, the B&B gets it all (and you'll have a better chance of getting a discount). I have negotiated special prices with this book (often for cash). You should find prices quoted here to be good through 2006 (except for major holidays and festivals). In popular weekend-getaway spots, you're unlikely to find a place to take you for Saturday night only. If my listings are full, ask for guidance. (Mentioning this book can help.) Owners usually work together and can call up an ally to land you a bed.

B&Bs are not hotels: If you want to ruin your relationship with your hostess, treat her like a hotel clerk. Americans often assume they'll get new towels each day. The Irish don't, and neither will you. Hang them up to dry and reuse.

B&Bs have plenty of stairs. Expect good exercise and be happy you packed light. Some B&Bs stock rooms with a hot-water pot, cups, tea bags, and coffee packets (if you prefer decaf, buy a jar at a grocery, and dump into a baggie for easy packing). Electrical outlets sometimes come with switches on the outlet to turn the current on or off; if your electrical appliance isn't working, flip the switch.

In B&Bs, no two showers are alike. Sometimes you'll encounter "telephone" showers—a handheld nozzle in a bathtub. Many B&Bs have been retrofitted with plumbing, and water is heated individually for each shower rather than by one central heating system. While the switch is generally left on, in some rooms you'll have a hot-water switch to consider. Any cord hanging from the ceiling is for lights or fans (not emergencies). Once in the shower, you'll find a multitude of overly clever mechanisms designed to somehow get the right amount and temperature of water. Good luck.

Cheap, Modern Hotels

Hotel chains, offering predictably comfortable accommodations at reasonable prices, are popping up in the center of big cities in Ireland.

These super-convenient hotels offer simple, clean, and modern rooms for up to four people (2 adults/2 children) for €80–120, depending on the location. Note that couples or families (up to 4) pay the same price for a room. Most rooms have a double bed, single bed, five-foot trundle bed, private shower, WC, and TV. Hotels often have an attached restaurant, good security, and a 24-hour staffed reception desk. Of course, they're as cozy as a Motel 6, but many travelers love them. You can book over the phone (or online) with a credit card, then pay when you check in. When you check out, just drop off the key, Lee.

If you choose to stay in these, book a room through their Web sites, as the room rates are often dramatically less for online bookings. The biggies are Jurys Inn (call their hotels directly or book online, reservations tel. 01/607-0000, U.S. tel. 800-423-6953, www.jurysdoyle.com), Comfort/Quality Inns (Republic of Ireland tel. 1-800-500-600, Northern Ireland tel. 0800-444-444, U.S. tel. 800-228-5150, www.choicehotels.com), and Travelodge (also has freeway locations for tired drivers, reservation center in Britain tel. 08700-850-950, www.travelodge.co.uk).

Making Reservations

It's possible to travel at any time of year without reservations, but given the high stakes, erratic accommodations values, number of people traveling with this book, and the quality of the gems I've listed, I highly recommend calling ahead for rooms at least a few days in advance as you travel.

When tourist crowds are down and you're traveling without reservations, you might make a habit of calling your hotel between 9:00 and 10:00 on the day you plan to arrive, when the hotel knows who'll be checking out and just which rooms will be available. I've taken great pains to list telephone numbers with long-distance instructions (see "Communicating," page 27; also see the appendix). Get a phone card and use it to confirm and reconfirm as you travel. A hotel receptionist will trust you and hold a room until 16:00 without a deposit, though some will ask for a credit-card number.

Honor your reservations or cancel by phone: Trusting travelers to show up is a huge, stressful issue and a financial risk for small B&B owners. I promised the owners of the places I list that you will be reliable when you make a telephone reservation; please don't let them (or me) down. If you'll be delayed or won't make it, simply call in. Americans are notorious for reserving B&Bs long in advance and never showing up (causing B&B owners to lose money—and respect for Americans). Being a little late is no problem if you are in telephone contact. Long-distance calls are cheap and easy from public phone booths.

Note that B&B owners will likely ask you the approximate time you'll arrive. Unlike hotels, most B&Bs don't have staff available to receive guests when they're out, so it helps them plan their days if they know when you're likely to show up.

While it's generally easy to find a room, a few national holidays jam things up (especially bank-holiday Mondays) and merit your making reservations long in advance (a list of holidays is in the appendix). Mark these dates in red on your travel calendar. Monday bank holidays are preceded by busy weekends; book the entire weekend in advance.

If you know exactly which dates you need and really want a particular place, reserve a room before you leave. To reserve from home, contact the hotel by e-mail, phone, or fax. To e-mail or fax, use the form in the appendix (also online at www.ricksteves.com /reservation). A two-night stay in August would be "two nights, 16/8/06 to 18/8/06." Europeans write the date day/month/year, and hotel jargon uses your day of departure. You'll often be asked for one night's deposit. Your credit-card number and expiration date will usually be accepted as a deposit, though you may need to send a signed traveler's check or a bank draft in the local currency.

Faxing your card number (rather than e-mailing it) keeps it private, safer, and out of cyberspace. If your credit card is the deposit, you can pay with your card or cash when you settle the bill. If you don't show up (or if you cancel with short notice), you'll be billed for one night.

Hotels in larger cities sometimes have strict cancellation policies (you might lose, say, a deposit if you cancel within 2 weeks of your reserved stay, or you might be billed for the entire visit if you leave early); ask about cancellation policies before you book.

On the road, reconfirm your reservations a day or two in advance for safety (or you may be bumped—really). Also, don't just assume you can extend. Take the time to consider in advance how long you'll stay.

Hostels

If you're traveling alone, hostelling is the best way to conquer hotel loneliness. Hostels are also a tremendous source of local and budget travel information. And if you hostel selectively, you'll enjoy historical and interesting buildings. You'll pay an average of €20 for a bed, €2 for sheets, and €3 for breakfast. Anyone of any age can hostel in Ireland. While there are no membership concerns for private hostels, IYHF hostels require membership. Those without cards simply buy one-night guest memberships for €2.50. You can book online for many hostels.

Ireland has hostels of all shapes and sizes. Choose your hostel selectively. They can be historic castles or depressing huts, serene and comfy or overrun by noisy school groups. Unfortunately, many of the International Youth Hostel Federation (IYHF) hostels have become overpriced, and, in general, I no longer recommend them. The only time I do is if you're on a very tight budget, want to cook your own meals, or are traveling with a group that likes to sleep on bunk beds in big rooms. But many of the informal private hostels are more fun, easygoing, and cheaper. These alternatives to IYHF hostels are more common than ever and allow you to enjoy the benefits of hostelling. Hostels of Europe (www.hostelseurope.com) and the Internet Guide to Hostelling (www.hostels.com) have good listings. Ireland's Independent Holiday Hostels (www.hostels -ireland.com) is a network of 145 independent hostels, requiring no membership and welcoming all ages. All IHH hostels are approved by the Irish Tourist Board.

EATING

Ireland has long been labeled the "land of potatoes," but you'll find modern-day Irish cuisine delicious and varied, from vegetables, meat, and dairy products to fresh- and salt-water fish. Try the local specialties wherever you happen to be eating.

The traditional breakfast, the "Irish Fry" (known in the North as the "Ulster Fry"), is a hearty way to start the day—with juice, tea or coffee, cereal, eggs, bacon, sausage, a grilled tomato, sautéed mushrooms, and optional black pudding (made from pigs' blood). Toast is served with butter and marmalade. This meal tides many travelers over until dinner. But there's nothing un-Irish about skipping the "fry"—few locals

actually start their day with this heavy traditional breakfast. You can simply skip the heavier fare and enjoy the cereal, juice, toast, and tea.

Many B&Bs don't serve breakfast until 8:00. If you need an early start, ask politely if it's possible. While they may not make you a cooked breakfast, they can usually put out cereal, toast, juice, and coffee.

Picnicking saves time and money. Try boxes of orange juice (pure, by the liter), fresh bread (especially Irish soda bread), tasty Cashel blue cheese, meat, a tube of mustard, local-eatin' apples, bananas, small tomatoes, a small tub of yogurt (it's drinkable), rice crackers, gorp or nuts, plain digestive biscuits (the chocolate-covered ones melt), and any local specialties. At open-air markets and supermarkets, you can get produce in small quantities. Supermarkets often have good deli sections, packaged sandwiches, and sometimes salad bars. I often munch a relaxed "meal on wheels" in a car, train, or bus to save 30 precious minutes for sightseeing.

At classier restaurants, look for "early-bird specials," allowing you to eat well and affordably, but early (around 17:30–19:00, last order by 19:00). At a sit-down place with table service, tip around 10 percent—unless the service charge is already listed on the bill (for details, see "Tips on Tipping," page 16).

Pub Grub and Beer

Pubs are a basic part of the Irish social scene, and whether you're a teetotaler or a beer guzzler, they should be a part of your travel here. Pubs, short for "public houses," serve as the community's living room and gossip center, as well as watering hole. Pub grub gets better every year—it's Ireland's best eating value. For around $12–15, you can get a basic budget hot lunch or dinner in friendly surroundings.

Pub menus consist of a hearty assortment of traditional dishes such as Irish stew (mutton with mashed potatoes, onions, carrots, and herbs), soups and chowders, coddle (bacon, pork sausages, potatoes, and onions stewed in layers), fish and chips, collar and cabbage (boiled bacon coated in bread crumbs and brown sugar, then baked and served with cabbage), boxty (potato pancake filled with fish, meat, or vegetables), and champ (potato mashed with milk and onions). Irish bread nicely rounds out a meal. In coastal areas, a lot of seafood is available, such as mackerel, mussels, and Atlantic salmon. There's seldom table service in Irish pubs. Order drinks and meals at the bar. Pay as you order, and don't tip.

I recommend certain pubs, and your B&B host is usually up-to-date on the best neighborhood pub grub. Ask for advice (but adjust for nepotism and cronyism, which run rampant).

When you say "a beer, please" in an Irish pub, you'll get a pint of Guinness (the black beauty with a blonde head). If you want a small beer, ask for a glass or a half-pint. Never rush your bartender when he's pouring a Guinness. It takes time—almost sacred time.

The Irish take great pride in their beer. At pubs, long hand pulls are used to draw the traditional, rich-flavored "real ales" up from the cellar. These are the connoisseur's favorites: They're

fermented naturally, vary from sweet to bitter, and often include a hoppy or nutty flavor. Experiment with obscure local microbrews; the best selection is at Dublin's Porter House (corner of Essex Street East and Parliament Street, tel. 01/671-5715). Short hand pulls at the bar mean colder, fizzier, mass-produced, and less interesting keg beers. Stout is dark and more bitter, like Guinness. If you don't like Guinness, try it in Ireland. It doesn't travel well and is better in its homeland. Murphy's is a very good Guinness-like stout, but a bit smoother and milder. For a cold, refreshing, basic, American-style beer, ask for a lager such as Harp. Ale drinkers swear by Smithwick's. Caffrey's is a satisfying cross between stout and ale. Try the draft cider (sweet or dry)...carefully. Teetotalers can order a soft drink.

Pubs are generally open daily from 11:00 to 23:30 and Sunday from noon to 22:30. Children are served food and soft drinks in pubs (sometimes in a courtyard or the restaurant section). You'll often see signs behind the bar asking that children vacate the premises by 20:00. You must be 18 to order a beer, and the Garda (police) are cracking down hard on pubs that don't enforce this. A cup of darts is free for the asking.

You're a guest on your first night; after that, you're a regular. A wise Irishman once said, "It never rains in a pub." The relaxed, informal atmosphere feels like a refuge from daily cares. Women traveling alone need not worry—you'll become part of the pub family in no time.

Craic (crack), the art of conversation, is the sport that accompanies drinking in a pub. People are there to talk. To encourage conversation, stand or sit at the bar, not at a table.

The Irish government passed a law in 2004 making all pubs in the Republic smoke-free. Smokers now take their pint outside, turning alleys into covered smoking patios. An incredulous Irishman responded to the new law by saying, "What will they do next? Ban drinking in pubs? We'll never get to heaven if we don't die."

Remember that since Northern Ireland is a different country (part of the United Kingdom), smoking is still legal in public places.

It's a tradition to buy your table a round, and then for each person to reciprocate. If an Irishman buys you a drink, thank him by saying, "Go raibh maith agat" (guh rov mah UG-ut). Offer him a toast in Irish—"Slainte" (SLAWN-chuh), the equivalent of "cheers." A good excuse for a conversation is to ask to be taught a few words of Gaelic.

Here's a goofy excuse for some *craic:* Ireland—small as it is—has many dialects. People from Cork are famous for talking very fast (and in a squeaky voice)—so fast that some even talk in letters alone. ABCD fish? (Anybody see the fish?) DR no fish. (There are no fish.) DR fish. (There are fish.) CDBDIs? (See the beady eyes?) OIBJ DR fish. (Oh aye, be Jeeze, there are fish.) For a possibly more appropriate spin, replace the fish with "bird" (girl). This is obscure, but your pub neighbor may understand and enjoy hearing it. If nothing else, you won't seem so intimidating to him anymore.

Traditional Irish Music

Traditional music is alive and popular in pubs throughout Ireland. "Sessions" (musical evenings) may be planned and advertised or impromptu. Traditionally, musicians just congregate and play for the love of it. There will generally be a fiddle, a flute or tin whistle, a guitar, a *bodhrán* (goatskin drum), and maybe an accordion or mandolin. Things usually get going around 21:30 or 22:00. Last call for drinks is around 23:30.

The music often comes in sets of three songs. The wind and string instruments embellish melody lines with lots of tight ornamentation. Whoever happens to be leading determines the next song only as the song the group is playing is about to be finished. If he wants to pass on the decision, it's done with eye contact and a nod. A *ceilidh* (KAY-lee) is an evening of music and dance...an Irish hoedown.

Send Me a Postcard, Drop Me a Line

If you enjoy a successful trip with the help of this book and would like to share your discoveries, please fill out the survey at www.ricksteves.com/feedback. I personally read and value all feedback.

Percussion generally stays in the background. The *bodhrán* (BO-run) is played with a small, two-headed club. The performer's hand stretches the skin to change the tone and pitch. You'll sometimes be lucky enough to hear a set of bones crisply played. These are two cow ribs (boiled and dried) that are rattled in one hand like spoons or castanets, substituting for the sound of dancing shoes in olden days.

Watch closely if a piper is playing. The Irish version of bagpipes, the *uilleann* (ILL-in) pipes are played by inflating the airbag (under the left elbow) with a bellows (under the right elbow) rather than with a mouthpiece like the Scottish Highland bagpipes. *Uilleann* is Gaelic for "elbow," and the sound is more melodic, with a wider range than the Highland pipes. The piper fingers his chanter like a flute to create individual notes, and uses the heel of his right hand to play chords on one of three regulator pipes. It takes amazing coordination to play this instrument well, and the sound can be haunting.

Occasionally, the fast-paced music will stop and one person will sing a "lament." Called *sean nos* (Gaelic for "old style"), this slightly nasal vocal style may be a remnant of the ancient storytelling tradition of the bards whose influence died out when Gaelic culture waned 400 years ago. This is the one time when the entire pub will stop to listen as sad lyrics fill the smoke-stained room. Stories—often of love lost, emigration to a far-away land, or a heroic rebel death struggling against English rule—are always heartfelt. Spend a lament studying the faces in the crowd.

A session can be magical or lifeless. If the chemistry is right, it's one of the great Irish experiences. The music churns intensely while members of the group casually enjoy exploring each other's musical style. The drummer dodges the fiddler's playful bow. Sipping their pints, they skillfully maintain a faint but steady buzz. The floor on the musicians' platform is stomped paint-free, and barmaids scurry artfully through the commotion, gathering towers of empty, cream-crusted glasses. Make yourself right at home, "playing the boot" (tapping your foot) under the table in time with the music. Talk to your neighbor. Locals often have an almost evangelical interest in explaining the music.

TRAVELING AS A TEMPORARY LOCAL

We travel all the way to Europe to enjoy differences—to become temporary locals. You'll experience frustrations. There are certain truths that we find God-given and self-evident, such as cold beer, ice in drinks, bottomless cups of coffee, "the customer's always right," easy shower faucets, and driving on the right-hand side of the road. One of the benefits of travel is the eye-opening realization that there are logical, civil, and even better alternatives. A willingness to go local ensures that you'll enjoy a full dose of Irish hospitality.

If there is a negative aspect to the image Irish have of Americans, it is that we are big, aggressive, impolite, rich, loud, and a bit naive. Americans tend to be noisy in public places, such as restaurants and trains. Our raised voices can demolish Europe's reserved and elegant ambience. Talk softly. While the Irish look bemusedly at some of our Yankee excesses—and worriedly at others—they nearly always afford us individual travelers all the warmth we deserve.

Judging from all the happy postcards I receive from travelers who have used this book, it's safe to assume you'll enjoy a great, affordable vacation—with the finesse of an independent, experienced traveler.

Thanks, and happy travels!

BACK DOOR TRAVEL PHILOSOPHY
From *Rick Steves' Europe Through the Back Door*

Travel is intensified living—maximum thrills per minute and one of the last great sources of legal adventure. Travel is freedom. It's recess, and we need it.

Experiencing the real Europe requires catching it by surprise, going casual... "Through the Back Door."

Affording travel is a matter of priorities. (Make do with the old car.) You can travel—simply, safely, and comfortably—nearly anywhere in Europe for $100 a day plus transportation costs (allow more for Dublin). In many ways, spending more money only builds a thicker wall between you and what you came to see. Europe is a cultural carnival, and, time after time, you'll find that its best acts are free and the best seats are the cheap ones.

A tight budget forces you to travel close to the ground, meeting and communicating with the people, not relying on service with a purchased smile. Never sacrifice sleep, nutrition, safety, or cleanliness in the name of budget. Simply enjoy the local-style alternatives to expensive hotels and restaurants.

Extroverts have more fun. If your trip is low on magic moments, kick yourself and make things happen. If you don't enjoy a place, maybe you don't know enough about it. Seek the truth. Recognize tourist traps. Give a culture the benefit of your open mind. See things as different but not better or worse. Any culture has much to share.

Of course, travel, like the world, is a series of hills and valleys. Be fanatically positive and militantly optimistic. If something's not to your liking, change your liking. Travel is addictive. It can make you a happier American as well as a citizen of the world. Our Earth is home to six billion equally important people. It's humbling to travel and find that people don't envy Americans. They like us, but, with all due respect, they wouldn't trade passports.

Globe-trotting destroys ethnocentricity. It helps you understand and appreciate different cultures. Regrettably, there are forces in our society that want you dumbed down for their convenience. Don't let it happen. Thoughtful travel engages you with the world—more important than ever these days. Travel changes people. It broadens perspectives and teaches new ways to measure quality of life. Many travelers toss aside their hometown blinders. Their prized souvenirs are the strands of different cultures they decide to knit into their own character. The world is a cultural yarn shop. And Back Door travelers are weaving the ultimate tapestry. Come on, join in!

REPUBLIC
OF IRELAND

REPUBLIC OF IRELAND

Though a relatively small island, Ireland has had a disproportionately large impact on the rest of the world. For hundreds of years, Ireland's greatest export has been its friendly yet feisty people. Geographically isolated in the damp attic of Dark Age Europe, Christian Irish monks tended the flickering flame of literacy, then bravely reintroduced it to the barbaric Continent. Later, pressure from wars and famines at home (combined with opportunities abroad) compelled many Irish to leave their island and scramble for a better life in far-flung America, Canada, and Australia.

The Republic of Ireland is just over 80 years old, but its inhabitants proudly claim their nation to be the only modern independent state to sprout from purely Celtic roots (the Romans never bothered to come over and organize the wild Irish). Through the persuasive and culturally enlightened approach of early missionaries such as St. Patrick, Ireland may also be the only country to have initially converted to Christianity without bloodshed. Irish culture absorbed the influences of Viking raiders and Norman soldiers of fortune, eventually enduring the 750-year shadow of English occupation.

Just a few decades ago, Ireland was an isolated agricultural economic backwater that had largely missed out on the Industrial Revolution. Membership in the European Community (precursor to the EU) 30 years ago began to turn things around, and the Irish government instituted far-sighted tax laws to entice foreign corporations to set up shop here.

Today, the Republic enjoys a renaissance as its Celtic Tiger economy—the strongest in the EU—attracts expatriate Irish and new foreign investment. And as the only English-speaking country to have adopted the euro currency, Ireland is an appealing place for U.S. corporations to set up shop as a beachhead on European turf. More than 40 percent of the Irish population is under 25 years old, leading many high-tech and pharmaceutical firms to take advantage of this young, well-educated labor force. Microsoft, Intel, Dell, Apple, Google, Compaq, and IBM all have

Republic of Ireland

outposts here (welcome to the "Silicon Bog"). Pfizer makes Viagra in Ringaskiddy, County Cork. And for the first time, Ireland has also become a destination for Third World emigrants seeking a better life...a switch from the days when Irish fled to start new lives abroad.

Other aspects of modern life are making inroads in traditional Ireland. In 2003, shops began charging customers 15 cents for plastic sacks for carrying goods, which has cut down on litter. In 2004, smoking was banned in all Irish pubs. Some pubkeepers grumble about lost business, but the smokers seem happy to take their pints out onto the street (at least in summer).

The resilient Irish character was born of dark humor, historical reverence, and an optimistic, "we'll get 'em next time" rebel spirit. Though the influence of the Catholic Church is less apparent these days, it still plays a major part in Irish life. The national radio and TV station, RTE, pauses for 30 seconds at noon and 18:00 to broadcast the chimes of the Angelus bells. The country is small enough that radio broadcasts manage to cover traffic snarls

Republic of Ireland Almanac

Official Name: The Republic of Ireland (locals say Ireland or Éire).

Population: Ireland's four million people (same as Kentucky) are of Celtic stock. They speak English, though Gaelic is spoken on the country's west coast. Nearly nine in 10 are nominally Catholic, though only one in three attends church.

Latitude and Longitude: 53°N and 8°W. The latitude is equivalent to Alberta, Canada.

Area: With 27,000 square miles—half the size of New York State—it occupies the southwestern 80 percent of the island of Ireland.

Geography: The isle is mostly flat, ringed by a hilly coastline. The climate is moderate, with cloudy skies about every other day.

Biggest Cities: The capital of Dublin (1 million) is the only big city; one in four Irish live in Dublin, and four in 10 live within 50 miles. Cork has 180,000, while Limerick and Galway have about 60,000.

Economy: The Gross Domestic Product is $125 billion (similar to Oregon's) and the GDP per capita is $32,000—one of Europe's highest, and 13 percent more than Britain's. Major money-makers include tourism and exports (especially to the U.S. and U.K.) of machines, medicine, Guinness, glassware, crystalware, and software. Traditional agriculture (potatoes and other root vegetables) is fading fast, but dairy booms.

Government: The elected president, Mary McAleese, appoints the president (Bertie Ahern), who is nominated by Parliament. The Parliament consists of the 60-seat Senate chosen by an electoral college, and the House of Representatives, with 166 seats apportioned after the people vote for a party. Major parties include Fianna Fail, Fine Gael, and Sinn Fein, the political arm of the (fading) IRA. Ireland is divided into 26 administrative counties—including Kerry, Clare, Cork, Limerick, and so on.

Flag: The Republic of Ireland's flag is made of three vertical bands of green, white, and orange.

The Average Irish: A typical Irish person is 5'6", 34 years old, has 1.87 kids, and will live to be 78. Every day, he or she drinks four cups of tea and spends $10 on alcohol.

nationwide, rather than citywide.

The vast majority of Irish people speak English, but you'll encounter Irish Gaelic if you venture to the western Irish fringe. The Irish love of conversation continually shines through. And the Irish welcome has roots in ancient Celtic laws of hospitality towards stranded strangers.

At first glance, Ireland's landscape seems unspectacular, with few mountains over 3,000 feet, and an interior consisting of grazing pastures and peat bogs. But its seductive beauty slowly grows on you. The gentle rainfall, called "soft weather" by the locals, really does create 40 shades of green—and quite a few rainbows as well. Ancient, moss-covered ring forts crouch in lush valleys, while stone-strewn monastic ruins and lone castle turrets brave the wind on nearby hilltops. Charming fishing villages dot the coast near rugged, wave-battered cliffs. Slow down to contemplate the checkerboard patterns created by the rock walls outlining the many fields. Examine the colorful small-town shop fronts that proudly state the name of the proprietor.

DUBLIN

With reminders of its stirring history and rich culture on every corner, Ireland's capital and largest city is a sightseer's delight. Dublin's fair city will have you humming, "Cockles and mussels, alive, alive-O."

Founded as a Viking trading settlement in the ninth century, Dublin grew to be a center of wealth and commerce, second only to London in the British Empire. Dublin, the seat of English rule in Ireland for 700 years, was the heart of a "civilized" Anglo-Irish area (eastern Ireland) known as "the Pale." Anything "beyond the Pale" was considered uncultured and almost barbaric...purely Irish.

The Golden Age of English Dublin was the 18th century, when the British Empire was on a roll, and the city was right there with it. Largely rebuilt during this Georgian era, Dublin—even with its tattered edges—became an elegant and cultured capital.

But nationalism, plus a realization of the importance of human rights, forever changed Dublin. The ideas of the French Revolution inspired Irish intellectuals to buck British rule and, after the Rebellion of 1798, life in Dublin was never quite the same. But the 18th century left a lasting imprint on the city. Squares and boulevards in the Georgian style (that's British for "neoclassical") gave the city an air of grandness. The National Museum, the National Gallery, and many government buildings are in the Georgian section of town. Few buildings (notably Christ Church and St. Patrick's cathedrals) survive from before this Georgian period.

In the 19th century, with the closing of the Irish Parliament, the Great Potato Famine, and the beginnings of the struggle for independence, Dublin was treated—and felt—more like a colony than a partner. The tension culminated in the Easter Rising of 1916, followed by independence from Britain and the tragic civil war. With many of its grand streets left in ruins, Dublin emerged as the capital of the only former colony in Europe.

While bullet-pocked buildings and dramatic statues keep memories of Ireland's recent struggle for independence alive, it's boom time now, and the city is looking to a bright future. Locals are enjoying the strong "Celtic Tiger" economy while visitors enjoy a big-town cultural scene wrapped in a small-town smile.

Planning Your Time

On a three-week trip through Ireland, Dublin deserves three nights and two days. Consider this aggressive sightseeing plan:

Day 1: 10:15–Follow the Trinity College guided walk; 11:00–Visit the Book of Kells and Old Library ahead of the mid-day crowds; 12:00–Browse Grafton Street and have lunch there or picnic on Merrion Square; 13:30–See Number Twenty-Nine Georgian House (closed Mon); 15:00–Head to the National Museum (also closed Mon); 17:00–Return to hotel, rest, have dinner—eat well for less during early-bird specials; 19:30–Go for an evening walk (musical or literary); 22:00–Drop in on Irish music in Temple Bar area.

Day 2: 10:00–Take the Dublin Castle tour; 11:00–Choose between self-guided O'Connell Street Stroll or guided historical walking tour; 13:00–Lunch; 14:00–Tour Kilmainham Gaol; 16:00–Visit Guinness Storehouse brewery and finish with view of city from their Gravity Bar; Evening–Catch a play, concert, or Comhaltas traditional music in Dun Laoghaire (DUN-leary).

ORIENTATION

(area code: 01)

Greater Dublin sprawls with a million people—a third of the country's population. But the center of touristic interest is a tight triangle between O'Connell Bridge, St. Stephen's Green, and Christ Church Cathedral. Within this triangle you'll find Trinity College (Book of Kells), Grafton Street (top pedestrian shopping zone), Temple Bar (trendy and touristy nightlife center), Dublin Castle, and the hub of most city tours and buses. The only major sights outside your easy-to-walk triangle are the Kilmainham Gaol and the Guinness Storehouse (both west of the center).

The River Liffey cuts the town in two. Focus on the southern half, where nearly all your sightseeing will take place. Dublin's wide main drag, O'Connell Street, starts north of the river at the Parnell monument and runs south, down to the central O'Connell Bridge. After crossing the bridge, it continues south as the major

Greater Dublin

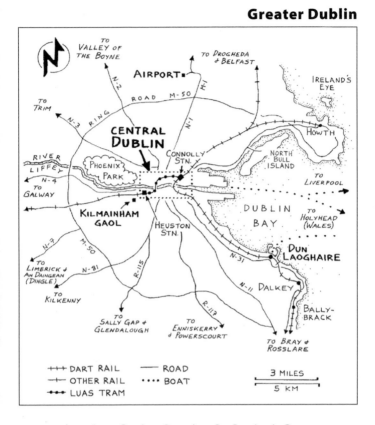

city axis (mostly as Grafton Street) to St. Stephen's Green.

The suburban port of Dun Laoghaire (described on page 87) lies south of Dublin, 20 minutes away by DART commuter train. Travelers connecting by ferry to Holyhead in Wales—or those just looking for a mellow town to sleep in outside of urban Dublin—can easily home-base here.

Tourist Information

Dublin's main tourist information office (TI) is a big shop with little to offer other than promotional fliers and long lines (Mon–Sat 9:00–17:30, Sun 10:30–15:00, located in a former church on Suffolk Street, 1 block off Grafton Street, tel. 01/605-7700, www .visitdublin.com). It has a car-rental agency, bus-info desk, sandwich bar, and traditional knickknacks. But perhaps its greatest value is the chance to peruse the rack opposite the info counter and pick up brochures for destinations throughout Ireland. There's also a TI at the airport (daily 8:00–22:00) and one at the Dun Laoghaire ferry terminal (Mon–Sat 10:00–13:00 & 14:00–18:00, closed Sun).

While you can buy the TI's lousy map for €0.50, its free newspaper, *Dubl!n*, has the same one on its staple page. The handy *Dublin's Top Visitor Attractions* booklet has a small map and the latest on all of the town's sights—many more than I list here (€2.50, sold at TI bookshop without any wait). For a schedule of happenings in town, check the minimal calendar of events inside *The Guide to Dublin* newspaper (free at TI).

The excellent *Collins Illustrated Dublin Map* (€6 at TIs and newsstands) is the ultimate city map, listing just about everything of interest, along with helpful opinions.

Dublin Pass: This mediocre sightseeing pass can be a good deal if you like to visit lots of sights quickly (€29/1 day, €49/2 days, €59/3 days, €89/6 days, sold at all 3 TIs, www.dublinpass .com). The pass might save you a little time, because it allows you to bypass ticket-buyer lines—though the lines at included sights generally aren't very long. It covers museums, churches, literature-related sights, and expensive stops like the Guinness Storehouse and the Old Jameson Distillery, plus the Aircoach airport bus (but not Airlink). However, the pass doesn't include the famous Book of Kells at Trinity College or any bus tours or walking tours, and many of the sights it claims to "cover" (such as the National Gallery and the Chester Beatty Library) are actually free.

Arrival in Dublin

By Train: Dublin has two train stations. **Heuston Station,** on the west end of town, serves west and southwest Ireland (30-min walk from O'Connell Bridge; take taxi or bus #90 instead, see below). **Connolly Station,** which serves the north, northwest, and Rosslare, is closer to the center (10-min walk from O'Connell Bridge). Each station has ATMs and lockers (small lockers-€4/ day, large-€6/day, 7-day maximum stay).

The two train stations are connected by the red line of the LUAS commuter train (see "Getting Around Dublin," below) and by bus. Bus #90 runs along the river, linking both train stations, the bus station, and the city center (€0.90, 6/hr).

When you're leaving Dublin and you want to reach Heuston Station from the city center, catch bus #90 on the south side of the river; to get to Connolly Station and Busaras Central Bus Station from the city center, catch #90 on the north side of the river.

By Bus: Bus Éireann, Ireland's national bus company, uses the **Busaras Central Bus Station** next to Connolly Station (10-min walk or short bus ride to the city center; see bus #90 info in "By Train," above).

By Plane: The airport (tel. 01/814-1111) has ATMs, change bureaus, car-rental agencies, baggage check, a café, and a super-market at the parking lot.

Getting Between the Airport and Downtown: Consider buying a €10 **Rambler** city-bus pass at the airport TI (see "Getting Around Dublin," below), which covers the Airlink bus into town—but read this first to see if Airlink is the best choice for your trip downtown. To get to the recommended accommodations in the **city center,** take Airlink bus #748 (not #747) and ask the driver which stop is closest to your hotel (€5, pay driver, 2/hr, 40 min, connects airport with Heuston Station and the Busaras Central Bus Station, near Connolly Station). **Dun Laoghaire** is also served by Airlink (bus #746). But for the **St. Stephen's Green** neighborhood, the Aircoach is a better bet (€7, covered by Dublin Pass but not Rambler city-bus pass, 4/hr, runs 5:30–22:30; pay driver and confirm best stop for your hotel, tel. 01/844-7118, www.aircoach.ie).

To get from the airport cheaply to downtown Dublin, take the **city bus** from the airport; buses marked #16A, #41, #41B, and #41C go to O'Connell Street (€1.75, exact change required, 4/hr, 55 min).

Taxis from the airport into Dublin cost about €25; to Dun Laoghaire, about €40.

By Ferry: Irish Ferries docks at the mouth of the River Liffey (at Dublin Docklands, near the town center), while the Stena Line docks at Dun Laoghaire (easy DART train connections into Dublin, 4/hr, 20 min). For more information, see "Transportation Connections," page 84.

Helpful Hints

High Costs: Thanks to its recent "Celtic Tiger" economic boom, Ireland now rivals Finland as the EU's most expensive country. A pint of beer in a Dublin pub can cost €4. Restaurants and lodging—other than hostels—are more expensive the closer you get to the touristy Temple Bar district (see cheaper options listed in "Sleeping," page 89). Look for pub grub "carvery" lunch or dinner options (usually around €10) and consider picnics once in a while. If you're staying at a big hotel, don't pay for the expensive optional €10–15 breakfast—you'll likely find a nearby local café that serves breakfast for half that.

Tourist Victim Support Service: This service can be helpful if you run into any problems (Mon–Sat 10:00–18:00, Sun 12:00–18:00, tel. 01/478-5295).

U.S. Embassy: It's on 42 Elgin Road in the Ballsbridge neighborhood (Mon–Fri 8:30–17:00 for passport concerns, closed Sat–Sun, tel. 01/668-7122 or 01/668-8777, http://dublin.usembassy.gov).

Festivals: St. Patrick's Day is a five-day extravaganza in Dublin (www.stpatricksday.ie). June 16 is Bloomsday, dedicated to the Irish author James Joyce and featuring the Messenger Bike Rally. On rugby weekends (about 4 per year), hotels raise their prices and are packed. Book ahead during festival times and for any weekend.

Internet Access: There are Internet cafés on nearly every street. At the Christ Church end of Temple Bar, try **Juice Net** (Mon–Fri 7:00–23:30, Sat 8:00–23:30, Sun 10:00–23:30, Essex Street West). Between Trinity College and St. Stephen's Green, **Central Cybercafé** is indeed central (Mon–Fri 9:00–22:00, Sat–Sun 10:00–21:00, 6 Grafton Street, tel. 01/677-8298). **Global Internet Café** is north of the River Liffey (Mon–Fri 8:00–23:00, Sat 9:00–23:00, Sun 10:00–23:00, 8 Lower O'Connell Street, tel. 01/878-0295).

Laundry: Patrick Street Launderette, a block southwest of Jurys Inn Christ Church on Patrick Street, is full-service only. Allow four hours and about €9 for a load (Mon–Fri 7:30–20:00, Sat 9:00–18:00, closed Sun, tel. 01/473-1779). The **All-American Launderette** offers self- and full-service options (Mon–Sat 8:30–19:00, Sun 10:00–18:00, 40 South Great George's Street, tel. 01/677-2779).

Car Rental: For Dublin car-rental information, see the appendix.

Getting Around Dublin

You'll do most of Dublin on foot.

By Bus: Big green buses are cheap and cover the city thoroughly. Most lines start at the four quays (pronounced "keys"), or piers, that are nearest to O'Connell Bridge. If you're away from the center, nearly any bus takes you back downtown. Tell the driver where you're going, and he'll ask for €0.90, €1.30, €1.50, or €1.75, depending on the number of stops. Bring exact change or lose any excess. Bus #90 connects the bus and train stations (see "Arrival in Dublin—By Train," above).

The bus office at 59 Upper O'Connell Street has free "route network" maps and sells two city-bus passes. The three-day **Rambler pass** costs €10 and covers the Airlink airport bus (but not Aircoach buses or DART trains). The three-day **Short Hop pass,** which costs €16, includes DART trains (but not Airlink or Aircoach buses). Passes are also sold at each TI (bus info tel. 01/873-4222).

By DART (Train): Speedy commuter trains run along the coast, connecting Dublin with Dun Laoghaire's ferry terminal and recommended B&Bs. Think of the DART line as a giant "C" that serves coastal suburbs from Bray in the south to Howth in the north (€1.90, €3.40 round-trips are valid the same day only, Eurail valid but uses a valuable flexi-day; for a longer stay, consider the €16 Short Hop 3-day bus and rail pass covering DART and

Dublin buses—see above, tel. 01/703-3504, www.irishrail.ie). For more information, see "Getting to Dun Laoghaire" on page 87.

By LUAS (Light Rail): The city's light-rail system has two main lines (red and green) that serve inland suburbs. The more useful line for travelers is the red line, connecting the Connolly and Heuston train stations at either edge of the Central 1 Zone. In between, the Busaras Central Bus Station and Smithfield Village stops can be handy (€1.30, 6/hr, runs 5:30–00:30 in the morning, tel. 1-800-300-604, www.luas.ie).

By Taxi: Cabbies are honest, plentiful, friendly, and good sources of information (€3.40 minimum, €0.50 per bag, figure up to €8 for most cross-town rides, €30 per hour for guided joyride).

TOURS

While the physical treasures of Dublin are lackluster by European standards, the city has a fine story to tell and people with a natural knack for telling it. It's a good town for walking tours, and the competition is fierce. Pamphlets touting creative walks are posted all over town. There are medieval walks, literary walks, 1916 Rebellion walks, Georgian Dublin walks, and more. The evening walks are great ways to meet other travelers.

▲▲**Historical Walking Tour**—This is your best introductory walk. A group of hardworking history graduates—many of whom claim to have done more than just kiss the Blarney Stone—enliven Dublin's basic historic strip (Trinity College, Old Parliament House, Dublin Castle, and Christ Church Cathedral). You'll get the story of their city, from its Viking origin to the present. Guides speak at length about the roots of Ireland's struggle with Britain. As you listen to your guide's story, you stand in front of buildings that aren't much to see, but are lots to talk about (May–Sept daily at 11:00 and 15:00, April and Oct daily at 11:00; Nov–March only Fri, Sat, and Sun at 11:00). All walks last two hours and cost €10 (but get the €8 "student" discount rate with this book in 2006, depart from front gate of Trinity College, private tours available, tel. 01/878-0227, mobile 087-830-3523, www.historicalinsights.ie).

1916 Rebellion Walks—This walking tour breathes gritty life into the most turbulent year in modern Irish history, when idealistic Irish rebels launched the Easter Uprising that eventually led to independence from Britain (€12, €2 discount with this book in 2006, 2 hours, daily mid-March–Oct Mon–Thu at 11:30, Fri–Sat at 11:30 and 14:30, Sun at 13:00, depart from International Bar at 23 Wicklow Street, mobile 086-858-3847, www.1916rising.com).

▲**Dublin Literary Pub Crawl**—Two actors take 30 or so tourists on a walk, stopping at four pubs. Half the time is spent enjoying their entertaining banter, which introduces the novice to the high

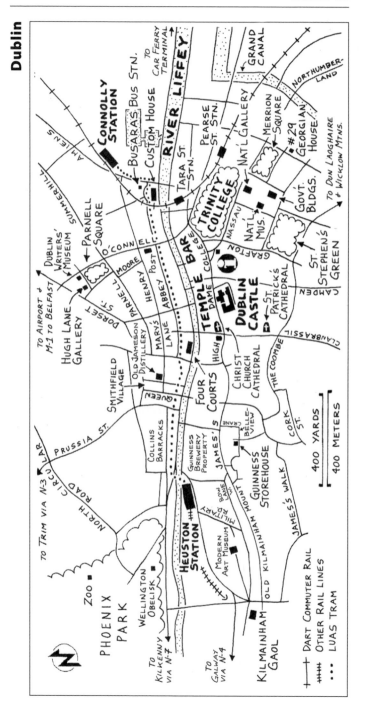

Dublin at a Glance

▲▲▲**National Museum** Interesting collection of Irish treasures from the Stone Age to today. **Hours:** Tue–Sat 10:00–17:00, Sun 14:00–17:00, closed Mon.

▲▲▲**Kilmainham Gaol** Historic jail used by the British as a political prison, today a moving museum to the suffering of the Irish people. **Hours:** Daily April–Sept 9:30–18:00, Oct–March 9:30–17:00.

▲▲▲**Book of Kells in the Trinity Old Library** Contains an exquisite illuminated manuscript, the most important piece of art from the Dark Ages. **Hours:** May–Sept Mon–Sat 9:30–17:00, Sun 9:30–16:30; Oct–April Mon–Sat 9:30–17:00, Sun 12:00–16:30.

▲▲**Trinity College** Ireland's most famous school, best visited with a 30-minute tour led by one of its students. **Hours:** Late May–Sept daily 10:15–15:45, weather permitting.

▲▲**Dublin Castle** The city's historic 700-year-old castle, featuring ornate English state apartments, tourable only with a guide. **Hours:** Mon–Fri 10:00–17:00, Sat–Sun 14:00–17:00.

▲▲**Grafton Street** The city's liveliest pedestrian shopping mall. **Hours:** Always open.

▲▲**Number Twenty-Nine Georgian House** Restored 18th-century house; tours provide an intimate glimpse of middle-class Georgian life. **Hours:** Tue–Sat 10:00–17:00, Sun 13:00–17:00, closed Mon.

▲▲**O'Connell Bridge** Landmark bridge spanning the River Liffey at the center of Dublin. **Hours:** Always open.

▲▲**O'Connell Street** Dublin's grandest promenade and main

craic (conversation) of Joyce, O'Casey, and Yeats. The two-hour tour is punctuated with 20-minute pub breaks (free time). While the beer lubricates the social fun, it dilutes the content of the evening (€12, €1 discount with this book in 2006, April–Nov daily at 19:30, plus Sun at noon; Dec–March Thu–Sun only; you can normally just show up, but call ahead July–Aug when it can fill up; meet upstairs in Duke Pub, off Grafton on Duke Street, tel. 01/670-5602, www.dublinpubcrawl.com).

drag, packed with history and ideal for a stroll. **Hours:** Always open.

▲**Dublin Experience** Decent but overpriced 45-minute slide-show offering a historic introduction to Dublin. **Hours:** June–Sept daily, showings on the hour 10:00–17:00, closed Oct–May.

▲**Chester Beatty Library** American expatriate's eclectic collection of mostly non-Western artifacts. **Hours:** May–Sept Mon–Fri 10:00–17:00, Sat 11:00–17:00, Sun 13:00–17:00; Oct–April closed Mon.

▲**National Gallery** Fine collection of top Irish painters and European masters. **Hours:** Mon–Sat 9:30–17:30, Thu until 20:30, Sun 12:00–17:30.

▲**St. Stephen's Green** Relaxing park surrounded by fine Georgian buildings. **Hours:** Always open.

▲**Merrion Square** Enjoyable and inviting park with a fun statue of Oscar Wilde. **Hours:** Always open.

▲**Temple Bar** Dublin's trendiest neighborhood, with shops, cafés, theaters, galleries, pubs, and restaurants—a great spot for live traditional music. **Hours:** Always open.

▲**Guinness Storehouse** The home of Ireland's national beer, with a museum of beer-making, a gallery of clever ads, and the spectacular Gravity Bar with panoramic city views. **Hours:** Daily 9:30–17:00.

▲**Gaelic Athletic Association Museum** High-tech museum of traditional Gaelic sports such as hurling and Irish football. **Hours:** Mon–Sat 9:30–17:00, Sun 12:00–17:00. On game Sundays, it's open only to Cusack stand ticket-holders.

▲▲**Traditional Irish-Music Pub Crawl**—This is similar to the Literary Pub Crawl, but it features music. You meet upstairs at 19:30 at Gogarty's Pub (Temple Bar area, corner of Fleet and Anglesea), and spend 40 minutes in each of the upstairs rooms of three pubs; there, you'll listen to two musicians talk about, play, and sing traditional Irish music. While having only two musicians makes the music a bit thin (Irish music aficionados will tell you you're better off just finding a good session), the evening—though touristy—is not gimmicky. It's an education in traditional Irish music. The musicians demonstrate a few instruments and really enjoy introducing rookies to their art (€12, €1 discount with this book in 2006, beer extra, April–Oct nightly, Nov and Feb–March Fri–Sat only, no tours Dec–Jan, allow 2.5 hours, expect up to 50 tourists, tel. 01/475-3313, www.musicalpubcrawl.com).

▲**Hop-on, Hop-off Bus Tours**—Two companies (Dublin City Tours and City Sightseeing/Guide Friday) offer hop-on, hop-off bus tours of Dublin, doing virtually identical 90-minute circuits, allowing you to get on or off at your choice of about 20 stops. Buses are mostly topless, with live running commentaries. Both companies go to Guinness Storehouse, but City Sightseeing/Guide Friday buses stop at Kilmainham Gaol (instead of Phoenix Park). Buy your ticket on board. Each company's map, free with your ticket, details various discounts you'll get at Dublin's sights (usually the Guinness Storehouse, Viking Splash tour, Old Jameson Distillery, Dublin Writers' Museum, Dublinia, Christ Church Cathedral, and others). Your ticket is valid for 24 hours from the time you buy it (daily, 4/hr from 9:30–18:30, until 17:30 off-season). **Dublin City Tour** runs the green-and-cream buses with drivers that do the narration (€12.50, tel. 01/873-4222). **City Sightseeing** (red buses) and **Guide Friday** (yellow buses) cost more but come with a guide and a driver, rather than a driver who guides (€14, tel. 01/872-9010, www.irishcitytours.com).

▲**Viking Splash Tours**—If you'd like to ride in a WWII amphibious vehicle—driven by a Viking-costumed guide who's as liable to spout history as he is to growl—this is for you. The tour starts with a group roar from the Viking within us all. At first, the guide talks as if he were a Viking ("When we came here in 841..."), but soon the patriot emerges as he tags Irish history onto the sights you pass. Near the end of the 75-minute tour (punctuated by occasional group roars at passersby), you don a life jacket for a slow spin up and down a boring canal. Kids who expect a Viking splash may feel they've been trapped in a classroom, but historians will enjoy the talk more than the gimmick (€17.50, daily Feb–Nov 10:30–17:00, none Dec–Jan, depart about hourly from Bull Alley beside St. Patrick's Cathedral and from the north side of St. Stephen's Green opposite Dawson Street, ticket office at 64–65 Patrick Street, on gray days boat is covered but still breezy—dress warmly, tel. 01/707-6000, www.vikingsplashtours.com).

SIGHTS

Trinity College
Founded in 1592 by Queen Elizabeth I to establish a Protestant way of thinking about God, Trinity has long been Ireland's most prestigious college. Originally the student body was limited to rich

Protestant males. Women were admitted in 1903, and Catholics—though allowed entrance by the school much earlier—were given formal permission to study at Trinity in the 1970s. Today, half of Trinity's 12,500 students are women, and 70 percent are culturally Catholic (although only about 20 percent of Irish youth are churchgoing).

▲▲**Trinity College Tour**—Trinity students organize and lead 30-minute tours of their campus (look for ticket seller on a stool

just inside the gate). You'll get a rundown of the mostly Georgian architecture; a peek at student life, both in the early days and today; and the enjoyable company of your guide, a witty Irish college kid (€10; includes €7.50 fee to see Book of Kells, where the tour leaves you; late May–Sept daily 10:15–15:45, departs roughly every 45 min, weather permitting, no tours off-season).

▲▲▲**Book of Kells in the Trinity Old Library**—The only Trinity campus interior welcoming tourists is the Old Library (just follow the signs), with its precious Book of Kells. The first-class *Turning Darkness into Light* exhibit puts the 680-page illuminated manuscript in its historical and cultural context, preparing you to see the original book and other precious manuscripts in the treasury. The exhibit is a one-way affair leading to the actual treasury, which shows only four books under glass in one display case. Make a point to spend at least half an hour in the exhibit (before reaching the actual Book of Kells). Especially interesting are the five-minute video clips showing the exacting care that went into transcribing the monk-uscripts and the ancient art of bookbinding.

Written on vellum (baby calfskin) in the late eighth century—by Irish monks on the island of Iona, Scotland—this enthu-

siastically decorated copy of the four Gospels was taken to the Irish monastery at Kells in A.D. 806 after a series of Viking raids. Arguably the finest piece of art from what is generally called the Dark Ages, the Book of Kells shows that monastic life in this far fringe of Europe was far from dark. It has been bound into four separate volumes, and at any given time, two of the four gospels are on display. The crowd around the one glass case with the treasures can be off-putting, but hold your own and get up close. You'll see four richly decorated, 1,200-year-old pages—two text and two decorated cover pages. The library treasury also displays two other books—likely the Book of Armagh (A.D. 807) and the Book of Durrow (A.D. 680)—neither of which can be checked out.

Next, a stairway leads upstairs to the 200-foot-long main chamber of the Old Library (from 1732), stacked to its towering ceiling with 200,000 of the library's oldest books. Here, you'll find one of a dozen surviving original copies of the **Proclamation of the Irish Republic.** Patrick Pearse read these words outside the General Post Office on April 24, 1916, starting the Easter Rising that led to Irish independence. Read the entire thing...imagining it was yours. Notice the inclusive opening phrase and the seven signatories (each of whom was executed). Another national icon is nearby: the oldest surviving Irish harp, from the 15th century.

Cost and Hours: €7.50; included in €10 Trinity College tour—see above; €11.30 combo-ticket covers *Dublin Experience* movie—see below; May–Sept Mon–Sat 9:30–17:00, Sun 9:30–16:30; Oct–April Mon–Sat 9:30–17:00, Sun 12:00–16:30 (tel. 01/608-2308). A long line often snakes out of the building. Minimize long waiting times by avoiding the midday crunch (roughly 11:30–14:30). For more on the Book of Kells, see page 346 in the Ireland: Past and Present chapter.

▲**Dublin Experience**—This 45-minute fancy slideshow, giving a historic introduction to Dublin, is one more tourist movie with the sound turned up. It's good—offering a fine, sweeping introduction to the story of Ireland—but pricey, riding on the coattails of the Book of Kells. But considering that the combo-ticket gets you this for half-price and lets you waltz past the Book of Kells ticket-buying line, it's not a bad value (€5, included in €11.30 combo-ticket with Book of Kells/Trinity Old Library, June–Sept daily showings on the hour 10:00–17:00, closed Oct–May, in modern arts building across from Trinity Old Library).

More Sights South of the River Liffey

▲▲**Dublin Castle**—Built on the spot of the first Viking fortress, this castle was the seat of British rule in Ireland for 700 years. Located where the Poddle and Liffey Rivers came together, making a black pool (*dubh linn* in Irish), Dublin Castle was the official residence of the viceroy who implemented the will of the British royalty. In this stirring setting, the Brits handed power over to Michael Collins and the Irish in 1922. Today, it's used for fancy state and charity functions. The 45-minute tours offer a room-by-room walk through the lavish state apartments of this most English of Irish palaces. The tour finishes with a look at the foundations of the Norman tower and the best remaining chunk

South Dublin

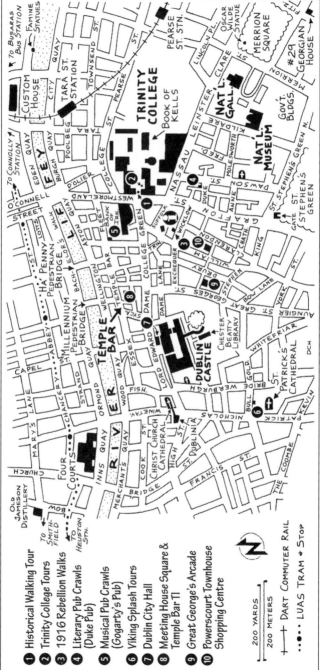

Map labels (as they appear on the map):

To Busaras Bus Station
Famine Statues
Custom House
City Quay
Tara St. Station
Townsend St.
Pearse St. Stn.
Lincoln Pl.
Oscar Wilde Statue
Merrion Square
Georgian House
#29 Georgian House
To Connolly Station
Eden Quay
Burgh Quay
Poolbeg Quay
Liffey
Trinity College
Book of Kells
Nat'l. Gall.
Nat'l. Museum
Gov't. Bldgs.
Leinster St.
Clare St.
Kildare St.
Molesworth St.
Frederick St.
O'Connell Street
D'Olier St.
Westmoreland St.
Fleet St.
Bank of Ire.
College Green
Nassau St.
Dawson St.
Anne St.
Duke St.
Wicklow St.
Exchequer St.
St. Stephen's Green
St. Stephen's Green Gate
Ha' Penny Pedestrian Bridge
Aston Quay
Bachelor's Walk
Millennium Pedestrian Bridge
Abbey St.
Capel St.
Mary's Lane
Chancery Lane
Strand St.
Ormond Quay
Wellington Quay
Temple Bar
Essex Quay
Wood Quay
Merchant's Quay
Inns Quay
Four Courts
Church St.
Old Jameson Distillery
To Smithfield
To Heuston Stn.
River Liffey
Fish. St.
Lord Edward St.
Dame St.
Dame Lane
Dublin Castle
Chester Beatty Library
Christ Church Cathedral
Wine Tav. St.
High St.
Nicholas St.
Dublinia
St. Patrick's Cathedral
Bull Alley
Bride St.
Werburgh St.
Kevin St.
Patrick St.
The Coombe
Francis St.
Cook St.
Bridge St.
Merchant's Quay
Cope St.
Temple Lane
Crow St.
Sycamore St.
Suffolk St.
King St.
Drury St.
George's St.
Great Georges St.
Stephen St.
Bow Lane
York St.
Aungier St.
Whitefriar St.
Golden Lane
DCH

Legend:
① Historical Walking Tour
② Trinity College Tours
③ 1916 Rebellion Walks
④ Literary Pub Crawls (Duke Pub)
⑤ Musical Pub Crawls (Gogarty's Pub)
⑥ Viking Splash Tours
⑦ Dublin City Hall
⑧ Meeting House Square & Temple Bar TI
⑨ Great George's Arcade
⑩ Powerscourt Townhouse Shopping Centre

200 YARDS
200 METERS

N

— DART Commuter Rail
•—• LUAS Tram + Stop

of the 13th-century town wall (€5, covered by Dublin Pass and by Heritage Card—see page 4, 2/hr, Mon–Fri 10:00–17:00, Sat–Sun 14:00–17:00, tel. 01/677-7129).

▲**Chester Beatty Library**—Chester Beatty was a rich American mining engineer who retired to Ireland in 1950, later becoming its first honorary citizen. He left his priceless and eclectic collection to his adopted homeland as a public charitable trust.

More an exotic parade of non-Irish treasures than a library, these two floors of rare texts and collectibles sprouted from over 2,000 years of Eastern religions, Islam, and Christianity. You'll see books carved out of jade, ornate snuff bottles, rhino-horn cups, and even the oldest surviving copy of St. Paul's letter to the Romans (A.D. 180). Other highlights include a graceful Burmese book written on palm leaves—bound together to unfold like an accordion—and a densely ornamental sunburst motif from a 500-year-old Iranian Quran (free entry, May–Sept Mon–Fri 10:00–17:00, Sat 11:00–17:00, Sun 13:00–17:00; Oct–April closed Mon, tel. 01/407-0750, www.cbl.ie). Enter the library via Dublin Castle's pedestrian arch, located across Dame Street from the Olympia Theatre; walk straight ahead crossing the courtyard/parking lot, turn right behind the church and castle turret, walk straight for 75 yards, and enter on the left, just past the walled gardens. It's in the modern addition to the Dublin Castle clock-tower building.

Dublin City Hall—The first Georgian building in this very Georgian city stands proudly overlooking Dame Street, in front of the gate to Dublin Castle. Built in 1779 as the Royal Exchange, it introduced the Georgian style (then very popular in Britain and the Continent) to Ireland. Step inside (it's free) to feel the prosperity and confidence of Dublin in her 18th-century glory days. In 1852, it became the City Hall. Under the grand rotunda, a cycle of heroic paintings tells the city's history. Pay your respects to the 18-foot-tall statue of Daniel O'Connell, the great orator and liberator who, in 1829, won emancipation for Catholics in Ireland from the much-despised Protestants over in London. The greeter sits like the Maytag repairman at the information desk, eager to give you more information. Downstairs is a simple *Story of the Capital* exhibition—storyboards and video clips of Dublin's history (€4, covered by Dublin Pass, free audioguides, coffee shop, Mon–Sat 10:00–17:00, Sun 14:00–17:00).

Dublinia—This exhibit tries valiantly to be a "bridge to Dublin's medieval past." The amateurish look at the medieval town starts with a walk through dim rooms of tableaus, followed by several halls of medieval exhibits, a scale model of old Dublin, and an interesting room devoted to medieval fairs. Then, at the top of the stairs, you get to enter the old synod (church council) hall, now devoted to exhibitions on Viking life in Dublin (€6, €10 combo-ticket includes Christ Church Cathedral—saves you €1, daily April–Sept 10:00–17:00, Oct–March 11:00–16:00, brass rubbing, coffee shop open in summer only, across from Christ Church Cathedral, tel. 01/679-4611).

Christ Church Cathedral—The first church on this spot was built of wood by King Sitric in Viking times (c. 1040). The present structure dates from a mix of periods: Norman and Gothic, but mostly Victorian neo-Gothic (1870s restoration work). The unusually large crypt under the cathedral—actually the oldest building in Dublin—contains stocks, statues, and the cathedral's silver (€5 donation to church, includes downstairs crypt silver exhibition, covered by Dublin Pass, €10 combo-ticket includes Dublinia, free brochure with self-guided tour, daily 10:00–17:00). Because of Dublin's British past, neither of its top two churches is Catholic. Christ Church Cathedral and the nearby St. Patrick's Cathedral are both Church of Ireland. In Catholic Ireland, these sights feel hollow. They're more famous than visit-worthy.

Evensong: At Christ Church Cathedral, a 45-minute evensong service is sung regularly several times a week (Wed-Thu at 18:00, Sat at 17:00, and Sun at 15:30; less regularly during the summer). The 13th-century St. Patrick's Cathedral, where Jonathan Swift (author of *Gulliver's Travels*) was dean in the 18th century, also offers evensong (Sun at 15:15, Mon–Fri at 17:30, but not on Wed in July–Aug).

▲▲▲**National Museum**—Showing off the treasures of Ireland from the Stone Age to modern times, this museum is itself a national treasure. Under one dome, it's wonderfully digestible. Ireland's Bronze Age gold fills the center. Up four steps, a prehistoric Ireland exhibit rings the gold. In a corner (behind a 2,000-year-old body), you'll find the treasury, with the museum's most famous pieces (brooches, chalices, and other examples of Celtic metalwork) and an 18-minute video (played on request) that gives an overview of Irish art through the 13th century. The collection's superstar is the gold, enamel, and amber eighth-century Tara Brooch. Jumping way ahead (and to the opposite side of the hall), a special corridor features *The Road to Independence,* with guns, letters, and death masks that recall the fitful birth of the "Terrible Beauty" (1900–1921, with a focus on the 1916 Easter Rising). The best Viking artifacts in town are upstairs (with the medieval collection). If you'll be visiting Cong (in Connemara, near Galway), seek out the original Cross of Cong (free entry, Tue–Sat 10:00–17:00, Sun 14:00–17:00, closed Mon, good café, Kildare Street 2, between Trinity College and St. Stephen's Green). Greatest-hits tours are given several times a day (€2, 40 min, tel. 01/677-7444—call in morning for tour schedule). For background information, read "Irish Art" on page 345 in the Ireland: Past and Present chapter.

▲**National Gallery**—Along with a hall that features the work of top Irish painters, this gallery has Ireland's best collection of European masters. It's impressive—although not nearly as extensive as those in London or Paris (free, covered by Dublin Pass, Mon–Sat 9:30–17:30, Thu until 20:30, Sun 12:00–17:30, Merrion Square West, tel. 01/661-5133, www.nationalgallery.ie). Guided tours run on weekends only (Sat at 15:00 only; Sun at 14:00, 15:00, and 16:00).

▲▲**Grafton Street**—Once filled with noisy traffic, today's Grafton Street is Dublin's liveliest pedestrian shopping mall. A five-minute stroll past street musicians takes you from Trinity College to St. Stephen's Green (and makes you wonder why American merchants are so terrified of a car-free street). Walking by a buxom statue of "sweet" Molly Malone (known by locals as "the tart with the cart"), you'll soon pass two venerable department stores: the Irish Brown Thomas and the English Marks & Spencer. An alley leads to the Powerscourt Townhouse Shopping Centre, which tastefully fills a converted Georgian mansion. The huge, glass-covered St. Stephen's Green Shopping Centre and the peaceful Green itself mark the top of Grafton Street.

▲**St. Stephen's Green**—This city park, originally a medieval commons, was enclosed in 1664 and gradually surrounded with fine Georgian buildings. Today, it provides 22 acres of grassy refuge for Dubliners. On a sunny afternoon, it's a wonderful world apart from the big city.

▲▲**Number Twenty-Nine Georgian House**—The carefully restored house at Number 29 Lower Fitzwilliam Street gives an intimate glimpse of middle-class Georgian life (which seems pretty high-class). From the sidewalk, descend the stairs to the basement-level entrance (corner of Lower Fitzwilliam and Lower Mount Streets, opposite southern corner of Merrion Square). Start with an interesting 15-minute video (you're welcome to bring in a cup of coffee from the café) before joining your guide, who takes you on a fascinating 35-minute walk through this 1790 Dublin home (€4.50, tours leave regularly, Tue–Sat 10:00–17:00, Sun 13:00–17:00, closed Mon, tel. 01/702-6165).

▲**Merrion Square**—Laid out in 1762, this square is ringed by elegant Georgian houses decorated with fine doors—a Dublin trademark—displaying ornate knobs and knockers. The park, once the exclusive domain of the residents, is now a delightful public escape. More inviting than St. Stephen's Green, it's ideal for a picnic. To learn what "snogging" is, walk through the park on a sunny day, when it's full of smooching lovers. Oscar Wilde, lounging wittily on a boulder on the corner nearest the town center and surrounded by his clever quotes, provides a fun photo op (see photo on page 350).

▲**Temple Bar**—This was a Georgian center of craftsmen and merchants. After falling on hard times in the 19th century, the area was a part of town with lower rents, attracting students and artists and giving the neighborhood a bohemian flair. With government tax incentives and lots of development money, the Temple Bar district has become a thriving cultural (and beer-drinking) hotspot.

This much-promoted center—with trendy shops, cafés, theaters, galleries, pubs with live music, and restaurants—feels like the heart of the city. It's Dublin's "Left Bank," and like in Paris, it's on the south shore of the river. It fills the cobbled streets between Dame Street and the River Liffey. ("Bar" means a walkway along the river.) The central **Meeting House Square** (just off Essex Street) hosts free street theater, as well as a lively organic-produce market and a book market (Sat 10:00–18:00). The square is surrounded by interesting cultural centers.

These days, the downside to Temple Bar is the noise and high prices. Crowded summer weekend nights can be a real zoo. Women in funky hats, part of loud "hen" (bachelorette) parties, promenade down the main drag as drunken dudes shout from pub doorways to get their attention. Be aware that a pint of beer here is fast approaching €5—at least €1 more than at less-glitzy pubs just a couple blocks away (north of the River Liffey or south of Dame Street).

For a listing of events and galleries, visit the **Temple Bar Information Centre** (12 East Essex Street, www.visit-templebar

.com). Rather than follow particular pub or restaurant recommendations (mine are under "Eating" on page 81), venture down a few side lanes off the main drag to see what looks good.

The pedestrian-only **Ha' Penny Bridge,** named for the halfpence toll people used to pay to cross it, leads from Temple Bar over the River Liffey to the opposite bank and more sights.

North of the River Liffey

▲▲**O'Connell Bridge**—This bridge spans the River Liffey, which has historically divided the wealthy, cultivated south side from the poorer, cruder, north side. While there's plenty of culture north of

North Dublin

North Dublin

TO AIRPORT

MOUNTJOY SQUARE

TO CROKE PARK & GAA MUSEUM

DUBLIN WRITERS MUSEUM

HUGH LANE GALLERY & FRANCIS BACON STUDIO

GARDEN OF REMEMBRANCE

SUMMERHILL

GATE THEATRE

DERMOT

MAC

CONNOLLY TRAIN STN.

PARNELL SQUARE

DORSET ST.

DOMINICK LOWER

PARNELL

ST. MARY'S PRO-CATHEDRAL

TALBOT

INNER DOCK

AMIENS

STREET MARKET

ABBEY THEATRE

HENRY

GENERAL POST OFFICE

MARY ST.

ABBEY LOWER

BUSARAS + CENTRAL BUS STATION

CUSTOM HOUSE QUAY

TO SMITHFIELD VILLAGE

ABBEY ST.

LOTTS ROW

EDEN QUAY

CUST. HOUSE QUAY

LIF

FEY

GEORGES DOCK

HA' PENNY BRIDGE

BACH. WALK

O'CONNELL BRIDGE

TARA ST. STATION

FAMINE MONUMENT

WOOD QUAY

ASTON QUAY

RIVER

TEMPLE BAR

TRINITY COLLEGE

PEARSE

200 YARDS
200 METERS

- ❶ Daniel O'Connell Statue
- ❷ James Larkin Statue
- ❸ Millennium Spire
- ❹ Father Matthew Statue
- ❺ Charles Stewart Parnell Monument
- ❻ Townhouse of Dublin
- ❼ Jurys Inn Custom House
- ❽ Comfort Inn
- ❾ Clifden House
- ❿ Charles Stewart Hotel
- ⓫ James Joyce Cultural Centre
- ⓬ Millennium Pedestrian Bridge

the river, even today "the north" is considered rougher and less safe.

From the bridge, look upriver (west) as far upstream as you can see. On the left in the distance, the **big concrete building**—considered an eyesore by locals—houses the city planning commission, which ironically is in charge of making sure new buildings are built in good taste. It squats on the still-buried precious artifacts of the first Viking settlement, established in Dublin in the ninth century.

Across the river stands the **Four Courts**—the Supreme Court building. It was shelled and burned in 1922, during the tragic civil war that followed Irish independence. The national archives office burned, and irreplaceable birth records were lost, making it difficult for those with Irish roots to trace their ancestry today. The closest bridge upstream—the elegant iron **Ha' Penny Bridge** (see photo on page 48)—leads left, into the Temple Bar nightlife district. Just beyond that old-fashioned, 19th-century bridge is Dublin's pedestrian **Millennium Bridge,** inaugurated in 2000. (Note that buses leave from O'Connell Bridge—specifically Aston Quay—for the Guinness Storehouse and Kilmainham Gaol.)

Turn 180 degrees and look downstream to see the tall **Liberty Hall** union headquarters—for now, the tallest building in the Republic (16 stories tall, some say in honor of the 1916 Easter Uprising)—and lots of cranes. Booming Dublin is developing downstream. The Irish (forever clever tax fiddlers) have subsidized and revitalized this formerly dreary quarter with great success. A short walk downstream along the north bank leads to a powerful series of modern statues memorializing the Great Potato Famine of 1845–1849.

▲▲O′Connell Street Stroll—Dublin's grandest street leads from O'Connell Bridge through the heart of north Dublin. From the 1740s, it has been a 45-yard-wide promenade. Ever since the first O'Connell Bridge connected it to the Trinity side of town in 1794, it's been Dublin's main drag. (But it was only named O'Connell after independence was won in 1922.) These days, construction reigns as the city makes the street more pedestrian-friendly. Though lined with fast-food and souvenir shops, O'Connell Street echoes with history. Take the following stroll (you can walk on the tree-lined median strip, which is wide, less crowded, and closer to the statues mentioned below):

Statues and monuments line O'Connell Street, celebrating great figures in Ireland's fight for independence. At the base of the street stands **Daniel O'Connell** (1775–1847), known as "the Liberator" for founding the Catholic Association and demanding Irish Catholic rights in the British Parliament.

Looking a block east down Abbey Street, you can see the famous **Abbey Theatre**—rebuilt after a fire into a nondescript, modern building. It's still the much-loved home of the Irish National Theatre.

The statue of **James Larkin** honors the founder of the Irish Transport Workers' Union. The one monument that didn't wave an Irish flag—a tall column crowned by a statue of the British hero of Trafalgar, Admiral Horatio Nelson—was blown up in 1966...the IRA's contribution to the local celebration of the Easter Rising's 50th anniversary. This spot is now occupied by the 300-foot-tall, stainless steel **Millennium Spire** that was finally completed in 2003. Dubious Dubliners have nicknamed it "the stiletto in the ghetto."

The **General Post Office** is not just any P.O. It was from here that Patrick Pearse read the Proclamation of Irish Independence in 1916, and kicked off the Easter Rising. The G.P.O. building itself—a kind of Irish Alamo—was the rebel headquarters and scene of a five-day bloody siege that followed the proclamation. Its pillars remain pockmarked with bullet holes. Step inside and trace the battle by studying the well-described cycle of 10 paintings that circle the main hall (open for business and sightseers Mon–Sat 8:00–20:00, closed Sun).

The busy **Moore Street Market** is nearby (Mon–Sat 8:00–18:00, closed Sun). To get there, detour left (west) two blocks after the Post Office down people-filled Henry Street, then wander to the right into the market. Many of its merchants have staffed the same stall for 30 years. Start a conversation. It's a great workaday scene. You'll see lots of mums with strollers—a reminder that Ireland is Europe's youngest country, with more than 40 percent of the population under the age of 25.

Back on O'Connell Street, cross back onto the median strip and continue your walk. The lampposts display the colorful, three-castle city seal. The Latin motto below the seal states, "Happy the city where citizens obey." Flames rise from the castles, symbolizing the citizens' zeal to defend Dublin.

St. Mary's Pro-Cathedral, a block east of O'Connell down Cathedral Street, is Dublin's leading Catholic church. But, curiously, it's not a cathedral, even though the pope declared Christ Church one in the 12th century—and later, St. Patrick's. (The Vatican has chosen to stubbornly ignore the fact that Christ Church and St. Patrick's haven't been Catholic for centuries.) Completed in 1821, it's done in the style of a Greek temple.

Continuing up O'Connell Street, you'll find a statue of **Father Matthew,** a leader of the temperance movement of the 1830s who, some historians claim, was responsible for enough Irish peasants staying sober to enable Daniel O'Connell to organize them into a political force. (Perhaps understanding this dynamic, the U.S.S.R. was careful to keep the price of vodka affordable.) The fancy Gresham Hotel is a good place for an elegant tea or beer.

A monument to **Charles Stewart Parnell** stands boldly at the top of O'Connell Street. The names of the four ancient provinces of Ireland and all 32 Irish counties (North *and* South, since this was erected before Irish independence) ring the monument, honoring the member of Parliament who nearly won Home Rule for Ireland in the late 1800s. (A sex scandal cost Parnell the support of the

Church, which let the air out of the movement for a free Ireland.)

Continue straight up Parnell Square East. At the **Gate Theatre** (on the left), Orson Welles and James Mason got their professional acting debuts.

The **Garden of Remembrance** (past Gate Theater, 1 block up on left, daily 8:30–18:00) honors the victims of the 1916 Rising. The park was dedicated in 1966 on the 50th anniversary of the uprising that ultimately led to Irish independence. The bottom of the cross-shaped pool is a mosaic of Celtic weapons, symbolic of how the early Irish would proclaim peace by throwing their weapons into a lake or river. The Irish flag flies above the park: green for Catholics, orange for Protestants, and white for the hope that they can live together in peace. Across the street...

The **Dublin Writers' Museum** fills a splendidly restored Georgian mansion. No other country so small has produced such a wealth of literature (see page 70). As interesting to fans of Irish literature as it is boring to those who aren't, this three-room museum features the lives and works of Dublin's great writers (€6.75, ask about €11 combo-ticket with James Joyce Museum in Dun Laoghaire, covered by Dublin Pass, Mon–Sat 10:00–17:00, Sun 11:00–17:00, June–Aug Mon–Fri until 18:00, helpful audioguide available, 18 Parnell Square North, tel. 01/872-2077). With hometown wits such as Swift, Yeats, Joyce, Wilde, and Shaw, Dublin has a checklist of residences and memorials to see. Aficionados of James Joyce's work may want to hike 400 yards east to visit the **James Joyce Cultural Centre** (€5, Mon–Sat 9:30–17:00, Sun 12:30–17:00, 35 North Great George's Street, tel. 01/878-8547). There's more Joyce memorabilia in Dun Laoghaire at the **James Joyce Museum** (see page 88). Next door to the Dublin Writers' Museum, the...

Hugh Lane Municipal Art Gallery, in a grand neoclassical building, has a fine, bite-sized selection of Pre-Raphaelite, French Impressionist, and 19th- and 20th-century Irish paintings (free, Tue–Thu 9:30–18:00, Fri–Sat 9:30–17:00, Sun 11:00–17:00, closed Mon, tel. 01/874-1903). Sir Hugh went down on the *Lusitania* in 1915; due to an unclear will, his collection is shared by this gallery and the National Gallery in London.

Tucked in the back of the gallery is the **Francis Bacon Studio,** reconstructed here in its original (messy) state from its London location at the time of the artist's death in 1992. Born in Dublin

Dublin's Literary Life

Dublin in the 1700s, grown rich from a lucrative cloth trade, was one of Europe's most cultured and sophisticated cities. The buildings were decorated in the Georgian style still visible today. The city's Protestant elite shuttled between here and London, bridging the Anglo-Irish cultural gap.

Jonathan Swift (1667–1745), the great satirical writer, was also dean of St. Patrick's Cathedral (1713–1745) and one of the city's eminent citizens. His most famous book, *Gulliver's Travels,* poked fun at religious hardliners and the pompous bureaucrats in London who shaped England's misguided Irish policies.

Around the turn of the 20th century, Dublin produced some of the world's great modern writers.

Oscar Wilde (1854–1900), born in Dublin and a graduate of Trinity College, wowed London with his quick wit, outrageous clothes, and flamboyant personality, and scandalized them when he was outed as being gay. He satirized upper-class Victorian society in comedic plays (like *The Importance of Being Earnest,* 1895) with characters who speak very elegantly about the trivial concerns of the idle rich.

William Butler Yeats (1865–1939), also born and raised in Dublin, captured the passion of the Irish independence movement. His poem "Easter Rising, 1916" contains the refrain that summed up how those events affected Ireland: "All are changed, changed utterly: A terrible beauty is born."

James Joyce (1882–1941) used to wander the back streets of Dublin, observing its seedier side, which he captured in a modern, stream-of-consciousness style. His famous novel *Ulysses,* set in a single day (June 16, 1904), follows Dubliners on an Odyssey through the city's pubs, hospitals, libraries, churches, and brothels.

And today, Ireland still produces some of the English language's greatest writers. **Seamus Heaney,** a Nobel- and Pulitzer Prize–winning poet, published a new translation of the Old English epic, *Beowulf*—wedding the old with the new.

For more on Irish literature, see page 349.

and inspired by Picasso, Bacon reflected his belief that "chaos breeds energy" in his shocking paintings. This compact space contains touch-screen terminals, display cases of personal items, and a few unfinished works. The 10-minute film interview of Bacon may fascinate like-minded viewers...and disquiet others (€7, same hours as rest of gallery).

Your walk is over. Here on the north end of town, it's

convenient to visit the Gaelic Athletic Association Museum at Croke Park Stadium (described on page 75, a 30-min walk or short taxi ride away). Otherwise, hop on your skateboard and return to the river.

Dublin's Smithfield Village

This neighborhood is worth a look for the Old Jameson Distillery whiskey tour, a Chimney Viewing Tower offering city views, and Dublin's most authentic traditional-music pub. The sights are clustered close together, two blocks northwest of the Four Courts—the Supreme Court building. For a decent bite to eat, try **Chief O'Neill's** restaurant, on the same square at the base of the chimney tower.

Old Jameson Distillery—Whiskey fans enjoy visiting the old distillery. You get a 10-minute video, a 20-minute tour, and a free shot in the pub. Unfortunately, the "distillery" feels fake and put together for tourists. The Bushmills tour in Northern Ireland (in a working factory, see page 295) and the Midleton tour near Cork (in the huge, original factory, page 151) are better experiences. If you do take this tour, volunteer energetically when offered the chance to take the "whiskey taste test" at the end (€8.75, covered by Dublin Pass, daily 9:00–18:00, last tour at 17:15, Bow Street, tel. 01/807-2355).

Jameson Distillery Chimney Viewing Tower—Built in 1895 for the distillery, the chimney is now an observatory. Ride the elevator 175 feet up for a Dublin panorama not quite as exciting as the view from the Guinness Storehouse's Gravity Bar (overpriced at €5, covered by Dublin Pass, Mon–Sat 10:00–17:00, Sun 11:00–17:00, tel. 01/817-3838).

Cobblestones Pub—Hiding in a derelict-looking building, this pub offers Dublin's least-glitzy and most-rewarding traditional music venue. The candlelit walls, covered with photos of honored trad musicians, set the tone with this understated sign: "Listening area, please respect musicians" (daily 17:00–23:45, trad-music sessions Mon–Wed at 21:30, Thu–Sat at 17:00, at north end of square, 100 yards from chimney tower, tel. 01/872-1799).

Outer Dublin

The jail and the Guinness Storehouse are the main sights outside of the old center. Combine them in one visit.

▲▲▲**Kilmainham Gaol (Jail)**—Opened in 1796 as both the Dublin County Jail and a debtors' prison, it was considered a model in its day. In reality, this jail was used frequently as a political prison by the British. Many of those who fought for Irish independence were held or executed here, including leaders of the rebellions of 1798, 1803, 1848, 1867, and 1916. National heroes

Charles Stewart Parnell
(1846–1891)

Parnell, who led the Irish movement for Home Rule, did time in Kilmainham Gaol. A Cambridge-educated Protestant and Member of Parliament, he had a vision of a modern and free Irish Republic filled mostly with Catholics but not set up as a religious state. Momentum seemed to be on his side. With the British Prime Minister of the time, William Gladstone, in favor of a similar form of Home Rule, it looked as if all of Ireland was ripe for independence. Then a sex scandal broke around Parnell and his mistress. The press, egged on by the powerful Catholic bishops (who didn't want a free but secular Irish state), battered away at the scandal until finally Parnell was driven from office. Sadly, after that, Ireland became mired in the Troubles of the 20th century: an awkward independence (1921) featuring a divided island, a bloody civil war, and sectarian violence ever since. It's said Parnell died of a broken heart. Before he did, this great Irish statesman requested to be buried outside of Ireland.

Robert Emmett and Charles Stewart Parnell each did time here. The last prisoner to be held here was Eamon de Valera, who later became president of Ireland. He was released on July 16, 1924, the day Kilmainham was finally shut down. The buildings, virtually in ruins, were restored in the 1960s. Today, it's a shrine to the Nathan Hales of Ireland.

Start your visit with a guided **tour** (1 hr, 2/hr, includes 25 min in prison chapel for a rebellion-packed video, spend waiting time in museum). It's touching to tour the cells and places of execution—hearing tales of terrible colonialism and heroic patriotism—alongside Irish schoolkids who know these names well. The museum is an excellent exhibit on Victorian prison life and Ireland's fight for independence. Don't miss the museum's dimly lit Last Words 1916 hall upstairs, which displays the stirring final letters that patriots sent to loved ones hours before facing the firing squad (€5, covered by Dublin Pass and Heritage Card—see page 4, daily April–Sept 9:30–18:00, Oct–March 9:30–17:00, last entry 1 hour before closing; €5 taxi; or bus #51b, #78a, or #79 from Aston Quay or Guinness Storehouse; tel. 01/453-5984). You could taxi to the jail, then catch the bus from there to the Guinness Storehouse (leaving the prison, take 3 rights, crossing no streets, to the bus stop and hop bus #51b or #78a). Another option is taking the City Sightseeing/Guide Friday hop-on, hop-off bus (see page 58), which stops at both the jail and the Guinness Storehouse.

▲**Guinness Storehouse**—A visit to the Guinness Storehouse is, for many, a pilgrimage. Arthur Guinness began brewing the famous stout here in 1759. By 1868, it was the biggest brewery in the world. Today, the sprawling brewery fills several city blocks. Around the world, Guinness brews more than 10 million pints a day. The home of Ireland's national beer welcomes visitors, for a price, with a sprawling modern museum, but there are no tours of the actual working brewery. The museum fills the old fermentation plant that was used from 1902 through 1988, vacated, and then opened in 2000 as a huge, shrine-like place. Step into the middle of the ground floor and look up. A tall beer-glass-shaped glass atrium—14 million pints big—leads past four floors of exhibitions and cafés to the skylight. Then look down at Arthur's original 9,000-year lease, enshrined under glass in the floor...at £45 per year it's been quite a bargain. Atop the building, the **Gravity Bar** provides visitors with a commanding 360-degree view of Dublin—with vistas all the way to the sea—and a free beer. The actual exhibit makes brewing seem more grandiose than it is and treats Arthur like the god of human happiness. Highlights are the cooperage (with old film clips showing the master wood-keg makers plying their now-extinct trade), a display of the brewery's clever ads, and the Gravity Bar, which really is spectacular (€14, covered by Dublin Pass, includes a €4 pint, daily 9:30–17:00, enter on Bellevue Street, bus #78a from Aston Quay near O'Connell Bridge, or bus #123 from Dame Street and O'Connell Street, tel. 01/408-4800). Both hop-on, hop-off bus tours stop here.

▲**Gaelic Athletic Association Museum**—The GAA was founded in 1884 as an expression of an Irish cultural awakening. It was created to foster the development of Gaelic sports, specifically Irish football and hurling, and to ban English sports such as cricket and rugby. It played an important part in the fight for independence. This museum, at the recently expanded 82,000-seat Croke Park Stadium, offers a high-tech, interactive introduction to Ireland's favorite games. Relive the greatest moments in hurling and Irish-football history. Then get involved. Pick up a stick and try hurling, kick a football, and test your speed and balance. A 15-minute film clarifies the connection between sports and Irish politics (€5.50, covered by Dublin Pass, Mon–Sat 9:30–17:00, Sun 12:00–17:00; on game Sundays, museum is open 12:00–18:00 to Cusack stand ticket-holders only, as other sections of stands are blocked from museum entry; museum located under the stands at Croke Park Stadium; from O'Connell Street, walk 20 min or catch bus #3, #11, #11a, #16, #16a, or #123; tel. 01/819-2323). The €9.50

museum-plus-stadium-tour option is worth it only for rabid fans who yearn to know which locker room is considered the unlucky one (1 hour, tour also covered by Dublin Pass).

Hurling or Irish Football at Croke Park Stadium—Actually seeing a match here, surrounded by incredibly spirited Irish fans, is a fun experience. Hurling is like airborne hockey with no injury timeouts, and Irish football is a rugged form of soccer. Matches are held on most Sunday afternoons May–September. Tickets (€20–55) are available at the stadium except during championships (tel. 01/836-3222, www.gaa.ie).

Greyhound Racing—For an interesting, lowbrow look at local life, consider going to the dog races and doing a little gambling (€8; generally Wed, Thu, and Sat at 20:00; Shelbourne Park, tel. 01/668-3502). Greyhounds race on the other days at Harold's Cross Racetrack (€8; Mon, Tue, and Fri at 20:00; tel. 01/497-1081).

SHOPPING

Shops are open roughly Monday–Saturday 9:00–18:00 and until 20:00 on Thursday. They have shorter hours on Sunday (if they're open at all). The best shopping area is Grafton Street, with its neighboring streets and arcades (such as the fun Great George's Arcade between Great George's and Drury Streets), and nearby shopping centers (Powerscourt Townhouse and St. Stephen's Green shopping centers). Francis Street creaks with antiques.

To visit a street market, consider Mother Redcaps (all day Fri–Sun, closed Mon–Thu, bric-a-brac, antiques, crafts, Back Lane, Christ Church neighborhood). For produce, noise, and color, visit Moore Street (Mon–Sat 8:00–18:00, closed Sun, near General Post Office). For raw fish, get a whiff of Michan Street (Tue–Sat 7:00–15:00, closed Sun–Mon, behind Four Courts building).

On Saturdays at Temple Bar's Meeting House Square, it's food in the morning (from 9:00) and books in the afternoon (until 18:00). Temple Bar, described on page 65, is worth a browse any day for its art, jewelry, new-age paraphernalia, books, music, and gift shops. For a bit of old-fashioned horse trading, check out the Smithfield Village horsefair (first Sun of each month in the square, next to Jameson Distillery Chimney Viewing Tower).

ENTERTAINMENT AND THEATER

Ireland has produced some of the finest writers in both English and Irish, and Dublin houses some of Europe's finest theaters. While Handel's *Messiah* was first performed in Dublin (1742), these days Dublin is famous for its rock bands (U2, Thin Lizzy, Sinead O'Connor, and Live Aid founder Bob Geldof's band the Boomtown Rats all got started here).

Abbey Theatre is Ireland's national theater, founded by W. B. Yeats in 1904 to preserve Irish culture during British rule (26 Lower Abbey Street, tel. 01/878-7222, www.abbeytheatre.ie). **Gate Theatre** does foreign plays as well as Irish classics (Cavendish Row, tel. 01/874-4045, www.gate-theatre.ie). The **Gaiety Theatre** offers a wide range of quality productions (King Street South, tel. 01/677-1717, www.gaietytheatre.com). **Point Theatre,** once a railway terminus, is now the country's top live-music venue (East Link Bridge, tel. 01/836-3633, www.thepoint.ie). At the **National Concert Hall,** the National Symphony Orchestra performs most Friday evenings (Earlsfort Terrace, off St. Stephen's Green, tickets €8–22, tel. 01/417-0077, www.nch.ie). Street theater takes the stage in Temple Bar on summer evenings.

Pub Action: Folk music fills the pubs and street entertainers are everywhere. The Temple Bar area thrives with music—traditional, jazz, and pop. Although it's pricier than the rest of Dublin, it really is *the* comfortable and fun place for tourists and locals (who come here to watch the tourists). **Gogarty's Pub** (corner of Fleet and Anglesea, tel. 01/671-1822) has top-notch sessions upstairs nightly from 21:00. Use this as a kick-off for your Temple Bar evening.

A 10-minute hike up the river west of Temple Bar takes you to a twosome with a local and less-touristy ambience. The **Brazen Head,** famous as Dublin's oldest pub, is a hit for an early dinner and late live music (nightly from 21:30, tel. 01/677-9549), with atmospheric rooms and a courtyard made to order for balmy evenings (on Bridge Street). **O'Shea's Merchant Pub,** just across the street, is encrusted in memories and filled with locals taking a break from the grind. They have live traditional music nightly (the front half is a restaurant, the magic is in the back half—enter on Bridge Street, tel. 01/679-3797).

To sample truly traditional Irish song and dance, consider heading to Comhaltas Ceoltoiri Éireann in nearby Dun Laoghaire (see page 88).

Pub Crawls: For guided pub crawls (focusing on either Irish literature or music), see page 54.

SLEEPING

Dublin is popular, and rooms can be tight. Book ahead for weekends any time of year, particularly in summer and during rugby weekends. Prices are often discounted on weeknights (Mon–Thu) and from November through February.

Big and practical places (both cheap and moderate) are most central near Christ Church Cathedral, on the edge of Temple Bar. For classy, older Dublin accommodations, you'll stay a bit farther out (east of St. Stephen's Green).

For a small-town escape with the best budget values, take the convenient DART train (at least 3/hr, 20 min) to nearby Dun Laoghaire (see page 87).

Near Christ Church Cathedral

These hotels face Christ Church Cathedral, a five-minute walk from the best evening scene (at Temple Bar), and 10 minutes from the sightseeing center (Trinity College and Grafton Street). The cheap hostels in this neighborhood have some double rooms. Full Irish breakfasts, which cost €10–15 at the hotels, are half the price at the many small cafés nearby; consider Bagel Haven or Chorus Café (see listings under "Eating," page 83).

$$ Harding Hotel is a hardworking, hardwood place with 53 simple yet intimate rooms (Sb-€64, Db-€89–106, Tb-€114–131, tell them Rick sent you and get 10 percent off in 2006, breakfast-€10; on weekends, request quiet upper-floor room away from fun ground-floor pub; Copper Alley, across street from Christ Church Cathedral, tel. 01/679-6500, fax 01/679-6504, www.hardinghotel .ie, info@hardinghotel.ie).

$$ Jurys Christ Church Inn (like its sisters in Galway and in Belfast) is central and offers business-class comfort in all of its

---

Sleep Code

(€1 = about $1.20 country code: 353, area code: 01)
S = Single, **D** = Double/Twin, **T** = Triple, **Q** = Quad, **b** = bathroom, **s** = shower only. Breakfast is included and credit cards are accepted unless otherwise noted.

To help you easily sort through these listings, I've divided the rooms into three categories, based on the price for a standard double room with bath:

$$$ **Higher Priced**—Most rooms €130 or more.
$$ **Moderately Priced**—Most rooms between €70–130.
$ **Lower Priced**—Most rooms €70 or less.

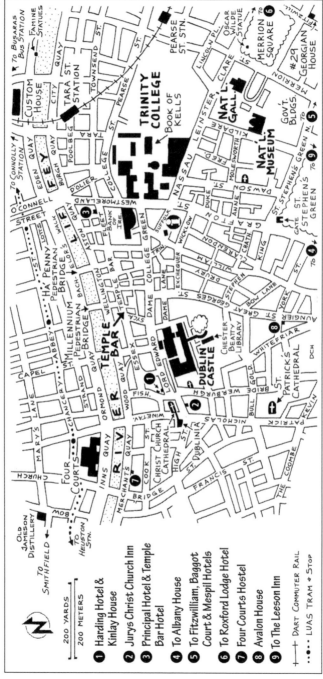

Dublin Accommodations

200 YARDS
200 METERS

1 Harding Hotel & Kinlay House
2 Jurys Christ Church Inn
3 Principal Hotel & Temple Bar Hotel
4 To Albany House
5 To Fitzwilliam, Baggot Court & Mespil Hotels
6 To Roxford Lodge Hotel
7 Four Courts Hostel
8 Avalon House
9 To The Leeson Inn

+ DART COMMUTER RAIL
•••• LUAS TRAM + STOP

182 identical rooms. This no-nonsense, American-style hotel chain has a winning keep-it-simple-and-affordable formula. If ye olde is getting old (and you don't mind big tour groups), there's no better value in town. All rooms cost the same: €112 Sunday–Thursday (or €122 Fri–Sat) for one, two, or three adults or two adults and two kids (breakfast extra). Each room has a modern bathroom, direct-dial telephone, and TV. Its three floors are strictly non-smoking. Request a room far from the noisy elevator (book long in advance for weekends, breakfast-€11, parking-€12/day, Christ Church Place, tel. 01/454-0000, fax 01/454-0012, U.S. tel. 800-423-6953, www.jurysdoyle.com, info@jurysdoyle.com). Another Jurys is near Connolly Station (see page 80).

$ Kinlay House, around the corner from Harding Hotel, is the backpackers' choice—definitely the place to go for cheap beds, a central location, and an all-ages-welcome atmosphere. This huge, red-brick, 19th-century Victorian building has 149 metal, prison-style beds in spartan, non-smoking rooms. There are singles, doubles, and four- to six-bed coed dorms (good for families), as well as a few giant dorms. It fills up most days. Call well in advance, especially for singles, doubles, and summer weekends (S-€44–66, D-€54–66, Db-€58–70, dorm beds-€18–28, includes continental breakfast, kitchen access, launderette-€7.50, Internet access-€4/hr, left luggage, travel desk, TV lounge, small lockers, lots of stairs, Christ Church, 2–12 Lord Edward Street, tel. 01/679-6644, fax 01/679-7437, www.kinlayhouse.ie, kinlay.dublin@kinlaygroup.ie).

$ Four Courts Hostel is a 236-bed hostel beautifully located immediately across the river from the Four Courts. It's within a five-minute walk of Christ Church Cathedral and Temple Bar. Bare and institutional (as hostels typically are), it's also spacious and well-run, with a focus on security and efficiency (dorm beds-€15–19, S-€45, Sb-€50, bunk D-€60, bunk Db-€66, includes small breakfast, non-smoking, elevator, Internet access, game room, laundry service, some parking, left luggage room, 15–17 Merchant's Quay, bus #748 from airport, #90 from Connolly Station or Busaras Central Bus Station, tel. 01/672-5839, fax 01/672-5862, www.fourcourtshostel.com, info@fourcourtshostel.com).

Between Trinity College and Temple Bar

$$$ Principal Hotel Fleet Street rents 70 decent rooms. For its size, it has a cozy ambience with character (Sb-€106–127, Db-€130–169, often mid-week deals, breakfast-€13.50, non-smoking rooms, request a quiet room off the street, 19–20 Fleet Street, tel. 01/670-8122, fax 01/670-8103, www.principalhotel.com, principalhotel@eircom.net). Rather than buying the spendy hotel breakfast, walk around the corner to Bewley's on Westmoreland Street (see listing under "Eating," page 81).

$$$ Temple Bar Hotel is a 130-room business-class place, very centrally located midway between Trinity College and the Temple Bar action (Sb-€80–150, Db-€120–195, Tb-€180–255, mid-week discounts, non-smoking rooms, Fleet Street, Temple Bar, tel. 01/677-3333, fax 01/677-3088, www.templebarhotel.com, reservations@tbh.ie).

$$ Trinity College turns its 800 student-housing rooms on campus into no-frills, affordable accommodations in the city center each summer (mid-June–Sept, S-€55, Sb-€66, D-€110, Db-€128, all doubles are twins, includes continental breakfast, cooked breakfast-€3 extra, tel. 01/608-1177, fax 01/671-1267, reservations @tcd.ie).

Near St. Stephen's Green

$$$ Albany House's 43 rooms come with classic furniture, high ceilings, Georgian elegance, and some street noise. Book early and request one of the four huge "superior" rooms, which are the same price as standard rooms (Sb-€100–130, Db-€140–180, €120 in slow times, Tb-€170–210, Una promises 10 percent off with this book in 2006, back rooms are quieter, non-smoking, just 1 block south of St. Stephen's Green at 84 Harcourt Street, tel. 01/475-1092, fax 01/475-1093, http://indigo.ie/~albany, albany@indigo.ie).

$$$ Baggot Court Guest House has 11 fine rooms but no lounge (Sb-€90–100, Db-€120–165, Tb-€160–220, non-smoking, free parking, 92 Lower Baggot Street, tel. 01/661-2819, fax 01/661-0253, www.baggotcourt.com, baggot@indigo.ie).

$$ The Fitzwilliam has an inviting lounge and rents 13 decent rooms cheaper than the Baggot Court, a block farther away (Sb-€90–100, Db-€120–165, 41 Upper Fitzwilliam Street, tel. 01/662-5155, fax 01/676-7488, www.fitzwilliamguesthouse.ie, info@fitzwilliamguesthouse.ie).

$ Avalon House, near Grafton Street, rents 281 backpacker beds (dorm beds-€12–22, S-€28–34, Sb-€30–37, twin D-€56–64, twin Db-€60–70, includes continental breakfast, elevator, Internet access in lobby, launderette, sells Ireland bus tickets, a few minutes off Grafton Street at 55 Aungier Street, tel. 01/475-0001, fax 01/475-0303, www.avalon-house.ie, info@avalon-house.ie).

Away from the Center, East of St. Stephen's Green

$$$ Roxford Lodge Hotel is a memorable splurge. In a quiet residential neighborhood a 20-minute walk from Trinity College, it has 20 tastefully decorated, Jacuzzi-laden rooms. The €275 executive suite is honeymoon-worthy (Sb-€90, Db-€140, Tb-€165, Qb-€200, secure parking, 46 Northumberland Road, tel. 01/668-8572, fax 01/668-8158, www.roxfordlodge.ie, roxfordlodge@eircom.net).

$$$ **Mespil Hotel** is a huge, modern, business-class hotel renting 256 identical three-star rooms (most with a double and single bed, phone, TV, voicemail, and modem hookup) at a good price with all the comforts. This is a cut above Jurys Inn, for a little more money (Sb, Db, or Tb-€99–155, breakfast-€12, elevator, non-smoking floors, Wi-Fi access, apartments for week-long stays, 10-min walk southeast of St. Stephen's Green or bus #10, Mespil Road, tel. 01/488-4600, fax 01/667-1244, www.leehotels .com, mespil@leehotels.com).

$$$ **The Leeson Inn,** with 22 crisply uncluttered rooms, stands proudly Georgian in a great location a five-minute walk south of St. Stephen's Green (Sb-€75–109, Db-€109–149, Tb-€129–169, Qb-€179–189; small first-come, first-served parking lot; 24 Lower Leeson Street, tel. 01/662-2002, fax 01/662-1567, www .leesoninndowntown.com, info@leesoninndowntown.com).

Near Connolly Station

$$ **Townhouse of Dublin,** with 80 small, stylish rooms (some with pleasant views into a central garden courtyard), hides behind a brick Georgian facade one block north of the Customs House (Sb-€55–75, Db-€102–125, Tb-€114–138; small first-come, first-served parking lot; 47–48 Lower Gardiner Street, tel. 01/878-8808, fax 01/878-8787, www.townhouseofdublin.com, info@townhouse .com)

$$ **Jurys Inn Custom House,** on Custom House Quay, offers the same value as the Jurys at the Christ Church neighborhood. Bigger (with 239 rooms) and not quite as well-located (in a boring neighborhood, a 10-min riverside hike from O'Connell Bridge), this Jurys is more likely to have rooms available (Db-€112 Sun–Thu, or €122 Fri–Sat, breakfast-€11, tel. 01/607-5000, fax 01/829-0400, U.S. tel. 800-423-6953, www.jurysdoyle.com, info@jurysdoyle.com).

$$ **Comfort Inn** has 92 plain-vanilla rooms that are short on character but long on dependable, modern comforts (€79–99 Sun–Thu, €99–189 Fri–Sat, cheaper if booked online, Great Denmark Street, tel. 01/873-7700, fax 01/873-7777, www.comfortinndublin .com, info@comfortinndublin.com).

$$ **Clifden House** is a good value, with 15 unpretentious, neatly kept rooms on a gritty Georgian street around the corner from once-swanky Mountjoy Square (Sb-€40–65, Db-€75–120, Tb-€100–140, Qb-€100–150, non-smoking, some parking in back, 32 Gardiner Place, tel. 01/874-6364, fax 01/874-6122, www .clifdenhouse.com, info@clifdenhouse.com).

$$ **Charles Stewart Hotel,** big and basic, offers lots of forgettable rooms, many of them long and narrow, with head-to-toe twins. But it's in a great location for a good price (Sb-€50–64, D-€60–80, Db-€65–95, Tb-€120–130, Qb-€120–150, frequent

mid-week discounts, includes cooked breakfast, just beyond top end of O'Connell Street at 5–6 Parnell Square East, tel. 01/878-0350, fax 01/878-1387, www.charlesstewart.ie, info@charlesstewart.ie).

EATING

As Dublin does its boom-time jig, fine, creative eateries are popping up all over town. While you can get decent pub grub for €12 on just about any corner, consider saving that for the countryside. (And there's no pressing reason to eat Irish in cosmopolitan Dublin.) The city's good restaurants are packed from 20:00 on, especially on weekends. Eating early (18:00–19:00) saves time and money, as many better places offer an early-bird special.

Eating Quick and Easy around Grafton Street

Cornucopia is a small, earth-mama-with-class, proudly vegetarian, self-serve place two blocks off Grafton. It's friendly and youthful, with hearty €9 lunches and €11 dinner specials (Mon–Sat 8:30–20:00, Sun 12:00–19:00, 19 Wicklow Street, tel. 01/677-7583).

O'Neill's offers dependable €10 carvery lunches in a labyrinth of a pub with a central location across from the main TI (daily 12:00–21:30, Suffolk Street, tel. 01/679-3656).

Graham O'Sullivan Restaurant and Coffee Shop, a cheap, cheery cafeteria, has soup, sandwiches, a salad bar, and an unpretentious ambience (Mon–Fri 8:00–18:30, Sat 8:30–17:30, Sun 10:00–16:30, 12 Duke Street). Two pubs on the same street—**The Duke** and **Davy Burns**—serve pub lunches. (The nearby Cathach Rare Books shop, at 10 Duke Street, displays a rare edition of *Ulysses* inscribed by Joyce, among other treasures, in its window.)

Bewley's Café is an old-time local favorite, offering light meals from €8 and full meals from €12. Sit on the ground floor among Art Deco lamps and windows by stained-glass artist Harry Clarke, or head upstairs to the bright atrium decorated by local art students (self-service Mon–Sat 8:00–22:00, Sun 9:00–20:00, 78 Grafton Street, tel. 01/672-7720). For a taste of witty Irish lunch theater, check out **Bewley's Café Theatre** upstairs, where you can catch an hour performance with soup and a sandwich for only €14 (Mon–Sat at 13:00 during a play's run, doors open 12:45, closed Sun, booking info tel. 086-878-4001, best to call ahead to see what's on).

Wagamama Noodle Bar, like its popular sisters in London, is a pan-Asian slurpathon with great and healthy noodle and rice dishes (€10–15) served by walkie-talkie-toting waiters at long communal tables (daily 12:00–23:00, no reservations, often a line, South King Street, underneath St. Stephen's Green Shopping Centre, tel. 01/478-2152).

Dublin Restaurants

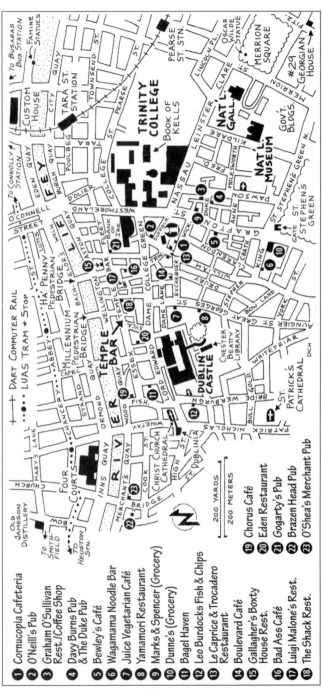

1. Cornucopia Cafeteria
2. O'Neill's Pub
3. Graham O'Sullivan Rest./Coffee Shop
4. Davy Burns Pub & The Duke Pub
5. Bewley's Café
6. Wagamama Noodle Bar
7. Juice Vegetarian Café
8. Yamamori Restaurant
9. Marks & Spencer (Grocery)
10. Dunne's (Grocery)
11. Bagel Haven
12. Leo Burdocks Fish & Chips
13. Le Caprice & Trocadero Restaurant
14. Boulevard Café
15. Gallagher's Boxty House Rest.
16. Bad Ass Café
17. Luigi Malone's Rest.
18. The Shack Rest.
19. Chorus Café
20. Eden Restaurant
21. Gogarty's Pub
22. Brazen Head Pub
23. O'Shea's Merchant Pub

South Great George's Street is lined with hardworking little eateries. **Juice** keeps vegetarians happy (daily 11:00–22:00, 73 South Great George's Street, tel. 01/475-7856).

Yamamori is a plain, bright, and modern Japanese place serving seas of sushi and noodles (€10 lunches daily 12:30–17:30, €14–19 dinners nightly 17:30–23:00, 71 South Great George's Street, tel. 01/475-5001).

Supermarkets: **Marks & Spencer** department store (on Grafton Street) has a fancy grocery store in the basement, with fine take-away sandwiches and salads (Mon–Fri 9:00–19:00, Thu until 21:00, Sat 9:00–19:00, Sun 12:00–18:30). Locals prefer **Dunne's** department store for its lower prices (Mon–Sat 8:30–19:00, Thu until 21:00, Sun 10:00–19:00, grocery in basement, in St. Stephen's Green Shopping Centre).

Eating Fast and Cheap near Christ Church Cathedral

Many of Dublin's **late-night grocery stores** (such as the Spar off the top of Dame Street on Parliament Street) sell cheap salads, microwaved meat pies, and made-to-order sandwiches. A €7 picnic dinner back at the hotel might be a good option after a busy day of sightseeing.

Bagel Haven does fresh bagel sandwiches and healthy fruit salads. Get yours to go, and enjoy a picnic with a Georgian view in one of Dublin's grassy squares (€4-5.50 breakfasts, €5–8 lunches, Mon–Fri 7:30–16:00, Sat 10:00–17:00, Sun 10:00–16:00, hidden beside Kinlay House on Cow's Lane, tel. 01/675-9900).

Chorus Café is a friendly little hole-in-the-wall diner, perfect for breakfast or lunch with a newspaper (€4–7 breakfasts, €5–9 lunches, Mon–Fri 7:30–16:30, Fishamble Street, next door to the site of the first performance of Handel's *Messiah*, tel. 01/616-7088).

Leo Burdocks Fish & Chips is tiny and popular with locals. Check out their celebrities-who-ate-here "wall of fame" while waiting in line outside (take-out only, daily 12:00–24:00, 2 Werburgh Street, off Christ Church Square).

Dining at Classy Restaurants and Cafés

These three restaurants are located within a block of each other, just south of Temple Bar and Dame Street, near the main TI.

Le Caprice is a fine, relaxing Italian place, with a wall of famous-people photos, a good wine selection, and a friendly staff (€20–27 meals, Tue–Sun 17:30–23:15, closed Mon, 12 St. Andrew Street, tel. 01/679-4050). Consider their €21 early-bird special if your plans allow for an early dinner (finish by 20:00).

Trocadero, across the street, serves beefy European cuisine to locals interested in a slow, romantic meal. The dressy, red-velvet interior is draped with photos of local actors. Come early or make a reservation. This place is a favorite with Dublin's theatergoers (€19–30 meals, Mon–Sat 17:00–24:00, closed Sun, 3 St. Andrew Street, tel. 01/677-5545). The three-course pre-theatre special is a fine value at €22 (17:00–19:00, leave by 20:00).

Boulevard Café is mod, local, trendy, and likeable, dishing up Mediterranean cuisine that's heavy on the Italian. Their salads, pasta, and sandwiches run about €8–11, and three-course lunch specials are €14 (Mon–Sat 12:00–16:00). Dinners cost around €15–23 (Mon–Sat 12:00–24:00, closed Sun, 27 Exchequer Street, smart to reserve for dinner, tel. 01/679-2131).

Eating at Temple Bar

Eden is a classy refuge serving a variety of contemporary Irish dishes in an airy space with a pleasant outdoor terrace (€20–27 dishes, €25 3-course pre-theatre menu before 19:00, daily 12:30–15:00 & 18:00–22:00, a half block off the busy tourist thoroughfare on Meeting House Square, tel. 01/670-5372).

Gallagher's Boxty House is touristy and traditional—a good, basic value with creaky floorboards and old Dublin ambience. Its specialty is boxties, the generally bland-tasting Irish potato pancake filled and rolled with various meats, veggies, and sauces. The "Gaelic Boxty" is liveliest (€14–25, also serves stews and corned beef, Mon–Fri 9:00–23:00, Sat–Sun 10:00–23:00, 20 Temple Bar, reservations wise, tel. 01/677-2762).

Bad Ass Café is a grunge diner (where Sinead O'Connor was once a waitress) serving cowboy/Mex/veggie/pizzas to old and new hippies. No need to dress up (€9 lunches and €13–18 dinners, kids' specials, daily 11:30–24:00, Crown Alley, just off Meeting House Square, tel. 01/671-2596).

Luigi Malone's, with its fun atmosphere and varied menu of pizza, ribs, pasta, sandwiches, and fajitas, is just the place to take your high-school date (€14–25 dishes, daily 12:00–23:00, corner of Cecila and Fownes Streets, tel. 01/679-2723).

The Shack, while a bit pricey and touristy, has a reputation for good quality. It serves traditional Irish, chicken, seafood, and steak dishes (€16–26 entrées, daily 11:00–23:00, in the center of Temple Bar, 24 East Essex Street, tel. 01/679-0043).

TRANSPORTATION CONNECTIONS

Note that trains and buses generally run less frequently on Sundays.

From Dublin by Train from Heuston Station to: Tralee (5/day, 3/day Sun, 4 hrs, talking timetable tel. 01/805-4266),

Ennis (2/day, 4 hrs), **Galway** (7/day, 3 hrs, talking timetable tel. 01/805-4222).

By Train from Connolly Station to: Rosslare (5/day, 3 hrs), **Portrush** (7/day, 2/day Sun, 5 hrs, transfer in Belfast), **Belfast** (8/day, 2 hrs, tel. 01/836-3333). The **Dublin–Belfast train** connects the two Irish capitals in two hours at 90 mph on one continuous, welded rail (€33 one-way, €48 round-trip; round-trip the same day only €35 except Fri and Sun). Train info: tel. 01/836-6222. Northern Ireland train info: tel. 048/9089-9400.

To Dun Laoghaire: See "Getting to Dun Laoghaire," below.

By Bus to: Belfast (6/day, 3 hrs), **Trim** (14/day, 1 hr), **Ennis** (11/day, 4.5 hrs), **Galway** (13/day, 3.5 hrs), **Limerick** (13/day, 3.5 hrs), **Tralee** (7/day, 6 hrs), **An Daingean** (4/day, 8 hrs, €23, transfer at Tralee). Bus info: tel. 01/836-6111.

Dublin Airport: The airport is well-connected to the city center seven miles away; for transportation options into the city, see "Arrival in Dublin," page 51. Airport info: tel. 01/814-1111, www.dublin-airport.com. For a list of airlines, see below and the appendix.

Tips for Drivers

Trust me, you don't want to drive in downtown Dublin. Cars are unnecessary to see the city, parking is expensive, and traffic will get your fighting Irish up. Save your car-rental days for cross-country travel between smaller towns and see this energetic city by taxi, bus, or on foot. If you're staying out in the suburbs (Dun Laoghaire), ask your innkeeper for the best place to park.

Drivers renting their car at Dublin airport (north of the city center), but not staying in Dublin, can bypass the worst of the big-city traffic by making use of the recently completed M-50 ring road to whisk themselves south or west.

Connecting Ireland and Britain

Spend a few minutes online researching your transportation options across the Irish Sea. Most airline and ferry companies routinely offer discounts (often as much as €10) for tickets purchased from their Web sites.

If you're going directly to London, flying is your best bet. Check **Ryanair** first (90 min, Irish tel. 01/609-7878, www.ryanair .com). Other options include **British Airways** (toll-free tel. in Ireland 1-800-626-747, in U.S. 800-247-9297, www.britishairways .com), **Aer Lingus** (tel. 01/886-8888, www.aerlingus.com), and **bmi british midland** (Irish tel. 01/407-3036, U.S. tel. 800-788-0555, www.flybmi.com). To get the lowest fares, ask about round-trip ticket prices and book months in advance (though Ryanair offers deals nearly all of the time).

Dublin and Liverpool: SeaCat has ferries for car and foot passengers (4 hrs, weekly via the Isle of Man, €28–32 one-way for foot passengers, tel. 800-805-055, www.steam-packet.com). Car-only ferries are operated by both P&O Irish Sea Ferries (7.5 hrs, daily, tel. 01/407-3434, www.poirishsea.com) and Norse Merchant (8 hrs, Mon–Sat, closed Sun, tel. 01/819-2999, www.norsemerchant.com). Check in one to two hours before the sailing time—call to confirm details.

Dublin and Holyhead: Irish Ferries sails between Dublin and Holyhead in North Wales (dock is a mile east of O'Connell Bridge, 5/day: 2 slow, 3 fast; slow boats—3.25 hrs, €30 one-way walk-on fare; fast boats—1.75 hrs, €35; Dublin tel. 01/638-3333, Holyhead tel. 08705-329-129, www.irishferries.com).

Dun Laoghaire and Holyhead: Stena Line sails a huge catamaran between Dun Laoghaire (near Dublin) and Holyhead in North Wales (3/day, 2 hrs €32–44 one-way walk-on fare, €4 extra if paying with credit card, reserve by phone—they book up long in advance on summer weekends, Dun Laoghaire tel. 01/204-7777, recorded info tel. 01/204-7799, can book online at www.stenaline.com).

Ferries to France

Irish Ferries connects Ireland (Rosslare) with France (Cherbourg and Roscoff) every other day (less often Jan–March). While Cherbourg has the quickest connection to Paris, your overall time between Ireland and Paris is about the same (20–25 hrs) regardless of which port is used on the day you sail. One-way fares range from €40 to €100. Eurailpass holders go half-price. In both directions, departures are generally between 16:00 and 17:00 and arrive late the next morning. While passengers can nearly always get on, reservations are wise in summer and easy by phone. If you anticipate a crowded departure, you can reserve a seat for €11. Doubles (or singles) start at €44–54 per person. The easiest way to get a bed (except during summer) is from the information desk upon boarding. The cafeteria serves bad food at reasonable prices. Upon arrival in France, buses and taxis connect you to your Paris-bound train (Irish Ferries: Dublin tel. 01/638-3333, recorded info tel. 01/661-0715, Paris tel. 01 44 94 20 40, www.irishferries.com, info@irishferries.com; European Ferry Guide: www.youra.com/ferry/intlferries.html).

Dun Laoghaire

Dun Laoghaire (DUN-leary) is seven miles south of Dublin. This beach resort, with the ferry terminal for Wales and easy connections to downtown Dublin, is a great small-town base for the big city.

The Dun Laoghaire harbor was strategic enough to merit a line of martello towers, built to defend against an expected Napoleonic invasion (one tower is now a James Joyce museum—see below). By the mid-19th century, its massive breakwaters were completed, protecting a huge harbor. Ships sailed regularly from here to Wales (60 miles away), and the first train line in Ireland connected the terminal with Dublin.

Getting to Dun Laoghaire

While buses run between Dublin and Dun Laoghaire, the **DART** commuter train is much faster (4/hr, 20 min, runs Mon–Sat about 6:30–23:30, Sun from 9:00, €1.90 one-way, €3.40 round-trips are good same day only, tel. 01/703-3504, www.irishrail.ie, Eurail valid but uses a flexi-day; for a longer stay, consider the €16 Short Hop 3-day bus and rail ticket covering DART and Dublin buses—see "Getting Around Dublin—By Dart," page 53). If you're coming from Dublin, catch a DART train marked "Bray" and get off at the Sandycove/Glasthule or Dun Laoghaire stop, depending on which B&B you choose. If you're leaving Dun Laoghaire, catch a train marked "Howth" to get to Dublin. Get off at the central Tara Street Station if you want to sightsee in Dublin; or ride it one stop further to Connolly Station (for train connections north, or Airlink bus connections to airport).

The **taxi** fare from Dun Laoghaire to central Dublin is about €25, to the airport about €40. Try ABC Taxi service (tel. 01/285-5444). With DART access into Dublin and cheap or sometimes free parking, this area is ideal for those with **cars** (which cost €3/hr or €20/day to park in Dublin).

ORIENTATION

A busy transportation hub, Dun Laoghaire has a coastline defined by its nearly mile-long breakwaters—reaching like two muscular arms into the Irish Sea. The breakwaters are popular for strollers, bikers, birders, and fishermen.

Tourist Information: The TI is in the ferry terminal (Mon–Sat 10:00–12:45 & 14:00–18:00 year-round, closed Sun).

Helpful Hints

Internet Access: U-surf.ie provides a fast connection (€4/hr, daily 10:00–22:00, Lower George's Street).

Post Office: It's on Lower George's Street (Mon–Fri 9:00–18:00, Sat 9:00–13:00).

Laundry: Try **Jeeves,** located in the village of Glasthule, a five-minute downhill walk from Sandycove/Glasthule DART station (Mon–Sat 8:30–18:00, closed Sun, full-service only, 34 Glasthule Road, next to Daniel's Restaurant and Wine Bar, tel. 01/230-1120).

Parking: If you don't have free parking at your B&B, try the pay-and-display street-parking system; buy a ticket at machines spaced along the street, and display it on dashboard (Mon–Fri 8:00–19:00, €1/hr, 3-hr max, free Sat–Sun).

Best Views: Hike out to the lighthouse, at the end of the interesting East Pier, or climb the spiral staircase at the James Joyce Museum/tower (see below).

SIGHTS

James Joyce Museum—This squat martello (masonry) tower at Sandycove was originally built to repel a Napoleonic invasion, but it became famous chiefly because of its association with James Joyce. The great author lived here briefly, and made it the setting for the opening of his novel, *Ulysses.* Today, the museum's round exhibition space is filled with literary memorabilia, including photographs and rare first editions. For a fine view, climb the claustrophobic, two-story spiral stairwell to reach the rooftop gun mount (€6.50, covered by Dublin Pass, ask about €11 combo-ticket with Dublin Writers' Museum, March–Oct Mon–Sat 10:00–13:00 & 14:00–17:00, Sun 14:00–18:00, closed Nov–Feb, tel. 01/280-9265).

The sandy little cove and rounded rocks beside the tower are a safe and clean swimming spot, a local favorite for kids of all ages.

ENTERTAINMENT

For an evening of pure Irish music, song, and dance, check out the **Comhaltas Ceoltoiri Éireann,** an association working to preserve this slice of Irish culture. It got started when Elvis and company threatened to steal the musical heart of the new generation. Judging by the pop status of traditional Irish music these days, Comhaltas accomplished its mission. Their "Seisiun" evening is a stage show mixing traditional music, song, and dance (€10, July–Aug Mon–Thu at 21:00, followed by informal music session at 22:30). On Fridays all year long, they have a *ceilidh* (KAY-lee), where everyone does set dances. This style, the forerunner of square dancing, evolved from the French Quadrille dances of 200 years ago with two couples making up a "set" (€8 includes friendly pointers, 21:30–00:30). At 21:00 on Tuesdays and Wednesdays (free) and Saturdays (€3), there are informal sessions by the fireside. All musicians are welcome. Performances are held in Cuturlann na Éireann, near the Seapoint DART stop, or take bus #7 from Dun Laoghaire, at 32 Belgrave Square, Monkstown (tel. 01/280-0295, www.comhaltas.com). Their bar is free and often filled with music.

SLEEPING

(€1 = about $1.20, country code: 353, area code: 01)

Near the Sandycove/Glasthule DART Station

These listings are within a couple of blocks of the Sandycove/Glasthule DART station and a 10-minute walk to the Dun Laoghaire DART station/ferry landing.

$$ Seaview B&B, a modern house run by Mrs. Kane, has three big, cheery rooms and a welcoming guests' lounge with a bright and friendly feeling (Db-€70–80 through 2006 with this book, cash only, non-smoking, just above Rosmeen Gardens at 2 Granite Hall, tel. & fax 01/280-9105, www.seaviewbedandbreakfast .com, seaviewbedandbreakfast@hotmail.com).

$$ Windsor Lodge rents four fresh, inviting rooms on a quiet street a block off the harbor and a block from the DART station (Db-€60–80, Tb-€90, family deals, cash only, non-smoking, 3 Islington Avenue, tel. 01/284-6952, winlodge@eircom.net, Mary O'Farrell).

$$ Ferry House is a family-friendly place with four high-ceilinged rooms on a quiet, dead-end street (Sb-€50–60, Db-€70–75, Tb-€100–110, Qb-€120, non-smoking, 15 Clarinda Park North just off Clarinda Park West, tel. 01/280-8301, fax 01/284-6530, www.ferryhousedublin.com, ferry_house@hotmail.com).

Near the Dun Laoghaire DART Station

$$ Lynden B&B, with a classy 150-year-old interior hiding behind a somber front, rents four big rooms (S-€40, Sb-€45-50, D-€62, Db-€72, 10 percent discount with this book in 2006, cash only, past Mulgrave Street to 2 Mulgrave Terrace, tel. 01/280-6404, fax 01/230-2258, lynden@iol.ie, Maria Gavin).

Dun Laoghaire

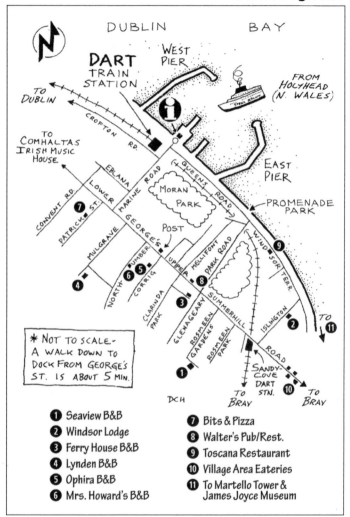

1 Seaview B&B
2 Windsor Lodge
3 Ferry House B&B
4 Lynden B&B
5 Ophira B&B
6 Mrs. Howard's B&B

7 Bits & Pizza
8 Walter's Pub/Rest.
9 Toscana Restaurant
10 Village Area Eateries
11 To Martello Tower &
James Joyce Museum

$ Ophira B&B is a historic house with five comfortably creaky rooms run by active diver, hiker, and biker John O'Connor (S-€30–35, Db-€60–70, Tb-€90, non-smoking, parking available, 10 Corrig Ave, tel. & fax 01/280-0997, www.ophira.ie, johnandcathy@ophira.ie).

$ Mrs. Howard's B&B has four big, well-worn rooms (S-€35, Sb-€40, D-€56, Db-€62, cash only, TV lounge, 36 Northumberland Avenue, tel. 01/280-3262, corahoward2003@yahoo.co.uk).

EATING

If staying in Dun Laoghaire, I'd definitely eat here and not in Dublin.

George's Street, Dun Laoghaire's main drag three blocks inland, has plenty of eateries and pubs, many with live music. **Walters Public House and Restaurant** is a bright, modern place above a pub, offering good food to a dressy crowd. The multi-terraced back patio of the pub is great for a drink on a warm evening (€16–24 meals, daily 17:30–22:30, 68 Upper George's Street, tel. 01/280-7442). A good bet for families is the kid-friendly **Bits and Pizza** (daily 12:00–22:30, off George's Street at 15 Patrick Street, tel. 01/284-2411).

Toscana, on the waterfront, is a popular little cubbyhole, serving hearty Italian dishes and pizza. Its prime location makes it easy to incorporate into your evening stroll (€11–24 meals, daily 12:00–22:00, 5 Windsor Terrace, dinner reservations smart, tel. 01/230-0890).

Glasthule (called simply "the village" locally, just down the street from the Sandycove/Glasthule DART station) has an array of fun, hardworking little restaurants. The big **Eagle House pub** dishes up hearty €10–19 pub meals in a wonderful atmosphere; it's a super, local joint for a late drink (Mon–Sat 12:30–21:30, Sun 12:30–19:30). The nearby **Daniel's Restaurant and Wine Bar** is less atmospheric, but it's also good (€18–24 meals, Tue–Sun 18:00–23:00, closed Mon, 34 Glasthule Road, tel. 01/284-1027). **Centra** market is right next door and has your picnic-makings (daily 7:00–23:00, Glasthule Road).

NEAR DUBLIN

Not far from urban Dublin, you'll find the stony skeletons of evocative ruins sprouting from the lush Irish countryside. The story of Irish history is told by ancient burial mounds, early Christian monastic settlements, huge Norman castles, and pampered estate gardens. These sights are separated into regions: north of Dublin (the Valley of the Boyne, including Brú na Bóinne and the town of Trim) and south of Dublin (Glendalough and the Wicklow Mountains).

North of Dublin: The Valley of the Boyne

The peaceful, green Valley of the Boyne, just 30 miles north of Dublin, has an impressive concentration of historical and spiritual sights: The enigmatic burial mounds at Brú na Bóinne are older than the Egyptian pyramids. At the Hill of Tara (seat of the high kings of Celtic Ireland), St. Patrick preached his most persuasive sermon. The valley also contains the first Vatican-endorsed monastery in Ireland and several of the country's finest high crosses. You'll see Trim's 13th-century castle—Ireland's biggest—built by Norman invaders, and you can wander the site of the historic Battle of the Boyne (1690), in which the Protestants turned the tide against the Catholics, and imposed British rule until the 20th century.

Valley of the Boyne

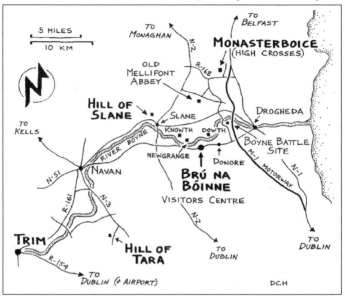

5 MILES
10 KM

TO BELFAST

TO MONAGHAN

MONASTERBOICE
(HIGH CROSSES)

N-2

R-168

OLD
MELLIFONT
ABBEY

HILL OF
SLANE

SLANE

DROGHEDA

TO KELLS

RIVER BOYNE

KNOWTH   DOWTH

NEWGRANGE

BOYNE BATTLE
SITE

N-51

NAVAN

DONORE

BRÚ NA
BÓINNE

M-1 MOTORWAY

N-1

R-161

N-3

VISITORS CENTRE

TRIM

N-2

HILL OF
TARA

TO
DUBLIN

TO
DUBLIN

R-154

TO
DUBLIN (& AIRPORT)

DCH

Planning Your Time

Of these sights, only Brú na Bóinne is worth ▲▲▲ (and deserves a good 3 hours). The others, while relatively meager physically, are powerfully evocative to anyone interested in Irish history and culture. Without a car, I'd visit only Brú na Bóinne, taking the shuttle bus from Dublin (see "Getting There" on page 96).

The region is a joy by car, because all of the described sights are within a 30-minute drive of each other. If you eat your Weetabix, you could do the entire region in a day. While sights are on tiny roads, they're well-marked with brown, tourist-friendly road signs, and you'll navigate best using an Ordnance Survey atlas.

As you plan your Ireland itinerary, keep in mind that if you're flying into or out of Dublin, and want to avoid the intensity and expense of that big city, you can use Trim as an overnight base (45-min drive from airport, see accommodations listings on page 101), and tour these sights from there.

Tours of the Valley of the Boyne

If you lack a car and like tours, consider one of these round-trip tours from Dublin.

Mary Gibbon's Tours visit both Brú na Bóinne (including inside the Newgrange tomb) and the Hill of Tara in a six-hour trip (€35, €30 if you flash this book in 2006, Mon–Fri only, 10:15 pick-up at Dublin TI on Suffolk Street, 10:25 pick-up at Royal

Dublin Hotel on O'Connell Street, home by 16:30, book direct rather than through TI, tel. 01/283-9973, www.newgrangetours .com, info@newgrangetours.com).

Over the Top Tours covers everything but Brú na Bóinne and Trim. Leaving Dublin at 9:00 and returning by 17:30, they stop at the Hill of Tara, the Hill of Slane (free time for lunch), Fourknocks (prehistoric tombs, less famous than Brú na Bóinne), the Battle of the Boyne site, and the monasteries of Monasterboice and Old Mellifont Abbey (€26, departing daily at 9:00 from Dublin TI on Suffolk Street, pick-up at 9:20 from Royal Dublin Hotel on O'Connell Street, 14-seat minibus, reservations required, hold seat by leaving credit-card number, toll-free tel. 1-800-424-252, Dublin tel. 01/838-6128, www.overthetoptours.com, info@overthetoptours.com).

Bus Eireann (AIR-an) alternates between two Valley of the Boyne itineraries depending on the day of the week, but they always go to Brú na Bóinne. During high season (May–Sept), they visit Brú na Bóinne, the Hill of Tara, and town of Trim on Tuesday, Thursday, and Sunday; on Monday, Wednesday, and Saturday, the tour includes Brú na Bóinne, Monasterboice, and the Old Mellifont Abbey (€30 for either route, price includes admission to Brú na Bóinne tombs, May–Sept tours run Sat–Thu, none on Fri; Oct–April on Thu and Sat only, departs Dublin's Busaras Central Bus Station at 10:00, returns to Busaras at 17:45, tel. 01/836-6111, www.buseireann.ie).

Brú na Bóinne

The famous archaeological site properly known as Brú na Bóinne— "dwelling place of the Boyne"—is also commonly referred to as "Newgrange" (actually one of the tombs). The well-organized site, worth ▲▲▲, centers on a state-of-the-art museum. Visitors are given appointments for shuttle buses that ferry small groups five minutes away, to one of two 5,000-year-old passage tombs where a guide gives a 30-minute tour. **Newgrange** is more famous, and allows you inside. **Knowth** (rhymes with south) opened more recently and is more extensive, but you can't go inside the tomb. At the turnstile, you'll buy a ticket to one or both sights, and be given bus departure times (if you plan to see both sights, note that buses depart 90 min apart). Newgrange sells out first, and comes with a longer wait. If you opt for Knowth, be sure to see the museum's replica of the Newgrange passage entrance (where a short tour and winter solstice light-show demo often occur upon request); the replica is connected to the video room. Each site is different enough and worthwhile, but for many, seeing just one is adequate. For information on the prehistoric art, see "Irish Art" in the Ireland: Past and Present chapter.

Newgrange is one single mound, the more restored of the Brú na Bóinne sites. Dating from 3200 B.C., it's 500 years older than the pyramids at Giza. While we know nothing of the builders, it most certainly was a sacred spot dealing with some kind of Sun God ritual. During the tour, you'll squeeze down a narrow passageway to a cross-shaped central chamber, located under a 20-foot-high igloo-type stone dome. Bones and ashes were placed here under 200,000 tons of stone and dirt to wait for a special moment. As the sun rose on the shortest day of the year (winter solstice, Dec 21), a ray of light would creep slowly down the 60-foot-long passageway. For 17 minutes it would light the center of the sacred chamber. Perhaps this was the moment when the souls of the dead would be transported to the afterlife via that mysterious ray of life-giving and life-taking light.

Knowth (the second Brú na Bóinne site) is a necropolis of several grassy mounds around one 85-yard-wide grand tomb. The big mound, covering 1.5 acres, has two passages aligned so that on the spring and fall equinox, rays from the rising and setting sun shine down the passageways to the center chamber. Neither of the passages is open to the public; but when you visit a room cut into the mound—designed to expose the interior construction layers—you get a glimpse down one of the passages. The Knowth site thrived from 3000 to 2000 B.C., with mysterious burial rituals and sun-tracking ceremonies to please the gods and ensure the regular progression of seasons for crops. The site then evolved into the domain of fairies and myths for the next 2,000 years, and became an Iron Age fortress in the early centuries after Christ. Around A.D. 1000, it was an all-Ireland political center, and, later, a Norman fortress was built atop the mound. You'll see plenty of mysteriously carved stones and new-feeling grassy mounds that you can look down on from atop the grand tomb.

Cost and Hours: Allow an hour for the excellent museum and an hour for each of the tombs you visit. The museum in the visitors center is included in the following prices: Newgrange-€5.50, Knowth-€4.25, both tombs-€9.75, covered by Heritage Card—see page 4 (May–Sept daily 9:00–18:30 or 19:00, slightly shorter hours off-season, Newgrange open year-round, Knowth open April–Oct only, tel. 041/988-0300).

Crowd-Beating Tips: Visits are limited, and on busy summer days those arriving in the afternoon may not get a spot (no reservations possible). In peak season, try to arrive by 9:30 to avoid a wait caused by big tour-bus crowds. Generally upon arrival you'll get a bus departure time for one or both of the passage-tomb sites (the last shuttle bus leaves 1.75 hours before closing). Spend your wait visiting the museum, watching the great seven-minute video, and munching lunch in the cheery cafeteria. You can't drive directly to the actual passage tombs.

Getting There: To reach the visitors center from Dublin by **car,** drive north on N1 to Drogheda, where signs direct you to the Brú na Bóinne Visitors Centre.

If you don't have a car and you're not taking a tour, hop on the Brú na Bóinne (Newgrange) **shuttle bus** that runs from Dublin directly to the visitors center (€15 round-trip, departs at 8:45 and 11:00 from TI on Suffolk Street or 9:00 and 11:15 from O'Connell Street, return trips depart at 13:00 and 16:00 from the visitors center, run by Over the Top Tours, book by phone, tel. 01/860-0405).

More Sights in the Valley of the Boyne

▲**Hill of Tara**—This was the most important center of political and religious power in pre-Christian Ireland. While aerial views show plenty of mysterious circles and lines, wandering with the sheep among the well-worn ditches and hills leaves you with more to feel than to see. Visits are made meaningful by an excellent 20-minute video presentation and the caring 20-minute guided walk that follows (always available upon request and entirely worthwhile).

You'll see the Mound of Hostages (a Bronze Age passage grave, c. 2500 B.C.), a couple of ancient sacred stones, a war memorial, and vast views over the Emerald Isle. While ancient Ireland was a pig-pile of minor chieftain-kings scrambling for power, the high king of Tara was king of the mountain. It was at this ancient stockade that St. Patrick directly challenged the authority of the high king. When confronted by the pagan high king, Patrick convincingly explained the Holy Trinity using a shamrock: three petals with one stem. He won the right to preach Christianity throughout Ireland, and the country had a new national symbol.

This now-desolate hill was also the scene of great modern events. In 1798, passionate young Irish rebels chose Tara for its defensible position, but were routed by better organized (and more sober) British troops. (The cunning British commander had sent three cartloads of whiskey along the nearby road earlier in the day, knowing the rebels would intercept it.) In 1843, the great orator and champion of Irish liberty Daniel O'Connell gathered more than 500,000 Irish peasants on this hill for his greatest "monster meeting"—a peaceful show of force demanding the repeal of the Act of Union with Britain. (In a bizarre final twist, a small group of British Israelites—who believed they were one of lost tribes of Israel, ending up in Britain—spent 1899 to 1901 recklessly digging up parts of the Hill in a misguided search for the Ark of the Covenant.)

Stand on the Hill of Tara. Think of the history it's seen, and survey Ireland. It's understandable why this "meeting place of heroes" continues to hold a powerful place in the Irish psyche (€2, covered by Heritage Card—see page 4, includes video and 20-min guided walk, mid-May–mid-Sept daily 10:00–18:00, last tour 17:00; otherwise, access to site is free but visitors center is closed; tel. 046/902-5903). Local guide Jean Thornton, who works on site, brings the lumpy mounds to life; if she's on duty, request her.

Old Mellifont Abbey—This Cistercian abbey (the first in Ireland) was established by French monks who came to the country in 1142 to bring the Irish monks more in line with Rome. (Even the abbey's architecture was unusual, marking the first time in Ireland that a formal, European-style monastic layout was used.) Cistercians lived isolated rural lives; lay monks worked the land, allowing the more educated monks to devote all their energy to prayer. After Henry VIII dissolved the abbey in 1539, centuries of locals used it as a handy quarry. Consequently, little survives beyond the octagonal lavabo, where the monks would ceremonially wash their hands before entering the refectory to eat. The lavabo gives a sense of the grandeur that the abbey once had. The excellent 45-minute tours, available upon request and included in your admission, give meaning to the site (€2, covered by Heritage Card—see page 4, May–Sept daily 10:00–18:00, last entry 17:15, no tours Oct–April when site is free and you can explore on your own, tel. 041/982-6459).

Monasterboice—This ruined monastery is visit-worthy for its round tower and its ornately carved high crosses—two of the best such crosses in Ireland. In the Dark Ages, these crosses, illustrated from top to bottom with Bible stories, gave monks a teaching tool as they preached to the illiterate masses. Today Monasterboice, basically an old graveyard, is always open and free.

The 18-foot-tall Cross of Murdock (Muiredach's Cross, A.D. 923, named after an abbot) is considered the best high cross in Ireland. The circle—which characterizes the Irish high cross—could represent the perfection of God. Or, to help ease pagans into Christianity, it may represent the sun, which was worshiped in pre-Christian Celtic society. Whatever its symbolic purpose, its real function was to support the crossbeam.

Face the cross (with the round tower in the background) and study the carved sandstone. The center panel shows the Last Judgment, with Christ under a dove, symbolizing the Holy Spirit. Those going to heaven are on Christ's right, and the damned are being ushered away by devils on his left. Working down, you'll see the Archangel Michael weighing souls, as the Devil tugs demonically at the scales; the adoration of the three—or four—Magi; Moses striking the rock; scenes from the life of David; and, finally, Adam, Eve, and the apple next to Cain slaying Abel. Imagine these carvings with their original, colorful paint jobs.

Find the even-taller cross nearest the tower. It seems the top section was broken off and buried, while the bottom part remained standing, enduring the erosive effect of Irish weather.

The door to the round tower was originally 15–20 feet above the ground (accessible by ladder). After centuries of burials, the ground level has risen.

Battle of the Boyne Site—One of Europe's great non-sights, this is simply the pastoral riverside site of the pivotal battle in which the Protestant British broke Catholic resistance, establishing Protestant rule over all Ireland and Britain. Drop into the information center next to the small parking lot and ask for a guided tour (free, May–Sept daily 10:00–18:00, last tour 17:00, closed Oct–April, tel. 041/984-9873). The attendant will generally take you on a 45-minute historic stroll around the Oldbridge Estate, on the south bank of the river.

It was here in 1690 that Protestant King William III, with his English and Dutch army, defeated his father-in-law, Catholic King James II, and his Irish and French army. King William's forces, on the north side of the Boyne, managed to cross the river, and by the end of the day, James was fleeing south in full retreat. He soon departed Ireland, but his forces fought on until their final defeat two years later. James the Second (called "James da Turd" by those who scorn his lack of courage and leadership) never returned, and died a bitter ex-monarch in France. King William of Orange's victory, on the other hand, is still celebrated in Northern Ireland every July 12th, with controversial marches by Unionist "Orangemen."

This site was bought in 1997 by the Office of Public Works as part of the Republic's governmental efforts to honor a site sacred to Unionists in Northern Ireland—despite the fact that the battle's outcome ensured Catholic subordination to the Protestant minority for the next 240 years.

Trim

The sleepy, workaday town of Trim, straddling the Boyne River, is marked by the towering ruins of Trim Castle. Trim feels littered with mighty ruins that seem to say, "This little town was big-time...700 years ago." The tall "Yellow Steeple" (over the river from the castle) is all that remains of the 14th-century Augustinian Abbey of St. Mary. A pleasant half-mile walk back toward Dublin takes you to the sprawling ruins of Saints Peter and Paul Cathedral (from 1206), once the largest Gothic church in Ireland. Across the old Norman bridge from the cathedral are the 13th-century ruins of the Hospital of St. John the Baptist.

If you're flying into or out of Dublin's airport and don't want to deal with big-city Dublin, Trim is perfect—an easy 45-minute, 30-mile drive away. You can rent a car at the airport and make Trim your first overnight base (getting used to driving on the other side of the road in easy country traffic), or spend your last night here before returning your car at the airport. Either way, you don't need or want a car in Dublin (where parking is expensive and sightseeing is best on foot, or by bus or taxi). If you have a car and are going from Trim to Dublin in the middle of your trip, try this compromise: Drive to Dublin's huge Phoenix Park, leave your car there for free, and then grab a Dublin City Tours hop-on, hop-off bus tour to shuttle you through big-city traffic (€12.50, see page 58).

ORIENTATION

Trim's main square is a traffic roundabout, and everything's within a block or two. Most of the shops and eateries are on or near Market Street, as well as banks, a supermarket, and the launderette (Mon–Sat 9:00–18:00, closed Sun, Watergate Street, tel. 046/943-7176). The post office is tucked in the back of the Spar Market (Mon–Fri 9:00–17:30, Sat 9:00–13:00, closed Sun, Emmet Street).

Tourist Information

The TI is right next to the castle entrance and includes a handy coffee shop. Drop in for a free map and take a moment to ask them about Mel Gibson's visit to film *Braveheart*. Check out the model of the castle transformed into the movie set (Mon–Sat 10:00–17:00, Sun 12:00–17:00, shorter hours off-season, Castle Street, tel. 046/943-7227).

Sights

▲▲**Trim Castle**—This is the biggest Norman castle in Ireland. Its mighty keep towers above a very ruined outer wall in a grassy

Trim

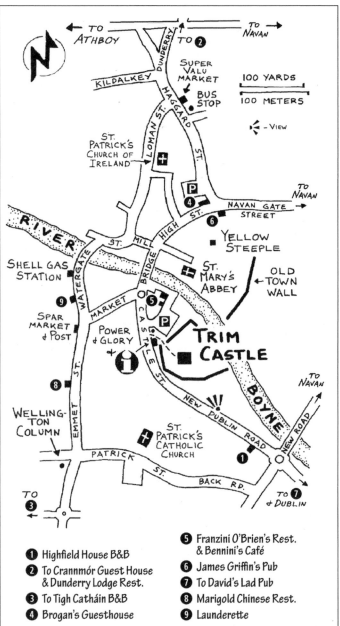

N

TO ATHBOY

TO NAVAN

TO NAVAN

KILDALKEY

DUNDERRY

LOMAN ST.

HAGGARD ST.

SUPER VALU MARKET

BUS STOP

100 YARDS

100 METERS

← VIEW

ST. PATRICK'S CHURCH OF IRELAND

P
4

NAVAN GATE STREET

TO NAVAN

HIGH ST.

6

MILL ST.

RIVER

WATERGATE ST.

MARKET ST.

BRIDGE ST.

YELLOW STEEPLE

ST. MARY'S ABBEY

OLD TOWN WALL

SHELL GAS STATION

9

SPAR MARKET & POST

5

P

POWER & GLORY

i

CASTLE ST.

TRIM CASTLE

BOYNE

TO NAVAN

8

EMMET ST.

WELLINGTON COLUMN

ST. PATRICK'S CATHOLIC CHURCH

NEW PUBLIN ROAD

NEW ROAD

TO NAVAN

PATRICK ST.

BACK RD.

1

TO DUBLIN

TO
3

TO
7

1 Highfield House B&B

2 To Crannmór Guest House & Dunderry Lodge Rest.

3 To Tigh Catháin B&B

4 Brogan's Guesthouse

5 Franzini O'Brien's Rest. & Bennini's Café

6 James Griffin's Pub

7 To David's Lad Pub

8 Marigold Chinese Rest.

9 Launderette

riverside park at the edge of the sleepy town. The current castle was completed in the 1220s, and served as a powerful Norman statement to the restless Irish natives. It remains an impressive sight—so impressive it was used in the 1994 filming of *Braveheart* (which was actually about Scotland's—not Ireland's—fight for freedom from the British).

The best-preserved walls ring the castle's southern perimeter and sport a barbican gate that contained two drawbridges. At the base of the castle walls, notice the cleverly angled "batter" wall—used by defenders who hurled down stones that banked off at great velocity into the attacking army.

The massive 70-foot-high central keep has 20 sides. Offering no place for invaders to hide, it was tough to attack. You can go inside only with the included 45-minute tour (2/hr). In a mostly hollow shell, you'll climb a series of tightly winding original staircases and modern, high catwalks, learn about life in the castle, and end at the top with great views of the walls and the countryside (€1.75 for castle grounds, €3.75 for entrance to keep and required tour, covered by Heritage Card—see page 4, roughly April–Oct daily 10:00–18:00, last entry 17:00, Nov–March Sat–Sun only 10:00–17:00, last entry 16:00, tour spots are limited, so call in peak season to save frustration of arriving to find nothing available, tel. 046/943-8619). Make time to take a 15-minute walk outside, circling the castle walls and stopping at the informative plaques that show the castle from each viewpoint during its gory glory days. Night strollers are treated to views of the castle hauntingly lit in blue-green hues.

The Power & Glory—This is a grade-schoolish 30-minute slide-show overview of the personalities and history of the castle, followed by an exhibit on life here in Norman times (€3.25, Mon–Sat 10:00–17:00, Sun 12:00–17:00, shorter hours off-season, in visitors center with TI next to castle, Castle Street, tel. 046/943-7227). The show and a free cup of coffee help to pass the time as you wait for your castle tour.

SLEEPING

To locate hotels, see the map on page 100.

In and Near Trim

$$ Brogan's Guesthouse offers 15 rooms divided between its rustic original front guest house and its modern annex out back

---

Sleep Code

(€1 = about $1.20, country code: 353, area code: 046)
S = Single, **D** = Double/Twin, **T** = Triple, **Q** = Quad, **b** = bathroom,
s = shower only. Credit cards are accepted and breakfast is
included unless otherwise noted.

   To help you easily sort through these listings, I've divided
the rooms into two categories, based on the price for a standard double room with bath:

$$ Moderately Priced—Most rooms more than €70.
 $ Lower Priced—Most rooms €70 or less.

(Sb-€45–55, Db-€72–80, Tb-€108–120, High Street, secure
parking, tel. 046/943-1237, fax 046/943-7648, www.brogans.ie,
info@brogans.ie).

$$ Highfield House B&B, across the street from the castle
and a five-minute walk from town, is a stately 175-year-old for-
mer maternity hospital, with hardwood floors and seven spacious,
high-ceilinged rooms (Sb-€48–50, Db-€76, Tb-€99–110, family-
friendly, free Internet access in lobby; overlooks roundabout where
Dublin Road hits Trim, just before castle at Maudlins Road; tel.
046/943-6386, fax 046/943-8182, www.highfieldguesthouse.com,
highfieldhouseaccom@eircom.net, Geraldine Duignan).

Countryside B&Bs: These two B&Bs are in the quiet countryside about a mile outside of Trim (phone ahead for driving
directions): At **$$ Crannmór Guest House,** north of town, Anne
O'Regan decorates five rooms with cheery color schemes, and her
husband knows all the best fishing holes (Sb-€46–50, Db-€68–72,
Tb-€96, Dunderry Road, tel. 046/943-1635, fax 046/943-8087,
www.crannmor.com, cranmor@eircom.net); southwest of town,
Mrs. Keane's **$ Tigh Catháin B&B** has four rooms with a comfy,
rural feel (Db-€64–70, cash only, Longwood Road, tel. 046/943-
1996, www.tighcathaintrim.com, mariekeane@esatclear.ie).

EATING

A country-market town, Trim offers basic meat-and-potatoes lunch
and dinner options. Don't waste time searching for gourmet food.
The restaurants and cafés along Market Street are friendly, whole-
some, and unpretentious (soup-and-sandwich delis close at 18:00).

   Your best cafeteria-style lunch bet is **Bennini's Café,** hid-
den beside the parking lot to the left of Trim Castle's entry gate
(Mon–Fri 9:00–17:30, Sat–Sun 10:00–17:30, French's Lane, tel.
046/943-8409).

Franzini O'Brien's, next door, is the only place in town with a fun dinner menu and enough business to make it work. They serve pasta, steak, fish, and fajitas in a modern, candlelit ambience. Nothing's Irish but the waiters (€15–25 dishes, Mon–Sat 18:30–22:00, Sun 17:00–21:00, French's Lane, tel. 046/943-1002).

If you feel like Chinese food, **Marigold** fits the bill (Mon–Sat 17:00–24:00, Sun 16:00–24:00, Emmet Street, tel. 046/943-8788).

For an expensive (€25–30) but tasty splurge of gourmet cooking out in the country, get driving directions to **Dunderry Lodge,** four miles north of Trim off the Dunderry Road (Mon–Sat 19:30–21:30, Sun 12:30–14:30 & 18:30–20:30, tel. 046/943-1671).

For an unvarnished pub experience, check out Trim's two best watering holes. **James Griffin's** (on High Street) is full of local characters, with Mr. Lenihan, who has run the place for 56 years, presiding. **David's Lad** is ideal if you like your beer experience unfiltered. Rock Hudson once dropped by for a pint while filming *Captain Lightfoot* on the bridge next door (closed Wed, at old Norman Bridge by cathedral ruins, 20-min walk out of town, but worth it).

Groceries: **Super Valu** has everything you need to create a picnic (Mon–Sat 8:00–21:00, Sun 7:00–19:30, Haggard Street). The smaller **Spar Market** has fewer choices (Mon–Sat 8:00–21:00, Sun 9:00–21:00, Emmet Street).

TRANSPORTATION CONNECTIONS

Trim has no train station; the nearest is in Drogheda on the coast, but there are no bus connections to Trim from there.

Buses from Trim to **Dublin** (14/day, 1 hr) pick you up next to the castle entry on Castle Street and in front of Tobin's News Shop on Haggard Street.

South of Dublin:
Glendalough and the Wicklow Mountains

The Wicklow Mountains, while only 10 miles south of Dublin, feel remote—enough so to have provided a handy refuge for opponents to English rule. Rebels who took part in the 1798 Irish uprising hid out here for years. When the frustrated British built a military road in 1800 to help flush out the rebels, the area became more accessible. Today, this same road—now the R115—takes you through the Wicklow area to Glendalough at its south end. While the valley is the darling of the Dublin day-trip tour organizers, it doesn't live up to the hype. But two blockbuster sights—Glendalough and the Gardens of Powerscourt—make a visit worth considering.

South of Dublin

Getting Around

By car or tour, it's easy. If you lack wheels, take a tour. It's not worth the trouble on public transport.

By Car: It's a delight. Take N-11 south from Dublin Bray, then R117 to Enniskerry, the gateway to the Wicklow Mountains. Signs direct you to the gardens and on to Glendalough. From Glendalough, if you're heading west, you can leave the valley (and pick up the highway to the west) over the famous but dull mountain pass called the Wicklow Gap.

By Tour from Dublin: Wild Wicklow Tours cover the region with an entertaining guide packing every minute with information and fun *craic* (conversation). With a gang of 29 packed into tight but comfortable mountain-gripping buses, the guide kicks into gear from the first pickup in Dublin. Tours cover Dublin's embassy row, Dun Laoghaire, the Bay of Dublin (with the mansions of

Ireland's rich and famous), the windy military road over scenic Sally Gap, and the Glendalough monasteries (€28, €25 for students, any of my readers can show this book and pay the student price in 2006, daily year-round, 9:10 pickup at Dublin TI on Suffolk Street, 10:00 pickup at Dun Laoghaire TI, stop for lunch at a pub—cost not included, return through Dun Laoghaire and on to Dublin by 17:30, Dun Laoghaire-ites could stay on the bus to continue into Dublin for the evening, advance booking required, tel. 01/280-1899, www.discoverdublin.ie).

Mary Gibbon's Tours visit both Glendalough and the Gardens of Powerscourt in a six-hour trip (€35, €30 with this book in 2006, 10:15 pick-up at Dublin TI on Suffolk Street, 10:25 pickup at Royal Dublin Hotel on O'Connell Street, home by 17:00, call ahead to reserve—especially in high season, book direct rather than through TI, tel. 01/283-9973, www.newgrangetours.com, info@newgrangetours.com).

Over the Top Tours bypass mansions and gardens to focus on Wicklow scenery. Stops include Glendalough, the Glenmacnass waterfall, and Blessington lakes (€24, 9:20 pickup at Gresham Hotel on O'Connell Street, 9:45 pickup at TI on Suffolk Street, return by 17:30, 14-seat minibus, reservations required, hold seat by leaving credit-card number, tel. 1-800-424-252, Dublin tel. 01/838-6128, www.overthetoptours.com).

Bus Eireann (AIR-an) visits the Gardens of Powerscourt, Glendalough, and Wicklow Gap, including admission prices to both Powerscourt and Glendalough (€30, mid-March–Oct daily; Nov–mid-Dec Wed, Fri, Sat only; no tours mid-Dec–mid-March; 10:30 pickup at Dublin's Busaras Central Bus Station, 11:00 pickup at Dun Laoghaire's TI, returns to Busaras at 17:45, tel. 01/836-6111, www.buseireann.ie).

SIGHTS

▲▲**Gardens of Powerscourt**—While the mansion's interior, only partially restored after a 1974 fire, isn't much, its meticulously kept aristocratic gardens are Ireland's best. The house was commissioned in the 1730s by Richard Wingfield, first viscount of Powerscourt. The gardens, created during the Victorian era (1858–1875), are called "the grand finale of Europe's formal gardening tradition...probably the last garden of its size and quality ever to be created." I'll buy that.

Upon entry, you'll get a flier laying

out 40-minute and 60-minute walks. The "60-minute" walk takes 30 minutes at a slow amble. With the impressive summit of the Great Sugar Loaf Mountain as a backdrop, and a fine Japanese garden, Italian garden, and goofy pet cemetery along the way, this attraction provides the scenic greenery I hoped to find in the rest of the Wicklow area. The lush movies *Barry Lyndon* and *The Count of Monte Cristo* were filmed in this well-watered aristocratic fantasy.

The Gardens of Powerscourt, a mile above the village of Enniskerry, cover several thousand acres within the 16,000-acre estate. The dreamy driveway alone is a mile long (€7 March–Oct, €5 Nov–Feb, daily 9:30–17:30 year-round, great cafeteria, tel. 01/204-6000, www.powerscourt.ie). Skip the associated waterfall (€4.50, 4 miles away).

▲▲**Military Road over Sally Gap**—This is only for those with a car. From the Gardens of Powerscourt and Enniskerry, go to Glencree, where you drive the tiny military road over Sally Gap and through the best scenery of the Wicklow Mountains. Look for the German military cemetery, built for U-Boat sailors who washed ashore in World War II. Near Sally Gap, notice the peat bogs and the freshly cut peat bricks drying in the wind. Many locals are nostalgic for the "good old days," when homes were peat-fire heated. At the Sally Gap junction, turn left, where a road winds through the vast Guinness estate. Look down on the glacial lake (Lough Tay) and the Guinness mansion (famous for jet-set parties). Nicknamed "Guinness Lake," the water looks like Ireland's favorite dark-brown stout, and the sand of the beach actually looks like the head of a Guinness beer. From here, the road meanders scenically down into the village of Roundwood and on to Glendalough.

▲▲**Glendalough**—The steep wooded slopes of Glendalough (GLEN-da-lock, "valley of the two lakes"), at the south end of Wicklow's military road, hides Ireland's most impressive monastic settlement. Founded by St. Kevin in the sixth century, the monastery flourished (despite repeated Viking raids) throughout the "Age of Saints and Scholars" until the English destroyed it in 1398. While it was finally abandoned during the Dissolution of the Monasteries in 1539, pilgrims kept coming, especially on St. Kevin's Day, June 3. (This might have something to do with the fact that a pope said seven visits to Glendalough had the same indulgence value as one visit to Rome.) While much restoration was done in the 1870s, most of the buildings date from the 8th–12th centuries.

The valley sights are split between the two lakes. The lower lake has the visitors center and the best buildings. The upper lake has scant ruins and feels like a state park, with a grassy lakeside picnic area and school groups. Walkers and hikers will enjoy a choice of nine different trails of varying lengths through the lush Wicklow countryside (longest loop takes 4 hours, hiking-trail maps available at visitors center).

Planning Your Time: Park free at the visitors center. Visit the center, wander the ruins (free) around the round tower, walk the traffic-free Green Road one mile to the upper lake, and then walk back to your car. Or you can drive to the upper lake (more free parking, except July–Aug, when it's €5). If you're rushed, skip the upper lake. Summer tour-bus crowds are terrible all day on weekends and 11:00–14:00 on weekdays.

Glendalough Visitors Centre: Start your visit here (€2.75, covered by Heritage Card—see page 4, mid-March–mid-Oct daily 9:30–18:00, mid-Oct–mid-March closes at 17:00, last entry 45 min before closing, tel. 0404/45325). The 20-minute video provides a good thumbnail background on monastic society in medieval Ireland. While the video is more general than specific to Glendalough, the adjacent museum room features this particular monastic settlement. The model in the center of the room re-creates the fortified village of the year 1050 (although there were no black-and-white Frisian cows in Ireland back then—they  would have been red). A browse through the interactive exhibits here shows the contribution these monks made to intellectual life in Dark Age Europe (such as illuminated manuscripts and Irish minuscule, a more compact alphabet developed in the 7th century).

From the center, a short and scenic walk along the Green Road takes you to the round tower.

The Monastic Village: Easily the best ruins of Glendalough gather around the famous 110-foot-tall round tower. Towers like this (usually 60–110 feet tall) were standard features in such settlements, functioning as bell towers, storage lofts, beacons for pilgrims, and last-resort refuges during Viking raids (though given enough warning, monks were safer hiding in the surrounding forest). They had a high door with a pull-up ladder. Several ruined churches (8th–12th centuries) and a sea of grave markers complete this evocative scene. Markers give short descriptions of the ruined buildings.

In an Ireland without cities, these monastic communities were mainstays of civilization. They were remote outposts where ascetics (with a taste for scenic settings) gathered to commune with God. In the 12th century, with the arrival of grander monastic orders such as the Franciscans and the Dominicans and with the growth of cities, these monastic communities were eclipsed. Today, Ireland is dotted with the reminders of this age: illuminated manuscripts, simple churches, carved crosses, and about 100 round towers.

Upper Lake: The Green Road continues one mile farther up the valley to the upper lake. The oldest ruins—scant and hard to find—lie near this lake. If you want a scenic Wicklow walk, begin here.

KILKENNY AND THE ROCK OF CASHEL

If you're driving from Dublin (on Ireland's east coast) to An Daingean (on Ireland's west coast), the best two stops to break the long journey are Kilkenny, often called Ireland's finest medieval town, and the Rock of Cashel, a thought-provoking early Christian site crowning the Plain of Tipperary. With a few extra days, there are additional worthwhile destinations along the southeast coast, such as Waterford and County Wexford (described in the next chapter). Folks with even more time can continue on the scenic southern coastal route west via Cobh, Kinsale, Kenmare, and the Ring of Kerry (covered in Kinsale/Cobh and Kenmare/Ring of Kerry chapters).

Kilkenny

Famous as "Ireland's loveliest inland city," Kilkenny gives you a feel for salt-of-the-earth Ireland. Its castle and cathedral stand like historic bookends on either end of a higgledy-piggledy High Street of colorful shops and medieval facades. It's nicknamed the "Marble City" for its nearby quarry (actually black limestone, not marble), and you can still see the white seashells fossilized within the black stone steps around town. While a small town today (fewer than 10,000 residents), Kilkenny has a big history. It used to be an important center—occasionally even the capital of Ireland in the Middle Ages.

Kilkenny is a good overnight for drivers wanting to break the journey from Dublin to An Daingean (necessary if you want to spend more time in the Wicklow area and at the Rock of Cashel).

Kilkenny and Cashel

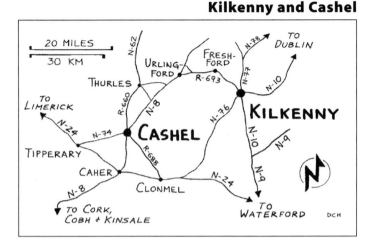

A night in Kilkenny comes with plenty of traditional folk music in the pubs (hike over the river and up John Street).

ORIENTATION

(area code: 056)

Tourist Information: The TI is a block off the bridge in the 16th-century Shee Alms poorhouse (Mon–Fri 9:00–18:00, Sat 10:00–18:00, closed Sun, Rose Inn Street, tel. 056/775-1500).

Arrival in Kilkenny: The train/bus station is four blocks from John's Bridge, which marks the center of town.

If arriving by car, the two handiest places to park are in the lot next to the castle (buy parking disks at local shops, closest is Kilkenny Crystal on Rose Inn Street across from west end of castle parking lot, €1 each, buy 1 for each hour you want to stay, 3 hours maximum in one parking space, scratch off your arrival time and leave it on your dash) or in the multistory parking garage on Ormonde Street (€1.20/hr, or just get the 5-day pass for €12 if staying overnight).

Helpful Hints

Internet Access and Bus Tickets: Café Net on Patrick Street sells bus tickets and surf time (€3/30 min, Mon–Fri 7:45–19:00, Sat 8:30–17:30, closed Sun; June–Aug also Sun 9:00–18:00, tel. 056/777-0051).

Post Office: It's on High Street (Mon–Fri 9:00–17:30, Sat 9:00–13:00, closed Sun).

Laundry: Hennessy's is at 18 Parliament Street (Mon–Sat 8:30–18:00, closed Sun).

Kilkenny

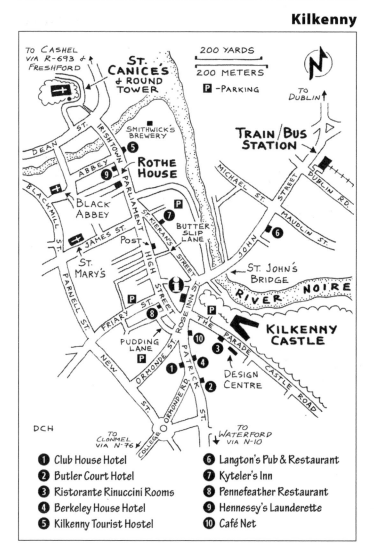

1 Club House Hotel
2 Butler Court Hotel
3 Ristorante Rinuccini Rooms
4 Berkeley House Hotel
5 Kilkenny Tourist Hostel
6 Langton's Pub & Restaurant
7 Kyteler's Inn
8 Pennefeather Restaurant
9 Hennessy's Launderette
10 Café Net

TOURS

Bus Tours—City Sightseeing's hop-on, hop-off bus tours cover the town in one hour, making 13 stops along the way (€10, pay driver, departs Kilkenny Castle at 10:30, 11:30, 12:30, 14:00, 15:00, 16:00, and 17:00, ticket valid 24 hours, www.city-sightseeing.com).

Local Guide—Pat Tynan offers hour-long guided town walks departing from the TI (€6, mid-March–Oct Mon–Sat at 10:30, 12:15, 15:00, and 16:30, Sun at 11:15 and 12:30; Nov–mid-March

Sat only 10:30, 12:15, and 15:00, mobile 087-265-1745, www
.tynantours.com).

SIGHTS

▲**Kilkenny Castle**—Dominating the town, this castle is a stony
reminder that the Anglo-Norman Butler family controlled the town
for 500 years. Tours start with a 12-minute video explaining how
the wooden fort built here by Strongbow in 1172 evolved into a 17th-

century château. Now restored
to its later Victorian splendor,
the highlight is the beautiful
family-portrait gallery putting you face-to-face with the
wealthy Butler family ghosts.
Tours, which start running 30
minutes after the castle opens
for the day, are first-come,
first-served, fill fast, and can be booked only for the same day (€5,
covered by Heritage Card—see page 4, daily June–Aug 9:30–19:00,
April–May 10:30–17:00, Sept 10:00–18:30, Oct–March 10:30–12:45
& 14:00–17:00, tel. 056/772-1450).

The **Kilkenny Design Centre,** across the street from the
castle in grand old stables, is full of local crafts and offers handy
cafeteria lunches upstairs (April–Dec Mon–Sat 10:00–19:00, Sun
11:00–19:00; Jan–March Mon–Sat 10:00–19:00, closed Sun; www
.kilkennydesign.com).

St. Canice's Cathedral—This 13th-century cathedral is early-
English Gothic, rich with stained glass, medieval carvings, and
floors paved in history. Check out the model of the old walled
town in its 1641 heyday (€3, €4 combo-ticket with tower, Mon–Sat
9:00–18:00, Sun 14:00–18:00, tel. 056/776-4971). The 100-foot-
tall round tower, built as part of a long-gone pre-Norman church,
recalls the need for a watchtower and refuge. The fun ladder-
climb to the top affords a grand view of the countryside (€2, €4
combo-ticket with cathedral, April–Sept Mon–Sat 9:00–18:00,
Sun 14:00–18:00; Oct–March Mon–Sat 10:00–16:00, Sun 14:00–
16:00).

Rothe House—This well-preserved Tudor merchant's house
expanded around interior courtyards as the prosperous family grew.
The museum, which also serves as the County Kilkenny genealogy center, runs a 15-minute video giving a glimpse of life here
in Elizabethan times (€3, April–Oct Mon–Sat 10:30–17:00, Sun
15:00–17:00; Nov–March Mon–Sat 13:00–17:00, Sun 15:00–17:00,
Parliament Street, tel. 056/772-2893).

SLEEPING

$$$ Club House Hotel is perfectly central. Originally a gentlemen's sporting club, it comes with old-time Georgian elegance; a palatial, well-antlered breakfast room; and 35 large, comfy bedrooms (Sb-€70–90, Db-€140–160, 10 percent discount with this book in 2006, Patrick Street, tel. 056/772-1994, fax 056/777-1920, www.clubhousehotel.com, clubhse@iol.ie).

$$ Butler Court, across the street and uphill from the Club House Hotel, offers eight modern rooms behind cheery yellow walls (Sb-€55–100, Db-€100–130, Tb-€160–180, accessible to wheelchair users, Patrick Street, tel. 056/776-1178, fax 056/779-0767, www.butlercourt.com, info@butlercourt.com).

$$ Ristorante Rinuccini, directly opposite the castle, has seven fine rooms off the street above the restaurant (Db-€100–120, Tb-€125–150, ask about possible midweek specials when booking, cheaper off-season, 1 The Parade, tel. 056/776-1575, fax 056/775-1288, www.rinuccini.com, info@rinuccini.com).

$$ Berkeley House, with 10 rooms across the street and downhill from Club House Hotel, is smaller, less expensive, and comfortable (Db-€80–120, Tb-€120–150, 5 Lower Patrick Street, tel. 056/776-4848, fax 056/776-4829, www.berkeleyhousekilkenny .com, berkeleyhouse@eircom.net).

$ Kilkenny Tourist Hostel, filling a fine Georgian townhouse in the town center, offers cheap beds, a friendly family room, a well-equipped members' kitchen, and a wealth of local information (dorm bed-€16, D-€40, Q-€72, cash only, laundry service-€5, 2 blocks from cathedral at 35 Parliament Street, tel. 056/776-3541, fax 056/772-3397, kilkennyhostel@eircom.net).

Sleep Code

(€1 = about $1.20, country code: 353, area code: 056)
S = Single, **D** = Double/Twin, **T** = Triple, **Q** = Quad, **b** = bathroom, **s** = shower only. All of these places include breakfast and accept credit cards.

To help you easily sort through these listings, I've divided the rooms into three categories, based on the price for a standard double room with bath:

  $$$ Higher Priced—Most rooms €130 or more.
   $$ Moderately Priced—Most rooms between €65–130.
    $ Lower Priced—Most rooms €65 or less.

EATING

Langton's serves quality Irish dishes under a Tiffany-skylight expanse (€10–12 lunches, €13–23 dinners, daily 8:00–22:30, 69 John Street, tel. 056/776-5133), while **Ristorante Rinuccini** provides your classy candlelit Italian fix (€10–16 lunches, €16–26 dinners, daily 12:00–14:30 & 18:00–22:30, 1 The Parade, tel. 056/776-1575).

Grab a quick, light lunch at the **Pennefeather Restaurant** above the Kilkenny Book Centre (Mon–Fri 9:00–17:30, Sat 9:00–17:00, closed Sun, 10 High Street, tel. 056/776-4063).

For basic pub grub in a timber-and-stone atmosphere, visit the fun 14th-century cellar under **Kyteler's Inn** and ask about their witch (daily 12:00–21:00, 27 St. Kieran's Street, tel. 056/772-1064). Try a pint of Smithwick's in its hometown.

TRANSPORTATION CONNECTIONS

From Kilkenny by Train to: Dublin (4/day, 2 hrs), **Waterford** (4/day, 45 min).

By Bus to: Dublin (7/day, 2 hrs), **Waterford** (2/day, 1 hr), **Tralee** (3/day, 5 hrs), **Galway** (6/day, 4.5 hrs).

Rock of Cashel

Rising high above the fertile Plain of Tipperary, the Rock of Cashel—worth ▲▲▲—is one of Ireland's most historic and evocative sights. Seat of the ancient kings of Munster (c. A.D. 300–1100), this is the where St. Patrick baptized King Aengus in about A.D. 450. Strategically located and perfect for fortification, the Rock was fought over by local clans for hundreds of years. Finally, in 1101, clever Murtagh O'Brien gave the Rock to the Church. His seemingly benevolent donation increased his influence with the Church, while preventing his rivals, the powerful McCarthy clan, from regaining possession of the Rock. As Cashel evolved into an ecclesiastical center, Iron Age ring forts and thatch dwellings gave way to the majestic stone church buildings enjoyed by tourists today.

Cost and Hours: €5, families-€11, covered by Heritage Card—see page 4, daily early June–mid-Sept 9:00–19:00; mid-March–early June and mid-Sept–mid-Oct 9:00–17:30;

mid-Oct–mid-March 9:00–16:30; last entry 45 minutes before closing. Parking will cost you €2.50 (buy parking ticket at machine inside lot).

Orientation: At the base of the Rock and next to the parking lot, you'll see WCs (none up on Rock) and the Bru Boru Cultural Centre (see page 121); you may want to visit the Centre to learn more about the Rock before you ascend.

It's a steep 50-yard walk up to the Rock itself. On this 200-foot-high outcropping of limestone, the first building you'll encounter is the 15th-century Hall of the Vicars Choral, housing the ticket desk, a tiny museum (with St. Patrick's original 12th-century high cross and a few replica artifacts), and a 20-minute video (2/hr, shown in the hall's former dormitory). You'll also find a round tower, an early Christian cross, a delightful Romanesque chapel, and a ruined Gothic cathedral, all surrounded by my favorite Celtic-cross graveyard. Bring a coat for the deceptively cool conditions on the high, windy, exposed Rock.

Crowd-Beating Tips: Summer crowds flock to the Rock (worst June–Aug 11:00–15:00). Try to plan your visit for early or late in the day. If you're here at a peak time, tour the Rock first and save the movie, museum, and Hall of the Vicars Choral for the end of your visit, when the tourist tide has receded. Otherwise, see the movie and museum first.

Tours: Call ahead for the tour schedule (included in entry price, 45 min, tel. 062/61437). Otherwise, set your own pace with the tour I've outlined below.

SELF-GUIDED TOUR

Exploring the Rock of Cashel

• *Follow this tour counterclockwise around the Rock. To start the tour, climb the stairs opposite the ticket desk.*

❶ **Hall of the Vicars Choral:** This is the youngest building on the Rock (early 1400s). It housed the minor clerics appointed to sing during cathedral services. These vicars—who were granted nearby lands by the archbishop—lived comfortably here with a large fireplace and white, lime-washed walls (to reflect light and act as a natural disinfectant). Window seats gave the blessedly literate vicars the best light to read by. The furniture is original, but the oak timber roof is a reconstruction, built to medieval specifications using wooden dowels instead of nails. The large wall tapestry, showing King Solomon with the Queen of Sheba, contains intentional errors—to remind viewers that only God can create perfection. The vicars, who formed a sort of corporate body to assist the bishop with local administration, used a special seal to authorize documents such as land leases. You can see an enlarged wooden

Rock of Cashel

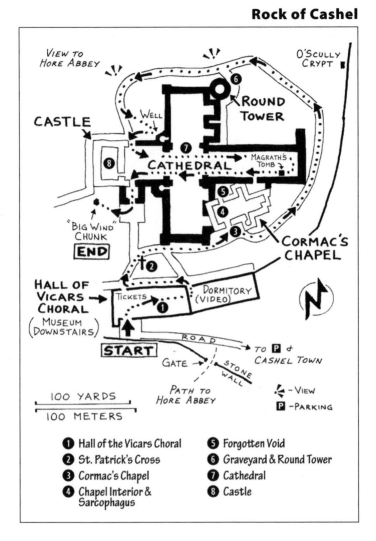

❶ Hall of the Vicars Choral	❺ Forgotten Void
❷ St. Patrick's Cross	❻ Graveyard & Round Tower
❸ Cormac's Chapel	❼ Cathedral
❹ Chapel Interior & Sarcophagus	❽ Castle

copy of the seal (hanging above the fireplace), depicting eight vicars surrounding a seated organist. It was a good system—until some of the greedier vicars duplicated the seal for their own use, forcing the archbishop to curtail its use.

• Go outside the hall and find...

❷ **St. Patrick's Cross:** St. Patrick baptized King Aengus at the Rock of Cashel around A.D. 450. Legend has it that St. Patrick, intensely preoccupied with the holy ceremony, accidentally speared the foot of the king with his crosier staff while administering the baptismal sacrament. But the pagan king stoically held his tongue until the end of the ceremony, thinking this was part of the painful process of becoming a Christian.

This 12th-century cross, a stub of its former glory, was carved to celebrate the handing over of the Rock to the Church 650 years after St. Patrick's visit. Typical Irish high crosses use a ring around the cross' head to support its arms and to symbolize the sun (making Christianity more appealing to the sun-worshipping Celts). But instead, this cross uses the Latin design: The weight of the arms is supported by two vertical beams on each side of the main shaft, representing the two criminals who were crucified beside Christ (today only one of these supports remains).

On my first visit, 25 years ago, the original cross still stood here. But centuries of wind and rain slowly eroded away important detail, so the cross was moved into the adjacent museum and replaced by this replica.

• *Turn your back on St. Patrick's Cross and walk about 100 feet slightly uphill along the gravel path beside the cathedral. Roughly opposite the far end of the Hall of the Vicars Choral is the entry to...*

❸ **Cormac's Chapel:** As the wild Celtic Christian church was reined in and reorganized by Rome 850 years ago, new archi-

tectural influences from continental Europe began to emerge on the remote Irish landscape. This small chapel— Ireland's first and finest Romanesque church, consecrated in 1134 by King Cormac MacCarthy—reflects this evolution. Travel in your imagination back to the 12th century, when this chapel and the tall round tower (described below) were the only stone structures on the Rock.

The "new" Romanesque style reflected the ancient Roman basilica floor plan. Its columns and rounded arches created an overall effect of massiveness and strength. Romanesque churches were like dark fortresses with thick walls, squat towers, few windows, and minimal decoration. Irish stone churches of this period (like the one at Glendalough in the Wicklow Mountains, or the Gallarus Oratory near An Daingean) were simple rectangular buildings with no ornate stone carving at all.

Tradition says that the chapel's easy-to-cut sandstone was quarried 12 miles away, and the blocks were passed from hand to hand back to the Rock. The two square towers resemble those in Regensburg, Germany, further suggesting that well-traveled medieval Irish monks brought back new ideas from the Continent.

• *The modern, dark-glass chapel door (always unlocked) is a recent addition to keep out nesting birds. Enter the chapel (remembering to close the door behind you) and let your eyes adjust to the low light.*

❹ **Chapel Interior:** Just inside the chapel is an empty stone **sarcophagus.** Nobody knows for sure whose body once lay here (possibly the brother of King Cormac MacCarthy). The damaged front relief is carved in the Scandinavian Urnes style. Vikings raided Ireland, intermarried with the Irish, and were melting into Irish society by the time this chapel was built. Some scholars interpret the relief design (a tangle of snakes and beasts) as a figure-eight lying on its side, looping back and forth forever, symbolizing the eternity of the afterlife.

With your back to the sarcophagus, let your eyes wander around the chapel interior. You're standing in the **nave,** lit by the three windows (partially blocked by the later cathedral) in the wall behind you. Overhead is a round vaulted ceiling with support ribs. The strong round arches support not only the heavy stone roof, but also the (unseen) second-story scriptorium chamber where monks once carefully copied manuscripts.

The **chancel arch,** studded with fist-sized heads, framed the altar (now gone). The lower heads are more grotesque, while those nearing the top become serene as they climb closer to God. The arch is off-center in relation to the nave, symbolic of Christ's head drooping to the side as he died on the cross.

Walk into the chancel and look up at the ceiling, examining the faint **frescoes,** a labor of love from 850 years ago. Frescoes are rare in Ireland because of the perpetually moist climate. (Mixing pigments into wet plaster worked better in dry climates like Italy.) Once vividly colorful, then fading over time, these frescoes were further damaged during the Reformation. Such ornamentation was considered vain by Protestants, who piously whitewashed over them. These surviving frescoes were discovered under multiple whitewash layers during painstaking modern restoration. The rich blue color came from lapis lazuli, an expensive gemstone imported from Asia.

• *Walk through the other modern, dark-glass doorway (don't let the birds in), opposite the door you used to enter the chapel. You'll find yourself in a...*

❺ **Forgotten Void:** This enclosed space (roughly 15 feet square) was created when the newer cathedral was wedged between the older chapel and the round tower. Once the main entrance into the chapel, this forgotten doorway is crowned by a finely carved tympanum decorating the arch above it. It's perfectly preserved because the huge cathedral shielded it from the elements. The large lion (symbol of St. Mark's gospel) is being hunted by a centaur archer (half man, half horse) wearing a Norman helmet (essential conehead attire in the late Middle Ages).

As you exit the chapel (turning left), take a look at the more exposed and weathered tympanum outside, above the south entrance. The carved bloated "hippo" is actually a bull, part of St. Luke's apocalyptic vision.

• *Tiptoe through the tombstones around the east end of the cathedral to the base of the round tower.*

❻ **Graveyard and Round Tower:** This graveyard still takes permanent guests—but only those put on a waiting list by their ancestors in 1930. A handful of these chosen few are still alive, and once they're gone, the graveyard will be considered full. The 20-foot-tall shaft at the edge of the graveyard, marking the O'Scully family crypt, was once crowned by an elaborately carved Irish high cross—destroyed during a lightning storm in 1976.

Look out over the **Plain of Tipperary**. Called the "Golden Vale," its rich soil makes it Ireland's most prosperous farmland. In St. Patrick's time, it was covered with oak forests. A path leads to the ruined 13th-century Hore Abbey in the fields below (free, always open and peaceful). The abbey is named for the Cistercian monks who wore simple gray robes, roughly the same color as hoarfrost.

Gaze up at the **round tower,** the first stone structure built on the Rock after the Church took over in 1101. The shape of these towers is unique to Ireland. Though you might think towers like this were used as a place to hide in case of invasion, they were used primarily as bell towers and lookout posts. (Enemies could smoke out anyone inside the tower, and with enough warning, monks were better off hiding in the countryside.) The tower stands 92 feet tall, with walls over three feet thick. The doorway, which once had a rope ladder, was built high up not only for security, but also because having it at ground level would have weakened the foundation of the top-heavy structure. The interior once contained wooden floors connected by ladders, and served as safe storage for the monk's precious sacramental treasures. The tower's stability is impressive when you consider its age, the winds it has endured, and the shallowness of its foundation (only 5 feet under present ground level).

Continue walking around the cathedral's north transept, noticing the square holes in the exterior walls. During construction, wooden scaffolding was anchored into these holes. On your way to the cathedral entrance, in the corner where the north transept joins the nave, you'll pass a small **well**. Without this essential water source, the Rock could never have withstood a siege, and would not have been as valuable to clans and clergy. In 1848, a chalice was dredged from the well, likely thrown there by fleeing medieval monks intending to survive a raid. They didn't make it. (If they had, they would have retrieved the chalice.)

• *Now enter the...*

❼ **Cathedral:** Traditionally, the choir of a church (where the clergy celebrate Mass) faces east, while the nave (where the congregation stands) stretches off to the west. Because this cathedral was squeezed between the pre-existing chapel, round tower, and drinking well, the builders were forced to improvise—giving it an extra-long choir and a cramped nave.

Built between 1230 and 1290, the church's pointed arches and high, narrow windows proclaim the Gothic style of the period (and let in more light than earlier Romanesque churches). Walk under the central bell tower and look up at the rib-vaulted **ceiling.** The hole in the middle was for a rope used to ring the church bells. The wooden roof is long gone. When Lord Inchiquin (Oliver Cromwell's general) attacked the town of Cashel in 1647, hundreds of townsfolk fled to the sanctuary of this cathedral and held out. Inchiquin packed turf around the exterior and burned it down, massacring those inside.

Ascend the **terraces** at the choir end of the cathedral, where the main altar once stood. Stand on the gravestones (of the 16th-century rich and famous) with your back to the open east wall (where the narrow windows have crumbled away) and look back down toward the nave. The right wall of the choir is filled with graceful Gothic windows, while the solid left wall hides Cormac's Chapel (which would have blocked any sunlight). The line of stone supports on the left wall once held the long, wooden balcony where the vicars sang. Closer to the altar, high on the same wall, is a small, rectangular window called the "leper's squint"—which allowed unsightly lepers to view the altar during Mass without offending the congregation.

The grand **wall tomb** on the left contains the remains of arch-

bishop Miler Magrath, the "scoundrel of Cashel," who lived to be 100. From 1570 to 1622, Magrath was the Protestant archbishop of Cashel while simultaneously profiting from his previous position as Catholic bishop of Down. He married twice, had lots of kids, confiscated the ornate tomb lid here from another bishop's grave, and converted back to Catholicism on his deathbed.

• *Walk back down to the far end of the nave and exit the cathedral on the left, through the porch entrance.*

❽ **Castle:** Back outside, stand beside the huge chunk of wall debris and try to picture where it might have fit in the ruins above. This end of the cathedral was converted into an archbishop's castle in the 1400s (shortening the nave even more). Looking high into the castle's damaged top floors, you can see the bishop's residence chamber and the secret passageways that were once hidden in the thick walls. Lord Inchiquin's cannons weakened the structure during the 1647 massacre, and in 1848, a massive storm (known as "Night of the Big Wind" in Irish lore) flung the huge chunk next to you from the ruins above.

In the mid-1700s, the Anglican Church transferred cathedral status to St. John's in town, and the archbishop abandoned the drafty Rock for a more comfortable residence, leaving the ruins that you see today.

SIGHTS

Near the Rock of Cashel

Bru Boru Cultural Centre—Nestled below the Rock of Cashel parking lot, next to the statue of the three blissed-out dancers, this center adds to your understanding of the Rock in its wider historical and cultural context. The highlight of the Sounds of History museum downstairs is the exhibit showing the Rock's gradual evolution from ancient ring fort to grand church ruins—projected down onto a large disc that visitors gather around.

Those headed for An Daingean's great traditional music scene will enjoy the surprisingly good 15-minute film introduction to Irish traditional music in the small museum theater (€5, June–Sept daily 9:00–20:30, Oct–May Mon–Fri 9:00–17:00, closed Sat–Sun, cafeteria, tel. 062/61122).

If you overnight in Cashel, consider taking in a performance of the Bru Boru musical dance troupe in the Centre's large upstairs theater (€16, mid-June–mid-Sept Tue–Sat at 21:00).

Town of Cashel—The huggable town at the base of the Rock affords a good break on the long drive from Dublin to An Daingean (**TI** open mid-March–Oct daily 9:30–17:30; Nov–mid-March Mon–Fri 9:30–17:30, closed Sat–Sun, tel. 062/62511). The Heritage Centre, next door to the TI, presents a modest six-minute audio explanation of Cashel's history around a walled town model.

SLEEPING

(€1 = about $1.20, country code: 353, area code: 062)
If you spend the night in Cashel, you'll be treated to views of the ruins beautifully illuminated at night.

$$ Legends Townhouse has seven pleasant rooms (some with views of the floodlit ruins) above a friendly restaurant in a convenient location near the base of the Rock (Sb-€50–60, Db-€110–128, non-smoking, parking, The Kiln, tel. 062/61292, www.legendsguesthouse.com, info@legendsguesthouse.com).

$ Rockville House, with six fine rooms, is close to the Rock (Sb-€39, Db-€50–55, Dominic Street, tel. 062/61760).

$ Abbey House, a bit farther toward town, has five comfortable rooms cheerily tended to by Ellen Ryan (Sb-€44, D-€55, Db-€70, Dominic Street, tel. & fax 062/61104, teachnamainstreach @eircom.net).

$ O'Brien's Holiday Lodge, well-kept and a step above most other hostels, is housed in an old stone grain warehouse behind the rock near Hore Abbey (dorm beds-€16, Db-€45–50, Tb-€60–70, camping spots-€7 per person, laundry service-€9, Dundrum Road R505, tel. 062/61003, fax 062/62797, obriensholidaylodge @eircom.net).

EATING

Grab a soup-and-sandwich lunch at tiny **Granny's Kitchen** (next to parking lot at base of Rock) or at snug **King Cormac's** (a block away at base of road up to Rock).

For lunch or dinner, **Pasta Milano's** neon-orange glow is easy to spot above a famine work-project wall (€12–19 meals, daily 12:00–23:00, Ladyswell Street, tel. 062/62729).

For a splurge dinner, consider the classy **Chez Hans** (2-course €25 early-bird menu before 19:30, otherwise €25–37 entrées, Tue–Sat 18:00–22:00, closed Sun–Mon, in an old church a block below the Rock, tel. 062/61177). The same folks also run the cheaper **Chez Hans Café** up the street, serving lunches only until closing (€10–14 meals, Tue–Sat 12:00–17:30, closed Sun–Mon).

Legends Restaurant offers good dinners with great night-time views of the lit-up Rock (2-course €20 early-bird menu before 19:30, Tue–Sat 18:00–21:30, closed Sun–Mon, The Kiln, behind hedge beside main parking lot, tel. 062/61292).

TRANSPORTATION CONNECTIONS

Cashel has no train station; the closest one is 13 miles away in the town of Thurles.

From Cashel by Bus to: Dublin (6/day, 3 hrs), **Kilkenny** (3/day, 2.5 hrs), **Waterford** (6/day, 2 hrs).

WATERFORD AND COUNTY WEXFORD

The best overnight stop in southeast Ireland is the historic Viking and Norman beachhead town of Waterford. From here, you can explore the varied sights of County Wexford. Throughout your travels, you'll see evidence of the region's Norman riots in its high concentration of family names with old Norman French prefixes: De Berg, De Claire, Fitzgilbert, Fitzsimmons, and so on.

Waterford

The oldest city in Ireland, Waterford was once more important than Dublin. Today, while tourists associate the town's name with its famous crystal, locals are quick to remind you that the crystal is named after the town and not vice versa. That said, Waterford is a plain, gray, workaday town. Pubs outnumber cafés, freighters offload cargo at the dock, and when radio stations offer dinner at McDonald's as a prize, people actually call in. It's a dose of real Ireland, which was, until a couple of generations ago, one of the poorest countries in Western Europe.

Planning Your Time
A day is more than enough time for Waterford. Visit the crystal factory on the south edge of town on your way in or out—to avoid the midday crowds (the TI at the factory has a free visitor's guide with a town map). In Waterford, your best activity is the historic walk (at 11:45 or 13:45 in peak season, see "Tours," below), followed by a visit to the Museum of Treasures and Reginald's Tower.

To feel the pulse of Waterford, hang out on the town's pedestrian square and stroll through its big, modern shopping mall.

ORIENTATION

(area code: 051)
Waterford's main drag runs along its ugly harbor, where you'll find the bus station and easy parking lots (€1.50/hr, €13 daily maximum, €5 overnight parking from 17:00–8:00, pay at automated station before driving out gate). All recommended accommodations and sights (except the Waterford Crystal Factory tour) are within a five-minute walk of the harbor. Both museums and the TI are on the harborfront. The stubby two-story Victorian clock tower marks the middle of the harbor as well as the pedestrian Barronstrand Street that runs a block inland to the town square.

Tourist Information

The TI is inside the old brick granary warehouse on Merchant's Quay (April–Oct Mon–Fri 9:00–18:00, Sat 10:00–18:00, closed Sun; Nov–March Mon–Sat until 17:00, closed Sun; tel. 051/875-823). As with all Irish TIs, it's basically a shop with a counter where clerks tell you about places that they endorse (i.e., get money from).

City Pass Ticket: If you're visiting all three participating town sights (Waterford Museum of Treasures-€6, Reginald's Tower-€2, and Waterford Crystal-€8), you can save nearly €6 in admissions by buying the €10.25 City Pass Ticket (sold at TI and each sight).

Helpful Hints

Internet Access: Voyager Internet is handy on the waterfront at 85 Parade Quay (€3/30 min, Mon–Sat 10:00–21:00, closed Sun, tel. 051/843-843).

Post Office: It's on Parade Quay (Mon–Fri 9:00–17:30, Sat 9:00–13:00, closed Sun).

Laundry: Snow White launderette is at 61 Mayor's Walk (Mon–Sat 9:30–13:30 & 14:30–18:00, closed Sun, tel. 051/858-905).

Taxis: Consider Street Cabs Ltd. (117 Parade Quay, tel. 051/877-778). Rapid Cabs operate local taxis (tel. 051/858-585) as well as Rapid Express coaches to Dublin's airport (tel. 051/872-149).

TOURS

▲▲**Waterford Historic Walking Tour**—Jack Burtchaell and his partners lead informative hour-long historic town walks that meet at the Waterford Museum of Treasures (behind TI) every day at 11:45 and 13:45 (just show up and pay €5 at the end, mid-March–mid-Oct only, tel. 051/873-711). The tour—really the most

Waterford

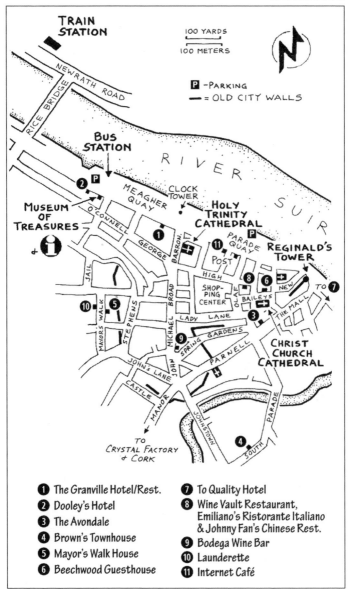

① The Granville Hotel/Rest.
② Dooley's Hotel
③ The Avondale
④ Brown's Townhouse
⑤ Mayor's Walk House
⑥ Beechwood Guesthouse
⑦ To Quality Hotel
⑧ Wine Vault Restaurant, Emiliano's Ristorante Italiano & Johnny Fan's Chinese Rest.
⑨ Bodega Wine Bar
⑩ Launderette
⑪ Internet Café

enjoyable thing to do in Waterford—is an entertaining walk from the TI to Reginald's Tower, giving you a good handle on the story of Waterford.

SIGHTS

Cathedral of the Holy Trinity—In 1793, the English king granted Ireland the Irish Relief Act, which, among other things, allowed the Irish to build Catholic churches and worship publicly. With Catholic France (30 million) threatening Britain (8 million) on one side, and Ireland (6 million) stirring things up on the other, the king needed to take action to lessen Irish resentment.

Granted their new freedom, the Irish built their interesting cathedral in 1796. It's Ireland's first Catholic post-Reformation church, and its only Baroque church. The building was funded by wealthy Irish wine merchants from Cadiz, Spain. Among its treasures are 10 Waterford Crystal chandeliers (free, daily 8:00–19:00).

Nearby: The cathedral faces **Barronstrand Street,** which leads from the clock tower on the harborfront to the pedestrian-friendly **town square.** The street separates the medieval town (on your left when the river is behind you) from the 18th-century city (on your right). A river once flowed here—part of the town's natural defenses just outside the old wall. The huge **shopping center** that dominates the old town was built right on top of the Viking town. In fact, the center is built over a church dating from 1150 that you can see at the bottom of the escalator (next to the kiddie rides).

▲**Reginald's Tower**—This oldest part of the oldest town in Ireland is named after Regnall, the first Viking leader of Waterford, who built a tower here in A.D. 914 and later founded Jorvik (York,

England). The tower you see today dates from 1003 and is supposedly Ireland's oldest intact building and its first made with mortar. It was the most important corner of the town wall. Inside you'll see a display of medieval coins, old city models, a few Viking artifacts, and a short video (€2, covered by City
Pass Ticket and Heritage Card—see page 4, includes guided tour any time upon request—ask for the 1-hour version, which adds a historic walk around the block to French's Church; daily June–Sept 10:00–18:30, Oct–May 10:00–17:00, last entry 75 min before closing, tel. 051/304-220).

▲▲**Waterford Museum of Treasures**—This museum presents, with the help of handheld audioguides, a grand sweep through the history of Ireland as seen from Waterford. It's housed, along

---

Waterford's History

The Vikings first came in 850 and established Waterford as their base for piracy. Since the spot is located at the gateway to the largest natural navigation system in Ireland, Viking ships could sail 50 miles into Ireland from here. Ireland had no towns at this time, only scattered monastic settlements and small gatherings of clans—perfect for rape, pillage, and plunder. Later, the Vikings decided to "go legal" and do their profiteering from an established trading base they named Vandrafjord ("safe harbor"...eventually Waterford). This became Ireland's first permanent town. It was from this base that the Norsemen invaded England.

In the 12th century, a deposed Irish king invited the Normans over from England, hoping to use their muscle to regain his land from a rival clan. The great warrior knight Strongbow came and never left, and that was the beginning of Ireland's long and troublesome relationship with the English. For the English, Waterford often proved to be a tough nut to crack. During Oliver Cromwell's "scorched earth" campaign of 1649–50, when the Cromwellian forces decimated Ireland, Waterford was the only Irish city to withstand his sieges.

---

with the TI, in an old stone grain warehouse where the original Waterford Crystal works stood (€6, covered by City Pass Ticket; April–Sept Mon–Sat 9:30–18:00, Sun 11:00–18:00; Oct–March Mon–Sat 10:00–17:00, Sun 11:00–17:00; last entry 1 hour before closing, tel. 051/304-500).

Christ Church Cathedral—The Protestant Cathedral, with 18th-century Georgian architecture, is the fourth church to stand here—see the exposed Gothic column six feet below today's floor level. In the Gothic church that once stood here, the Norman conquerer Strongbow married the Gaelic princess Aoife in 1170, granting him the title of King of Leinster and planting England's first roots in Ireland.

Wander over to the macabre tomb of 15th-century mayor James Rice, bearing a famous epitaph: "I am what you will be, I was what you are, pray for me." To emphasize the point, he requested that his body be dug up one year after his death (1482) and his partially decomposed remains be used to model his likeness, now seen on the tomb's lid...complete with worms and frogs (€3, generally open daily 10:00–17:00).

▲▲**Waterford Crystal Factory**—With a tradition dating back to 1783, Waterford is the largest and one of the most respected glass-works in the world. Its fine hour-long tours take visitors through the entire production process and offer a close-up look at many of

Thomas Francis Meagher
(1823–1867)

Waterford's favorite son had a short but amazing life. Born to a conservative Waterford mayor, Meagher joined Daniel O'Connell's nonviolent movement to repeal the Act of Union with Britain. Impatient with the slow-moving political process, he joined the radical Young Irelander movement and became an inspiring speaker. He went to France in 1848 and came back with the first Irish tricolor flag—a gift from the French representing the Catholics (green), the Protestants (orange), and peaceful coexistence between them (white). Involved in a failed uprising, Meagher was sentenced to hang (and then drawn and quartered), but his sentence was commuted to life in prison in Tasmania. Meagher escaped Tasmania in 1852 aboard an American whaling ship and sailed to San Francisco. He then went overland to New York, where he studied law and eventually became a lawyer. After he made a trip to Nicaragua to study the feasibility of building a canal or railway across the isthmus, the American Civil War broke out. Returning to New York, Meagher was made a general and raised a regiment of Irish immigrants that he led famously into battle for the Union at Antietam and Fredricksburg. After the war, he became the first governor of the Montana territory. Then 44-year-old Thomas Francis Meagher fell off a riverboat and drowned in the Missouri River. His body was never found.

the plant's 1,600 employees hard at work.

While you ride a bus to one end of the factory, your guide

orients you. Then you see a huge furnace—which has been burning nonstop for 30 years—where the dipping, blowing, and shaping take place. (It's powered by natural gas, piped in 90 miles from Kinsale.) Next you see the etching. Workers, after a five-year apprenticeship, make the art of crystal blowing and cutting look easy. Each glass piece goes through more than 30 sets of hands before it's ready for sale. Waterford proudly sells no seconds. Due to tiny blemishes detected by quality control, about a third of the pieces are smashed and re-melted. (Workers are paid by the successful piece.) The tour finishes with an opportunity to actually meet a cutter, see his diamond-bladed wheel in action, and ask questions. Then you land in the glittering salesroom surrounded by hard-to-pack but easy-to-ship temptations. Before leaving, go upstairs above the gift shop to see the copies of famous sports trophies (they make backups of their most important commissions...just in case).

Cost and Hours: €8, covered by City Pass Ticket, March–Oct daily 8:30–18:00, last tours leave at 16:00 sharp, but shop stays open until 18:00; Nov–Feb daily 9:00–17:00, last tours leave at 15:15 sharp, no tours Sat–Sun. A handy TI is next to the cafeteria at the back of the reception area.

Tours: Tours are liveliest weekdays before 15:30. Except for a skeleton crew working for the benefit of the tours, the factory is pretty quiet after 16:00 and on weekends. Minimize crowds by coming early and avoiding the afternoon rush. If arriving late, call to confirm tour times (tel. 051/332-500, www.waterfordvisitorcentre.com).

Getting There: The factory is conveniently located on the N25 Cork road about two miles south of the city center. There are easy city bus connections from the waterfront.

SLEEPING

Waterford is a working-class town. Cheap accommodations are fairly rough. Fancy accommodations are venerable old places facing the water.

$$$ The Granville Hotel is Waterford's top, most historic hotel, grandly overlooking the center of the harborfront. The place is plush, from its Old World lounges to its extravagant rooms

---

Sleep Code

(€1 = about $1.20, country code: 353, area code: 051)
S = Single, **D** = Double/Twin, **T** = Triple, **Q** = Quad, **b** = bathroom, **s** = shower only. Unless otherwise noted, breakfast is included and credit cards are accepted.

To help you easily sort through these listings, I've divided the rooms into three categories, based on the price for a standard double room with bath:

  $$$ **Higher Priced**—Most rooms €100 or more.
   $$ **Moderately Priced**—Most rooms between €65–100.
    $ **Lower Priced**—Most rooms €65 or less.

(Sb-€70–90, Db-€160–195, Tb-€150–200, ask about "corporate discounts," Meagher Quay, tel. 051/305-555, fax 051/305-566, www.granville-hotel.ie, stay@granville-hotel.ie).

$$$ Dooley's Hotel, a more modern business-class place with big motel-style rooms on the harbor, can be less expensive (Sb-€80–120, Db-€170–190, Tb-€195–240, often discounted much lower, Merchant's Quay, tel. 051/873-531, fax 051/870-262, www.dooleys-hotel.ie, hotel@dooleys-hotel.ie).

$$$ Quality Hotel, part of the dependable hotel chain, has large, comfortable rooms and very little personality (Sb-€70–90, Db-€120–180, Canada Street, parking, tel. 051/856-600, fax 051/856-605, www.qualityhotelwaterford.com, info@qualityhotelwaterford.com).

$$ The Avondale, facing a noisy street a block inland from Reginald's Tower, rents seven fine rooms (Sb-€40–60, Db-€60–80, Qb-€110, no breakfast served, 2 Parnell Street, tel. 051/852-267, www.staywithus.net, info@staywithus.net, Margaret and John Fogarty).

$$ Brown's Townhouse is a charming, Victorian-style, six-room place where guests share one big, homey breakfast table. It's on a quiet residential street a 10-minute walk from the city center (Sb-€45–70, Db-€72–110, Qb-€120–160, 10 percent discount for stays of 2 or more nights and cash payment, 29 South Parade, Internet access in lobby, parking, tel. 051/870-594, fax 051/871-923, www.brownstownhouse.com, info@brownstownhouse.com, Siobhan McConnell).

$ Mayor's Walk House is a well-worn, grandmotherly place that takes you right back to the 1950s. Bob and Jane Hovenden rent four economical yet pleasant rooms (S-€27, D-€48, T-€72, cash only, 12 Mayor's Walk, tel. & fax 051/855-427, mayorswalkbandb@eircom.net).

$ Beechwood Guesthouse, sitting quietly next to Christ Church Cathedral, has three cozy little rooms in a great location (S-€45, D-€55–60, cash only, non-smoking, 7 Cathedral Square, tel. 051/876-677, mbryan05@yahoo.co.uk, Mary Ryan).

EATING

For something livelier than tired pub grub, consider three good restaurants (wine bar, Italian, and Chinese) that share a tiny street behind Reginald's Tower. All are small, popular, and serve an early-bird special (2 or 3 courses for €15–20 before 19:00). **The Wine Vault**—a cellar wine shop by day—offers decent European cuisine and seafood with a good selection of wines from its 18th-century cellar (lunches Tue–Sat 12:30–14:30, dinners Mon–Sat 17:30–22:30, closed Sun, tel. 051/853-444); you're welcome to climb into the wine cellar below the restaurant. **Emiliano's Ristorante Italiano** (lunches Sat–Sun 12:30–14:30, dinners Tue–Sun 17:00–22:30, closed Mon, tel. 051/820-333) and **Johnny Fan's Chinese Cuisine and Seafood** (Mon–Sat 12:30–14:30 & 17:30–23:30, Sun 13:00–15:00 & 18:00–23:00, tel. 051/879-535) are both next door and lively with locals.

The relaxed **Bodega** is my favorite wine bar, run by laid-back Cormac in a warm-glow Mediterranean atmosphere (Tue–Sun 12:00–14:30 & 18:00–22:00, closed Mon, 54 John Street, tel. 051/844-177).

The carvery at **The Granville Hotel** is your easiest lunch option, given its central location (daily 12:30–14:30, otherwise good bar food daily 10:30–19:00, Meagher Quay).

Pub Grub: Waterford's staple food seems to be pub grub. Several typical pubs serve dinner in the city center. For your musical entertainment, just wander around, read the notices, and follow your ears. You'll find plenty of live action on George Street, Barronstrand Street, and Broad Street.

TRANSPORTATION CONNECTIONS

From Waterford by Train to: Dublin (6/day, 3 hrs), **Kilkenny** (5/day, 45 min), **Rosslare** (2/day, 1.5 hrs).

By Bus to: Cork (13/day, 2.25 hrs), **Kilkenny** (2/day, 1 hr), **Rosslare** (5/day, 1.25 hrs), **Wexford** (5/day, 1 hr). Waterford bus station info: tel. 051/879-000.

County Wexford

The southeast corner of Ireland is peppered with pretty views and historic sites easily accessible to drivers as a day trip from Waterford. While most of the sights are mediocre, five (each within an hour's drive of Waterford) are worth considering.

The dramatic Hook Head Lighthouse—capping an intriguing and remote peninsula—comes with lots of history and a great tour. The Kennedy Homestead is a pilgrimage site for Kennedy fans. The *Dunbrody* Famine Ship in New Ross gives a sense of what 50 days on a coffin ship with dreams of "Americay" must have been like. The Irish National Heritage Park in Wexford is a Stone Age Knott's Berry Farm. And the National 1798 Visitors Centre at Enniscorthy explains the roots of the Irish struggle for liberty.

Planning Your Time

New Ross, Enniscorthy, and Wexford are each less than 30 minutes apart, connected by fast roads. The Kennedy Homestead is a

County Wexford

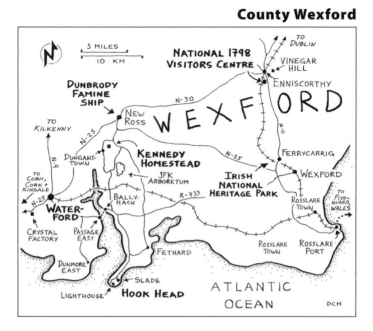

10-minute drive from New Ross, and the lighthouse is a 45-minute trip to the end of the Hook Peninsula. All are well-signposted and easy to find. Connecting Dublin with Waterford, you could visit many of these sights in a best-of-County Wexford day en route. On a quick trip, the sights are not worth the trouble by public transit. If you'll be spending the night, Enniscorthy and New Ross are blue-collar towns (with decent hotels and B&Bs) that provide a good glimpse of Ireland.

If connecting Hook Head and Waterford, use the car-ferry shortcut from Passage East to Ballyhack (€3.50, 5-min crossing, runs continuously, daily April–Sept 7:00–22:00, Oct–March 7:00–20:00).

SIGHTS

If you plan on visiting more than one of the following Wexford sights (except the Kennedy Homestead), take advantage of the "Southeast Explorer" pass discount coupons, which offer 20 percent off each sight (ask for it at the first sight you visit).

▲**Hook Head Lighthouse**—This is the oldest operating lighthouse in Northern Europe. According to legend, St. Dubhan arrived in the sixth century and discovered the bodies of shipwrecked sailors. Dismayed, he and his followers began tending a fire on the headland to warn future mariners. What you see

today is essentially 12th-century, built by the Normans (who first landed 5 miles up the east coast at Baginbun Head in 1169). They established Waterford Harbor as a commercial beachhead to the rich Irish countryside that they intended to conquer. This beacon assured them safe access.

Today's lighthouse is 110 feet tall and looks modern on the outside (it was automated in 1996, and its light can be seen 23 miles out to sea). But it's 800 years old, built on a plan inspired by the lighthouse of Alexandria in Egypt—one of the seven wonders of the ancient world.

Since it's a working lighthouse, it may be toured only with a guide or escort. Fine 30-minute tours leave about hourly. Inside, with its black-stained, ribbed, vaulted ceilings and stout, 10-foot-thick walls, you can almost feel the presence of the Benedictine monks who tended a coal-burning beacon at the top for the Normans. Climbing 115 steps through four levels rewards you with a breezy, salt-air view from the top.

When Oliver Cromwell arrived here to secure the English claim to this area, he considered his two options and declared he'd take strategic Waterford "by Hook or by Crooke." Hook is the long peninsula with the lighthouse. Crooke is a little village on the other side (just south of Passage East).

Cost, Hours, Services: €5.50, March–Oct daily 9:30–17:30, last tour usually at 17:00, closed Nov–Feb, call to check tour times before driving out (tel. 051/397-055).

There's a decent cafeteria and a shop with fliers explaining other sights on the peninsula. Kids-at-heart can't resist climbing out on the rugged rocky tip of the windy Hook Head.

▲**Kennedy Homestead**—Patrick Kennedy, JFK's great-grandfather, left Ireland in 1858. Distant relatives have turned his property into a little museum/shrine for Kennedy pilgrims. Physically, it's not much: A barn and a wing of the modern house survive from 1858. JFK dropped in by helicopter in June of 1963, a few months before he was assassinated. You'll view two short videos: five minutes of Kennedy's actual visit to the farm and a 16-minute newsreel tracing the events of his 1963 trip through Ireland (both fascinating if you like Kennedy stuff). Then Patrick Grennan, a distant Kennedy relative himself whose grandmother hosted the tea here for JFK, gives you a 15-minute tour. Finally you're free to peruse the barn, lined with Kennedy-in-Ireland memorabilia and detailing the history of the Kennedy dynasty. While it's just a private home, anyone interested in the Kennedys will find it worth driving the treacherous narrow lane to see.

Cost, Hours, Location: €4, July–Aug daily 10:00–17:00, May–June and Sept 11:30–16:30, by appointment after hours, in slow times, and Oct–April (no big deal, as it's their home), tel. 051/388-264, www.kennedyhomestead.com. It's four miles south of New Ross near Dunganstown (look for sign off of R733, long one-lane road). Don't confuse the Kennedy Homestead with the nearby JFK Arboretum. The arboretum is lovely if you like trees and plants. It's a huge park with 4,500 species of trees and a grand six-county view—but no Kennedy history.

▲▲*Dunbrody* **Famine Ship**—Permanently moored in the tiny port of New Ross, this was built as a reminder of the countless

hungry Irish who sailed to America on ships like this. The *Dunbrody* is a full-scale reconstruction of a 19th-century three-masted bark built in Quebec in 1845. It's typical of the trading vessels that sailed empty to America to pick up goods, but during the famine found they could make a little money on the westward voyage. Extended families camped out for 50 days on bunk beds no bigger than a king-size mattress. Often, boats like this would arrive in America with only 50 percent of their original human cargo—hence the nickname "coffin ships."

After a 10-minute video about the building of the ship, you'll follow an excellent guide through the ship and encounter a couple of grumpy passengers who tell vivid tales about life aboard. Roots-seekers are welcome to peruse their computerized file of one million names of immigrants who sailed from 1846 through 1865.

Cost, Hours, Location: €6.50, 45-min tours go 2/hr, daily April–Oct 9:00–18:00, Nov–March 10:00–17:00, last tour leaves one hour before closing (tel. 051/425-239, www.dunbrody.com). The *Dunbrody* is in New Ross, near the Kennedy Homestead. Parking is easy and free on Sundays, but during work hours you'll need to feed the €1/hr parking meters in the lot.

▲**Irish National Heritage Park**—This 35-acre wooded park, which contains an 1857 tower commemorating local boys killed in the Crimean War, features replicas of buildings from each era of Irish history. Ireland's countless ancient sights are generally unrecognizable ruins—hard to re-create in your mind. This park is intended to help out. You'll find buildings and settlements illustrating life in Ireland from the Stone Age through the 12th-century Norman Age. As a bonus, you'll see animal-skin clad characters doing their prehistoric thing—gnawing on meat, weaving, making arrowheads, and so on.

Your visit begins with a 12-minute video followed by a 90-minute tour. During 13 stops, your guide explains the various civilizations. The highlight is a monastic settlement from the age when Europe was dark and Ireland was "the island of saints and scholars." While you can wander around on your own, the place is a bit childish (there's nothing actually old here) and only worthwhile if you take the included tour.

Cost, Hours, Location: €7.50, daily 9:30–18:30, until 17:30 in winter, last entry 90 minutes before closing, tours go hourly (tel. 053/20733). It's clearly signposted on the west end of Wexford—you'll hit it before entering town on the N11 Enniscorthy road.

National 1798 Visitors Centre—Located in Enniscorthy, this museum creatively tells the story of the rise of revolutionary thinking in Ireland, which led to the ill-fated rebellion of 1798. Enniscorthy was the crucial Irish battleground of a populist revolution (inspired by the American and French Revolutions) that witnessed the bloodiest days of the doomed 1798 uprising. The material is compelling for anyone intrigued by struggles for liberty, but there's little more here than video clips of reenactments and storyboards on the walls.

Leaving the center, look east across the Slaney River, which divides Enniscorthy, and you'll see a hill with a stumpy tower on it. This is Vinegar Hill. The tower is the old windmill that once flew the green rebel flag. Drive to the top for the views that the rebels had of the surrounding British forces. The doomed rebels desperately tried to hold the high ground with no shelter from the merciless British artillery fire.

Cost, Hours, Location: €6, April–Oct Mon–Fri 9:30–18:00, Sat–Sun 11:00–18:00; Nov–March Mon–Fri until 16:00, closed Sat–Sun, last entry one hour before closing (tel. 054/37596). Enniscorthy is 12 miles north of Wexford town. The Visitors Center is the town's major sight and well signposted.

KINSALE AND COBH

County Cork, on Ireland's south coast, is fringed with historic port towns and scenic peninsulas. The typical tour-bus route here includes Blarney Castle and Killarney—places where most tourists wear nametags. A major mistake many tourists make is allowing destinations into their itineraries simply because they're famous (in a song or as part of a relative's big-bus-tour memory). If you have the misfortune to spend the night in Killarney, you'll understand what I mean. The town is a sprawling line of green Holiday Inns littered with pushy shoppers looking for three-leaf clovers.

Rather than kissing the spit-slathered Blarney Stone, spend your time in County Cork enjoying the bustling, historic maritime towns of Kinsale and Cobh.

Planning Your Time

Kinsale makes a great home base for enjoying the County Cork coast. From Kinsale, you can wade through the salty history of Cobh. Travelers approaching this region from Waterford can easily visit Ardmore and the Old Midleton Whiskey Distillery. Those departing this region for the Ring of Kerry or An Daingean can stop by Blarney Castle and Macroom en route.

Kinsale

While nearby Cork is the biggest town in south Ireland, Kinsale (15 miles south) is actually more historic, certainly cuter, and delightful to visit. Thanks to the naturally sheltered bay barbed

Kinsale and Cobh Area

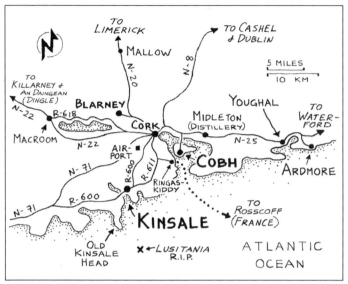

by a massive 17th-century star fort, you can submerge yourself in maritime history, from the Spanish Armada to Robinson Crusoe to the *Lusitania*. Apart from all the history, Kinsale has a laid-back Sausalito feel with a touch of wine-sipping class.

Planning Your Time

Kinsale is worth two nights and a day. The town's two tiny museums open at 10:00 and will occupy you until the 11:15 town walking tour. After lunch at the Fishy Fishy Café, head out to Charles Fort for great bay views and insights into British military life in colonial Ireland. On the way back, stop for a pint at the Bulman Bar. Finish the day with a gourmet dinner and live music in a pub. Those on the blitz tour can give Kinsale five hours—see the fort, wander the town, and have a nice lunch—before driving on.

ORIENTATION

(area code: 021)

Kinsale, because of its great natural harbor, is older than Cobh (Cork's harbor town). While the town is prettier than the actual harbor, the harbor was its reason for being. Today Kinsale is a wealthy resort of 2,000 residents. The town's long and skinny old center is part modern marina and part pedestrian-friendly medieval town—an easy 15-minute stroll from end to end.

Kinsale's History

Kinsale's remarkable harbor has made this an important port since prehistoric times. The bay's 10-foot tide provided a natural shuttle service for Stone Age hunter-gatherers: They could ride it at two miles per hour twice a day the eight miles up and down the River Bandon. In the Bronze Age, when people discovered that it takes tin and copper to make bronze, tin came from Cornwall and copper came from this part of Ireland. From 500 B.C. to A.D. 500, Kinsale was a rich trading center. The result: Lots of Stonehenge-type monuments are nearby (the best is Drombeg Stone Circle, a 1-hour drive west).

Kinsale's importance peaked during the 16th, 17th, and 18th centuries, when sailing ships ruled the waves, turning countries into global powers. Kinsale was Ireland's most perfect natural harbor and the gateway to both Spain and France—potentially providing a base for either of these two powers in cutting off English shipping. Because of this, two pivotal battles were fought here in the 17th century: in 1601 against the Spanish, and in 1690 against the French. Two great forts were built to combat these threats from the Continent. England couldn't rule the waves without ruling Kinsale.

To understand the small town of Kinsale, you need to understand the big picture: Around 1500, the pope gave the world to Spain and Portugal. With the Reformation breaking Rome's lock on Europe, maritime powers such as England were ignoring the pope's grant. This was important because trade with the New World and Asia brought huge wealth in spices (necessary for curing meat), gold, and silver. England threatened Spain's New World piñata, and Ireland was Catholic. Spain had an economic and a religious reason to defend the pope and Catholicism. The showdown between Spain and England for mastery of the seas (and control of all that trade) was in Ireland. The excuse: to rescue the dear Catholics of Ireland from the treachery of Protestant England (as if democracy and not oil were the rationale for the modern conflict in the Middle East).

Tourist Information

The TI is as central as can be, at the head of the harbor across from the bus stop (July–Aug Mon–Sat 9:00–19:00, Sun 10:00–17:00; March–June and Sept–Nov Mon–Sat 9:30–17:30, closed Sun; shorter hours Dec–Feb; tel. 021/477-2234). It has a free town map and brochures outlining a world of activities in the vicinity.

Arrival in Kinsale

Since Kinsale doesn't have a train station, you'll arrive by bus (the stop is at Esso gas station on Pier Road at south end of town) or

So the Irish disaster unfolds. The powerful Ulster chieftains Hugh O'Neill and Red Hugh O'Donnell and their clans had been on a roll in their battle against the English. With Spanish aid, they figured they could actually drive the English out of Ireland. In 1601, the Spanish Armada dropped off 5,000 soldiers, who established a beachhead in Kinsale. After the ships left, the Spaniards were pinned down in Kinsale by the English commander (who, breaking with the martial etiquette, actually fought in the winter). Virtually the entire Irish fighting force left the north and marched through a harsh winter to the south coast, thinking they could liberate their Spanish allies and win freedom from England.

The numbers seemed reasonable (10,000 Englishmen versus 5,000 Spaniards as 5,000 Irish clansmen approached). The Irish attacked on Christmas Eve in 1601. But, holding the high ground around fortified and Spanish-occupied Kinsale, a relatively small force of English troops could keep the Spaniards hemmed in, leaving the bulk of the English force to outnumber and rout the fighting Irish. The Irish resistance was broken and its leaders fled to Europe (the "flight of the Earls"). England made peace with Spain and began the "plantation" of mostly Scottish Protestants in Ireland (the seeds of today's Troubles in Ulster). England ruled the waves and it ruled Ireland. The lesson: Kinsale is key. England eventually built two huge, star-shaped fortresses to ensure control of the narrow waterway, a strategy it would further develop in later fortifications built at Gibraltar and Singapore.

Kinsale's maritime history continues. Daniel Defoe used the real-life experience of Scottish privateer Alexander Selkirk, who departed from Kinsale in 1703 and was later marooned alone on a desert island, as the basis for his book *Robinson Crusoe*. And it was also just 10 miles offshore from Old Kinsale Head that the passenger liner *Lusitania* was torpedoed by a German submarine in 1915, killing 1,200 and sparking America's entry into World War I.

by car. Park your car and enjoy the town on foot. While Kinsale's windy medieval lanes are narrow and congested, parking is fairly easy. There's a big lot at the head of the harbor behind the TI (€2/hr, €12/day, overnight 18:00–9:00 €10 extra) and a big, safe, and free parking lot across the street from St. Multose Church at the top of town, a three-minute walk from most recommended hotels and restaurants. Streetside parking requires a disk (purchase at a newsstand such as Boland's, on corner of Emmet Place and Pierce Street, €0.50/hr, 2-hour maximum 10:30–18:00). The outlying streets, a five-minute stroll from all the action, have wide-open parking.

Helpful Hints

Banking: The two banks in town are Allied Irish Bank on Pearse Street and Bank of Ireland on Emmett Street (both open Mon 10:00–17:00, Tue–Fri 10:00–16:00, closed Sat–Sun).

Internet Access: Finishing Services is your best bet (€6/hr, Mon–Fri 9:00–17:30, Sat 10:00–17:00, closed Sun, 71 Main Street, tel. 021/477-3571).

Post Office: It's on Pearse Street (Mon–Fri 9:00–17:30, Sat 9:00–13:00, closed Sun).

Laundry: The Cullinane launderette washes and dries in a day, but gets my vote for the most expensive laundry in Ireland (€15 minimum per load, no self-service, Mon–Fri 9:00–18:00, Sat 9:00–17:30, closed Sun, Market Street, tel. 021/477-2875). Don't let them take you to the cleaners—if possible, wait to do it in another town.

Bike Rental: The Hire Shop rents bikes (€12/day), plus power tools and fishing gear (Mon–Fri 8:30–18:00, Sat 9:00–18:00, Sun 11:00–17:00, 18 Main Street, tel. 021/477-2875, mobile 086-881-2354).

Taxi: Kinsale Cabs has regular cab service and minibuses available (Market Square, tel. 021/477-2642).

TOURS

▲▲Don Herlihy's Historic Town Walk—To understand the important role Kinsale played in Irish, English, and Spanish history, join Don Herlihy on a fascinating 90-minute walking tour (€7, daily April–mid-Oct at 11:15 from the TI, private tours possible, tel. 021/477-2873). Don is a joy to hear as he creatively brings to life Kinsale's place in history and makes the stony sights more than just buildings. Don collects for the tour at the end, giving anyone disappointed in his talk an easy escape midway through. Don's walk is Kinsale's best single attraction.

Ghost Walk Tour—This is not just any ghost tour; it's more comedy than horror. Two actors weave funny stunts and stories into a loose history of the town, offering a thoroughly entertaining hour (€9, May–Sept Mon–Fri at 21:00, leaves from Tap Tavern, mobile 087-948-0910 or 086-855-5043). This tour doesn't overlap with Don Herlihy's more serious historic town walk (above).

SIGHTS

Kinsale Town Wander—Stroll the old part of town. The medieval walled town's economy was fueled by the harbor, where ships came to be stocked. The old walls—which followed what is now O'Connell Street and Main Street—defined the original town.

Kinsale

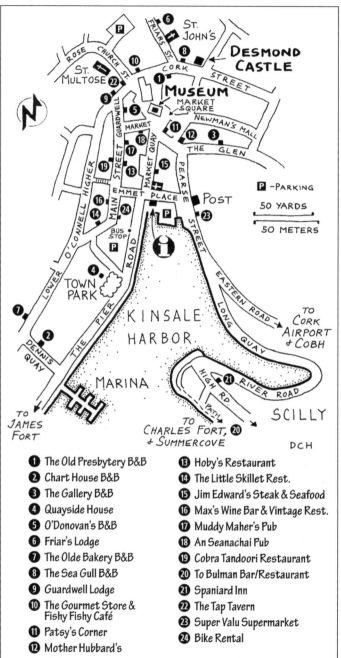

1. The Old Presbytery B&B
2. Chart House B&B
3. The Gallery B&B
4. Quayside House
5. O'Donovan's B&B
6. Friar's Lodge
7. The Olde Bakery B&B
8. The Sea Gull B&B
9. Guardwell Lodge
10. The Gourmet Store & Fishy Fishy Café
11. Patsy's Corner
12. Mother Hubbard's
13. Hoby's Restaurant
14. The Little Skillet Rest.
15. Jim Edward's Steak & Seafood
16. Max's Wine Bar & Vintage Rest.
17. Muddy Maher's Pub
18. An Seanachai Pub
19. Cobra Tandoori Restaurant
20. To Bulman Bar/Restaurant
21. Spaniard Inn
22. The Tap Tavern
23. Super Valu Supermarket
24. Bike Rental

The windy Main Street traces the original coastline. Walking this, you'll see tiny lanes leading to today's harbor. These originated as piers—just wide enough to roll a barrel down to an awaiting ship. The wall detoured inland to protect the St. Multose Church, which dates from Norman times (back when worshippers sharpened their swords on the doorway of the church—check it out). After James and Charles Forts were built in the 1600s, the wall became obsolete—and also boxed in the town, preventing further expansion. The townspeople disassembled the wall and used its ready-cut stones to build out the piers in the harbor.

What seems like part of the old center was actually built later on land reclaimed from the harbor. The town is a kind of quarry, with shale hills ideal for a ready supply of fill. Notice the mudflats in the harbor at low tide. Clear-cutting of the once-plentiful oak forest upriver (for ship building and barrel making) hastened erosion and silted up the harbor. By the early 1800s—when British ships needed lots of restocking for the Napoleonic Wars—Kinsale's port was slowly dying, and nearby Cobh's deepwater port took over the lion's share of shipping.

▲▲**Charles Fort**—Kinsale is protected by what was Britain's biggest star-shaped fort—a state-of-the-art defense when artillery made the traditional castle obsolete. The British occupied it until Irish independence in 1922. Its interior buildings were torched in 1923 by anti-treaty IRA forces to keep it from being used by Free State troops during the Irish Civil War. Guided 45-minute tours (depart on the hour, confirm  at entry) engross you in the harsh daily life of the 18th-century British soldier. Before or after your tour, peruse the exhibits in the barracks and walk the walls.

For a coffee, beer, or meal nearby, stop by the Bulman Bar (see "Eating," page 147) in Summercove, where the road runs low near the water on the way back to town. And to actually see how easily the forts could bottle up this key harbor, stop for the grand harbor view at the high point on the road back into town (above Scilly, just uphill from the Spaniard pub).

Cost, Hours, Location: €3.50, covered by Heritage Card (see page 4), daily mid-March–Oct 10:00–18:00, Nov–mid-March 10:00–17:00, last entry 45 min before closing, half a mile south of town in Summercove, tel. 021/477-2263.

James Fort—Older, overgrown, and filling a peaceful park, James Fort is Kinsale's other star fort, guarding the bay opposite Charles Fort. Built in the years just after the famous 1601 battle, this fort is more ruined, less interesting, and less visited than Charles Fort. Its satellite blockhouse sits below the fort at the water's edge opposite Summercove and controlled a strong chain that could be raised to block ships from reaching Kinsale's docks.

Easily accessible by car or bike, it's two miles south of town along Pier Road on the west shore of the bay (cross bridge and turn left; you'll dead-end at Castle Park Marina, where you can park or leave your bike). It's up the hill behind the Dock pub.

▲**Desmond Castle**—This 15th-century fortified Norman customs house has had a long and varied history. It was the Spanish armory during their 1601 occupation of Kinsale. Nicknamed "Frenchman's Prison," it served as a British prison and once housed 600 prisoners of the Napoleonic Wars (not to mention earlier American Revolutionary War prisoners captured at sea—who were treated as rebels, not prisoners, and chained to the outside of the building as a warning to any rebellion-minded Irish). In the late 1840s, it was a famine-relief center. Today the evocative little ruin comes with a scant display of its colorful history and the modest one-room Museum of Wine highlighting Ireland's little-known connection to the international wine trade. In the Middle Ages, Kinsale was renowned for its top-quality wooden casks. Developing strong trade links with Bordeaux, local merchants traded their dependable empty casks for casks full of wine.

Cost, Hours, Location: €2.75, covered by Heritage Card (see page 4), mid-April–Oct daily 10:00–18:00, last entry 17:15, tours given on request, closed Nov–mid-April, Cork Street, tel. 021/477-4855.

▲**Kinsale Regional Museum**—In the center of the old town, traffic circles the old town market, which later became a courthouse and is now the Regional Museum. Drop by at least to read the fun 1788 tax code for all Kinsale commercial transactions (outside at the front door). The modest museum is worth a quick visit for its fun mishmash of domestic and maritime bygones. It also gives a good perspective on the controversial *Lusitania* tragedy. Kinsale had maritime jurisdiction over the waters 10 miles offshore, where the luxury liner was torpedoed in 1915. Hearings were held here in the courthouse shortly afterward to investigate the causes of the disaster—which helped propel America into World War I—and to paint the German Hun as a bloodthirsty villain. Claims by Germany that the *Lusitania* was illegally carrying munitions seem to have been borne out by the huge explosion and rapid sinking of the vessel. But perhaps even more interesting, in the side room, is the boot of the 8-foot 3-inch Kinsale giant, who lived here in the late 1700s.

Cost, Hours, Location: €2.50, Wed–Sat 10:30–17:30, Sun 14:00–17:15, closed Mon–Tue, Market Square, tel. 021/477-7930.

SLEEPING

Kinsale is a popular place in summer for yachters and golfers (who don't flinch at paying $300 for 18 holes out on the exotic Old Head of Kinsale Golf Course). It's wise to book ahead. I've listed peak-season prices. These places include breakfast and are all within a five-minute walk of the town center.

$$$ **The Old Presbytery** is a fine, quiet house a block outside of the commercial district, with a goofy floor plan and 10 pleasant rooms. Well-listed in most guidebooks, it has lots of American guests. The breakfasts are a delight, and Noreen McEvoy runs the place with a passion for excellence (Db-€85–160 depending on room size, family Qb-€160, 2 Qb suites with no breakfast and minimum 3-night stay-€170, private parking, 43 Cork Street, tel. 021/477-2027, fax 021/477-2166, www.oldpres.com, info @oldpres.com).

$$$ **Friar's Lodge** is a newly built shingled hotel, perched up the hill past St. John's Catholic church. What its 18 spacious rooms lack in Old World character, they make up for in modern, dependable quality (Sb-€55–80, Db-€90–120, Tb-€135–180, Qb-€180–240, Wi-Fi access, private parking, Friar Street, tel. 021/477-7384, fax 021/477-4363, www.friars-lodge.com, mtierney@indigo.ie).

$$$ **Chart House B&B** is a luxurious Georgian home renting a tidy little single and three grand, sumptuous doubles. It's a block off the harbor at the marina end of the old town. This non-smoking, quiet, and well-run place is top-end in every respect—high ceilings, chandeliers, and a plush living room (Sb-€40–50, Db-€110–170 depending on size and season, 6 Dennis Quay, tel. 021/477-4568, fax 021/477-7907, www.charthouse-kinsale.com, charthouse@eircom.net, Mary O'Connor).

$$ **The Gallery,** a bright and funky five-room place with

Sleep Code

(€1 = about $1.20, country code: 353, area code: 021)
S = Single, **D** = Double/Twin, **T** = Triple, **Q** = Quad, **b** = bathroom, **s** = shower only. Unless otherwise noted, breakfast is included and credit cards are accepted.

To help you easily sort through these listings, I've divided the rooms into three categories, based on the price for a standard double room with bath:

$$$ **Higher Priced**—Most rooms €110 or more.
$$ **Moderately Priced**—Most rooms between €80–110.
$ **Lower Priced**—Most rooms €80 or less.

stylish decor, is run by Tom and Carole O'Hare with a fresh informality—you can have ice cream for breakfast. He's a jazz pianist and she's an artist (Db-€90–110, family Qb-€140–180, public parking out back, The Glen, tel. 021/477-4558, www.gallerybnb .com, carole@gallerybnb.com).

$$ Quayside House is a grand, blocky building overlooking a small park and the bay along Pier Road. Mary Cotter rents six rooms and offers a warm welcome (Db-€65–100, Tb-€120–150, family Qb-€130–160, Pier Road, tel. 021/477-2188, fax 021/477-2664, www.euroka.com/quayside, quaysidehouse@eircom.net).

$ O'Donovan's B&B has six rooms in a 400-year-old building made cheery and welcoming by Eileen and Michael O'Donovan. It's right in the charming medieval center—and triple-paned windows ensure a quiet stay (S-€40, D-€64, Db-€70, non-smoking, 8 Guardwell Street, tel. 021/477-2428, odonovans_bb@iolfree.ie).

$ The Olde Bakery B&B makes you feel at home, with six quilt-bedded rooms and a cozy breakfast at the kitchen table cooked up by Tom and Chrissie Quigley (D-€60–65, Db-€70–76, cash only, non-smoking, laundry service available, 56 Lower O'Connell Street, tel. 021/477-3012, www.theoldebakery.com, theoldebakery@oceanfree.net).

$ The Sea Gull, perched up the hill right next to Desmond Castle, offers six well-worn rooms run by Mrs. Mary O'Neill, who also runs The Tap Tavern down the hill (S-€35–40, Db-€65–70, Tb-€95, 10 percent discount with this book in 2006, cash only, Cork Street, tel. 021/477-2240, marytap@iol.ie).

$ Guardwell Lodge is a big, boxy, building at the top of the old center, with 64 rooms connected by a prison-like series of stairways and catwalks in its inner courtyard. While almost a hostel, it has no hostel-type regulations or restrictions. Its stark but modern and comfortable rooms (each with a fine bathroom) are far and away the best budget beds in this ritzy town. Avoid any rooms ending in "B," which house noisy water pumps in their closets for their three neighboring rooms (€16–20 beds in 4-bed dorms, Sb-€30, Db-€55–60, Tb-€60, no breakfast, all bedding provided, fully equipped self-service kitchen, TV lounge, request quiet room on church side, Guardwell Street, tel. 021/477-4686, fax 021/477-4684, www.guardwelllodge.com, info@guardwelllodge.com).

EATING

As Ireland's self-proclaimed gourmet capital, Kinsale manages to merge friendly old-fashioned Irish hospitality with quality restaurant options. Local competition is fierce, and restaurants offer creative and tempting menus. You don't have to have a big budget or a cultured palate to enjoy the range of choices available—everything from simple chowder-and-sandwich lunches to memorable fish-and-steak dinner feasts.

Lunch

The Gourmet Store and Fishy Fishy Café is *the* place for a good lunch. It's like eating in a fish market surrounded by the day's catch and a pristine stainless-steel kitchen. Marie and her white-aproned staff hustle wonderful steaming piles of beautifully presented seafood to eager customers (€20 specials, cash only, daily 12:00–15:45 for lunch only, closed Sun off-season, across from church on Guardwell Street, tel. 021/477-4453). Look at the lobster tank and ponder this: Several years ago, a soft-hearted, fat-walleted Buddhist tourist bought up the entire day's supply of live lobster (worth over €600) and set them free in the bay. They've refilled the tank since.

For cheap and cheery, try the cramped **Patsy's Corner** or local breakfast hangout, **Mother Hubbard's.** Both are near Market Square and serve sandwiches, baguettes, or salads with coffee for under €10.

For a picnic, gather supplies at the **Super Valu** supermarket (Mon–Sat 8:30–21:00, Sun 10:00–21:00, Pearse Street).

Good Dinners in the Old Center

The Little Skillet feels intimate, with tasty food and a romantic, rough-stone-and-timber atmosphere. You'll find all the old-time Irish favorites with traditional Irish music, fresh and seasonal veggies, and absolutely no French fries (€17–20 dinners, 3-course €25 early-bird meal before 19:30, daily 12:00–14:30 & 18:00–22:30, Main Street, tel. 021/477-4202).

Hoby's Restaurant, another well-established favorite, offers modern cuisine in a quiet, candlelit room. It's popular with people from Cork coming down for a special night out (3-course €25 dinners, daily 18:00–22:00, Main Street, tel. 021/477-2200).

At **Jim Edward's Steak & Seafood,** one kitchen keeps eaters happy in both the bar and the restaurant. Choose between a noisy maritime ambience in the restaurant (€19–29 meals) or dark and mellow in the bar (€11–18 meals). While cheaper and less gourmet than other Kinsale eateries, it offers decent steaks, seafood, and vegetables (bar daily 12:30–22:00, restaurant daily 18:00–22:00, Market Quay, tel. 021/477-2541).

Several candlelit wine-bar restaurants vie for your attention along the gently curving Main Street. **Max's Wine Bar** has a respected French chef (tel. 021/477-2443). **Vintage** looks like, feels like, and is the most expensive place in town (daily from 18:30, closed Jan, reservations recommended, near Max's, tel. 021/477-2502).

Pubs with decent kitchens abound, serving casual dinners (€10–18) in a funky atmosphere. Many follow dinner with live music. Consider **Muddy Maher's** (daily 12:00–15:00 & 18:00–21:00, Main Street, tel. 021/477-4602) and **An Seanachai** (daily 12:00–21:00, Market Street, tel. 021/477-7077).

For a break from Irish cooking, check out **Cobra Tandoori** for tasty Indian cuisine (€14–18 dinners daily 16:30–23:30, 69 Main Street, tel. 021/477-7911).

Fine Food Near Charles Fort

The **Bulman Bar and Restaurant** serves seafood with seasonal produce. The mussels are especially tasty; on a balmy day or evening, diners take a bucket and a beer out to the seawall. This is the only real way to eat on the water in Kinsale (€10 lunches, €22–26 meals upstairs in fancy restaurant, daily 12:30–21:30, 200 yards toward Kinsale from Charles Fort in hamlet of Summercove, tel. 021/477-2131). The pub, strewn with fun decor and sporting a big fireplace, is also good for a coffee or beer after your visit to the fort.

Without a car (and weather permitting), enjoy Kinsale's best 45-minute stroll back into town with great harbor views on the Scilly Walk paved pedestrian trail (trailhead on left after you climb 200 yards up steep road toward town, look for stone steps and old black iron turnstile).

Live Pub Music

Kinsale's pubs are packed with atmosphere and live music (though not always traditional Irish). Rather than target a certain place, simply walk the area between Guardwell, Pearse Street, and the Market Square. Pop into each pub that has live music, and then settle into your favorite. Several of the pubs wind deep into buildings. On a Thursday night, I found six places with live music thriving at 23:00 along this proposed loop. **An Seanachai** (SHAN-ah-key) means "storyteller" in Gaelic, but it's now known for its music (Main Street). **The Tap Tavern** has music on Thursday nights (just below St. Multose Church).

Irish music purists will be rewarded if they take the five-minute taxi ride (€7 one-way) out to the **Bulman Bar** near the base of Charles Fort. This is Kinsale's best pub for traditional Irish music sessions (Tue, Thu, Sun at 21:30, Wed folk session at 21:30, get there well before 21:00 to ensure a seat, see above). Otherwise, get your trad fix at the tiny **Spaniard Inn,** a 10-minute walk out to the Scilly peninsula across the harbor from town. Its eye-catching golden walls fill the center of a hairpin turn on the crest of the peninsula (Wed at 21:30, you'll stand all night unless you arrive by 20:30, tel. 021/477-2436).

TRANSPORTATION CONNECTIONS

Like many worthwhile corners of Ireland, Kinsale is not accessible by train. The closest train station is in Cork, 15 miles north. But buses run frequently between Kinsale (stop is at Esso gas station on Pier Road, south end of town) and Cork's bus station (10/day, 45 min, €6 one-way, €10 round-trip).

In Cork, the bus station and train station are a 10-minute walk apart. Cork's bus station (corner of Merchant's Quay and Parnell Place) is on the south bank of the Lee River, just over the nearest bridge from Cork's train station (north of the river on Lower Glanmire Road).

By Bus from Cork to: Dublin (6/day), **Galway** (12/day), **Tralee** (8/day), and **Kilkenny** (9/day). Bus info: tel. 021/450-8188.

Cobh

If your ancestry is Irish, there's a good chance that this was the last Irish soil your ancestors had under their feet. Cobh (cove)

was the major port of Irish emigration in the 19th century. Of the six million Irish who have emigrated to America, Canada, and Australia since 1815, nearly half left from Cobh.

The first steam-powered ship to make a transatlantic crossing departed from Cobh in 1838—cutting the journey time from 50 days to 18. When Queen Victoria came to Ireland for the first time in 1849, Cobh was the first Irish ground she set foot on. Giddy, the town renamed itself "Queenstown" in her honor. It was still going by that name in 1912, when the *Titanic* made its final fateful stop here before heading out on its maiden (and only) voyage. To celebrate their new independence from British royalty in 1922, locals changed the name back to its original Irish name: Cobh.

ORIENTATION

Cobh sits on a large island in Cork harbor. The town's inviting waterfront is colorful yet salty, with a playful promenade. The butcher's advertisement reads, "always pleased to meet you and always with meat to please you." Stroll past the shops along the water. Ponder the *Lusitania* memorial on Casement Square and the modest *Titanic* memorial nearby on Pearse Square. A hike up the hill to the towering neo-Gothic St. Colman's Cathedral rewards you with a fine view of the port.

Tourist Information: The TI is in the Old Yacht Club on the harbor (Mon–Fri 9:30–17:30, Sat–Sun 13:00–17:00, tel. 021/481-3301, www.cobhharbourchamber.ie). You can buy parking disks here or in local shops (€0.50/hr, 2-hour maximum parking anywhere in Cobh).

TOURS

"Titanic Trail" Tours—Michael Martin leads 75- to 90-minute walking tours of Cobh that give you unexpected insights into the tragic *Titanic* voyage, Spike Island (Ireland's Alcatraz), and Cobh's maritime history (€8.50, includes free pint in pub at end of tour, daily at 11:00, June–Aug also at 14:00, meet at Commodore Hotel, private tours available, tel. 021/481-5211 or mobile 087-276-7218, www.titanic-trail.com).

SIGHTS

▲**The Queenstown Story**—Cobh's major sightseeing attraction, filling its harborside Victorian train station, is an earnest attempt to make the city's emigration and history interesting. The topics—the famine, Irish emigration, Australia-bound prison ships, the sinking of the *Lusitania,* and the ill-fated voyage of the *Titanic*—are fascinating enough to make this museum a worthwhile stop. But the museum itself, while kid-friendly, is weak on actual historical artifacts. It reminds me of a big, interesting history picture book with the pages expanded and tacked on the wall (€5, daily May–Oct 10:00–18:00, Nov–April 10:00–17:00, last entry 1 hour before closing, tel. 021/481-3591).

Those with Irish roots to trace are welcome to use the Heritage Centre's genealogy search service (www.cobhheritage.com, cobhher@indigo.ie).

SLEEPING

(€1 = about $1.20, country code: 353, area code: 021)
The following listings are all centrally located near the harbor, less than a five-minute walk from the Queenstown Story.

$$$ Waters Edge Hotel has bright modern rooms and a pleasant harbor-view restaurant (Sb-€55–90, Db-€100–160, Tb-€120–160, Yacht Club Quay, tel. 021/481-5566, www.watersedgehotel.ie, info@watersedgehotel.ie).

$$$ Commodore Hotel is a grand 150-year-old historic landmark. This place was once owned by the wealthy German Humbert family, who opened it up to *Lusitania* refugees after the 1915 sinking. Its high-ceilinged rooms creak with Victorian character (Sb-€70–92, Db-€115–142, Tb-€175–210, Westbourne Place, tel. 021/481-1277, fax 021/481-1672, www.commodorehotel .ie, commodorehotel@eircom.net).

$ Ard na Laoi is a friendly place with five modest rooms (Sb-€45–50, Db-€68, Tb-€99, Westbourne Place, tel. 021/481-2742).

TRANSPORTATION CONNECTIONS

By Car: Driving to Cobh from Cork or Waterford, leave N25 about eight miles east of Cork, following the little R624 over a bridge, onto the Great Island, and directly into Cobh.

Kinsale to Cobh is 25 miles, takes an hour, and involves catching a small ferry. Leave Kinsale north on R600 toward Cork. Just south of Cork and its airport, go east on R613. You will be following little car-ferry signs, but they ultimately take you to the wrong ferry (Ringaskiddy—to France). After you hit N28, take R610 to Monkstown and then Glenbrook, where a (poorly sign-posted) shuttle ferry takes you to Carrigloe on the Great Island (5 min, €3.50 ride). Once on the island, turn right and drive a mile or two into Cobh. In Cobh, follow the Heritage Centre signs to The Queenstown Story, where you'll find easy parking right at the museum (buy parking disks at nearby TI, €0.50/hr, 2-hour maximum).

By Plane: Cork Airport has become an increasingly handy entry point into (or exit point from) Ireland. Located four miles south of Cork city (on the N-27/R600 road to Kinsale, a 30-minute drive away), it offers connecting flights from London Heathrow on Aer Lingus, London Stansted on Ryanair, and Edinburgh on Aer Arann. More distant connections can be made from Frankfurt, Amsterdam, Paris, Prague, and Málaga (tel. 021/431-3131, www .corkairport.com).

More Sights in and near County Cork

These sights are convenient stops when connecting Kinsale and Cobh with Waterford (to the east) or the Ring of Kerry (to the west).

Between Waterford and Kinsale

If you're driving from Waterford (previous chapter) to Cobh and Kinsale, you can easily visit these sights just off N25 (listed roughly from east to west).

Ardmore—This funky little beach resort, with a famous ruined church and round tower, is a handy stop (just west of Youghal, 3 miles south of N25 between Waterford and Cobh). A couple of buses run daily from Ardmore to Cork and to Waterford.

This humble little port town is just a line of pastel houses that appear frightened by the sea. Its beach claims (very modestly) to be "the most swimmable in Ireland." The beachside **TI,** housed in an alien spacecraft, has a flier laying out a historic walk (June–Aug Mon–Sat 11:00–13:00 & 14:00–17:00, Sun 15:00–17:00, closed Sept–May, tel. 024/94444).

The town's historic claim to fame: Christianity came to Ireland here first (thanks to St. Declan, who arrived in A.D. 416— 15 years before St. Patrick). As if to proclaim that feat with an 800-year-old exclamation mark, one of Ireland's finest examples of a round tower stands perfectly intact, 97 feet above an evocative graveyard and a ruined church (noted for the faint remains of some early Christian carvings on its west facade). You can't get into the tower—the entrance is 14 feet off the ground.

Sleeping in Ardmore (area code: 024): **$ Duncrone B&B** has vividly colorful rooms run by Jeanette Dunne (Sb-€38–45, Db-€60, Tb-€90, a half-mile outside of town, up past the round tower, tel. 024/94860, www.duncronebandb.com, info@duncronebandb .com). **$$ Round Tower Hotel,** a sedate traditional place, is a safe bet in town (Sb-€60, Db-€110, on R673 leading west out of town, tel. 024/94494).

▲**Old Midleton Distillery**—Sometime during your Ireland trip, even if you're a teetotaler, you'll want to tour a whiskey distillery. Of the three major distillery tours (this one, Jameson in Dublin, and Bushmills in North

Ireland), the Midleton experience is the most interesting. After a 10-minute video, you'll walk with a guide through a great old 18th-century plant on a 45-minute tour; see waterwheel-powered crankshafts and a 31,000-gallon copper still—the largest of its kind in the world; and learn the story of whiskey. Predictably, you finish in a tasting room and enjoy a free not-so-wee glass. The finale is a Scotch/Irish whiskey taste test. Your guide will take two volunteers for this. Don't be shy—raise your hand like an eager little student and enjoy an opportunity to taste the different brands.

Cost, Hours, Location: Tour-€9, daily 9:00–18:00 year-round, last tour at 17:00, 2/hr in summer, 3/day in winter (tel. 021/461-3594, www.whiskeytours.ie). It's 12 miles east of Cork in Midleton, about a mile off N25, the main Cork–Waterford road. There's easy parking—just drive right into the distillery lot. A cafeteria is on site.

Between Kinsale and Killarney

If you're driving between Kinsale and the Ring of Kerry (see next chapter), you can easily visit these sights (listed from east to west).

Blarney Stone and Castle—The town of Blarney is of no importance, and the 15th-century Blarney Castle is an empty hulk (with no effort at making it meaningful or interesting). It's only famous as the place of tourist pilgrimage, where busloads line up to kiss a stone on its top rampart and get "the gift of gab." The stone's origin is shrouded in myth (it was either brought back from the Holy Land by crusaders, or perhaps was part of Scotland's royal Stone of Scone). The best thing about this lame sight is the opportunity to watch a cranky man lower lemming tourists over the edge, belly up and head back, to kiss the stone while his partner snaps a photo—which will be waiting for you to purchase back at the parking lot. After a day of tour groups mindlessly climbing up here to perform this ritual, the stone is literally slathered with spit and lipstick.

The tradition goes back to the late 16th century, when Queen Elizabeth I was trying to plant loyal English settlers in Ireland to tighten her grip on the rebellious island. She demanded that the Irish clan chiefs recognize the crown, rather than the clan chiefs, as the legitimate titleholder of all lands. One of those chiefs was Cormac MacCarthy, Lord of Blarney Castle (who was supposedly loyal to the queen). He was smart enough never to disagree with the Queen—instead, he would cleverly avoid acquiescing to her demands by sending a never-ending stream of lengthy and deceptive excuses, disguised with liberal doses of flattery (while subtly maintaining his native Gaelic loyalties). In her frustration, the Queen declared his endless words nothing but "blarney." Walking back, you'll cross a stream littered with American pennies—as if the good-luck fairy can change them into euros.

Cost, Hours, Location: €7, Mon–Sat 9:00–18:00, Sun 9:30–17:00, later in peak season, shorter hours in winter, free parking lot, helpful TI, tel. 021/438-5252. It's five miles northwest of Cork, the major city in south Ireland. Looking for shopping galore?

Adjacent Blarney Woolen Mills has it all (right next to the castle parking lot).

Macroom—This colorful, inviting market town is a handy stop between Cork and Killarney. The ghostly gateway of its ruined castle (once owned by the father of the William Penn who founded Pennsylvania) overlooks its entertaining main square, where you'll find plenty of parking. This makes for an excellent coffee or lunch stop midway between Cork and Killarney. The Next Door Café, next to the Castle Hotel, serves a good, fast lunch.

KENMARE AND THE RING OF KERRY

X 2

It's no wonder that, since Victorian times, visitors have been attracted to this dramatic chunk of Ireland. Mysterious ancient ring forts stand sentinel on mossy hillsides. A beloved Irish statesman maintained his ancestral estate here, far from 19th-century power politics. And early Christian hermit monks left a lonely imprint of their devotion, in the form of simple stone dwellings, atop an isolated rock crag far from shore...a holy retreat on the edge of the known world.

In this region, the ideal overnight stop is the colorful, tidy town of Kenmare—the best springboard for diving into the famous Ring of Kerry.

Kenmare

Cradled in a lush valley, this charming little town (known as Neidin, or "little nest," in Gaelic) hooks you right away with its rows of vividly colored shop fronts and go-for-a-stroll atmosphere. Its fresh appearance made it Ireland's "Tidy Town" winner in 2000, and the nearby finger of the gentle sea feels more like a large lake (called the Kenmare River, just to confuse things). Far from the assembly-line tourism of Killarney town, Kenmare also makes a great launchpad for enjoying the sights of the Iveragh (eev-er-AH) Peninsula—known to shamrock-lovers everywhere as "The Ring of Kerry."

Planning Your Time

All you need in compact Kenmare is one night and a couple of hours to wander the town. Check out the Heritage Centre (in the back rooms of the TI) to get an overview of the region's rich history. Visit the Kenmare Lace and Design Centre (above TI, entry next door) to get a close look at the famously delicate lace. Hands-on access to an ancient stone circle is just a five-minute walk to the edge of town. Finish up by taking a peek inside Holy Cross Church to see the fine ceiling woodwork. Call it an early night to get a jump on the Ring of Kerry in the morning.

ORIENTATION

(area code: 064)

In carefully planned Kenmare, "X" marks the spot. The upper (northern) half of the X contains the town square (flea market Wed and Fri in summer), with adjacent TI and Heritage Centre, as well as a cozy park.

The lower (southern) half of the X contains three one-way streets, forming a busy triangle of shops, lodging, and restaurants.

Use the tall Holy Cross Church spire to get your bearings (next to the northeast parking lot, public WCs across the street). The two shopping streets in the lower half look alike. If you see the steeple at the end of the street, you're on Henry Street...if not, you're on Main Street. Shelbourne Street is the quiet third leg of the triangle, with a small parking lot.

Tourist Information: The helpful TI is on the town square (May–Sept Mon–Sat 9:00–18:00, Sun 10:00–18:00, closed Oct–April, tel. 064/41233).

Helpful Hints

Banking: Bank of Ireland faces the town square, and Allied Irish Bank takes up the corner of Henry and Main streets (both open Mon 10:00–17:00, Tue–Fri 10:00–16:00, closed Sat–Sun).

Internet Access: Kenmare's dang slow terminals are in the front shop of the post office (see below), with longer hours than the P.O. (€1/10 min, Mon–Fri 8:30–17:30, Sat 10:00–13:00, closed Sun; July–Aug Mon–Fri until 20:00).

Post Office: It's on Henry Street, at the intersection with Shelbourne Street (Mon–Fri 9:00–13:00 & 14:00–17:30, Sat 10:00–13:00, closed Sun).

Laundry: Try O'Shea's Cleaners and Launderette (Mon–Fri 8:30–18:00, Sat 9:30–18:00, closed Sun, a half-mile north of town on N71 in Kenmare Business Park, tel. 064/41394).

Kenmare's History: Axes, Xs, Nuns, and Lace

Bronze Age people (2000 B.C.), attracted to this valley for its abundant game and fishing, stashed their prized **axe heads** and daggers in hidden hoards. Nearly 4,000 years later (in 1930), a local farmer from the O'Sullivan clan pried a bothersome boulder from one of his fields and discovered it to be a lid for a collection of rare artifacts that are now on display in the National Museum in Dublin (the "Killaha hoard"). The O'Sullivans (Gaelic for "descendants of the one-eyed") were for generations the dominant local clan, and you'll still see their name on many Kenmare shop fronts.

Oliver Cromwell's bloody Irish campaign (1649) subdued Ireland, but never reached Kenmare. However, his chief surveyor, William Petty, knew good land when he saw it and took a quarter of what is now County Kerry as payment for his valuable services marking the "lands down" on maps. His heirs, the Lansdownes, created Kenmare as a model 18th-century estate town and developed its distinctive **"X" street plan**. William Petty-Fitzmaurice, the first Marquis of Lansdowne and landlord of Kenmare, became the British Prime Minister who negotiated the peace that ended the American War of Independence in 1783.

Sister Margaret Cusack, a.k.a. Sister Mary Francis Clare, lived in the town from 1862 to 1881, becoming the famous **"Nun of Kenmare."** Her controversial religious life began when she decided to become an Anglican nun after her fiancé's sudden death. Five years later, she converted to Catholicism, joined the Poor Clare order as Sister Mary Francis Clare, and moved with the order to Kenmare. She became an outspoken writer who favored women's rights and lambasted the tyranny of the landlords during the famine. She eventually took church funds and attempted to set herself up as abbess of a convent in Knock. Her renegade behavior led to her leaving the Catholic faith, converting back to Protestantism, writing an autobiography, and lecturing about the "sinister influence of the Roman church."

After the devastation of the Great Potato Famine (1845–1849), an industrial school was founded in Kenmare to teach trades to destitute youngsters. The school, run by the Poor Clare sisters, excelled in teaching young girls the art of **lace-making.** Inspired by lace created earlier in Italy, Kenmare lace caught the eye of Queen Victoria and became much coveted by Victorian society. Examples of it are now on display in the Victoria and Albert Museum (London), the Irish National Museum (Dublin), and the U.S. National Gallery (Washington, D.C.).

Bike Rental: Finnegan's Corner rents bikes for €15 per day and has route maps (July–Aug Mon–Sat 10:00–20:00, Sept–June until 18:00, closed Sun, leave ID for deposit, 37 Henry Street, across from post office, tel. 064/41083).

Parking: The town's two largest public parking lots (free overnight) cling to the two main roads departing town to the north (otherwise street parking is allowed for 2 hours).

Taxi: Try Murnane Cabs (mobile 087-236-4353) or Kenmare Koach and Kab (mobile 087-248-0800).

TOURS

Finnegan's Guided Coach Tours—The company runs a variety of local day tours, departing from the TI at 10:00 and returning by 17:00 (route depends on day: Ring of Kerry on Mon, Wed, and Fri; Ring of Beara on Tue; Glengarrif and Garnish Island on Thu; €25 for any tour, reserve a day in advance, can book private tours for small groups with enough notice, tel. 064/41491, mobile 087-248-0800, www.kenmarecoachandcab.com).

SIGHTS AND ACTIVITIES

Heritage Centre—This museum, in the back rooms of the TI, consists of a series of storyboards and a model of the planned town. A 20-minute visit here explains the nearby ancient stone circle, as well as the history of Kenmare's lace-making fame and notorious nun (free, May–Sept Mon–Sat 9:00–18:00, Sun 10:00–18:00, closed Oct–April, tel. 064/41233).

Kenmare Lace and Design Centre—A single large room (above the TI) displays the delicate lacework that put Kenmare on the modern map. From the 1860s until World War I, the Poor Clare convent at Kenmare became the center of excellence for Irish lace-making. Inspired by antique Venetian lace, but creating their own unique designs, nuns taught needlepoint lace-making as a trade to girls in a region struggling to get back on its feet in the wake of the catastrophic famine. Queen Victoria commissioned five pieces of lace in 1885, and by the end of the century, tourists began visiting Kenmare on their way to Killarney. Nora Finnegan, who runs the Centre, usually has a work in progress to demonstrate the complexity of fine lace-making to visitors (free, May–mid-Oct Mon–Sat 10:00–13:00 & 14:00–17:30, closed Sun; mid-Oct–April

Mon, Wed, and Sat 10:30–13:30, closed Tue, Thu–Fri, and Sun, tel. 064/42636 or 064/42978).

Druid Stone Circle—Of the 100 stone circles that dot southwest Ireland (counties Cork and Kerry), this is one of the biggest and most accessible (5-min walk from TI). It's over 3,000 years old, and it may have been used both as a primitive calendar and a focal point for rituals. The circle has a diameter of 50 feet and consists of 15 stones ringing a large center boulder (probably a burial monument). Experts think that this stone circle tracked the position of the setting sun to determine the annual solstices, marking the longest and shortest days of the year (to help early settlers know when to plant their crops).

To get to the circle from the city center, face the TI and turn left, walking 200 yards down Market Street, passing a row of cute 18th-century houses on your right. Beyond the row of houses, veer right through an unmarked modern gate mounted in stone columns, and continue 50 yards down the paved road. You'll see the circle on your right (free, always open).

Holy Cross Church—Finished in 1864, this is Kenmare's grand Catholic church. It's worth visiting to see the ornate wooden ceiling with 10 larger-than-life angels (carved in Germany's Black Forest). Town lore says that after the church was finished, Father O'Sullivan had the spire topped with a cock to crow over the nearby office of the landlord's agent (who had once denied him the land for a church).

Horseback Riding—River Valley Riding Stables offers day treks for all levels of experience through beautiful hill scenery in the Roughty River Valley (€20/hr, discounts for groups, located about 7 miles east of Kenmare off R569 near Kilgarvan, tel. 064/85360, jamescanavan@hotmail.com).

Boating and Hiking—Star Sailing rent boats, offers sailing lessons, and organizes hill walks. Hop on a small two-person sailboat (€25/hr) or canoe (€10/hr), kick around in a kayak (€8/hr), or take sailing lessons (€20/hr or €35/3 hrs). Phone ahead to reserve boats or ask about hikes (located 5 miles southwest of Kenmare on R571 on Beara Peninsula, courtesy shuttle can pick you up in Kenmare, tel. 064/41222, www.staroutdoors.ie; adjacent Con's Restaurant is open daily 12:00–21:00).

Golfing—Another way to experience Ireland's 40 shades of green is to splurge on a scenic day on the links. The Kenmare Golf Club is right on the edge of town (green fees Mon–Fri €45, Sat–Sun €55, on R569 to Cork, tel. 064/41291), or try the Ring of Kerry Golf and Country Club (€80 green fees, 4 miles west of town on N70, pre-booking advisable on weekends, tel. 064/42000, www.ringofkerrygolf.com).

Kenmare

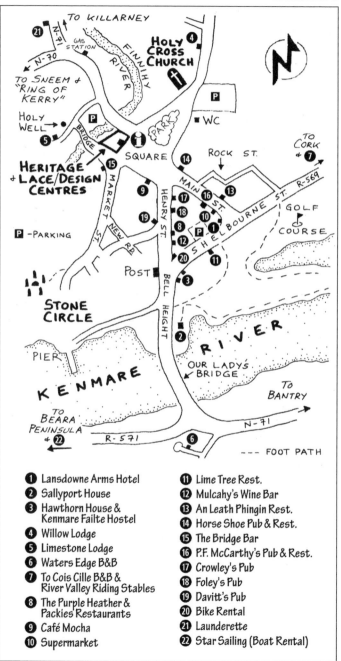

1. Lansdowne Arms Hotel
2. Sallyport House
3. Hawthorn House & Kenmare Failte Hostel
4. Willow Lodge
5. Limestone Lodge
6. Waters Edge B&B
7. To Cois Cille B&B & River Valley Riding Stables
8. The Purple Heather & Packies Restaurants
9. Café Mocha
10. Supermarket
11. Lime Tree Rest.
12. Mulcahy's Wine Bar
13. An Leath Phingin Rest.
14. Horse Shoe Pub & Rest.
15. The Bridge Bar
16. P.F. McCarthy's Pub & Rest.
17. Crowley's Pub
18. Foley's Pub
19. Davitt's Pub
20. Bike Rental
21. Launderette
22. Star Sailing (Boat Rental)

SLEEPING

$$$ Lansdowne Arms Hotel is a centrally located, 200-year-old historical landmark with large, crisp rooms (Fri–Sun: Sb-€100, Db-€150, Tb-€225; Mon–Thu: Sb-€80, Db-€130, Tb-€195; most rooms non-smoking, parking, corner of Main and Shelbourne Streets, tel. 064/41368, fax 064/41114, www.lansdownearms.com, info@lansdownearms.com).

$$$ Sallyport House is an elegantly quiet house filled with antique furniture that's been in Helen Arthur's family for generations. Ask her to point out the foot-worn doorstep that was salvaged from the local workhouse and built into her stone chimney (Sb-€120, Db-€140–170, Tb-€200–210, closed Nov–mid-March, non-smoking, no kids, parking, 5-min walk south of town before crossing Our Lady's Bridge, tel. 064/42066, fax 064/42067, www.sallyporthouse.com, port@iol.ie).

$$ Hawthorn House sports fine woodwork in its eight neat rooms, courtesy of Mr. O'Brien, who's also a carpenter (Db-€80–90, Tb-€100–120, Qb-€100–130, parking, Shelbourne Street, tel. 064/41035, fax 064/41932, www.hawthornhousekenmare.com, info@hawthornhousekenmare.com, Mary and Noel O'Brien).

$$ Willow Lodge has seven comfortable rooms, some with Jacuzzi-equipped bathtubs (Sb-€50–80, Db-€75–85, Tb-€120–126, non-smoking, parking, just beyond Holy Cross Church, tel. 064/42301, willowlodgekenmare@yahoo.com, Gretta Gleeson-O'Byrne).

$$ Limestone Lodge is rock-solid, with five homey rooms and a holy well just a stone's throw from the front door. Ask hostess Siobhan Thoma to show off her handmade lace (Sb-€30–35, Db-€60–70, Tb-€86–92, parking, 5-min walk from town over

---

Sleep Code

(€1 = about $1.20, country code: 353, area code: 064)
S = Single, **D** = Double/Twin, **T** = Triple, **Q** = Quad, **b** = bathroom, **s** = shower only. Breakfast is included; credit cards are accepted unless otherwise noted.

To help you easily sort through these listings, I've divided the rooms into three categories, based on the price for a standard double room with bath:

$$$ **Higher Priced**—Most rooms €100 or more.
  $$ **Moderately Priced**—Most rooms between €65–100.
   $ **Lower Priced**—Most rooms €65 or less.

Finnihy Bridge then left beyond parking lot, tel. 064/42541 or 087/757-4411).

$ Waters Edge B&B rests on a forest hillside a mile south of town overlooking the estuary. It has four clean, colorful rooms and a kid-pleasing backyard (Sb-€35–40, Db-€52–58, Tb-€75–78, cash only, non-smoking, parking, tel. 064/41707, mobile 087-413-4235, vnk@gofree.indigo.ie). To get here, drive south over Our Lady's Bridge, stay on the road (bearing left), take the first driveway on the right, go a couple hundred yards up the bumpy paved road, then at the end of the white wall (on left), turn right onto the gravel lane and drive a hundred yards to the dead-end.

$ Cois Cille B&B (koysh kila, means "near church") is a friendly, old-fashioned place half a mile east of town. It offers three cute rooms and an inviting "grandmother's house" atmosphere (Db-€60, Tb-€90, cash only, non-smoking, parking, 15-min walk from center down Kilgarvan Road, next to old church ruin, tel. 064/42683, Sheila Harrington).

$ Kenmare Failte Hostel (fawl-chuh) maintains 40 budget beds in a well-kept, centrally located building with more charm than most hostels (dorm beds-€15 in rooms without bath, €4 more in rooms with bath, D-€38, Db-€46, T-€48, Tb-€60, Q-€64, Qb-€76, closed Nov–March, tel. 064/42333, fax 064/42466, www .neidin.net/failtehostel, failtefinn@eircom.net).

EATING

This friendly little town offers plenty of quality choices, but try to get a table early, as many finer places book up later in the evening during the summer. Pub dinners are a good value and easier on the budget, but might not serve meals as late as restaurants. Soup-and-sandwich lunch options are easy to find.

Lunch

The Purple Heather makes great salads and omelets (€8–19 meals, Mon–Sat 11:00–19:00, closed Sun, Henry Street, tel. 064/41016, run by same people who own classy Packies restaurant—recommended below).

Hey there, bub—**Davitt's** pub does not flub hearty grub (€12–23 meals, daily 8:00–22:00, Henry Street, tel. 064/42741).

Café Mocha is a basic €4 sandwich shop where you can flop on a sofa and munch (Mon–Fri 9:00–17:30, Sat–Sun 10:00–17:00, tel. 064/42133).

Super Valu supermarket is a good place to stock up for a Ring of Kerry picnic (Mon–Thu 8:00–20:00, Fri 8:00–21:00, Sat 8:00–19:00, Sun 9:00–17:00, Main Street).

Dinner

The **Lime Tree Restaurant** occupies the former Lansdowne Estate office, which gave more than 4,000 people free passage to America in the 1840s. These days, it serves delicious, locally caught seafood dishes and has a classy art gallery upstairs (€17–25 meals, April–Oct daily 18:30–22:00, closed Nov–March, reservations smart, Shelbourne Street, tel. 064/41225).

Packies is a popular, expensive bistro with a leafy, low-light interior and few empty seats. Their scallops get rave reviews (€17–32 meals, Mon–Sat 18:00–22:00, closed Sun, reservations smart, Henry Street, tel. 064/41508).

Mulcahy's Wine Bar has a jazz-mellowed ambience and gourmet dishes nurtured by chef Bruce Mulcahy, whose brother Louis is a well-known potter on the An Daingean Peninsula (€18–28 meals, daily 18:30–22:00, 36 Henry Street, tel. 064/42383, mobile 087-236-4449).

An Leath Phingin (on LAF fing-in, means the "half-penny") combines rough rock walls with steep, narrow stairs to create a fun, relaxed atmosphere for tasty pasta and pizza (€13–20 meals, Thu–Mon 18:00–22:00, closed Tue–Wed, 35 Main Street, tel. 064/41559).

Horse Shoe Pub and Restaurant, specializing in steak and spare ribs, somehow turns rustic farm-tool decor into a romantic candlelit sanctuary (€15–25 meals, daily 17:00–22:00, Main Street, tel. 064/41553).

The Bridge Bar goes for a smart, sophisticated look, with dependable pub lunches and filling dinners (€8–12 lunches daily 12:00–15:00, €14–23 dinners served Thu–Mon 17:30–21:30, €18 3-course early-bird dinners before 19:00, no dinners Tue–Wed, on square where Market Street meets Bridge Street, tel. 064/40613).

P.F. McCarthy's Pub and Restaurant offers salad or sandwich lunches and filling dinner fare (€11–18 meals, Mon 12:00–16:00, Tue–Sat 12:00–21:00, closed Sun, 14 Main Street, tel. 064/41516).

Music in Pubs

Wander Henry Street and stick your head in wherever you hear something you like. Music usually starts at 21:30 and ranges from Irish traditional sessions to sing-along strummers. **Crowley's** is an atmospheric little shoebox of a pub with an unpretentious clientele. **Foley's** jug-stacked window invites you in for a folksy songfest. Across the street, **Davitt's** competes for your ears.

TRANSPORTATION CONNECTIONS

From Kenmare

Kenmare has no train station (the nearest is in Killarney, 20 miles away) and only a few bus connections. Most buses transfer in Killarney.

From Kenmare by Bus to: Killarney (4/day, 1 hr), **An Daingean** (3/day, 3.25 hrs, change in Tralee or Killarney), **Tralee** (4/day, 2 hrs), **Kinsale** (3/day, 5 hrs), **Dublin** (3/day, 7.5 hrs).

From Killarney

If you're traveling in the region without a car, be ready to grit your teeth and run the transportation gauntlet in over-touristed Killarney. The Killarney bus and train stations cling like afterthoughts to opposite sides of the Killarney Outlet Centre mall. Got some layover time between connections? Walk straight out of the front of the mall for five minutes, and check out High Street and New Street, examples of what rampant commercialism can do to a once-charming village. Then get the heck out of Dodge.

A **taxi** ride from the Killarney bus or train station to Muckross House will cost around €12 one-way. There is no bus service to Muckross House.

For a quick peek at the Ring of Kerry from Killarney, Bus Eireann drives the loop (stops only to pick-up and drop off travelers en route, no sightseeing stops) from June to mid-September, departing the Killarney bus station at 8:30 and returning to Killarney at 12:30. You can catch this same bus earlier at 7:50 from Tralee and get back to Tralee by 13:45.

You may want to do some homework prior to your arrival. For bus schedules, call 01/836-6111 or visit www.buseireann.ie; for train schedules, call 01/836-6222 or visit www.irishrail.ie.

From Killarney by Bus to: Kenmare (5/day, 45 min), **Tralee** (16/day, 1.5 hrs), **An Daingean** (6/day, 2.5 hrs, change in Tralee), **Shannon Airport** (6/day, 3.5 hrs), **Dublin** (5/day, 6 hrs, change in Limerick).

From Killarney by Train to: Tralee (5/day, 45 min), **Cork** (5/day, 1.5 hrs), **Waterford** (2/day, 3 hrs), **Dublin** (5/day, 3.5 hrs).

Ring of Kerry

The Ring of Kerry (the Iveragh Peninsula) has been the perennial breadwinner of Irish tourism for decades now. Lassoed by a winding coastal road (the Ring), this mountainous, lake-splattered region is undeniably striking. But as annual flocks of visitors have grown, the area has strained to balance the demand for tourist

Ring of Kerry

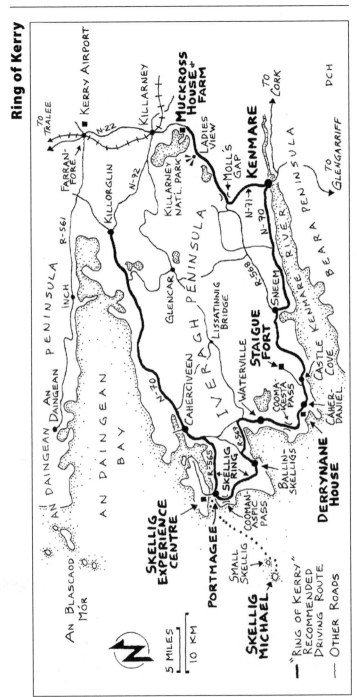

access with the preservation of the rural charms that everyone has come to see. In towns such as Killarney, the battle has already been lost—what remains there of real Ireland is buried under a pile of postcards and ceramic leprechauns galore.

But fearless motorists, armed with a good map and a reliable alarm clock, can sidestep the crowds and chow down on the most visit-worthy tidbits in this feast of Irish sightseeing.

Planning Your Time

More than twice the size of the An Daingean Peninsula (see next chapter) and backed by a muscular tourism budget that promotes every sight as a "must-see," the Iveragh Peninsula can seem overwhelming. Be selective and don't let them pull the turf over your eyes.

By Car: You can drive the Ring (primarily on N70) in one long but satisfying day. Travelers linking overnights in Kinsale and An Daingean can insert a night between them in Kenmare (a good base to enjoy the best of the Ring of Kerry).

On a one-day visit to the Ring, I'd leave Kenmare before 9:00 and allow time for stops at Staigue Ring Fort (45 min), Derrynane House (1.25 hrs), and the Skellig Experience Centre (1 hr).

Photographers and ambitious early birds may want to take in the adjacent Skellig Ring as well (1 hr). Consider taking along a picnic lunch to be enjoyed from the car at a scenic pullout (the parking lot at Coomakesta Pass has terrific views), or grab a quick pub-grub lunch in a town halfway around. Waterville has plenty of lunch options (try Brod's Bar at Lodge Hotel right on the waterfront, tel. 066/947-4436) and a wide beachfront park. If you're considering a boat trip out to the craggy island of Skellig Michael, you'll need to add another day to allow for an overnight in the Portmagee area...and hope for good weather (see page 173).

By Tour: You can take a €25 day-long bus tour of the Ring from Kenmare with Finnegan's Guided Coach Tours (Mon, Wed, and Fri; see page 157). Ring of Kerry tours also go from the supertouristy but well-connected town of Killarney (TI tel. 064/31633).

Driving the Ring of Kerry (Made Less Scary)

Given the fact that every other tourist and his clan seem hell-bent on taking a battering-ram bus tour of this scenic, often narrow, 120-mile loop road, careful pre-planning of your route is time well spent. Study an *Ordnance Survey Atlas* (€12.50, sold in most TIs

Ring of Kerry vs. the An Daingean Peninsula

If I could beam a traveler to any one spot in Ireland, it would have to be An Daingean. It just seems to have the right balance of magically delicious Irish charms. But you're more likely to have heard of the justifiably famous Ring of Kerry. To help you decide how to best spend your time, here's a brief snapshot of both.

The An Daingean Peninsula's western tip is a joy to explore via the scenic Ceann Sleibhe loop drive (30 miles, see page 198). The Ring of Kerry (120 miles, see page 163) is also delightful, though its beauty is sometimes marred by too many tour buses. There are abundant archaeological sights to see on the An Daingean Peninsula, and they all feel very intimate and accessible. The Ring of Kerry drive, however, is much longer, so many travelers find themselves only glossing over the most worthwhile sights.

An Daingean town is alive with traditional music pubs, an active fishing harbor, and the sturdy cultural atmosphere of a Gaeltacht, a Gaelic preserve; you can easily spend three fun nights here. In comparison, Kenmare's a colorful-yet-quiet base town—simply a refresher before tackling the Ring (spend a relaxing night here; spend another out in Portmagee if planning a visit to Skellig Michael).

Near An Daingean, the heather- and moss-covered hump of the An Blascaod Mór (Great Blasket Island) and the excellent Ionad An Blascaod Mór (Great Blasket Centre) offer insights into the storytelling traditions and simple lives of hardy fisherfolk who—until 50 years ago—lived at the tip of the An Daingean Peninsula. Off the tip of the Ring of Kerry, the rocky ledges of Skellig Michael and the worthwhile Skellig Experience Centre near Portmagee preserve the harsh environment and social isolation sought out by devoutly inspired medieval hermit monks.

Muckross House (page 168), and the beautiful lake views of Killarney National Park, are part of the eastern segment of the Ring of Kerry. But they're easy to visit en route from Kinsale to An Daingean, if you don't have enough time to commit to the entire Ring of Kerry drive.

Both regions are beyond the reach of the Irish train system and require a car or bus service to access. Both offer memorable scenery, great restaurants, warm B&B hospitality, and similar prices. But An Daingean is a winner that rarely disappoints. If you have some wiggle room in your vacation, stitch an extra night or two onto your itinerary to swing through the Ring of Kerry. But lock in your An Daingean time first.

and bookstores in Ireland). The *Fir Tree Aerial* series makes a useful map that covers both the Iveragh and An Daingean Peninsulas, giving you a bird's-eye feel for the terrain (€8, sold in many TIs and bookstores in County Kerry).

Unlike the much shorter Slea Head loop on the neighboring An Daingean Peninsula (see next chapter), which can only be driven clockwise, the Ring of Kerry loop can be driven in either direction.

Think of the Ring as a rectangle (with Kenmare in the lower-right corner) and consider the following: Most tour buses depart from Killarney in a virtual convoy and spend the day chugging counter-clockwise around the loop. Rather than getting stuck behind a slow, view-blocking behemoth, drive the loop clockwise (as many locals do). Since you'll be driving on the left side of the road, the dramatic coastal views (on your left) will never be obstructed by passing vehicles.

If you're approaching the region from Kinsale and Cobh, the best scenario is to visit Muckross House first, giving you a great  Killarney lakes experience without wasting time in plastic Killarney town. Then go south on N71 to see some of the Ring's best mountain scenery at Ladies View and Moll's Gap (WCs beside parking lot) before descending into Kenmare to spend the night. Drivers from Kinsale who skip Blarney and have lunch at Muckross House can be in Kenmare by mid-afternoon. The flat inland N72 section of the Ring from Killorglin to Killarney (the upper-right corner of the rectangle) is least worthwhile and can be skipped. This leaves you with less of the Ring to tackle the following day. If you depart Kenmare before 9:00 (staying on N70 all the way around to Killorglin, adding the Skellig Ring if you can), you'll have time to enjoy the Ring and still make it to An Daingean town by 19:00. If you don't get an early start, you'll feel rushed and stressed.

Fill up on gas in Kenmare (Esso filling station and Centra market at junction where N70 Sneem road meets N71 Killarney road). Gas is cheaper here than out on the Ring.

The downside of all this is that you'll need to be an alert and courteous driver as you unexpectedly encounter oncoming bus traffic. Buses have the right-of-way. Not all of the Ring road is narrow, but the most challenging stretch is the rugged, curvy coastal section between Derrynane and Waterville (the lower-left corner of the rectangle). There are lots of scenic-view pullouts, but it will be up to you to back up to the nearest wide spot in the road to let a less-nimble bus get through a tight curve.

If you get an early start out of Kenmare, however, you should be through the narrowest stretches of road by the time the bus convoys approach from the opposite direction. I like to duck the heavy bus traffic by enjoying the peaceful, bus-free Skellig Ring in the middle of the day (roughly 11:30–13:30), when the worst traffic lumbers by on N70.

For Irish driving tips, see page 24 in the Introduction.

Muckross House

Perhaps the best Victorian stately home you'll see in Ireland, Muckross House (built in 1843) is magnificently set at the edge of Killarney National Park.

This regular stop on the tour-bus circuit includes several sights in one: the mansion, a set of traditional farms showing rural life in the 1930s, a fine garden idyllically set on a lake, and an information center for the national park. The Victorian period was the 19th-century boom time, when the sun never set on the British Empire and the Industrial Revolution (born in England) was chugging the world into the modern age. Of course, Ireland was a colony  back then, with big-shot English landlords. (The English gentry lived very well, while a third of Ireland's population starved in the famine of 1845–1849. Read the Muckross House lord's defense on page 43 of the fine souvenir book.) Be sure to take the 45-minute guided **tour** that gives meaning to the house (included with admission, offered regularly throughout the day).

Muckross House feels lived in—with fine Victorian furniture cluttered around the fireplace under Waterford Crystal chandeliers and lots of antlers. You'll see Queen Victoria's bedroom (ground floor, since she was afraid of house fires). They spent a couple of years preparing for her visit in 1861, but she stayed only three nights.

The house exit takes you through an **information center** for Killarney National Park, with a relaxing 15-minute video on "Ireland's premier national park," featuring lots of geology, flora, and fauna (free, shown on request).

The **garden** is a hit for those with a green thumb, and a €1.50 guide booklet makes the nature trails interesting. A bright, modern cafeteria (with indoor/outdoor seating) faces the garden. The adjacent crafts shop shows weaving and pottery in action.

Muckross Traditional Farms, designed to give the Muckross stop a little heft, consists of six different farmhouses showing off life in the 1930s. Several farms come with a person ready to feed you a little home-baked bread and reminisce about the old days. If you've yet to see an open-air folk museum, this might be worthwhile—otherwise it's pretty lightweight. The farms are strung along a mile-long road with an old bus shuttling those who don't want to hike (free, 4/hr).

Cost and Hours: €5.50 for house, €8.25 includes house and old farms, covered by Heritage Card—see page 4. House open daily 9:00–17:30, July–Aug until 19:00, shorter hours in winter; farms open May–Sept only; tel. 064/31440.

Getting There: Muckross House is conveniently located for a break on the long ride from Cork or Cashel to An Daingean or Kenmare. From Killarney, follow signs to Kenmare, where you'll find Muckross House three miles south of town. As you approach from Killarney, you'll see a small parking lot two miles before the actual parking lot. This is used by horse-and-buggy bandits to hoodwink tourists into thinking they have to pay to clip-clop to the house. Giddy-up on by and you'll find a big, safe, and free lot right at the mansion.

Staigue Fort

One of the largest and best-preserved of Ireland's ring forts, Staigue (STAY-ig) is an imposing sight rising out of a desolate high valley. The circular drystone walls were built sometime between 500 B.C. and A.D. 300 without the aid of mortar or cement. About 80 feet  across, with walls 12 feet thick at the base and up to 20 feet high, this brutish structure would have taken a hundred men six months to complete. Expert opinion is divided, but most believe that the people who built it would have retreated here at times of tribal war, bringing their valuable cattle inside to protect them from ancient rustlers. Others see the round design as a kind of amphitheater, where local clan chieftains would have gathered for important meetings or rituals. However, the ditch surrounding the outer walls suggest a defensive, rather than ceremonial, function. Without written records, we can only imagine the part this mute ghost played in ancient dramas.

Before you see the fort, pay a visit to the **Staigue Fort Exhibition Centre** to gain an appreciation for the deceptively simple structure. Inside the Centre, you'll find a tiny museum, a detailed fort model, and a 10-minute film putting it all into historical context (put €1 admission fee in honor box beside gate at base of fort, Easter–Sept daily 10:00–21:00, closed Oct–Easter, tel. 066/947-5127, coffee shop and WCs).

Getting There: The fort is beside the main N70 road, on the right. Just after passing through the hamlet of Castle Cove, look for signs to "Staigue" on the right leading up into the interior. You'll find the fort (always open) at the top of a 2.5-mile-long rural access road.

Derrynane House

This is the home of Daniel O'Connell, Ireland's most influential pre-independence politician, whose tireless nonviolent agitation gained equality for Catholics 175 years ago. The coastal lands of the O'Connell estate that surround Derrynane House are now a national historic park. A visit here is a window onto a man who not only liberated Ireland from the last oppressive anti-Catholic penal laws, but who also first developed the idea of a grassroots movement, organizing on a massive scale to achieve political ends without bloodshed (see sidebar on page 171).

The house has a quirky floor plan that can be confusing, so pick up a laminated guide at the front desk. Ask about the next scheduled 20-minute audiovisual show, which fleshes out the highlights of O'Connell's turbulent life and makes the contents of the house more interesting.

In the exhibition room downstairs is a glass case containing the pistols that were used in O'Connell's famous duel. Beside them are his black gloves, one of which he always wore on his right pistol hand when he went to Mass (out of remorse for the part it played in taking a man's life). The drawing room upstairs is lined with family portraits and contains his ornately carved chair with tiny harp strings and wolfhound collars made of gold. On a wall in the upstairs bedroom is a copy of O'Connell's famous speech imploring the Irish not to riot when he was arrested. Then visit the coach house (out back, beside the tearoom) to see the enormous grand chariot that carried O'Connell through throngs of joyous Dubliners after his release from prison in 1844. He added the small chapel wing to the house in gratitude to God for his prison release.

The grounds of the estate are pleasant enough for a 20-minute stroll to the beach and back, but not at the expense of making you rush through the remainder of your Ring of Kerry day.

Cost and Hours: €2.75, covered by Heritage Card—see page 4, May–Sept Mon–Sat 9:00–18:00, Sun 11:00–19:00; April and

Daniel O'Connell
(1775–1847)

Born in Cahersiveen and elected in Ennis as the first Catholic member of the British Parliament, O'Connell was the hero of Catholic emancipation in Ireland. Educated in France at a time when the anti-Catholic penal laws limited schooling for Irish Catholics in Ireland, he witnessed the carnage of the French Revolution. Upon his return to Ireland, he saw more bloodshed during the futile Rebellion of 1798. He chose law as his profession and reluctantly killed a man who challenged him to a duel. Abhorring all this violence, O'Connell dedicated himself to peacefully gaining equal rights for Catholics in an Ireland dominated by a wealthy Protestant minority. He formed the Catholic Association with a one-penny-per-month membership fee and quickly gained a huge following (especially among the poor) with his persuasive speaking skills. Although Catholics weren't allowed to hold office, he ran for election to Parliament anyway and won a seat in 1828. His unwillingness to take the anti-Catholic Oath of Supremacy initially kept him out of Westminster, but the moral force of his victory caused the government to give in and concede Catholic emancipation the following year. Known as "the Liberator," he was making progress toward his next goal of repealing the Act of Union with Britain when the Potato Famine hit in 1845. O'Connell died two years later in Genoa on his way to Rome, but his ideals lived on: His Catholic Association was the model that taught the fundamentals of political organization to the Irish who later emigrated and rose within American big-city political "green machines."

Oct Tue–Sun 13:00–17:00, closed Mon; Nov–March Sat–Sun 13:00–17:00, closed Mon–Fri; last entry 45 min before closing, tel. 066/947-5113.

Getting There: Just outside the town of Derrynane, pick up a handy free map of the estate from the little TI inside the brown Wave Crest market (TI open May–Sept daily 9:00–20:00, closed Oct–April, tel. 066/947-5188; market is a great place to buy a picnic). One mile after the market, take a left and follow the signs into Derrynane National Historic Park. Visit the ogham stone (below) on your way to the house.

Ogham Stone: On the grounds of Derrynane House is a fine example of an ogham stone. Such pillars were erected by Irish clans around the time of Christ to mark boundaries, or possibly graves of nobility. Ogham (AHG-um) was the first written language of the Irish, inspired by contacts with the Roman alphabet.

The notches and diagonal lines carved into the corner of the stone (facing the bay) represent letters of the Irish alphabet. To find the stone as you approach the Derrynane House grounds, watch for a small, brown sign next to a rusty little gate on your left pointing to a stone 25 feet off the road (a mile after turning off N70, just before the *Entering National Park* sign).

Skellig Ring

This narrow little 20-mile ring road is an unspoiled jewel dangling off the end of the Ring of Kerry necklace. It's a lovely (but time-consuming) bonus for travelers wanting to lose the crowds. The Skellig Ring is bus-free and takes an hour to drive (cars do it in either direction). If you time it right, you'll be out here in the middle of the day—as the worst of the tour-bus traffic goes by on N70. Be ready to pull over to allow occasional oncoming traffic to pass.

Driving the Skellig Ring

Leave the Ring of Kerry (N70) by turning left onto R567 about three miles north of Waterville, following the brown "Skellig Ring" signs to Ballinskelligs. The road north from Ballinskelligs to Portmagee is not numbered but is easy to follow, rewarding adventurous motorists with dramatic views of the two Skellig rocks seven miles offshore. A rugged dose of scenic coastal Ireland graces the foreground. St. Finan's Bay lies about halfway around, with a pleasant little picnic-friendly beach (but no WCs). Popping up unexpectedly near the bay is the small Skelligs Chocolate factory, inviting visitors in for a sample and proclaiming their chocolates to be "never boring, always reliably gorgeous,

and sometimes a little different—just like the Irish!" (April–Oct Mon–Fri 10:00–17:00, Sat–Sun 12:00–17:00, tel. 066/947-9119, www.skelligschocolate.com).

In 1944, a U.S. Navy B-24 Liberator on U-Boat patrol crashed into the summit of Skellig Michael, killing all aboard. A simple memorial can be found a mile down the undulating dead-end spur road running south along the coast from St. Finan's Bay. The very steep switchback road, climbing north out of St. Finan's Bay, tests your clutch skills (honk at blind hairpin corners to alert oncoming cars) and leads to a spectacular viewpoint on the ridgetop at Coomanaspic Pass. Locals claim this is the highest place you can drive a car in Ireland. The An Daingean Peninsula and Na Blascaodai (Blasket Islands) are often visible off to the north. From here, put it in low gear and coast down the other side of the ridge, passing a pretty little roadside shrine to the Virgin Mary before arriving in Portmagee. The R565 leads you back to the Ring of Kerry.

Visiting Skellig Michael

If you have more time, consider venturing out to the pointy, secluded island of Skellig Michael. To do it right, visit the Skellig Experience Centre, spend the night in or near Portmagee, and take a boat to the island the next day (book the cruise ahead; see page 174).

Portmagee

Just a short row of snoozy buildings lining the bay, Portmagee is the best harbor for boat excursions out to the Skellig Islands. It's a quiet village with a handful of B&Bs, two pubs, a bakery, a market, and no ATMs. A 100-yard-long bridge connects it to the gently rounded Valencia Island, where you'll find the Skelligs Experience Centre (on the left at the Valencia end of the bridge; see below). A public parking lot is at the Portmagee end of the bridge, with award-winning WCs (no kidding: Irish Toilet of the Year 2002 runner-up plaque proudly displayed). The first transatlantic cable (for telegraph communication) was laid from Valencia Island in 1866. The tiny post office hides inside O'Connell's Market (Mon–Fri 9:00–17:30, Sat 9:00–13:00, closed Sun).

SLEEPING

(€1 = about $1.20, country code: 353, area code: 066)
$$ Moorings Guest House feels like a small hotel, with 14 rooms, a pub and a fine restaurant downstairs, and the most convenient location in town, 50 yards from the end of the pier (Db-€80–90, tel. 066/947-7108, fax 066/947-7220, www.moorings.ie, moorings@iol.ie, Gerard and Patricia Kennedy).

At the homey **$ Island View B&B,** Kathleen O'Donoghue bakes the daily bread in her antique stove, and can arrange a boat trip out to the Skelligs (S-€30, Db-€60, Tb-€80, a half-mile south of Portmagee on the road to St. Finan's Bay, tel. 066/947-7188, mobile 087-926-1492, www.islandviewguesthouse.com).

$ Beach Cove B&B offers four comfortable rooms in splendid isolation four miles south, over lofty Coomanaspic ridge from Portmagee, beside the pretty beach at St. Finan's Bay. Charming

Bridie O'Connor will arrange a boat trip out to the Skelligs for you. Her adjacent cottage out back has two double rooms and a kitchen, making it ideal for families (Sb-€40, Db-€64, Tb-€85, tel. 066/947-9301, mobile 087-202-1820, www.stayatbeachcove .com, beachcove@eircom.net).

EATING

These options all line the waterfront (between pier and bridge to Valencia Island). **The Moorings** is an expensive restaurant with great seafood caught literally just outside its front door (€18–29 dinners, Tue–Sun 18:00–22:00, closed Mon, reservations smart, 50 yards to the left coming off the pier, tel. 066/947-7108). The **Bridge Bar,** right next door and under the same ownership, does traditional pub grub but stops serving food a bit early. Call ahead to check on their traditional music and dance schedule (€12–17 meals, daily 12:00–20:00, live music Fri and Sun nights, tel. 066/947-7108). The **Fisherman's Bar** is less pretentious, with more locals and cheaper prices (€10–18 meals, daily 10:00–21:30, immediately on the right coming off the pier, tel. 066/947-7103). **O'Connell's Market** is the only grocery (Mon–Sat 9:00–21:30, Sun 10:00–18:00, 100 yards east of the pier, roughly halfway to the bridge). **Skellig Mist Bakery** can make basic lunch sandwiches to take on Skellig boat excursions (daily 9:00–17:00, a couple of doors farther toward the bridge from the market, tel. 066/947-7250).

Skellig Experience Centre

You'll better appreciate a visit to Skellig Michael if you explore this modest museum first (if you're taking a boat to the island, visit here the afternoon before). Straightforward exhibits explain the unique bird life of the Skellig Islands, as well as the underwater creatures surrounding them. The highlight is the historical coverage of the tenacious early Christian community that somehow sustained itself on these rocks at the edge of the world for five centuries. A 15-minute audiovisual show fills in the blanks. Follow it up with a coffee or sandwich in the tearoom, and you've got wind back in your sails. A visit here is also worth considering if a tight schedule or bad weather prevents you from an actual visit to the Skelligs (€5, audioguide €0.50 extra, daily July–Aug 10:00–19:00, May–June and Sept 10:00–18:00, March–April and Oct 10:00–17:00, closed Nov–Feb, call ahead in off-season as hours may vary, on Valencia Island beside bridge linking it to Portmagee, tel. 066/947-6306, www.skelligexperience.com).

Two-hour **boat trips,** circling both Skellig Michael and Little

Skellig (but without putting people ashore on them), are available for those who want a close look without the stair climb and vertigo that go with an actual visit to the island (€20, sailing daily about 15:00 and returning by 17:00, weather permitting, depart from Valencia Island pier 50 yards below the Skellig Experience Centre—which you can call for details, see phone number above).

Skellig Michael

A trip to this jagged, isolated pyramid—the Holy Grail of Irish monastic island settlements—rates as a truly memorable ▲▲▲ experience. After visiting Skellig Michael a hundred years ago, Nobel Prize–winning Irish author George Bernard Shaw called it "the most fantastic and impossible rock in the world."

Rising seven miles offshore, the Skelligs (Gaelic for "splinter") are two gigantic slate-and-sandstone rocks crouched aggressively on the ocean horizon. The larger of the two, Skellig Michael, is over 700 feet tall and a mile around, with a tiny cluster of abandoned beehive huts clinging near its summit like stubborn barnacles. The smaller of the two, Little Skellig, is home to a huge colony of gannets (like a large, graceful seagull with a 4-foot wingspan), protected by law from visitors setting foot on shore.

Skellig Michael (dedicated to the archangel) was first inhabited by ultra-pious sixth-century Christian monks. Inspired by earlier hermit monks in the Egyptian desert, they sought the purity of isolation to get closer to God. Neither Viking raids nor winter storms could dislodge them as they patiently built a half-dozen small stone igloo-like dwellings and a couple of tiny oratories. Their remote cliff-terrace perch is still connected to the sea 600 feet below by an amazing series of rock stairs. Viking Olav Trygvasson, who later became King of Norway and introduced Christianity to his country, was baptized here in 956.

Chiseling the most rudimentary life out of solid rock, the monks lived a harsh, lonely, disciplined existence that endured for over 500 years. They collected rainwater in cisterns and lived off fish and birds. To supplement their meager existence, they gathered bird eggs and feathers to trade with passing boats for cereals, candles, and animal hides (used for clothing and for copying scripture). They finally moved their holy community ashore to Ballinskelligs in the early 1100s.

Time—which dragged for medieval monks—flies by for modern visitors to Skellig Michael. Since you'll have only a few hours to explore the island, begin by surmounting the seemingly unending series of stone stairs to the monastic ruins. Plan on 600 vertical feet of uneven stone stairs with no handrails. Save most of your film for the way down. Those who linger too long below risk missing the enlightening 20-minute free talk among the beehive huts given by Office of Public Works guides (who camp on the island from April–Oct) soon after a few boats arrive. Afterward, poke your

head into some of the huts and try to imagine the dark, damp, and devoted life of a monk here over 1,000 years ago. After rambling through the ruins, you can give in to photo frenzy as you wander back down the stairs.

When you reach the saddle between the two main peaks, gaze at the tallest spire (called the Needle's Eye) and visualize a horizontal natural stone outcrop that once extended from near the summit. A cross was carved into the end of it, and devout pilgrims would crawl out to kiss it as part of their penitential duty. It finally fell 700 feet into the sea in 1977 without loss of life.

The two lighthouses on the far side of the island are now automated, and access to them has been blocked off. There are no WCs or modern shelters of any kind on Skellig Michael—you're roughing it in a remote and magical place for several hours.

If you visit between late April and early August, you'll be surrounded by fearless rainbow-beaked puffins, who nest here in underground burrows. Their bizarre swallowed cooing sounds like a distant chainsaw. These portly little birds live off fish, and divers have reported seeing them 20 feet underwater in pursuit of their prey.

Your return boat journey usually includes a pass near Little Skellig, which looms like an iceberg with a white coat of guano—courtesy of the 20,000 gannets that circle overhead like feathered confetti. Although these large birds have four-foot wing spans, they suddenly morph into sleek darts when pursuing a fish, piercing the water from over 100 feet above. You're also likely to get a glimpse of gray seals lazing on rocks near the water's edge.

Getting to Skellig Michael: To book a boat trip from Portmagee, contact **Murphy's Sea Cruise** (€35, office across from O'Connell's Market, tel. 066/947-7156, mobile 087-234-2168 or 087-645-1909, www.esatclear.ie/~skelligsrock, murphyseacruise @esatclear.ie), **Joe Roddy** (tel. 066/947-4268 or mobile 087-120-9924, www.skelligstrips.com), or **Brendan Casey** (tel. 066/947-2437).

Landing on Skellig Michael is highly weather-dependent. If the seas are too choppy, the boats cannot safely put people ashore on the concrete island pier (a bit like jumping off a trampoline onto an ice rink). Excursions are scheduled to run daily from Easter to late September, but experienced boat captains say they are able to put visitors ashore roughly five days out of seven in an average summer week.

Your best bet is to reserve a room near Portmagee that fits your itinerary, then call a few days in advance to make a boat reservation. Keep your fingers crossed for good weather. Contact the boat operator on the morning of departure to get the final word. If the seas are too rough, he can tell from Portmagee and will make a decision that morning whether or not to go (rather than taking passengers halfway out, then aborting).

Boat trips normally depart Portmagee at 10:30. The crossing takes an hour, and passengers are put ashore from roughly 11:30 until 14:00. That gets people back into Portmagee by 15:00 (with enough time to drive on to An Daingean). There is a total fleet of 15 small boats (from Portmagee, Ballinskelligs, Waterville, and Valencia Island) that have permits to land on Skellig Michael. Each boat can carry a dozen passengers. This limits the number of daily visitors and minimizes the impact on the sensitive island ecosystem.

Bring your camera, a sandwich lunch (easy to buy at Skellig Mist Bakery in Portmagee—see page 174), water, sunscreen, rain gear, and comfortable hiking shoes for rocky terrain.

AN DAINGEAN PENINSULA

(Dingle Peninsula)

The An Daingean Peninsula, the western-most tip of Ireland, offers just the right mix of far-and-away beauty, ancient archaeological wonders, and isolated walks or bike rides—all within convenient reach of its main town. An Daingean town (pronounced "on DANG-un," called Dingle in English) is just large enough to have all the necessary tourist services and a steady nocturnal beat of Irish folk music.

Although crowded in summer, An Daingean still feels like the fish and the farm really matter. Forty fishing boats sail from An Daingean, tractor tracks dirty its main drag, and a faint whiff of peat fills its nighttime streets.

For more than 25 years, my Irish dreams have been set here on this sparse but lush peninsula, where locals are fond of saying, "The next parish is Boston." There's a feeling of closeness to the land on An Daingean. When I asked a local if he was born here, he thought for a second and said, "No, it was about six miles down the road." When I told him where I was from, a faraway smile filled his eyes, and he looked out to sea and sighed, "Ah, the shores of Americay." I asked his friend if he'd lived here all his life. He said, "Not yet."

An Daingean feels so traditionally Irish because it's a Gaeltacht, a region where the government subsidizes the survival of the Irish language and culture. While English is always there, the signs,

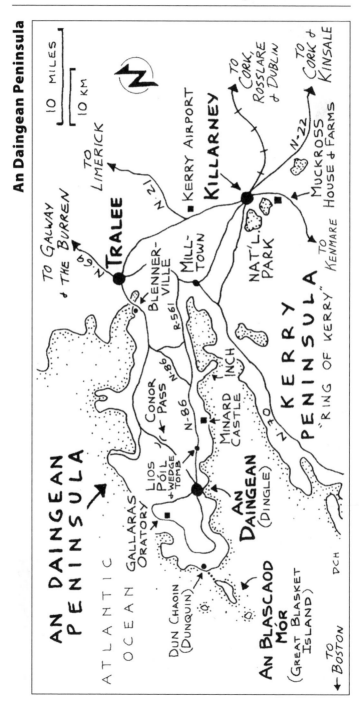

menus, and songs come in Gaelic. Children carry hurling sticks to class, and even the local preschool brags "ALL Gaelic."

Of the peninsula's 10,000 residents, 1,500 live in An Daingean town. Its few streets, lined with ramshackle but gaily painted shops and pubs, run up from a rain-stung harbor always busy with fishing boats and leisure sailboats. Traditionally, the buildings were drab gray or whitewashed. Thirty years ago, Ireland's "tidy town" competition prompted everyone to paint their buildings in playful pastels.

It's a peaceful town. The courthouse (1832) is open one hour a month. The judge does his best to wrap up business within a half hour. During the day you'll see teenagers—already working on ruddy beer-glow cheeks—roll kegs up the streets and into the pubs in preparation for another night of music and *craic* (fun conversation and atmosphere).

An Daingean Town

Planning Your Time

For the shortest visit, give An Daingean two nights and a day. It takes six to eight hours to get there from Dublin, Galway, or the boat dock in Rosslare. By spending two nights, you'll feel more like a local on your second evening in the pubs. You'll need the better part of a day to explore the 30-mile loop around the peninsula by bike, car, or tour bus (see "Circular Tour" on page 197). To do any serious walking or relaxing, you'll need two or three days. It's not uncommon to find Americans slowing way, way down in An Daingean town.

ORIENTATION

(area code: 066)
An Daingean—extremely comfortable on foot—hangs on a medieval grid of streets between the harborfront (where the Tralee bus stops) and Main Street (3 blocks inland). Nothing in town is more than a five-minute walk away. Street numbers are used only when more than one place is run by a family of the same name. Most locals know most locals, and people on the street are fine sources of information. Remember, locals love their soda bread, and tourism provides the butter. You'll find a warm and sincere welcome.

Tourist Information

The TI is a privately owned, for-profit business—little more than a glorified shop with a green staff who know the town, but not much about the rest of the peninsula (July–Aug daily 9:00–19:00,

An Daingean's History

The wet sod of An Daingean is soaked with medieval history. In the darkest depths of the Dark Ages, peace-loving, bookish monks fled the chaos of the Continent and its barbarian raids. They sailed to the drizzly fringe of the known world—places like An Daingean. These monks kept literacy alive in Europe. Charlemagne, who ruled much of Europe in the year 800, imported Irish monks to be his scribes.

It was from this peninsula that the semi-mythical explorer/monk, St. Brendan, is said to have set sail in the sixth century in search of a legendary western paradise. Some think he beat Columbus to North America by nearly a thousand years.

An Daingean was a busy seaport in the late Middle Ages. An Daingean and Tralee (covered later in this chapter) were the only walled towns in Kerry. Castles stood at the low and high ends of An Daingean's Main Street, protecting the Normans from the angry and dispossessed Irish outside. An Daingean was a gateway to northern Spain—a three-day sail due south. Many 14th- and 15th-century pilgrims left from An Daingean for the revered Spanish church, Santiago de Compostela, thought to house the bones of St. James.

In An Daingean's medieval heyday, locals traded cowhides for wine. When An Daingean's position as a trading center waned, the town faded in importance. In the 19th century, it was a linen-weaving center. Until 1970, fishing dominated, and the only visitors were scholars and students of old Irish ways. In 1970, the movie *Ryan's Daughter* introduced the world to An Daingean (known then as Dingle). The trickle of An Daingean fans has grown to a flood as word of its musical, historical, gastronomical, and scenic charms—not to mention its friendly dolphin—has spread.

June and Sept–Oct daily 9:30–17:30; Nov–May Mon–Tue and Thu–Sat 10:00–17:00, closed Sun and Wed; on Strand Street by the water, tel. 066/915-1188). For more knowledgeable help, drop by the Mountain Man shop (on Strand Street, see "An Daingean Activities," page 183) or talk to your B&B host.

Helpful Hints

Before You Go: The local Web site (www.dingle-peninsula.ie) lists festivals and events.

Crowds: Crowds trample An Daingean's charm throughout July and August. The absolute craziest are the Dingle Races (2nd weekend in Aug), Dingle Regatta (3rd weekend in Aug), and the Blessing of the Boats (end of Aug, beginning of Sept).

An Daingean Area

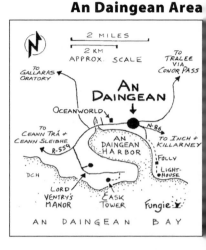

The first Mondays in May, June, and August are bank holidays, giving Ireland's workers three-day weekends—and ample time to fill up An Daingean. The town's metabolism (prices, schedules, activities) rises and falls with the tourist crowds, so October through April is sleepy.

Money: Two banks in town, both on Main Street, offer the same rates (Mon 10:00–17:00, Tue–Fri 10:00–16:00, closed Sat–Sun) and have cash machines. The TI happily changes cash and traveler's checks at mediocre rates. Expect to use cash (rather than credit cards) to pay for most peninsula activities.

Internet Access: Dingle Internet Café is on Main Street (€2.60/ 30 min, April–Sept Mon–Sat 10:00–22:00, Sun 14:00– 20:00, shorter hours Oct–March, tel. 066/915-2478, www .dingleinternetcafe.ie).

Post Office: It's on Main Street near Benners Hotel (Mon–Fri 9:00–17:30, Sat 9:00–13:00, closed Sun).

Laundry: Dingle Cleaners is full-service only—drop off before 10:00 and pick up dried and folded laundry late that afternoon (€12 minimum, priced by load size, Mon–Sat 9:30–18:00, closed Sun, beside Moran's Market and gas station, tel. 066/915-0680, mobile 087-793-5621).

Bike Rental: Bike-rental shops abound. The cheapest is at Kirrary B&B (€8/day, Greys Lane, see "Sleeping," page 193) or try Paddy's Bike Hire (€10/day or €1 more for 24 hrs, €12 for better bikes, daily 9:00–19:00, on Dykegate next to Grapevine Hostel, tel. 066/915-2311). Foxy John's (Main Street), Mountain Man (no helmets), and the Ballintaggert Hostel also rent bikes. If you're biking the peninsula, get a bike with skinny street tires, not slow and fat mountain-bike tires. Plan on leaving €10 plus a driver's license or passport as a security deposit.

Taxi: Try Diarmuid Begley in An Daingean (mobile 087-250-4767) or Tom Kearney out in Dun Chaoin (mobile 087-933-2264).

Parking: If you're not staying overnight (i.e., parking at your B&B), then use the waterfront parking lot extending west from the TI (€0.80/hr, pay at meter in lot and display on dashboard, daily 8:00–18:00).

An Daingean Activities: The Mountain Man, a hiking shop run by a local guide, Adrian Curran, is a clearinghouse for information on hiking, biking, horseback riding, climbing, peninsula tours, and trips to the Na Blascaodai, or Blasket Islands (the shop is the An Daingean town contact for the Dun Chaoin–Na Blascaodai boats and shuttle-bus rides to the harbor—see "Na Blascaodai," page 205). Give them a call a few days ahead of time to see which guided, scenic, mountain day-hikes are scheduled (daily July–Sept 9:00–21:00, Oct–June 9:00–18:00, just off harbor at Strand Street, tel. 066/915-2400, www.themountainmanshop.com).

Travel Agency: Maurice O'Connor at Galvin's Travel Agency can book plane tickets, as well as boat rides to France (Mon–Fri 9:30–18:00, Sat 9:30–17:00, closed Sun, John Street, tel. 066/915-1409).

Farmers Market: On most Saturdays (10:00–14:00), local farmers fill the St. James churchyard on Main Street with their fresh produce and homemade marmalade.

SIGHTS AND ACTIVITIES

▲▲The Harry Clark Windows of Diseart—Just behind An Daingean's St. Mary Church stands St. Joseph's Convent and Diseart (dee-SHART), containing a beautiful neo-Gothic chapel built in 1884. The sisters of this order, who came to An Daingean in 1829 to educate local girls, worked heroically during the famine. During Mass in the chapel, the Mother Superior would sit in the covered stall in the rear, while the sisters—filling the carved stalls—chanted responsively.

The chapel was graced in 1922 with 12 windows—the work of Ireland's top stained-glass man, Harry Clark. Long appreciated only by the sisters, these special windows—showing six scenes from the life of Christ—are now open to the public. The convent has become a center for sharing Christian Celtic culture and spirituality (free, Mon–Fri 9:30–13:00 & 14:00–17:00, closed Sat–Sun, tel. 066/915-2476, www.diseart.ie).

Enjoy a meditative 15 minutes following the free audioguide that explains the chapel one window at a time. The scenes (clockwise from the back entrance) are: the visit of the Magi, the Baptism of Jesus, "Let the little children come to me," the Sermon on the Mount, the Agony in the Garden, and Jesus appearing to Mary Magdalene. Each face is lively and animated in the imaginative, devout, medieval, and fun-loving art of Harry Clark, whom locals talk about as if he's the kid next door.

▲**Fungie**—In 1983, a dolphin moved into An Daingean Harbor and became a local celebrity. Fungie (FOON-gee, with a hard *g*) is now the darling of the town's tourist trade and one reason you'll find so many tour buses parked along the harbor. With a close look at Fungie as bait, tour boats are thriving. The hardy little boats motor seven to 40 passengers out to the mouth of the harbor, where they troll around looking for Fungie. You're virtually assured of seeing the dolphin, but you don't pay unless you do (€12, kids-€6, 1-hr trips depart 10:00–19:00 depending on demand, behind TI at Dolphin Trips office, tel. 066/915-2626). To actually swim with Fungie, rent wetsuits at Brosnan's B&B (Cooleen Street, tel. 066/915-1967) and catch the early-morning 8:00–10:00 trip (€50 includes boat trip and wetsuit—unless you've packed your own).

▲**Oceanworld**—The aquarium offers a little peninsula history, 300 different species of fish in thoughtfully described tanks, and the easiest way to see Fungie the dolphin...on video. Walk through the tunnel while fish swim overhead. You'll see local fish as well as a colorful Amazon collection. The aquarium's mission is to teach, and you're welcome to ask questions. The petting pool is fun. Splashing attracts the rays, which are unplugged (€10, families-€27, daily July–Aug 10:00–20:30, May–June and Sept 10:00–18:30, Oct–April 10:00–17:00, cafeteria, just past harbor on west edge of town, tel. 066/915-2111, www.dingle-oceanworld.ie).

▲**Short Harbor Walk from An Daingean**—For an easy stroll along the harbor out of town (and a chance to see Fungie, 90 min round-trip), head east from the roundabout past the Esso station. Just after Bambury's B&B, take a right, following signs to Skelligs Hotel, and go left at the Irish Coast Guard station on the bay. At the beach, climb the steps over the wall and follow the seashore path to the mouth of An Daingean Harbor (marked by a tower—some 19th-century fat cat's folly). Ten minutes beyond that is a lighthouse. This is Fungie's neighborhood. If you see tourist boats out, you're likely to see the dolphin. The trail continues to a dramatic cliff.

The Harbor: The harbor was built on land reclaimed (with imported Dutch expertise) in 1992. The string of old stone shops facing the harbor was the loading station for the narrow-gauge railway that hauled the fish from An Daingean to Tralee (1891–1953). Make a point to walk out to the end of the breakwater—newly paved and illuminated at night. The Eask Tower on the distant hill is a marker that was built in 1847 during the famine as a make-work project. In pre-radar days, it helped ships locate An Daingean's hidden harbor. The fancy mansion across the harbor is Lord Ventry's 17th-century manor house (see "Circular Tour," page 199).

Sailing—The Dingle Marina Centre offers diving, sailing, traditional currach rowing, and a salty little restaurant. Sailors can join the club for a day to sail (€22, July–Aug, tel. 066/915-1984). Currachs—stacked behind the building—are Ireland's traditional lightweight fishing boats, easy to haul and easy to make. Cover a wooden frame with canvas (originally cowhide) and paint with tar—presto.

Horseback Riding—Dingle Horse Riding takes out beginners (€25/hr for a trail ride) and experienced riders on four-hour (€95) and longer six-hour (€130) excursions. Bob along beaches or mountains on an English-style ride (call ahead to book, tel. 066/915-2199, www.dinglehorseriding.com).

Dingle World of Leisure—This is a health club for adults and a good rainy-day option for kids, offering bowling (€18–30/hr depending on time of day), arcades games, a swimming pool, and a children's indoor playground (daily July–Sept 11:00–23:00, Oct–June 11:00–20:00, just off John Street, tel. 066/915-0660, www.dingleworldofleisure.com).

Dingle Pitch & Putt—For 18 scenic holes and a driving range, hike 10 minutes past Oceanworld (€6 includes gear, driving range €6 for 100 balls, April–Oct daily 10:00–20:00, closed Nov–March, over bridge take first left and follow signs, Milltown, tel. 066/915-2020).

Golf—Located out west, near the tip of the An Daingean peninsula in the town of Baile an Fheirtearaigh (9 miles from An Daingean town), Ceann Sibeal/Dingle Links offers a round of golf in a hard-to-beat setting (€50–75 green fees, open daily, tel. 066/915-6255, www.dinglelinks.com).

Shopping—An Daingean is filled with shops showing off local craftsmanship. The **West Kerry Craft Guild**—a co-op selling the work of 15 local artists—is a delight even if you're just browsing. The prices here are very good since you're buying directly from the artists (daily June–Aug 10:00–18:00, Sept–May 11:00–17:00, 18 Main Street, tel. 066/915-2976, www.gailearaibeag.com). The **Niamh Utsch Jewelry** shop on Green Street is much respected for its unique work. **Dingle Crystal,** also on Green Street, features Sean Daly and his Waterford-trained crystal-cutting skills. Sean prides himself on his deeper, sharper design cuts (cutting demonstrations daily, tel. 066/915-1550, www.dinglecrystal.ie). **Lisbeth Mulcahy Weaver,** filled with traditional but stylish woven wear, is also the An Daingean sales outlet of the well-known potter from out on Ceann Sleibhe, or Slea Head (Mon–Fri 9:00–18:00, Sat–Sun 10:00–18:00, Green Street, tel. 066/915-1688).

The Voyage of St. Brendan

It has long been part of Irish lore that St. Brendan the Navigator (A.D. 484–577) and 12 followers sailed from the southwest of Ireland to the "Land of Promise" (what is now North America) in a currach—a wood-frame boat covered with ox hide and tar. According to a 10th-century monk who poetically wrote of the journey, St. Brendan and his crew encountered a paradise of birds, were attacked by a whale, and suffered the smoke of a smelly island in the north before finally reaching their Land of Promise.

The legend and its precisely described locations still fascinate modern readers. A British scholar of navigation, Tim Severin, re-created the entire journey from 1976 to 1977. He and his crew set out from Brendan Creek in County Kerry in a currach. The prevailing winds blew them to the Hebrides, the Faeroe Islands, Iceland, and finally to Newfoundland. While this didn't successfully prove that St. Brendan sailed to North America, it did prove that he could have.

St. Brendan fans have been heartened by an intriguing archaeological find in Connecticut. Called the "Gungywamp," the site includes a double circle of stones and a beehive-like chamber built in the same manner as the stone *clochans* huts on the An Daingean Peninsula. The Gungywamp beehive chamber has been carbon-dated to approximately A.D. 600. Outside the chamber, a stone slab is inscribed with a cross that resembles the unique style of the Irish cross.

According to his 10th-century biographer, "St. Brendan sailed from the Land of Promise home to Ireland. And from that time on, Brendan acted as if he did not belong to this world at all. His mind and his joy were in the delight of heaven."

East of An Daingean Town

▲**Minard Castle**—Three miles southwest of the town of Abhainn an Scail (Annascaul), off the Lios Póil (Lispole) Road, is the largest fortress on the peninsula. Built by the Knights of Kerry in 1551, Minard Castle was destroyed by Cromwell in about 1650. With

its corners undermined by Cromwellian explosives, it looks ready to split—it's no longer safe to enter this teetering ruin.

From the outside, look for the faint scallop in the doorway, the symbol of St. James. Medieval pilgrims would stop here before making a seafaring pilgrimage from An Daingean to St. James' tomb at Santiago de Compostela in northern Spain. Imagine the floor plan of the castle: ground floor for animals and storage; main floor with fireplace; then living-quarters floor; and, on top, the defensive level.

The setting is dramatic, with the Ring of Kerry across the way and Storm Beach below. The beach is notable for its sandstone boulders that fell from the nearby cliffs. Grinding against each other in the wave and tidal action, the boulders eroded into cigar-shaped rocks. Pre-Christian Celts would carry them off and carve them into ogham stones to mark clan boundaries (for more on ogham stones, see page 204).

Next to the fortress, look for the "fairy fort," a Stone-Age fort from about 500 B.C.

▲**Puicin Wedge Tomb**—While pretty obscure, this is worth the trouble for its evocative setting. Above the hamlet of Lios Póil (Lispole) in Doonties, park your car and hike 10 minutes up a ridge. At the summit is a pile of rocks made into a little room with one of the finest views on the peninsula. Beyond the Ring of Kerry you may just make out the jagged Skellig Rock, noted for its sixth-century monastic settlement (see page 175).

Inch Strand—This four-mile sandy beach, shaped like a half moon, was made famous by the movie *Ryan's Daughter*. It's rated a "Blue Flag" beach for its clean water and safe swimming (usually has lifeguard in summer).

NIGHTLIFE

▲▲▲**Music in An Daingean Pubs**—Even if you're not into pubs, take a nap and then give these a whirl. An Daingean is renowned among traditional musicians as a place to get work ("€40 a day, tax-free, plus drink"). The town has piles of pubs. There's music every night and rarely a cover charge. The scene is a decent mix of locals, Americans, and Germans. Music normally starts around 21:30, and the last call for drinks is "half eleven" (23:30), sometimes later on weekends. For a seat near the music, arrive early. If the place is chockablock, power in and find breathing room in

the back. By midnight, the door is usually closed and the chairs are stacked. For more information, see "Traditional Irish Music" on page 38 in the Introduction.

While two pubs, the **Small Bridge Bar** (An Droichead Beag) and **O'Flaherty's,** are the most famous for their good beer and folk music, make a point to wander the town and follow your ear. Smaller pubs may feel a bit foreboding to a tourist, but people—locals as well as travelers—are out for the *craic*. Irish culture is very accessible in the pubs; they're like highly interactive museums waiting to be explored. But if you sit at a table, you'll be left alone. Stand or sit at the bar and you'll be engulfed in conversation with new friends. Have a glass in an empty, no-name pub and chat up the publican. Pubs are no longer smoky, but can be stuffy and hot, so leave your coat home. The more offbeat pubs are more likely to erupt into leprechaun karaoke.

Pub Crawl: The best pub crawl start is along Holyground Street to **O'Flaherty's.** Quietly intense owner Fergus O'Flaherty, a fixture since my first visit to An Daingean, sings and plays a half dozen different instruments during nightly traditional music sessions. His domain has a high ceiling and is dripping in old-time photos and town memorabilia—it's touristy but lots of fun. Moving up Strand Street, find lively **Murphy's,** offering rock as well as ballads and traditional music. A few doors farther down, **John Benny Moriarty's** has dependably good traditional music sessions, with John himself joining in on accordion when he's not pouring pints.

Then head up Green Street. **Dick Mack,** across from the church, is nicknamed "the last pew." This is a tiny leather shop by day, expanding into a pub at night, with several rooms, a fine snug (private booth, originally designed to allow women to drink discreetly), reliably good beer, and strangely fascinating ambience. Notice the Hollywood-type stars on the sidewalk recalling famous visitors. Established in 1899, the grandson of the original Dick Mack now runs the place. A painting in the window shows Dick Mack II with the local gang.

Green Street climbs to Main Street, where two more Dick Mack–type places are filled with locals deep in conversation (but no music): **Foxy John's** (a hardware shop by day) and **O Currain's** (across the street, a small clothing shop by day).

A bit higher up Main Street is **McCarthy's Pub,** a smoke-stained relic. It's less touristy and has occasional traditional music sessions on its little stage. Wander downhill to the **Small Bridge** Bar at the bottom. With live music nightly, it's popular for good reason. While the tourists gather around the music, poke around the back and do an end run around the wall, which leads to a window nook actually closest to the musicians. Occasionally musicians sell CDs of their tunes, which can be a nice keepsake of your time in Ireland.

Off-Season: From October through April, the bands play on, though at fewer pubs: Small Bridge Bar (live music nightly), John Benny Moriarty's (Mon, Wed, Thu), McCarthy's (Fri, Sat), and Murphy's (Sat).

Music Shops: Danlann Gallery sells musical instruments and woodcrafts (Mon–Fri 10:00–18:00, later in summer, "flexible" on weekends, owner makes violins, Green Street). Dingle Bodhrans sells homemade traditional goatskin drums and gives lessons (1-hour lesson-€40, Mon–Sat 10:30–18:00, closed Sun, Green Street, enter red iron gate of small alley opposite church, tel. 087-245-7689, Andrea).

Folk Concerts—Top local musicians offer a quality evening of live, acoustic, classic Irish music in the fine little St. James Church on Main Street (€10 advance purchase, €14 at the door; Mon, Wed, and Fri at 19:30, May–Sept only; mobile 087-982-9728, see sign on church gate or drop by Murphy's Ice Cream shop for details). If you're not a night owl (music in pubs doesn't begin until 21:30) or prefer not to be packed into a pub with the distractions of conversation, then this is your best opportunity to hear Irish traditional music in a more controlled environment.

Dancing—Some pubs host "set dancing" with live music. Your two best possibilities are the Small Bridge Bar or John Benny Moriarty's pub (see above), but ask at the TI for more suggestions.

Theater—An Daingean's great little theater is The Phoenix on Dykegate. Its film club (50–60 locals) meets here Tuesdays year-round at 20:30 for coffee and cookies, followed by a film at 21:00 (€6 for film, anyone is welcome). The leader runs it almost like a religion, with a sermon on the film before he rolls it. The regular film schedule for the week is posted on the door.

SLEEPING

$$$ Heaton's Guesthouse, big, peaceful, and American in its comforts, is on the water just west of town at the end of An Daingean Bay—a five-minute walk past Oceanworld on The Wood. The 16 thoughtfully appointed rooms come with all the amenities (Db-€86–130, suite Db-€130–180, creative breakfasts, parking, The Wood, tel. 066/915-2288, fax 066/915-2324, www .heatonsdingle.com, heatons@iol.ie, Cameron and Nuala Heaton).

$$$ Castlewood House is a palatial refuge playfully competing with Mom and Dad Heaton's place next door. Each of its 12 tasteful rooms has unique furnishings. The breakfast room and patio have wonderful views of An Daingean Harbor (Sb-€60–105, Db-€100–148, Tb-€135–165, parking, The Wood, tel. 066/915-2788, fax 066/915-2110, www.castlewooddingle.com, castlewoodhouse@eircom.net, Brian and Helen Heaton).

$$$ Benners Hotel was the only place in town a hundred years ago. It stands bewildered by the modern world on Main Street, with sprawling public spaces and 52 abundant, overpriced rooms (Db-€200 July–Aug, €160 May–June, €150 Sept–May,

Sleep Code

(€1 = about $1.20, country code: 353, area code: 066)
S = Single, **D** = Double/Twin, **T** = Triple, **Q** = Quad, **b** = bathroom,
s = shower only. Prices vary with the season, with winter
cheap and August tops. Breakfast is included and credit cards
are accepted unless otherwise noted.

To help you easily sort through these listings, I've divided
the rooms into three categories, based on the price for a standard double room with bath:

$$$ **Higher Priced**—Most rooms €100 or more.
$$ **Moderately Priced**—Most rooms between €60–100.
$ **Lower Priced**—Most rooms €60 or less.

discounts on Web site, tel. 066/915-1638, fax 066/915-1412, www
.dinglebenners.com, info@dinglebenners.com).

$$ Greenmount House sits among chilly palm trees in the
countryside at the top of town. A five-minute hike up from the town
center, this guest house commands a fine view of the bay and moun-
tains. John and Mary Curran run one of Ireland's best B&Bs, with
five superb rooms (Db-€75–100—highest price through the sum-
mer) and seven sprawling suites (Db-€100–150) in a modern build-
ing with lavish public areas and breakfast in a solarium (reserve in
advance, no children under age 8, most rooms at ground level, park-
ing, top of John Street, tel. 066/915-1414, fax 066/915-1974, www
.greenmount-house.com, info@greenmount-house.com).

$$ Captain's House B&B is a shipshape place in the town
center, fit for an admiral, with eight classy rooms, peat-fire lounges,
a stay-a-while garden, and a magnificent breakfast in the conserva-
tory. Mary, whose mother ran a guest house before An Daingean
was discovered, loves her work and is very good at it (Sb-€50–60,
Db-€80–100, great suite-€140–160, The Mall, tel. 066/915-1531,
fax 066/915-1079, captigh@eircom.net, Jim and Mary Milhench).

$$ Alpine Guest House looks like a monopoly hotel, but
that means it's comfortable and efficient. Its 13 spacious, bright,
and fresh rooms come with wonderful sheep-and-harbor views, a
cozy lounge, a great breakfast, and friendly owners (Db-€72–95,
Tb-€90–130, prices vary with room size and season, 10 percent
discount with this book through 2006, no smoking, parking, Mail
Road, tel. 066/915-1250, fax 066/915-1966, www.alpineguesthouse
.com, alpinedingle@eircom.net, Paul). Driving into town from
Tralee, you'll see this a block uphill from the An Daingean round-
about and Esso station.

An Daingean Accommodations and Services

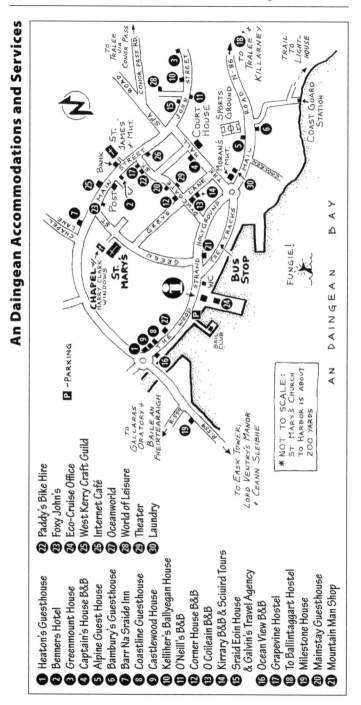

1. Heaton's Guesthouse
2. Benners Hotel
3. Greenmount House
4. Captain's House B&B
5. Alpine Guest House
6. Bambury's Guesthouse
7. Barr Na Sraide Inn
8. Coastline Guesthouse
9. Castlewood House
10. Kelliher's Ballyegan House
11. O'Neill's B&B
12. Corner House B&B
13. O Coileain B&B
14. Kirrary B&B & Sciuird Tours
15. Sraid Eoin House
    & Galvin's Travel Agency
16. Ocean View B&B
17. Grapevine Hostel
18. To Ballintaggart Hostel
19. Milestone House
20. Mainstay Guesthouse
21. Mountain Man Shop

22. Paddy's Bike Hire
23. Foxy John's
24. Eco-Cruise Office
25. West Kerry Craft Guild
26. Internet Café
27. Oceanworld
28. World of Leisure
29. Theater
30. Laundry

$$ Bambury's Guesthouse, big and modern with views of grazing sheep and the harbor, rents 12 airy, comfy rooms (Db-€70–110, prices depend on size and season, family deals; coming in from Tralee it's on your left on Mail Road, 2 blocks before Esso station; tel. 066/915-1244, fax 066/915-1786, www .bamburysguesthouse.com, info@bamburysguesthouse.com).

$$ Milestone House is a 15-minute walk out of town (at mile 0.8 on the "Circular Tour" in this chapter—see page 199). It has warmly decorated rooms, great views of An Daingean Harbor, and an ancient boundary stone in the front yard. Friendly Barbara Carroll is a font of sightseeing tips (Sb-€45–50, Db-€70–75, Tb-€105–115, Qb-€120–140, parking, tel. & fax 066/915-1831, www. iol.ie/~milstone, milestonedingle@eircom.net).

$$ Mainstay Guesthouse is smack dab in the center of town, with 14 modest rooms, a cheery breakfast area, and an inviting back garden (Sb-€48–58, Db-€76–96, Tb-€114–144, non-smoking, tel. 066/915-1598, fax 066/915-2376, www.mainstaydingle.com, info@mainstaydingle.com, Gus and Ruth Cero).

$$ Barr Na Sraide Inn, central and hotelesque, has 26 comfortable rooms (Sb-€40–60, Db-€70–100, Tb-€105–150, family deals, self-service laundry, bar, parking, past McCarthy's pub, Upper Main Street, tel. 066/915-1331, fax 066/915-1446, www .barrnasraide.com, barrnasraide@eircom.net).

$$ Coastline Guesthouse, on the water next to Heaton's Guesthouse (listed above), is a modern place with seven bright, spacious rooms (Db-€76–96, Tb-€100–140, 10 percent discount with this book in 2006—except July and Aug, non-smoking, parking, The Wood, tel. 066/915-2494, fax 066/915-2493, www .coastlinedingle.com, coastlinedingle@eircom.net, Vivienne O'Shea).

$$ Kelliher's Ballyegan House is a big, plain building with six fresh, comfortable rooms on the edge of town and great harbor views (Db-€70, Tb-€100, cash only, non-smoking, parking, Upper John Street, tel. 066/915-1702, Hannah and James Kelliher).

$$ O'Neill's B&B is a homey, friendly place with six decent rooms on a quiet street at the top of town (Db-€70 with this book in 2006, family deals, cash only, strictly non-smoking, parking, John Street, tel. 066/915-1639, oneills@godingle.com, Mary O'Neill).

$$ Corner House B&B is my longtime An Daingean home. It's a simple, traditional place with five large, uncluttered rooms run with a twinkle and a grandmotherly smile by Kathleen Farrell (S-€45, D-€80, T-€100, plenty of plumbing but it's down the hall, cash only, reserve with a phone call and reconfirm a day or two ahead, central as can be on Dykegate Street, tel. 066/915-1516). Mrs. Farrell, one of the original three B&B hostesses in a town now filled with them, is a great storyteller.

$$ Collins B&Bs: The following two B&Bs, which take up a quiet corner in the town center, are run by the same Collins—Coileain in Gaelic—family that does archaeological tours of the peninsula (see "Sciuird Archaeology Tours," page 204). Both offer fine rooms (O Coileain's are a bit bigger), cheap bike rental (€8/day), identical prices (Db-€70–76), and a homey friendliness. **O Coileain B&B** is run by a young family—Rachel, Michael, and their two cute little girls (tel. 066/915-1937, archeo@eircom .net). **Kirrary B&B,** just over the fence, is grandma's place, with a homey charm (good place to rent bikes, tel. 066/915-1606, collinskirrary@eircom.net, Eileen Collins).

$$ Sraid Eoin House offers four modest but pleasant top-floor rooms above Galvin's Travel Agency (Db-€65–70, Tb-€90–100, 10 percent discount with cash and this book in 2006, John Street, tel. 066/915-1409, fax 066/915-2156, sraideoinhouse@hotmail.com, friendly Kathleen and Maurice O'Connor).

$ Ocean View B&B rents three tidy rooms (two with views) in a humble little waterfront row house overlooking the bay (S-€30, D-€50, 5-min walk from center, 100 yards past Oceanworld at 133 The Wood, tel. 066/915-1659, thewood@gofree.indigo.ie, Mrs. Brosnan).

Hostels: **$ Grapevine Hostel** is clean and friendly, quietly yet very centrally located, with a cozy fireplace lounge and a fine members' kitchen. Each four- to eight-bed dorm has its own bathroom. Dorms are coed, but there's a girls-only room (28 beds, €15–17 per person, Db-€40, laundry-€5, open all day, Dykegate Lane, tel. 066/915-1434, www.grapevinedingle.com, hostel@grapevinedingle.com, run by Siobhan—sheh-vahn).

$ Ballintaggart Hostel, a backpackers' complex, is housed in a stylish old manor house used by Protestants during the famine as a soup kitchen (for those hungry enough to renounce Catholicism). It comes complete with laundry service (€8), a classy study, a family room with a fireplace, and a resident ghost (138 beds, €14 in 10-bed dorms, €18 beds in Qb, Db-€52–65, 3- to 6-person family room-€65–75, no breakfast but there's a kitchen, a mile east of town on Tralee Road, tel. 066/915-1454, fax 066/915-2207, www .dingleaccommodation.com, info@dingleaccommodation.com). Ask the Tralee bus to drop you here before arriving in An Daingean. A taxi into An Daingean costs €6.

EATING

For a rustic little village, An Daingean is swimming in good food.

Budget Tips: The **Super Valu** supermarket/department store, at the base of town, has everything and stays open late (Mon–Sat 8:00–21:00, Sun 8:00–19:00, daily until 22:00 in July–Aug).

An Daingean Restaurants and Pubs

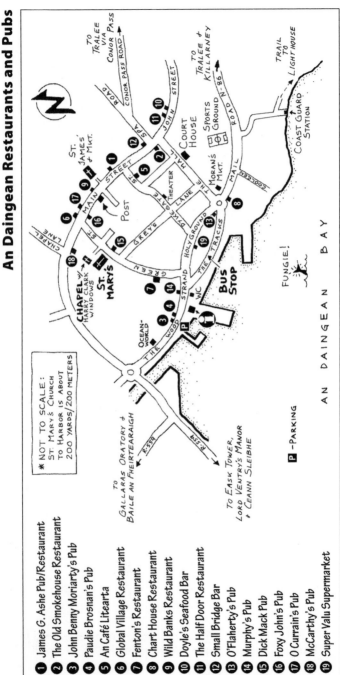

1 James G. Ashe Pub/Restaurant
2 The Old Smokehouse Restaurant
3 John Benny Moriarty's Pub
4 Paudie Brosnan's Pub
5 An Café Litearta
6 Global Village Restaurant
7 Fenton's Restaurant
8 Chart House Restaurant
9 Wild Banks Restaurant
10 Doyle's Seafood Bar
11 The Half Door Restaurant
12 Small Bridge Bar
13 O'Flaherty's Pub
14 Murphy's Pub
15 Dick Mack Pub
16 Foxy John's Pub
17 O Currain's Pub
18 McCarthy's Pub
19 Super Valu Supermarket

Smaller groceries, such as **Centra** on Main Street (Mon–Sat 8:00–21:00, Sun 8:00–18:00), are scattered throughout the town. Consider a grand-view picnic out on the end of the newer pier (as you face the harbor, it's the pleasure-boat pier on your right).

Fancy restaurants serve early-bird specials from 18:00 to 19:00. Many "cheap and cheery" places close at 18:00, and pubs do good €12–15 dinners all over town. Most pubs stop serving food around 21:00 (to make room for their beer drinkers).

James G. Ashe Pub and Restaurant, an old-fashioned joint, is popular with locals for traditional Irish food at great prices. Try their beef-and-Guinness stew (€10–15 lunches, €15–22 dinners, lunch 12:00–16:00, dinner 18:00–21:00, Main Street, tel. 066/915-0989).

The Old Smokehouse, serving happy locals in a rustic woody setting, offers the best moderate-value meals in town, with fresh An Daingean Bay fish and good vegetables (lunch daily 12:30–14:30, €16–27 dinner plates daily 18:00–21:30, corner of Main Street and The Mall, tel. 066/915-1061).

John Benny Moriarty's is a waterfront pub dishing up traditional Irish fare (food daily 12:30–21:30, music after 21:30, The Pier). **Paudie Brosnan's** pub, a few doors down, has fresh mussels.

An Café Litearta, a likeable eatery hidden behind an inviting bookstore, serves tasty soup and sandwiches to a good-natured crowd of Gaelic-speakers (daily 10:00–18:00, tel. 066/915-2204, Dykegate Street).

At the **Global Village Restaurant,** Martin Bealin concocts his favorite dishes, gleaned from his travels around the world. It's an eclectic, healthy, meat-eaters' place popular with locals for its interesting cuisine (€18–25 dinners, good salads and great Thai curry, July–Aug daily 17:00–21:30; Sept–June Thu–Tue 18:00–21:30, closed Wed, top of Main Street, tel. 066/915-2325 or mobile 087-917-7700).

Fenton's is a good place for seafood meals with a memorable apple-and-berry-crumble dessert (€22–32 main courses, 3-course meals for €28, early-bird specials before 19:00, Tue–Sun 18:00–21:30, closed Mon, reservations smart, on Green Street down the hill below the church, tel. 066/915-2172 or mobile 087-247-2487).

The **Stone House Restaurant,** on the Ceann Sleibhe (Slea Head) loop, offers good meals in a great atmosphere. It's a good choice for those looking for an out-of-the-way dinner and a 20-minute scenic drive. It's right across the road from the Dunbeg fort at mile 12.5 on the "Circular Tour"—see page 200 (open Wed–Mon 12:30–15:30 for €8–12 lunches and 18:30–22:00 for €17–23 dinners, closed Tue, dinner reservations essential, tel. 066/915-9970).

All Roads Lead to An Daingean

The western half of the An Daingean Peninsula is part of the Gaeltacht, where locals speak the Irish (Gaelic) language. In an effort to ward off English-language encroachment, all road sign place names were controversially changed to Irish in the spring of 2005. Note that many businesses in An Daingean town are keeping easy-to-pronounce "Dingle" in their names (to make it easier for tourists), and the rest of Ireland outside of the Gaeltacht regions still refer to this region as Dingle. But when you're in the Gaeltacht, it's helpful to know the Gaelic names.

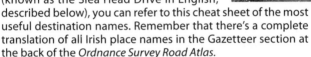

As you travel along Ceann Sleibhe (known as the Slea Head Drive in English; described below), you can refer to this cheat sheet of the most useful destination names. Remember that there's a complete translation of all Irish place names in the Gazetteer section at the back of the *Ordnance Survey Road Atlas.*

Gaelic Name	Pronounced	English Name
An Daingean	*on DANG-un*	Dingle
Ceann Tra'	*k'yown (rhymes with crown) thraw*	Ventry
Ceann Sleibhe	*k'yown SHLAY-veh*	Slea Head
Dun Chaoin	*doon qween*	Dunquin
Na Blascaodai	*nuh BLAS-kud-ee*	Blasket Islands
An Blascoad Mór	*on BLAS-kade moor*	Great Blasket Island
Baile an Fheirtearaigh	*BALL-yuh on ur-TEER-ig*	Ballyferriter
Mainistir Riaise	*MON-ish-ter REE-isk*	Reasc Monastery
Gallaras	*GAHL-russ*	Gallarus
Cill Mhaoilcheadair	*kill moyle-KAY-dir*	Kilmalkedar
Abhainn an Scail	*ow'een on skahl*	Anascaul
Tra' Li	*thraw lee*	Tralee

An Daingean's Four Fancy Restaurants

Chart House Restaurant serves contemporary cuisine with a menu dictated by what's fresh and seasonal. Settle back into the sharp, clean, lantern-lit harborside ambience (€17–28 dinners, June–Sept daily 18:30–22:00, Oct–May closed Tue, at roundabout at base of town, tel. 066/915-2255).

Wild Banks Restaurant is named for nearby fishing grounds, and Chef Laura Walker does a great job preparing the local catch. There's a nice wine selection, and the white-chocolate crème brûlée dessert gets raves (€19–26 dinners, €24 early-bird 3-course meals before 20:00, Thu–Tue 18:00–21:30, closed Wed, halfway down Main Street, tel. 066/915-2888).

Two of An Daingean's long-established top-notch restaurants—**Doyle's Seafood Bar** (more famous, with excellent seafood and service, tel. 066/915-1174) and **The Half Door** (heartier portions, also open for lunch Mon–Sat 12:30–14:00, tel. 066/915-1600)—are neighbors on John Street. They're in the guidebooks for good reason, and therefore filled with tourists. Both have the same dinner hours (Mon–Sat 18:00–21:30, closed Sun), offer an early-bird special (2-course meal-€26, 18:00–19:00), and take reservations (wise).

TRANSPORTATION CONNECTIONS

The nearest train station is 30 miles away in Tralee (Tra' Li in Gaelic).

From An Daingean by Bus to: Galway (5/day, 6.5 hrs), **Dublin** (4/day, 8 hrs, transfer in Tralee), **Rosslare** (2/day, 9 hrs), **Tralee** (6/day, 75 min, €9 one-way, €15 round-trip); fewer departures on Sundays. Most bus trips out of An Daingean require at least one or two (easy) transfers. An Daingean has no bus station and only one bus stop, on the waterfront behind the Super Valu supermarket (bus info tel. 01/830-2222 or Tralee station at 066/712-3566). For more information, see "Transportation Connections" in Tralee, page 211.

By Car: Drivers choose two roads into town: the easy southern route or the much more dramatic, scenic, and treacherous Conor Pass (see "Transportation Connections" in Tralee, page 212). It's 30 miles from Tralee either way.

An Daingean Peninsula Circular Tour

A sight worth ▲▲▲, the An Daingean Peninsula loop trip is about 30 miles (47 km) long and must be driven in a clockwise direction. It's easy by car, or it's a demanding four hours by bike—if you don't stop. Bikers should plan on an early start (preferably by 9:00) to allow for enough sightseeing and lunch/rest time.

While you can take the basic guided tour of the peninsula

An Daingean Peninsula Circle Tour

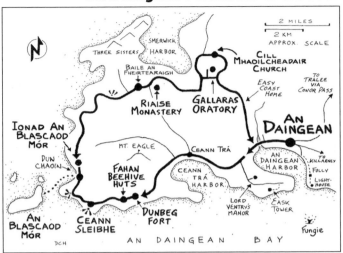

(see "Tours," page 204), the route described in this section makes it unnecessary. A fancy map is also unnecessary with my instructions. I've keyed in distances to help locate points of interest. Just like Ireland's speed-limit signs, Ireland's car speedometers and odometers have gone 100 percent metric in recent years. I've given distances below in kilometers so you can follow along with your rental-car odometer. Most Irish odometers give distances to tenths of a kilometer right above the kilometer total.

If you're driving, as you leave An Daingean, check your odometer (reset to zero if you can) at Oceanworld. Even if you get off track or are biking, derive distances between points from my kilometer listings. To get the most out of your circle trip, read through this entire section before departing. Then go step by step (staying on R559 and following the brown *Ceann Sleibhe/Slea Head Drive* signs). Roads are very congested in August.

The An Daingean Peninsula is 10 miles wide and runs 40 miles from Tralee to Ceann Sleibhe. The top of its mountainous spine is Mount Brandon—at 3,130 feet, the second-tallest mountain in Ireland. While only tiny villages lie west of An Daingean town, the peninsula is home to 500,000 sheep.

Leave An Daingean town west along the waterfront (0.0 km at Oceanworld). There's an eight-foot tide here. The seaweed was used to make formerly worthless land arable. (Seaweed is a natural source of potash—organic farming before it was trendy.) Across the water, the fancy Milltown House B&B (with flags) was Robert Mitchum's home for a year during the filming of *Ryan's Daughter*. Look for the narrow mouth of this blind harbor (where Fungie frolics) and the Ring of Kerry beyond that. An Daingean Bay is so hidden, ships needed the tower (1847) on the hill to find its mouth.

0.7 km: At the roundabout, turn left over the bridge. The hardware-store building on the right was a corn-grinding mill in the 18th century.

1.3 km: The Milestone B&B is named for the stone pillar (*gallaun* in Gaelic) in its front yard. This may have been a prehistoric grave or a boundary marker between two tribes. The stone goes down as far as it sticks up. The peninsula, literally an open-air museum, is dotted with more than 2,000 such monuments dating from the Neolithic Age (4000 b.c.) through early Christian times. Another stone pillar stands in the field across the street in the direction of the yellow manor house of Lord Ventry (in the distance).

Lord Ventry, whose family came to An Daingean as post–Cromwellian War landlords in 1666, built this mansion in about 1750. Today it houses an all-Gaelic boarding school for 140 high-school girls.

As you drive past the Ventry estate, you'll pass palms, magnolias, and exotic flora introduced to An Daingean by Lord Ventry. The Gulf Stream is the source of the mild climate (it never snows), which supports subtropical plants. Consequently, fuchsias—imported from Chile and spreading like weeds—line the roads all over the peninsula and redden the countryside June–September. And over 100 inches of rain a year gives this area its "40 shades of green."

4.6 km: Stay off the "soft margin" as you enjoy views of Ceann Tra' Bay, its four-mile-long beach (to your right as you face the water), and distant Skellig Michael, which you'll see all along this part of the route. Skellig Michael—jutting up like France's Mont St. Michel—contains the rocky remains of an sixth-century monastic settlement (see page 175). Next to it is a smaller island, Little Skellig—a breeding ground for gannets (seagull-like birds with 6-foot wingspans). In 1866, the first transatlantic cable was laid from nearby Valentia island to Newfoundland. It was in use until 1965. Mount Eagle (1,660 feet), rising across the bay, marks the end of Ireland. In the village of Ceann Tra' (Ventry in English), Gaelic is the first language. The large hall at the end of the village is used as a classroom where big-city students come on field trips to be immersed in the Gaelic language.

5.2 km: The rushes on either side of the road are the kind used to make the local thatched roofs. Thatching, which nearly died out because of the fire danger, is more popular now that anti-flame treatments are available. It's not the cheap alternative, however; it's expensive to pay the few qualified craftsman thatchers that remain in Ireland. Black-and-white magpies fly.

8.6 km: The Irish football star Paidi O Se (Paddy O'Shea) is a household name in Ireland. He won eight all-Ireland football titles for Kerry as a player. He then trained the Kerry team for many years and now runs the pub on the left. (Easy beach access from here.)

9.2 km: The blue house hiding in the trees 100 yards off the road on the left (view through the white gate, harder to see in summer when foliage is thickest) was kept cozy by Tom Cruise and Nicole Kidman during the filming of *Far and Away*.

10.7 km: *Taisteal go Mall* means "go slowly"; there's a red-colored, two-room schoolhouse on the right (20 students, 2 teachers). On the left is the small Celtic and Prehistoric Museum, a strange private collection of prehistoric artifacts with no real connection to An Daingean (overpriced at €4, daily 10:00–18:00).

11.1 km: The circular mound on the right is a late Stone Age ring fort. In 500 B.C., it was a petty Celtic chieftain's headquarters, a stone-and-earth stockade filled with little stone houses. These survived untouched through the centuries because of superstitious beliefs that they were "fairy forts." While this is unexcavated, recent digging has shown that people have lived on this peninsula since 4000 B.C.

11.7 km: Look ahead up Mount Eagle at the patchwork of stone-fenced fields.

12.5 km: Dunbeg Fort, a series of defensive ramparts and ditches around a central *clochan*, though ready to fall into the sea, is open to tourists. There are no carvings to be seen, but the small *(beg)* fort *(dun)* is dramatic (€2.50, daily 9:30–19:00, May–Aug open until 20:00, descriptive handout). Forts like this are the most important relics left from Ireland's Iron Age (500 B.C.–A.D. 500). Since erosion will someday take this fort, it has been excavated.

Along the road, you'll see a new stone-roofed house built to blend in with the landscape and the region's ancient rock-slab architecture (A.D. 2000). It's the Stone House Restaurant, serving good lunches (daily 12:30–15:30 and dinners 18:30–22:00, tel. 066/915-9970).

12.6 km: Just 50 yards up the hill is a cottage abandoned by a family named Kavanaugh 150 years ago during the famine. It still contains their original furniture. Gabriel Kavanaugh proudly displays his Kerry livestock in an adjacent pen, including some local red deer—once plentiful, but now rare (€3, May–Sept daily 9:30–18:00, tel. 066/915-6241).

13.4 km: A group of beehive huts, or *clochans,* is a short walk uphill (€2, daily 9:30–19:00, WC). These mysterious stone igloos, which cluster together within a circular wall, are a better sight than the similar group of beehive huts a mile down the road. Look over the water for more Skellig views.

Farther on, you'll ford a stream. There has never been a bridge here; this bit of road—nicknamed the "upside-down bridge"—was designed as a ford.

14.9 km: Pull off to the left at this second group of beehive huts. Look downhill at the rocky field—in the movie *Far and Away*, that's where Lord Ventry evicted (read: torched) peasants from their cottage. Even without Hollywood, this is a bleak and god-forsaken land. Look above at the patches of land slowly made into farmland by the inhabitants of this westernmost piece of Europe. Rocks were cleared and piled into fences. Sand and seaweed were laid on the clay, and in time it was good for grass. The created land, if at all tillable, was generally used for growing potatoes; otherwise it was only good for grazing. Much has fallen out of use now. Look across the bay at the Ring of Kerry in the distance and ahead at the Na Blascaodai (Blasket Islands in English).

16.1 km: At Ceann Sleibhe (Slea Head), marked by a crucifix, a pullout, and great views of the Na Blascaodai (described on page 205), you turn the corner on this tour. On stormy days, the waves are "racing in like white horses."

16.9 km: Pull into the little parking lot (at *Dun Chaoin* sign) to view the Na Blascaodai and Dunmore Head (the westernmost

point in Europe) and to review the road-side map (which traces your route) posted in the parking lot. The scattered village of Dun Chaoin (Dunquin in English) has many ruined rock homes abandoned during the famine. Some are fixed up, as this is a popular place these days for summer homes. You can see more good examples of land reclamation, patch by patch, climbing up the hillside. Mount Eagle was the first bit of land Charles Lindberg saw after crossing the Atlantic on his way to Paris in 1927. Villagers here were as excited as he was—they had never seen anything so big in the air. Ahead, down a road on the left, a plaque celebrates the 30th anniversary of the filming of *Ryan's Daughter*.

19.3 km: Na Blascaodai's residents had no church or cemetery on the island. This was their cemetery. The famous Blascaod storyteller Peig Sayers (1873–1958) is buried in the center. At the next intersection, drive down the little lane that leads left (100 yards) to a small stone marker (hiding in the grass on the left) commemorating the 1588 shipwreck of the *Santa Maria de* *la Rosa* of the Spanish Armada. Below that is the often-tempestuous Dun Chaoin Harbor, from which the Na Blascaodai ferry departs. Island farmers—who on a calm day could row across in 20 minutes—would dock here and hike 12 miles into An Daingean to sell their produce. When transporting sheep, farmers would lash the sheep's pointy little hoofs together and place them carefully upside down in the currach—so they wouldn't puncture the frail little craft's canvas skin.

19.4 km: Back on the main road, follow signs to the Ionad An Blascaod Mór (Great Blasket Centre).

22.3 km: Leave the Ceann Sleibhe/Slea Head Road left for the Ionad An Blascaod Mór (described on page 206).

23.1 km: Back at the turnoff, head left (sign to Louis Mulcahy Pottery).

24.5 km: Passing land that was never reclaimed, think of the work it took to pick out the stones, pile them into fences, and bring up sand and seaweed to nourish the clay and make soil for growing potatoes. Look over the water to the island aptly named the "Sleeping Giant"—see his hand resting happily on his beer belly.

24.9 km: The view is spectacular. Ahead, on the right, study the top fields, untouched since the planting of 1845, when the potatoes didn't grow, but rotted in the ground. The faint vertical ridges of the potato beds can still be seen—a reminder of the famine (easier to see a bit later). Before the famine, 40,000 people lived on this peninsula. After the famine, the population was so small that there was never again a need to farm so high up. Today, only 10,000 live on the peninsula. Coast downhill. The distant hills are crowned by lookout forts built back when Britain expected Napoleon to invade.

30 km: The town of Baile an Fheirtearaigh (Ballyferriter), established by a Norman family in the 12th century, is the largest on this side of An Daingean. The pubs serve grub, and the old schoolhouse is a museum (€2.50, May–Sept daily 10:00–18:00, closed off-season, tel. 066/915-6333). The early-Christian cross next to the schoolhouse looks real. Tap it...it's fiberglass—a prop from *Ryan's Daughter.*

31.4 km: At the T-junction, signs direct you to An Daingean (11 km) either way. Go left, via Gallaras (and still following Ceann Sleibhe/Slea Head Way). Take a right over the bridge, still following signs to Gallaras.

32 km: Just beyond the bridge, you'll pass the Tigh Bhric pub and market (great pub-grub lunches, tel. 066/915-6325). Just a few yards before the sign to Mainistir Riaise (Raise Monastery), detour right up the lane. After 0.3 km (up the unsigned turnout on your right), you'll find the scant remains of the walled Raise Monastery (dating from the 6th–12th centuries). The inner wall divided the community into sections for prayer and business (cottage industries helped support the monastery). In 1975, only the stone pillar was visible, as the entire site was buried. The layer of black felt marks where the original rocks stop and the excavators' reconstruction begins. The stone pillar is Celtic (c. 500 B.C.). When the Christians arrived in the fifth century, they didn't throw out the Celtic society. Instead, they carved a Maltese-type cross over the Celtic scrollwork. The square building was an oratory (church—you'll see an intact oratory at the next stop). The round buildings would have been *clochans*—those stone igloo-type dwellings. One of the cottage industries operated by the monastery was a double-duty kiln. Just outside the wall (opposite the oratory, past the duplex *clochan,* at the bottom end), find a stone hole with a passage facing the southwest wind. This was the kiln—fanned by the wind, it was used for cooking and drying grain. Locals would bring their grain to be dried and ground, and the monks would keep a 10 percent tithe. With the arrival of the Normans in the 12th century, these small religious communities were replaced by relatively big-time state and church governments.

32.8 km: Return to the main road, continue to the right.

34.6 km: At the big hotel (Smerwick Harbor), turn left following the sign to Gallaras (Gallarus Oratory in English).

35.6 km: At the big building (with camping sign), go right and follow the sign for the oratory where you'll find a small tourist center with a coffee shop, WC, and video theater. For €3 you get a 17-minute video overview of An Daingean Peninsula's historic sights (daily May–Sept 9:00–21:00, Oct–April 9:00–19:00).

The Gallaras Oratory, built about 1,300 years ago, is one of Ireland's best-preserved early-Christian churches. Shaped like an upturned boat, its finely fitted drystone walls are still waterproof. Notice the holes once used to secure covering at the door and the fine alternating stonework on the corners.

From the oratory, return to the main road and continue, following the brown *Ceann Sleibhe/ Slea Head Drive* sign.

37.7 km: Turn right at the fork and immediately take a right (at the blue shop sign) at the next fork. Pass a 19th-century church on the right (it's been converted into a private residence).

39.5 km: The ruined church of Cill Mhaoilcheadair (Kilmalkedar in English) was the Norman center of worship for this end of the peninsula. It was built when England replaced the old monastic settlements in an attempt to centralize their rule. The 12th-century Irish Romanesque church is surrounded

by a densely populated graveyard (which has risen noticeably above the surrounding fields over the centuries). In front of the church, you'll find the oldest medieval tombs, a stately early Christian cross (substantially buried by the rising graveyard and therefore oddly proportioned), and a much older ogham stone. This stone, which had already stood here 900 years when the church was built, is notched with the mysterious Morse code–type ogham script used from the third to seventh centuries. It marked a grave, indicating this was a pre-Christian holy spot. The hole was drilled through the top of the stone centuries ago as a place where people would come to seal a deal—standing on the graves of their ancestors and in front of the house of God, they'd "swear to God" by touching thumbs through this stone. You can still use this to renew your marriage vows (free, B.Y.O. spouse). The church fell into ruin during the Reformation. As Catholic worship went underground until the early 19th century, Cill Mhaoilcheadair was never rebuilt.

40.2 km: Continue uphill, overlooking the water. You'll pass another "fairy fort" (Ciher Dorgan) on the right dating back to 1000 B.C. (free, go through the rusty "kissing gate").

41.7 km: At the crest of the hill, enjoy a three-mile coast back into An Daingean town (in the direction of the Eask Tower).

46.3 km: *Tog Bog E* means "take it easy." At the T-junction, turn left. Then turn right at the roundabout.

47.5 km: You're back into An Daingean town. Well done.

TOURS

▲▲**Sciuird Archaeology Tours**—Sciuird (SCREW-id, Irish for "excursion") tours are offered by a father-son team with An Daingean history—and a knack for sharing it—in their blood. Tim Collins, a retired An Daingean police officer, and his son Michael give serious 2.5-hour minibus tours (€20, departing at 10:30 and 14:00, depending upon demand). Drop by the Kirrary B&B (at Dykegate and Grey's Lane) or call 066/915-1606 to put your name on the list. Call early. Tours fill quickly in summer. Off-season (Oct–April), you may have to call back to see if the necessary six people signed up to make a bus go. While skipping the folk legends and the famous sights (such as Ceann Sleibhe, or Slea Head in English), your guide will drive down tiny farm roads (the Gaelic word for road literally means "cow path"), over hedges, and up ridges to hidden Celtic forts, mysterious stone tombs, and forgotten castles with sweeping seaside views. The running commentary gives an intimate peek into the history of An Daingean and their sound system allows you to hear clearly, no matter where you sit. They do two completely different tours: west (Gallaras Oratory) and east (Minard Castle and a wedge tomb). I enjoyed both. Dress for the weather. In a gale storm with horizontal winds, Tim kept saying, "You'll survive it."

More Minibus Tours—Moran's Tour, which does a quickie minibus tour around the peninsula, offers meager narration and a short stop at the Gallaras Oratory (€17 to Ceann Sleibhe, normally May–Sept at 10:00 and 14:00 from An Daingean TI, 2.5 hrs; Moran's is at Esso station at roundabout, tel. 066/915-1155 or mobile 087-275-3333). There are usually enough seats, though it's best to book a day ahead. But if no one shows up, consider a private Moran taxi trip around the peninsula (€70 for 4 people, cabbie narrates 2.5-hour ride).

Eco-Cruises—Dingle Marine Eco Tours offers a 2.5-hour birds-and-rocks boat tour of the peninsula. The guided tour sails either east toward Minard Castle or west toward the Na Blascaodai (€30, runs April–Sept only, departs 16:00 weather permitting, office around corner from TI, tel. 066/915-0768).

Na Blascaodai (Blasket Islands)

This rugged group of six islands off the tip of An Daingean Peninsula seems particularly close to the soul of Ireland. The population of An Blascaod Mór (Great Blasket Island), home to as many as 160 people, dwindled until the government moved the last handful of residents to the mainland in 1953. Life here was hard. Each family had a cow, a few sheep, and a plot of potatoes. They cut their peat from the high ridge and harvested fish from the sea. There was no priest, pub, or doctor. These people formed the most traditional Irish community of the 20th century—the symbol

of antique Gaelic culture.

A special closeness to an island—combined with a knack for vivid storytelling—is inspirational. From this primitive but proud fishing/farming community came three writers of international repute whose Gaelic work—basically tales of life on An Blascaod Mór—is translated into many languages. You'll find *Peig* (by Peig Sayers), *Twenty Years a-Growing* (Maurice O'Sullivan), and *The Islander* (Thomas O'Crohan) in shops everywhere.

In the summer, there's a café and hostel (open May–Sept, mobile 086-852-2321) on An Blascaod Mór, but it's little more than a ghost town overrun with rabbits on a peaceful, grassy, three-mile-long poem.

Getting to the Na Blascaodai

The 40-passenger Na Blascaodai ferry runs hourly, and in summer, every half hour, depending on weather and demand (€20 round-trip, April–Sept 10:00–17:00, no boats Oct–March). There may be a bus from An Daingean town to Dun Chaoin—leaving in the morning and picking up in the late afternoon—coordinated with the ferry schedule (also €17 taxi service by Moran, tel. 066/915-1155; Dun Chaoin ferry tel. 066/915-6422 or 066/915-4864). Dun Chaoin has a fine hostel (tel. 066/915-6121).

In summer, a fast 12-passenger boat called the *Peig Sayers* runs between An Daingean town and  the Na Blascaodai. The ride (which may include a quick look at Fungie the dolphin) traces the spectacular coastline all the way to Ceann Sleibhe (Slea Head), in a boat designed to slice expertly through the ocean chop. Because of the tricky landing at An Blascaod Mór's primitive and tiny boat ramp, any substantial swell can make actually going ashore impossible (€30 same-day round-trip, departs from the sailing pier in An Daingean at 9:00, 11:00, 13:00, and 15:00, includes 40-min ride with free time to explore island; or €80 overnight trip, includes dinner, a bed in the island's hostel, and breakfast; for info, call Mary at 066/915-1344 or mobile 087-672-6100). The fast boat called *Loch an Iasc* offers similar service from An Daingean (tel. 066/915-0678 or mobile 086-254-7512).

▲▲**Ionad An Blascaod Mór (Great Blasket Centre)**—This state-of-the-art Blascaod and Gaelic heritage center gives visitors the best look possible at the language, literature, and way of life of Na Blascaodai's inhabitants. See the fine 20-minute video (shows on the half hour), hear the sounds, read the poems, browse through old photos, and then gaze out the big windows at those rugged islands and imagine. Even if you never got past limericks, the poetry of these people—so pure and close to each other and nature—will have you dipping your pen into the cry of the birds (€3.50, covered by Heritage Card—see page 4, Easter–Oct daily 10:00–18:00, July–Aug until 19:00, closed Nov–Easter, cafeteria, on the mainland facing the islands, well-signposted, tel. 066/915-6444). Visit this center before visiting the islands.

Tralee

While Killarney is the tour-bus capital of County Kerry, Tralee (Tra' Li in Irish Gaelic) is its true leading city. Except for the tourist complex around the TI and during a few festivals, Tralee feels like a bustling Irish town. A little outdoor market combusts on The Square (Thu–Sat).

Tralee's famous Rose of Tralee International Festival, usually held in mid-August, is a celebration of arts and music, culminating in the election of the Rose of Tralee—the most beautiful woman at the festival. While the rose garden in the Castle Gardens surrounding the TI is in bloom from summer through October, Tralee's finest roses are going about their lives in the busy streets of this workaday town.

ORIENTATION

(area code: 066)
For the tourist, the heart of Tralee is Ashe Memorial Hall, housing the TI and the Kerry the Kingdom museum, located near the rose garden and surrounded by the city park. Beyond the park is the Aqua Dome and steam railway that, if you were here 50 years ago, would chug-chug you to An Daingean. Today, it goes only to the touristy windmill.

Tourist Information
The TI is hidden under the east end of Ashe Memorial Hall, which also houses the Kerry the Kingdom museum (TI open July–Aug Mon–Sat 9:00–19:00, Sun 9:00–18:00; May–June Mon–Sat 9:00–18:00, closed Sun; Sept–April Mon–Sat 9:00–17:00, closed Sun; also closed Sat in Jan–Feb, tel. 066/712-1288).

Arrival in Tralee
From the train and bus station (both are located in the same building, with bike rental available), the Ashe Memorial Hall is a 10-minute walk through the center of town. Exit the station right, take a near-immediate left on Edward Street, then turn right on

Tralee

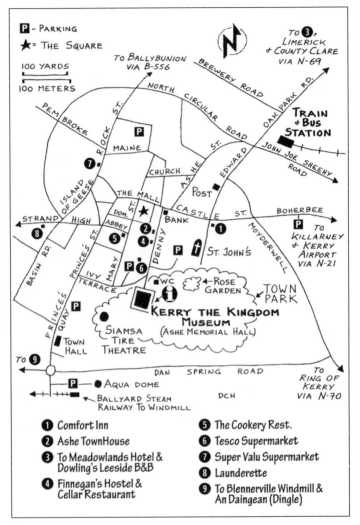

P - Parking
★ = The Square

1 Comfort Inn
2 Ashe TownHouse
3 To Meadowlands Hotel & Dowling's Leeside B&B
4 Finnegan's Hostel & Cellar Restaurant
5 The Cookery Rest.
6 Tesco Supermarket
7 Super Valu Supermarket
8 Launderette
9 To Blennerville Windmill & An Daingean (Dingle)

Castle Street and left on Denny. The hall is at the end of Denny. Drivers should knock around the town center until they find a sign to the TI. Parking on the street requires a disk (€1.20/hr, sold at TI and newsstands—have them date it for you—or from exact-change machines on the street).

Helpful Hints

Post Office: It's on Edward Street (Mon–Fri 9:00–17:30, Sat 9:00–13:00, closed Sun).

Laundry: The launderette on Strand Street charges €10 for an average load (Mon–Sat 9:30–18:30, closed Sun, 103 Strand Street).

Taxis: Try Speedy Cab (tel. 066/712-7411) or Behan Cab (tel. 066/712-6296).

Day Trips from Tralee: For those without their own wheels, **An Daingean** town is an easy day trip from Tralee in summer. Bus Eireann departs from the Tralee bus and train station at 9:00, putting you in An Daingean at 10:15; the bus returns from An Daingean at 16:00, getting you back to Tralee at 17:15 (June–mid-Sept only). You can also take a blitz bus tour of the **Ring of Kerry:** Bus Eireann departs the Tralee bus station at 7:50, drives the N70 Ring route, and gets you back to Tralee at 13:45 (runs late June–early Sept, stops only to off-load and pick-up, no sightseeing stops en route).

SIGHTS

▲▲**Kerry the Kingdom**—This is the place to learn about life in Kerry. The museum has three parts: Kerry slide show, museum, and medieval-town walk. Get in the mood by relaxing for 15 minutes through the Enya-style, continuous slideshow of Kerry's spectacular scenery, then wander through 7,000 years of Kerry history in the museum (well described, no need for free headphones). The Irish say that when a particularly stupid guy moved from Cork to Kerry, he raised the average IQ in both counties—but this museum is pretty well-done. It starts with good background on the archaeological sites of An Daingean and goes right up to a video showing highlights of the Kerry football team (a fun look at Irish football—more like rugby than soccer). The lame finale is a stroll back in time on a 1450 re-creation of Tralee's Main Street (€8, June–Aug daily 9:30–17:30; April–May and Sept–Dec Tue–Sat 9:30–-17:00, closed Sun–Mon; Jan–March Tue–Fri 10:00–16:30, closed Sat–Mon, tel. 066/712-7777, www.kerrymuseum.ie). The Café Park Gate makes a handy basic lunch stop (under Ashe Memorial Hall, beside TI, same hours). Before leaving, horticulture enthusiasts will want to ramble through the rose garden in the adjacent park.

Blennerville Windmill—On the edge of Tralee, just off the An Daingean road, spins a restored mill originally built in 1800. Its eight-minute video tells the story of the windmill, which ground grain to feed Britain as the country steamed into the Industrial Age (€5 gets you a 1-room emigration exhibit, the video, and a peek at the spartan interior of the working windmill, April–Oct daily 9:30–17:30, closed Nov–March, tel. 066/712-1064).

A restored narrow-gauge steam railway runs hourly between Tralee's Ballyard Station (near the Aqua Dome swim center) and the windmill (€5 round-trip, 15 min each way, tel. 066/712-1064). In the 19th century, Blennerville was a major port for America-bound emigrants. It was also the home port where the *Jeannie Johnston* was built. This modern-day replica of a 19th-century ship is now sailing the world, explaining the Irish emigrant experience.

Siamsa Tíre Theatre—The National Folk Theater of Ireland, Siamsa Tíre (shee-EM-sah TEE-rah), stages two-hour dance and theater performances based on Gaelic folk traditions. The songs are in Irish, but there's no dialogue (€19.50, April–Oct Mon–Sat at 20:30, next to Kingdom of Kerry building in park, tel. 066/712-3055, www.siamsatire.com, siamsaboxoffice@eircom.net).

Swimming—The Aqua Dome is a modern-yet-fortified swim center—the largest indoor water world in Ireland—at the An Daingean end of town, near the Ashe Memorial Hall. Families enjoy the huge slide, wave pool, and other wet amusements (adults-€10, kids-€9, locker-€1, bring your own towels, July–Aug Mon–Fri 10:00–22:00, Sat–Sun 11:00–20:00, shorter hours off-season, tel. 066/712-8899 or 066/712-9150).

Music and Other Distractions—Tralee has several fine pubs within a few blocks of each other (on Castle Street and Rock Street) offering live traditional music most evenings. There's greyhound racing (Fri–Sat year-round plus Tue in summer, 20:00–22:15, ten 30-second races every 15 min, 10-min walk from station or town center, tel. 066/718-0008). Entry to the track costs €7—plus what you lose gambling. At just about any time of day, you can drop into a betting office to check out the local gambling scene.

SLEEPING

(€1 = about $1.20, country code: 353, area code: 066)
The Comfort, Ashe, and Finnegan's accommodations are central. Meadowlands and Dowling's Leeside B&B are across the street from each other, a 10-minute walk from the train station (take Oakpark Road) or a €4 cab ride.

$$$ Meadowlands is a classy 58-room guest house with a bar that serves great pub meals. If you want to splurge in Tralee, do it here (Db-€160–200, suites-€250–300, parking, Oakpark Road, tel. 066/718-0444, fax 066/718-0964, www.meadowlands-hotel .com, info@meadowlandshotel.com).

$$ Comfort Inn has 45 predictable quality rooms in the center of town. They charge by the room, making triples and family quads a good deal (April–Sept Db/Tb/Qb-€69–99, a bit more on festival or holiday dates, cheaper off-season rates, full Irish breakfast-€8.50, continental breakfast-€4.50, some parking, Castle Street, tel. 066/712-1877, fax 066/712-2273, www.choicehotelsireland .ie, comfortinntralee@eircom.net).

$$ Ashe TownHouse, built in 1826, is a solid Georgian relic, sporting 12 brightly restored rooms in the heart of town (Sb-€40–45, Db-€70–80, Tb-€85–95, Qb-€100–120, 15 Denny Street, tel. & fax 066/712-1003, www.accommodation-kerry.com, theashetownhouse@eircom.net).

$ Dowling's Leeside B&B is a tidy, modest house hosted by charming Maura and Seamus Dowling, with four comfy rooms that feel surrounded by trees even though they're on a busy street (tiny Sb-€35, Db-€60–66, Tb-€76, private parking, Oakpark Road, tel. 066/712-6475, dowlingsbandb@hotmail.com).

$ Finnegan's Hostel, in a stately Georgian house, is a block from TI at 17 Denny Street (€16 beds in 4-, 6-, 8-, or 10-bed dorms, Sb-€20, Db-€40, tel. 066/712-7610, www.finneganshostel.com, finneganshostel@eircom.net).

EATING

The Cookery is consistently good (€10 lunches Tue–Sat 12:30–17:30, €15–24 dinners Tue–Sat 18:00–22:00, closed Sun–Mon, a block off The Square, 16 Abbey Street, tel. 066/712-8833). Or try candle-lit **Finnegans Cellar** (€14–24 dinners, daily 17:30–22:30, 17 Denny Street, tel. 066/718-1400). Shop for a picnic at **Tesco,** the big grocery off The Square (Mon–Sat 8:00–22:00, Sun 10:00–20:00), or at **Super Valu** on Rock Street (Mon–Sat 8:00–22:00, Sun 8:00–19:00).

TRANSPORTATION CONNECTIONS

Day-trippers, beware: The station has lockers, but not enough.

From Tralee by Train to: Dublin (5/day, 3/day on Sun, 4 hrs, €55), **Rosslare** (1/day except Sun, 5 hrs, €51). Train info: tel. 066/712-3522.

By Bus to: An Daingean (6/day, less off-season and on Sun, 75 min, €9 one-way, €15 round-trip), **Galway** (8/day, 4 hrs), **Limerick** (9/day, 2 hrs), **Doolin/Cliffs of Moher** (2/day, 5 hrs), **Ennis** (8/day, 3 hrs, change in Limerick), **Rosslare** (2/day, 7 hrs, €24), **Shannon** (8/day, 2.5 hrs), **Dublin** (7/day, 6 hrs). Tralee's bus station is at the train station. Bus info: tel. 066/712-3566.

Car Rental: Duggan's Garage Practical Car Hire rents Fiat Puntos (€111/48 hrs, includes everything but gas, must be at least 25 years old, 2 blocks from train station on Ashe Street, tel. 066/712-1124, fax 066/712-7527).

Airports

Kerry Airport, a 45-minute drive from An Daingean town (just off the main road from Killarney to Tralee), offers connecting flights from **Dublin** on Aer Arann, **London Stansted** on Ryanair (www.ryanair.com), and even **Frankfurt-Hahn** on Ryanair (tel. 066/976-4644, www.kerryairport.ie).

Shannon Airport, the major airport in Western Ireland, has direct flights to **Dublin** (2–3/day, 30 min) and **London** (6/day, 1 hr). Ryanair and Aer Lingus (www.aerlingus.ie) fly out of Shannon. The airport has a TI (daily 6:30–17:30, June–Sept until 19:30, tel. 061/471-664). Airport info: tel. 061/471-444.

Shannon Airport also has easy bus connections to **Limerick** (nearly hrly, 1 hr, can continue to Tralee—2 hrs, and An Daingean—1.25 hrs more), **Ennis** (nearly hrly, 45 min), and **Galway** (every 2 hrs, 2 hrs). Bus info: tel. 061/313-333, www.buseireann.ie.

Route Tips for Drivers

From Tralee to An Daingean: Drivers choose between the narrow, but very exciting, Conor Pass road or the faster, easier, but still narrow N86 through Lougher and Abhainn an Scail (Anascaul). On a clear day, Conor Pass comes with incredible views over Tralee Bay and Brandon Bay, the Na Blascaodai (Blasket Islands), and the open Atlantic. Pull over at the summit viewpoint to look down on An Daingean town and harbor. While in Kerry, listen to Radio Kerry FM 97. To practice your Gaelic, tune in to FM 94.4.

Between Tralee and Galway/Burren/Doolin: The Killimer–Tarbert ferry connection allows those heading north for the Cliffs of Moher (or south for An Daingean) to avoid the 80-mile detour around the Shannon River. If you're going straight to Galway, the inland Limerick route is faster. But the ferry route is more scenic and direct to the Cliffs of Moher and the Burren (1 trip/hr, 20 min, €14/carload, April–Sept departs Mon–Sat on the half-hour 7:30–21:30 going north and on the hour 7:00–21:00 going south, on Sun the first departures are 9:30 going north and 9:00 going south, Oct–March last departures at 19:00, no need to reserve, tel. 065/905-3124, www.shannonferries.com).

GALWAY

Galway feels like a boomtown—rare in Western Ireland. With 60,000 people, it's the county's main city, a lively university town, and the region's industrial and administrative center. Amid the traditional regions of Connemara and the Aran Islands, it's also a Gaelic cultural preserve.

Galway offers tourists plenty of traditional music, easy train connections to Dublin (1/hr, 2.5 hrs, €30), and a convenient jumping-off point for a visit to the Aran Islands.

While Galway has a long and interesting history, its British overlords (who ruled until 1921) had little use for anything important to the Irish heritage. Consequently, precious little from old Galway survives. What does remain has the interesting disadvantage of being built in the local limestone, which, even if medieval, looks like modern stone construction. The city's quincentennial celebration in 1984 prompted a spirit of preservation.

What Galway lacks in sights it makes up for in ambience. Spend an afternoon just wandering its medieval streets, with their delightful mix of colorful facades, labyrinthine pubs, weather-resistant street musicians, and steamy eateries.

Blustery Galway heats up after dark, with fine theaters and a pub scene that attracts even Dubliners. Visitors mix with old-timers and students as the traditional music goes round and round.

If you hear a strange language on the streets and wonder where those people are from...it's Irish, and so are they.

Planning Your Time

Galway's sights are little more than pins on which to hang the old town. The joy of Galway is its street scene. You can see its sights in three hours, but without an evening in town, you've missed the best. Many spend three nights and two days: one for the town and another for a side-trip to the Burren, the Aran Islands, or Connemara (see next chapter). Tour companies make day trips to all three regions cheap and easy.

ORIENTATION

(area code: 091)
The center of Galway is Eyre Square. Within two blocks of the square, you'll find the TI, Aran boat offices, a tour pick-up point, the best cheap beds, and the train station. The train and bus station butt up against the Great Southern Hotel, a huge gray railroad hotel that overlooks and dominates Eyre Square. The lively old town lies between Eyre Square and the river. From Eyre Square, Williamsgate Street leads right through the old town (changing names several times) to Wolfe Tone Bridge. Nearly everything you'll see and do is within a few minutes' walk of this spine.

Tourist Information: The TI, located a block from the bus/train station in the ground floor of the Forster Court Hotel, has a bookshop and many booking services (June–Sept daily 9:00–17:45, Oct–May Mon–Sat 9:00–17:45, Sun 9:00–12:45, tel. 091/537-700, www.irelandwest.ie). Pick up the TI's free weekly *What's Going On* or *Galway Magazine* (€3, persistent readers will find several maps and walking tours amid the ads).

Arrival in Galway

Trains and most buses share the same station, virtually on Eyre Square (which has the nearest ATMs). To get to the TI, go left on Station Road as you exit the station (toward Eyre Square), then turn right on Forster Street. Some buses from Dublin and Dublin's airport use the Forster Street Bus Park, next to the TI.

For drivers, the most central and handiest parking garage is under Jurys Inn in the town center. To park nearby for free, try across the bridge along the Claddagh Quay or by the Siamsa Theatre. Otherwise, you'll have to buy a pay-and-display ticket and put it on your dashboard (€1.50/hr, buy from machines on street).

Helpful Hints

Crowd Control: Expect huge crowds—and higher prices—during the Galway Arts Festival (July 17–30 in 2006), Galway Oyster Festival (4 days near end of Sept), and the three sets of Galway Races (a week in late July/early Aug).

Markets: On Saturday, a fun market clusters around St. Nicholas' Church (all day, but best 9:00–12:00).

Internet Access: The e-2008 Internet Café is located next to the

Galway's History

The medieval fishing village of Galway went big time when the Normans captured the territory from the O'Flaherty family in 1234. Making the town a base, the Normans invited in their Angle friends, built a wall (1270), and kicked out the Irish. Galway's Celtic name (Gaillimh) comes from an old Irish word, *gall,* which means "foreigner." Except for a small section in the Eyre Square Shopping Centre and a chunk at the Spanish Arch, that Norman wall is gone. In the 14th century, 14 merchant families, or tribes, controlled Galway's commercial traffic, including the lucrative wine trade with Spain and France. These English families constantly clashed with the local Irish. Although the wall was built to "keep out the O's and the Macs," it didn't always work. A common prayer at the time was, "From the fury of the O'Flahertys, good Lord deliver us."

Galway's support of the English king helped it prosper. But with the rise of Oliver Cromwell, Galway paid for that prosperity. After sieges in 1651 by Cromwell's troops and in 1691 by the Protestant King William of Orange, Galway declined. It wasn't until the last half of the 20th century that it regained some of its importance and wealth.

Park House Hotel (€2.10/30 min, daily 9:00–24:00, Forster Street). There are also several good places along High Street near Jurys Inn.

Post Office: You'll find it on Eglinton Street (Mon–Fri 9:00–17:30, Sat 9:00–13:00, closed Sun).

Laundry: Launderland is close to the recommended B&Bs on College Road (Mon–Fri 8:30–18:30, Sat 9:00–18:00, closed Sun, €8 drop-off, Forster Court, 2-min walk up hill from TI, tel. 091/568-393).

Bike Rental: Mountain Trail rents a variety of mountain bikes (€10/day, Mon–Sat 9:00–18:00, closed Sun, Cornerstore Middle Street, tel. 091/569-888, www.biketoursireland.com).

TOURS

▲**Walking Tours**—Grandmotherly **Kay Davis** enjoys taking small groups on two-hour walks through old Galway (by appointment only). She covers Eyre Square, the cathedral, and the old town, and then finishes up at the Spanish Arch (€8, June–Sept, tel. 091/792-431).

The **City of the Tribes** tour covers the major sights in a two-hour walk, then finishes with a group meal and traditional music session in a 16th-century building (€25, departs TI June–Sept daily

Galway

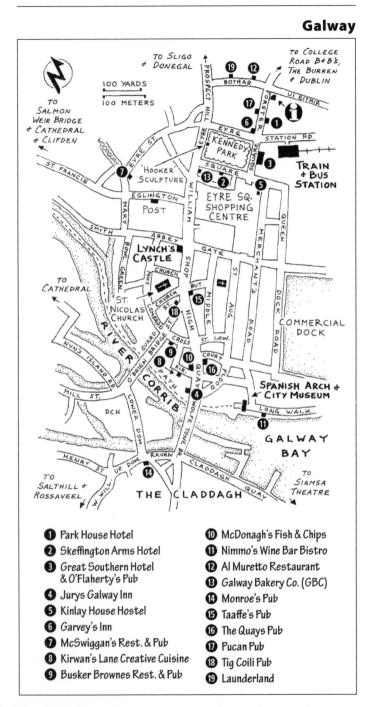

1 Park House Hotel
2 Skeffington Arms Hotel
3 Great Southern Hotel & O'Flaherty's Pub
4 Jurys Galway Inn
5 Kinlay House Hostel
6 Garvey's Inn
7 McSwiggan's Rest. & Pub
8 Kirwan's Lane Creative Cuisine
9 Busker Brownes Rest. & Pub
10 McDonagh's Fish & Chips
11 Nimmo's Wine Bar Bistro
12 Al Muretto Restaurant
13 Galway Bakery Co. (GBC)
14 Monroe's Pub
15 Taaffe's Pub
16 The Quays Pub
17 Pucan Pub
18 Tig Coili Pub
19 Launderland

at 10:00, 12:00, and 14:00, tel. 091/566-858).

The Other Galway walking tours focus on Galway's medieval folklore, mythology, gore, and ghosts (€10, departs TI May–Sept Mon–Fri at 15:00, Sat–Sun at 11:00, 13:00, and 15:00, mobile 087-778-2887 or 087-984-4887).

▲**Hop-on, Hop-off City Bus Tours**—Several companies run guided, 60-minute, hop-on, hop-off double-decker buses from the TI or Eyre Square, making nine stops—including the cathedral, Salthill, and the Spanish Arch. You can get off and explore and hop back on later (€10, daily 10:30–16:30, 4/day, buses usually depart every 90 min from TI on Forster Street).

SIGHTS

Medieval Galway's "Latin Quarter"

From the top of Eyre Square, Williamsgate Street (named for the old main gate of the Norman town wall that once stood here) is the spine of medieval Galway, leading downhill straight to the Corrib River. While the road changes names several times (William, Shop, High, and Quay Streets), it leads generally downhill and straight past these sights:

Lynch's Castle—Now the Allied Irish Bank, Galway's best 16th-century fortified townhouse was the home of the Lynch family—the most powerful of the town's 14 tribes. More than 60 Lynch mayors ruled Galway in the 16th and 17th centuries.

Collegiate Church of St. Nicholas—This church, located a half-block off the main street on the right, is the finest surviving medieval building in town (1320) and is dedicated to St. Nicholas of Myra, the patron saint of sailors. Columbus is said to have worshipped here in 1477, undoubtedly while contemplating a scary voyage. Its interior is littered with obscure town history (€3 donation for admission). On most Saturdays (and Sun June–Aug only), a wonderful market surrounds the church.

The Quay Pub—The pub, once owned by "Humanity Dick," an 18th-century Member of Parliament who was the original animal-rights activist, is worth a peek inside for its lively interior. The lane just before it leads to the...

Druid Theatre—This 100-seat theater offers top-notch contemporary Irish theater. Drop by to see if anything's playing tonight (€15–18 tickets, Chapel Lane, tel. 091/568-617, www.druidtheatre.com).

Spanish Arch and City Museum—Overlooking the Corrib River, these make up the best surviving chunk of the old city wall. The Spanish Arch (1584), the place where Spanish ships would unload their cargo, is a reminder of Galway's former importance in trade. Fragments of old Galway are kept in the recently expanded museum (€3, May–Sept daily 10:00–13:00 & 14:00–17:00; Oct–April Wed–Sun 11:00–13:00 & 14:00–17:00, closed Mon–Tue, call to verify price and hours, tel. 091/567-641).

Corrib River Sights—At the Corrib River, you'll find a riverside park perfect for a picnic (or get take-out from the town's best chippie, McDonagh's, across the street). Over the river (southeast of the bridge) is the modern housing project that, in the 1930s, replaced the original Claddagh. Claddagh (CLA-dah) was a picturesque, Gaelic-speaking fishing village with a strong tradition of independence—and open sewers. This gaggle of thatched cottages actually functioned as an independent community with its own "king" until the early 1900s.

The old Claddagh village has since disappeared, but the tradition of its popular ring (sold all over town) lives on. The Claddagh ring shows two hands holding a heart that wears a crown. The heart represents love, the crown is loyalty, and the hands are friendship. If the ring is worn with the tip of the heart pointing toward the wrist, it signifies that the wearer is married or otherwise taken. However, if the tip of the heart points toward the fingertip, it means the wearer is available.

Look at the monument (just before the bridge) given to Galway by the people of Genoa, celebrating Columbus' visit here in 1477. (That acknowledgment, from a town known in Italy for its stinginess, helps to substantiate the murky visit.) From the bridge, look up the river. The green copper dome marks the city's Cathedral of St. Nicholas (described below). Down the river is a tiny harbor with a few of Galway's famous square-rigged "hooker" fishing ships tied up and on display. Called hookers for their hook-and-line fishing, these sturdy yet graceful boats were later used for transporting turf from Connemara until improved roads and electricity made them obsolete. Beyond that, a huge park of reclaimed land is popular with the local kids for Irish football and hurling. From there, the promenade leads to the resort town of Salthill.

More Sights in Galway

▲**Eyre Square**—In the Middle Ages, this was a green just outside the town wall. The square is named for the mayor who gave the land to the city in 1710. While still called Eyre Square, it now contains John F. Kennedy Park—established in memory of the Irish-American president's visit in 1963, a few months before he was assassinated. (Though Kennedy is celebrated as America's first Irish-Catholic president, there have been several presidents who are descendants of Protestant Ulster stock.) On a sunny day, grassy Eyre Square is a popular hangout. Walk to the rust-colored Quincentennial Fountain (built in 1984 to celebrate the 500th anniversary of the incorporation of the city). The sails represent Galway's square-rigged fishing ships and the vessels that made Galway a trading center so long ago. The Browne Doorway, from a 1627 fortified townhouse, is a reminder of the 14 family tribes that once ruled the town (see Lynch's Castle, listed above, to get a feel for an intact townhouse). Each had a town castle—much like the towers that characterize the towns of Tuscany with their feuding noble families. So little survives of medieval Galway that the town makes a huge deal of any surviving window or crest. The cannons are from the Crimean War (1854). The statue is of Patrick O'Connor, Galway's favorite Gaelic poet, who'd sit on a limestone wall, as sculpted, recording the local life.

The Eyre Square Shopping Centre—a busy, modern shopping mall (see the arcaded entry from the square)—leads to a surviving piece of the old town wall that includes two reconstructed towers (and an antiques market).

▲▲**Cathedral of St. Nicholas**—Opened by American Cardinal Cushing in 1965, this is one of the last great stone churches built in Europe. The interior is a treat—mahogany pews set on green Connemara marble floors under a Canadian cedar ceiling.

The acoustically correct cedar enhances the church's fine pipe organ. Two thousand worshippers sit in the round facing the central altar. A Dublin woman carved 14 larger-than-life Stations of the Cross. The carving above the chapel (left of entry) is from the old St. Nicholas church. Explore the modern stained glass. Find the Irish holy family—with Mary knitting and Jesus offering Joseph a cup of tea. The window depicting the Last Supper is particularly creative—find the 12 apostles.

Next, poke your head into the side chapel with a mosaic of Christ's resurrection (if you're standing in the nave facing the main altar, it's on the left and closest to the front). Take a closer look at the profiled face to the right of Christ—the one looking up while praying with clasped hands. It's JFK, nearly a saint in Irish eyes at the time this cathedral was built.

Church bulletins at the doorway tell of upcoming Masses and

Galway Legends

Because of the dearth of physical old stuff, the town milks its legends. Here are a few you'll encounter repeatedly:

• In the 15th century, the mayor, one of the Lynch tribe, condemned his son to death for the murder of a Spaniard. When no one in town could be found to hang the popular boy, the dad—who loved justice more than his son—did it himself.

• Columbus is said to have stopped in Galway in 1477. He may have been inspired by tales of the voyage of St. Brendan, the Irish monk who is thought by some (mostly Irish) to have beaten Columbus to the New World by nearly a thousand years.

• On the main drag you'll find a pub called the King's Head. It was originally given to the man who chopped off the head of King Charles I in 1649. For his safety, he settled in Galway—about as far from London as an Englishman could get back then.

concerts (located across Salmon Weir Bridge on outskirts of town, tel. 091/563-577).

Salmon Weir Bridge—This bridge was the local "bridge of sighs." It led from the courthouse (opposite the church) to the prison (torn down to build the church—unlikely in the U.S.). Today the bridge provides a fun view of the fishing action. Salmon run up this river most of the summer (look for them). Fishermen, who wear waders and carry walking sticks to withstand the strong current, book long in advance to get half-day appointments for a casting spot.

Canals multiplied in this city (sometimes called the "Venice of Ireland") to power more water mills.

Outer Galway

▲**Galway Irish Crystal Heritage Center**—This is an impressive-sounding name for a sight in a grand building made-to-order for big bus groups. Still, this cheap tour (handy for drivers) is the place to see the making of Irish crystal. After a guided tour through the museum and a quick look at craftsmen cutting crystal (Mon–Fri only), you sit for 10 minutes while a video subliminally sells you crystal and wows you with Galway sights. The museum gives you a good rundown on Claddagh village and a chance to see a large hooker named *Fiona*. Tours run every half hour and are much more interesting on weekdays (€4, Mon–Fri 9:00–17:30, Sat 10:00–17:30, Sun 11:00–17:00, good cafeteria, 5 min out of Galway on Dublin road N6, or take Merlin Park bus—every 20 min—from Eyre Square, tel. 091/757-311, www.galwaycrystal.ie).

▲**Salthill**—This small resort packs pubs, discos, a splashy water park, amusement centers, and a fairground up against a fine mile-long beach promenade. At the Atlantaquaria aquarium, which features solely Irish water life, kids can help feed the fish at 15:00 (€8, daily 9:00–17:00, touch tanks, The Promenade, tel. 091/585-100, www.nationalaquarium.ie). For beach time, a relaxing sunset stroll, late-night traditional music, or later-night disco action, Salthill hops. To get to Salthill, catch bus #1 from Eyre Square in front of the AIB bank, next to the Great Southern Hotel (€1.20, runs 7:00–23:00).

Dog Racing—Join the locals and cheer on the greyhounds on Thursday, Friday, and Saturday evenings from 20:00 to 22:00 (€8, barking distance from my recommended B&Bs, a 10-min walk from Eyre Square, tel. 091/562-273).

NIGHTLIFE

Folk Theater—Galway's folk theater, **Siamsa,** features Irish music, folk drama, singing, and dancing, including the step dancing popularized by Riverdance (€20, late-June–Aug Mon–Fri at 20:45, no shows on weekends, Claddagh Hall, Nimmo's Pier, tel. 091/755-479 or mobile 087-662-9292, www.siamsatire.com).

▲**Traditional Irish Music in Pubs**—Galway, like An Daingean and Doolin, is a mecca for good Irish music (nightly 21:30–23:30). Unlike An Daingean and Doolin, this is a university town (enrollment: 12,000), and many pubs are often overrun with noisy students. Still, the chances of landing a seat close to a churning band surrounded by new Irish friends are good any evening of the year. Touristy and student pubs are found and filled along the main drag down from Eyre Square to the Spanish Arch, and across Wolfe Tone Bridge along William Street West and Dominick Street. Across the bridge, start at **Monroe's,** with its vast, music-filled interior (live music nightly at 21:30, set-dancing Tue at 21:30, Dominick Street, tel. 091/583-397). Several other pubs within earshot also feature almost-nightly traditional music.

Pubs known for Irish music along the main drag include **Tig Coili** (sessions Mon–Sat at 18:00 and 21:00, Sun at 14:00 and 21:00, intersection of Main Guard Street and High Street, tel. 091/561-294), **Taaffe's** (nightly music sessions at 17:00 and 21:30, Shop Street, across from St. Nicholas Church, tel. 091/564-066) and **The Quays** (traditional music Mon–Thu at 21:30, Fri–Sun at 17:00, young scene, Quay Street, tel. 091/568-347).

Pucan Pub, a cauldron of music and beer drinking with an older crowd—including lots of tourists—is worth a look (music nightly at 22:00, sometimes traditional, just off Eyre Square on Forster Street, tel. 091/561-528).

SLEEPING

There are three price tiers for most beds in Galway: high season (Easter–Oct), off-season, and charge-what-you-like festivals and race weekends (see "Crowd Control," page 214). I've listed high-season rates. B&Bs simply play the market. If you're on a tight budget, call around and see where the prices are. All B&Bs include a full fried breakfast. For locations, see the map on page 216.

Hotels

For a fancy hotel, Park House Hotel offers the best value. For a budget hotel, go to Jurys. For cheap beds, hit the hostel.

$$$ Park House Hotel, a plush, business-class hotel, is ideally located a block from the train station and Eyre Square. Its 84 spacious rooms come with all the comforts you'd expect (Db-€150–185 is the "corporate rate" you should get most of the year, ask if there's a discount, Sun night is slow and rooms can rent for Db-€125, good restaurant, elevator, free garage, helpful staff, Forster Street, tel. 091/564-924, fax 091/569-219, www.parkhousehotel.ie, parkhousehotel@eircom.net).

$$$ Skeffington Arms Hotel, which feels more Irish (and a bit smokier) than the Park House or Jurys, escapes most of the tour-group scene because it has only 23 rooms. Centrally located on Eyre Square, it's furnished in a dark-wood Victorian style (Db-€118–150, pub downstairs, Eyre Square, tel. 091/563-173, fax 091/561-679, www.skeffington.ie, reception@skeffington.ie).

$$$ Great Southern Hotel, filled with palatial Old World elegance and 99 rooms, marks the end of the Dublin–Galway train line and the beginning of Galway. Since 1845, it has been Galway's landmark hotel...JFK stayed here in 1963 (Db-€180–280, some discounts during slow times, best rates by booking online, breakfast-€15 extra, sauna, stuffy staff, at the head of Eyre Square, tel. 091/564-041, fax

---

Sleep Code

(€1 = about $1.20, country code: 353, area code: 091)
S = Single, **D** = Double/Twin, **T** = Triple, **Q** = Quad, **b** = bathroom, **s** = shower only. All of these places accept credit cards.

To help you easily sort through these listings, I've divided the rooms into three categories, based on the price for a standard double room with bath:

$$$ **Higher Priced**—Most rooms €100 or more.
$$ **Moderately Priced**—Most rooms between €60–100.
$ **Lower Priced**—Most rooms €60 or less.

091/566-704, www.gshotels.com, res@galway-gsh.com).

$$ Garvey's Inn, with 18 comfortable but occasionally smoky rooms right across from the station, offers the best price on Eyre Square. Mrs. Garvey adds a personal touch that bigger places can't offer (Sb-€55–65, Db-€100–130, above a great pub, tel. 091/562-224, fax 091/562-526, www.garveysinn.com, info@garveysinn .com).

$$ Jurys Galway Inn has 130 American-style rooms in a modern hotel, centrally located where the old town hits the river. The big, bright rooms have two double beds and huge modern bathrooms. You'll pay the same per room whether it's for a single, a couple, three adults, or a family of four (€72–106 Sun–Thu, €99–115 Fri–Sat depending on season, continental breakfast-€9 extra per person, full Irish breakfast-€11, elevator, lots of tour groups, 3 non-smoking floors, parking-€9, Quay Street, tel. 091/566-444, fax 091/568-415, U.S. tel. 800-423-6953, www.jurysdoyle.com, jurysinngalway@jurysdoyle.com).

$ *Hostel:* Kinlay House is a no-nonsense place just 100 yards from the train station, with 220 beds (1–8 beds per room) in bare, clean, and simple rooms, including 15 doubles/twins. Easygoing people of any age feel welcome here, but if you want a double, book well ahead—several months in advance for weekends (dorm bed-€16–22, Db-€54, elevator, self-service kitchen, Internet access in lobby, launderette, baggage storage, on Merchants Road, just off Eyre Square, tel. 091/565-244, fax 091/565-245, www.kinlayhouse .ie, kinlay.galway@usit.ie).

B&Bs

Drivers following city-center signs into Galway pass right by a string of B&Bs just after the greyhound-racing stadium. These are about an eight-minute walk from Eyre Square (from the station, walk up Forster Street, which turns into College Road). All of the listings are on College Road except for the lowest-priced listing (Flanagan's). The Petra House and Four Seasons are the best values. For locations, see the map on page 224.

$$$ Ardawn House is a classy B&B with nine comfortable rooms (Sb-€70, Db-€80–140, Qb-€160, College Road, near stadium on right, tel. 091/568-833, fax 091/563-454, www.galway .net/pages/ardawn-house, ardawn@iol.ie).

$$ Petra House, a peaceful-feeling brick building, rents six great rooms, including a family room. The owners, Joan and Frank Maher, keep everything lovingly maintained. Breakfasts are a highlight (Sb-€50–65, Db-€80–90, elegant sitting room, next door to Ardawn House—listed above, 29 College Road, tel. & fax 091/566-580, www.galway.net/pages/petra-house, petrahouse@eircom.net).

Galway B&Bs

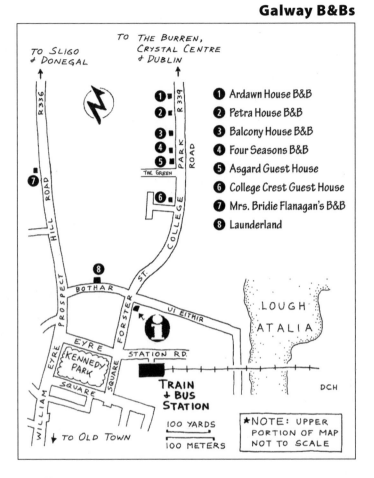

TO SLIGO & DONEGAL

TO THE BURREN, CRYSTAL CENTRE & DUBLIN

R 336

R 339

COLLEGE PARK ROAD

THE GREEN

HILL ROAD

PROSPECT

BOTHAR

COLLEGE ST.

FORSTER ST.

UI EITHIR

EYRE

KENNEDY PARK

STATION RD.

SQUARE

LOUGH ATALIA

TRAIN & BUS STATION

DCH

WILLIAM

↓ TO OLD TOWN

100 YARDS
100 METERS

★NOTE: UPPER PORTION OF MAP NOT TO SCALE

1 Ardawn House B&B
2 Petra House B&B
3 Balcony House B&B
4 Four Seasons B&B
5 Asgard Guest House
6 College Crest Guest House
7 Mrs. Bridie Flanagan's B&B
8 Launderland

$$ Four Seasons B&B is well-kept, with seven inviting rooms hosted by Eddie and Helen Fitzgerald (Sb-€50–60, Db-€75–89, Tb-€100–130, Qb-€110–150, parking, 23 College Road, tel. 091/564-078, fax 091/569-765, www.galway.net/pages /fourseasons, 4season@gofree.indigo.ie).

$$ College Crest Guest House, my closest recommended B&B to town, has 12 big, fresh rooms and a cushy lounge (Sb-€60–70, Db-€80–90, Tb-€120, non-smoking, parking, 5 College Road, tel. & fax 091/564-744, www.collegecrest.com, info@collegecrest .com).

$$ Asgard Guest House offers eight restful rooms and an appealing glass-atrium breakfast room (Sb-€45–55, Db-€70–80, Tb-€90–105, 21 College Road, tel. & fax 091/566-855, www.galway .net/pages/asgard, asgard@eircom.net, Geraldine Lohan).

$$ Balcony House B&B rents nine pleasant rooms (Db-€70–100, Tb-€105–140, Qb-€140–160, 27 College Road, tel. & fax 091/563-438, www.aaabalconyhouse.com, Michael and Teresa Coyne).

$ On Prospect Hill Road: This road (leaving Eyre Square from Richardson's Bar on Prospect Hill Road) is lined with small row houses, including **Mrs. Bridie Flanagan's B&B,** a humble, friendly old home with a welcoming living room and four bedrooms—two big and two cramped. Tom Flanagan met a fascinating variety of stars and politicians during his 45 years at the Great Southern Hotel (tiny D-€50, fine Db-€60, T-€70, cash only, 85 Prospect Hill, tel. 091/561-515).

Salthill

$$ Carraig Beag B&B, the classiest, friendliest, and most peaceful of all, is a big brick home on a residential street a block off the beach just beyond the resort town of Salthill. Catherine Lydon, with the help of her husband Paddy, rents six big, bright, fresh, and comfy rooms with a welcoming living room and a communal breakfast table (Sb-€50–65, Db-€65–80, family room-€75–130; 8-min drive from Galway, follow the beach past Salthill, take second right after golf course on Knocknacarra Road and go 2 blocks to 1 Burren View Heights, tel. 091/521-696, thelydons@eircom .net, www.dirl.com/galway/salthill/carraig-beag.htm). The #2 bus (€1.25, 3/hr) goes from Eyre Square (picks up in front of Skeffington Arms pub) to the Knocknacarra stop at the B&B's doorstep. Catherine can arrange for day-tour pickups at her place.

EATING

This college town is filled with colorful, inexpensive eateries. People everywhere seem to be enjoying their food. Each of these places is at the bottom of the old town, within a block or two of Jurys Inn. For locations, see the map on page 216.

Kirwan's Lane Creative Cuisine, considered Galway's best restaurant, is a dressy place where reservations are required (€20 lunches, €22–30 dinners, Mon–Sat 12:30–14:30 & 18:00–22:30, closed Sun, on Kirwan's Lane a block from Jurys, tel. 091/568-266).

Busker Brownes has three eateries in a sprawling place popular for its good, cheap food. Enter on Cross Street for the restaurant (and walk to the back for better seating), or enter on Kirwan's Lane for the ground-floor pub; upstairs from the pub is the third section (€9–21 meals, daily 11:00–21:00, "Sunday-morning jazz session" at 13:00, Cross Street and Kirwan's Lane, tel. 091/563-377).

McDonagh's Fish & Chips is a favorite "chipper." It has a fast, cheap section and a classier restaurant. If you're determined to try Galway oysters, remember that they're in season September–through April only. Other times you'll eat Pacific oysters—which doesn't make much sense to me (€10 lunch, €13–24 in restaurant, Mon–Sat 12:00–15:00 & 17:00–22:00, chipper open Sun 17:00–22:00 but restaurant closed, 22 Quay Street, tel. 091/565-001).

Nimmo's Wine Bar Bistro lurks peacefully in an old stone warehouse behind the Spanish Arch with terrific €6 fish soup and a diverse wine list. The candlelit ambience is great even for a cup of coffee (€14–25 meals, Tue–Thu and Sun 17:30–22:00, Fri–Sat 12:30–15:00, closed Mon, Long Walk Street, tel. 091/561-114).

McSwiggan's, with a downstairs pub and upstairs restaurant, is a maze of wooden stairways, brick walls, and hidden alcoves, serving hearty traditional Irish meals (€11–18 lunches, €14–22 dinners, daily 11:30–22:30, Eyre Street, tel. 091/568-917).

Al Muretto serves friendly Italian trattoria-style meals, just a five-minute walk towards town from my College Road B&B listings (€11–23 meals, daily 12:30–23:00, facing Bothar 50 yards up from corner with Forster, tel. 091/561-996).

O'Flaherty's Pub has a sports-bar feel and affordable pub grub (€10–18 meals, daily 12:30–21:30, under Great Southern Hotel on Eyre Square, tel. 091/509-621).

The **Galway Bakery Company (GBC)** is a popular and basic place for a quick Irish meal (€8–12 meals in ground-floor cafeteria, pricier restaurant upstairs, daily 8:00–21:00, 7 Williamsgate Street, near Eyre Square, tel. 091/563-087).

Supermarket: **Dunne's** is accessed through the Eyre Square Shopping Centre or around the corner at tiny Castle Street, off the pedestrian street called Williamsgate (Mon–Sat 9:00–18:30, Thu–Fri until 21:00, Sun 12:00–18:00, supermarket in basement). Lots of smaller grocery shops are scattered throughout town.

Medieval Banquet: If you have a car, consider a **Dunguaire Castle medieval banquet** in Kinvarra, a 30-minute drive south of Galway (see page 238). The 17:30 banquet can be done very efficiently as you're driving into or out of Galway (B&Bs accommodate late arrivals if you call).

TRANSPORTATION CONNECTIONS

From Galway by Train to: Dublin (7/day, 3 hrs). For **Belfast, Tralee,** and **Rosslare,** you'll change in or near Dublin. Train info: tel. 091/561-444.

By Bus to: Ennis (14/day, 1.25 hr), **Doolin/Cliffs of Moher** (4/day, 2 hrs), **Limerick** (14/day, 2 hrs), **Rosslare** (2/day, 6.5 hrs), **Belfast** (4/day, 7 hrs), **Dublin** (13/day, 3.5 hrs, €14; also see Citylink, below). Bus info: tel. 091/562-000.

Citylink (tel. 091/564-164, www.citylink.ie) runs cheap and fast bus service from Galway's Forster Street Bus Park to **Dublin** (Tara Street DART Station, 7/day, 3 hrs, €12), **Dublin Airport** (14/day, 3.5 hrs, €17), or **Shannon Airport** (5/day, 1.5 hrs, €13).

By Car: For ideas on driving from Galway to Derry or Portrush in Northern Ireland, see "Between Galway and Derry" on page 260).

NEAR GALWAY

In three different directions, Galway has interesting sights: County Clare and the Burren to the south, the Aran Islands to the west, and the Connemara region to the north.

To see the Burren by car, visit it en route between Galway and An Daingean (or take a tour from Galway). The Aran Islands (use public transportation) and Connemara (easy by car or tour) each take a day.

Bus Tours of the Burren and Connemara

Two Galway companies—Lally and O'Neachtain—run all-day, €25 tours of nearby regions. Tours of the Burren do a loop south of Galway, covering Kinvarra, Aillwee Cave, Poulnabrone Dolmen, and the Cliffs of Moher. Tours of Connemara include the *Quiet Man* Cottage, Kylemore Abbey, Clifden, and the "Famine Village." Tours go most days from about 10:00 to 17:30 (depart near Galway's TI, call to confirm exact itinerary: Lally tel. 091/562-905, www.lallytours.com; O'Neachtain tel. 091/553-188, www.oneachtaintours.com). Drivers take cash only; to pay with a credit card, book at the TI.

County Clare and the Burren

Those connecting An Daingean in the south with Galway in the north can entertain themselves along the way by joyriding through the fascinating landscape and tidy villages of County Clare. Ennis,

County Clare and the Burren

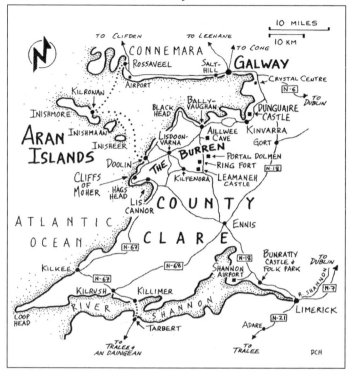

the major city of the county, with a medieval history and a market bustle, is a workaday Irish town ideal for anyone tired of the tourist crowds. The dramatic Cliffs of Moher overlooking the Atlantic offer tenderfeet a thrilling hike. The Burren is a unique, windblown limestone wasteland that hides an abundance of flora, fauna, caves, and history. For your evening entertainment, you can join a tour-bus group in a castle for a medieval banquet at Kinvarra or meet up with traditional Irish music enthusiasts from around Europe for tin whistling in Doolin.

Planning Your Time

By **train** and **bus,** your gateways to this region are Ennis from the south and Galway from the north (consider a tour from Galway; see "Bus Tours of the Burren and Connemara," above).

By **car,** the region can be an enjoyable daylong drive-through or a destination in itself. None of the sights has to take much time. But do get out and walk a bit.

If driving from An Daingean to Galway, I'd recommend this day plan rather than the main road via Limerick: Drive north from Tralee via Listowel to catch the Tarbert–Killimer car ferry (avoiding Limerick traffic and the 80-mile drive around the Shannon estuary; see "Route Tips" at the end of An Daingean chapter), then drive the coastal route to the Cliffs of Moher for an hour break. The scenic drive through the Burren, with a couple of stops and a tour of the caves, takes about two hours. There's a 17:30 medieval banquet at Dunguaire Castle near Kinvarra (just 30 min south of Galway, see Kinvarra section below).

Tips: Visit an ATM in Ennis or Galway before you enter this region (there are no ATMs in Doolin, Lisdoonvarna, Kilfenora, or Ballyvaughan). Skip the **Bunratty Castle and Folk Museum.** I'd leave this most commercial and least lively of all European open-air folk museums to the jet-lagged, big-bus American tour groups (located just a potty stop from the Shannon Airport, past Limerick on the road to Ennis).

Cliffs of Moher

A visit to the Cliffs of Moher ("more"), a ▲▲▲ sight, is one of Ireland's great natural thrills. For five miles, the dramatic cliffs soar as high as 650 feet above the Atlantic.

You can get here by bus from Galway (2/day in summer, 1.5 hrs, €15 round-trip). Drivers park at the lot for €4. You'll find the TI next to the parking lot (May–Sept daily 9:30–17:30, closed Oct–April, tel. 065/708-1171). The adjacent shop, cafeteria, and WCs are open 9:30–17:30 year-round. Walk 200 yards to the cliff's edge, past harpists and accordion players, and along a low wall of the local Liscannor slate. Notice the squiggles made by worms, eels, and snails long ago when the slate was still mud on the sea floor. O'Brien's Tower, built in 1853, marks the highest point of the cliffs (€1.50 tower entry not worth it).

For the best thrill, read the warning, consider the risk (wind gusts can be sudden, strong, and fatal), then step over the slate barrier and down onto the stone platform. Here there are no crowds. If you're a risk-taking fool, belly out and take a peek over the ledge.

You'll find yourself in a dramatic world where the only sounds are the waves, the wind, the gulls, and your stomach signaling frantically for help. There's a particularly peaceful corner of the platform over on the far right. On the far left, watch the birds play in the updrafts. In the distance, on windy days, the Aran Islands can be seen wearing their white necklace.

Before leaving the area, drivers could take 10 minutes to check out the holy well of St. Brigid, located beside the tall column about two miles south of the cliffs on the main road to Liscannor. In the short hall leading into the hillside spring, you'll find a treasure of personal and religious memorabilia left behind by devoted visitors seeking cures and blessings. The simple gray column outside was a folly erected 150 years ago by a local landlord with money and ego to burn.

Cruises: To get a different perspective of the cliffs (up instead of down), you can cruise along their base between Doolin and Liscannor. **Cliffs of Moher Cruises** makes the 75-minute voyage past sea stacks and crag-perched birds. Boats depart from the main pier in Doolin (same dock as Aran Islands boat) or from Liscannor (in Liscannor, find the dock by following signs for Cliffs of Moher cruises near Vaughan's pub). A free shuttle bus takes you back to whichever port you departed from (€20, daily April–Oct, 1/day from Liscannor, 3/day from Doolin, weather and tides permitting, call or go online to check sailing schedule and to reserve, tel. 065/707-5949, mobile 087-245-3239, www.mohercruises.com).

Doolin

This town is a strange phenomenon. Tourists go directly from Paris or Munich to Doolin. It's on the tourist map for its traditional music. A few years ago, this was a mecca for Irish musicians. They came together here to jam before a few lucky aficionados. But now the crowds and the foreigners are overwhelming the musicians, and the quality of music is not as reliable. Still, as Irish and European music-lovers alike crowd the pubs, the *bodhrán* beat goes on.

Doolin has plenty of accommodations and a Greek-island-without-the-sun ambience. The "town" is just a few homes and shops strung out along a valley road from the tiny harbor. Locals generally divide the town into an Upper Village and Lower Village. The Lower Village is the closest thing to a commercial center.

Doolin is famous for these three pubs, all featuring Irish folk music: Nearest the harbor, in the Lower Village, is **O'Connor's Pub** (tel. 065/707-4168). A mile farther up the road, the Upper Village straddles a bridge with the other two destination pubs, **McGann's** (tel. 065/707-4133) and **McDermott's** (tel. 065/707-4328). Music starts in the pubs between 21:30 and 22:00, finishing around midnight. Get there before 21:00 if you want a place to sit, or pop in later and plan on standing. On my last trip, I hit Doolin on a mediocre music night. The *craic* is fine regardless. Pubs serve decent dinners before the music starts. (**Dial-A-Cab** is a handy service for folks without wheels wanting to link a night of fun in Doolin with a bed in Lisdoonvarna; mobile 086-812-7049 or 087-290-2060.)

The Michael Russell Heritage Centre in Doolin may eventually become a museum of traditional music. For now, some *ceilidh* dances are held here. Ask at a pub if anything's scheduled.

From Doolin, you can hike or bike (rentals in town) up Burren Way for three miles to the Cliffs of Moher. (Get advice locally on the trail condition and safety). Doolin also offers boat cruises along the Cliffs of Moher (see page 231).

SLEEPING

$$ Harbour View B&B is a fine modern house with six rooms, a mile from the Doolin fiddles, overlooking the valley. Mrs. Cullinan keeps the guests' living room stocked with books and games (Sb-€50, Db-€64, Tb-€85, larger family-room deals, includes classy breakfast, on main road halfway between Lisdoonvarna and Cliffs of Moher, next to Statoil gas station, tel. 065/707-4154, fax 065/707-4935, www.harbourviewdoolin.com, clarebb@eircom.net).

$ Doolin Hostel, right in Doolin's Lower Village, caters creatively to the needs of backpackers in town for the music (dorm

---

Sleep Code

(€1 = about $1.20, country code: 353, area code: 065)
S = Single, **D** = Double/Twin, **T** = Triple, **Q** = Quad, **b** = bathroom, **s** = shower only. Breakfast is included and credit cards are accepted unless otherwise noted.

To help you easily sort through these listings, I've divided the rooms into categories, based on the price for a standard double room with bath:

$$$ **Higher Priced**—Most rooms €70 or more.
 $$ **Moderately Priced**—Most rooms between €50–70.
  $ **Lower Priced**—Most rooms €50 or less.

bed-€14, Db-€40, Qb-€68, Lower Village, tel. & fax 065/707-4421, www.doolinhostel.com, doolinhostel@iol.net).

EATING

My two favorite restaurants are both in the Upper Village; both have simple decor and excellent seafood (and more). **Bruach na haille** is next door to McGann's pub (€13–19 dinners, €11 early-bird specials before 20:00, daily 18:00–22:00, tel. 065/707-4120). The **Lazy Lobster,** across from McDermott's pub, is equally good, but costs a bit more (€19–25 meals, Tue–Sun 18:30–21:30, closed Mon, tel. 065/707-4085).

TRANSPORTATION CONNECTIONS

From Doolin by Bus to: Galway (4/day, 2 hrs), **Ennis** (3/day, 60–90 min).

By Ferry to the Aran Islands: The boats from Doolin to the Aran Islands (described below) can be handy, but are often canceled or run late. Even a balmy day can be too windy (or the tide can be too low) to allow for a sailing from Doolin's crude little

port. If you're traveling by car and have time limits, don't risk sailing from Doolin. Without a car, you can travel on from the Aran Islands to Galway by the bigger boats, so Doolin might work for you. But it's a longer trip to Inishmore, so consider an overnight stay on the islands. If you do have a car, note that parking is free beside the pier (even overnight).

There are three ferry companies in Doolin with similar schedules competing hard for your business. While they all promise to get you to Inishmore in under an hour, every one of my crossings in the past five years has included a stop on Inisheer en route, making the actual crossing time about 90 minutes. **Doolin Ferries** has been at it longest (to Inishmore: €18 one-way, €25 same-day round-trip, 2/day, 1.5 hrs, leaving at 10:00 and 13:00, returning at 11:30 and 16:00; to Inisheer: €10 one-way, €16 same-day round-trip, 5/day, 30 min, leaving every 90 min, 10:00–17:30; tel. 065/707-4455, www.doolinferries.com). **Aran Island Fast Ferries** claim to get you there quicker (tel. 065/707-4550, www.aranislandsfastferries .com). And the **Jack B** is your third option (tel. 065/707-5949 or mobile 087-245-3239, www.mohercruises.com). No matter which company you choose, it's smart to phone a day or two ahead to confirm schedules and prices.

Lisdoonvarna

This town of 1,000 was known for centuries for its spa and its matchmakers. Today, except for a couple of September weeks during its Matchmaking Festival, it's pretty sleepy. (The bank is only open 1 day a week.) Still, it's more of a town than Doolin and, apart from festival time, less touristy. Lisdoonvarna has good traditional music in its pubs. I'd stay here, rather than in Doolin, and commute.

Sleeping in Lisdoonvarna (area code: 065): $$ Ballinsheen House perches on a hill with five tastefully decorated rooms and a pleasant glassed-in breakfast terrace (Sb-€33–40, Db-€54–64, Tb-€75–96, Qb-€100–120, parking, 5-min walk north of town on N67 Galway Road, tel. 065/707-4806, mobile 087-656-9434, fax 065/707-4859, Mary Gardiner). **$$ Marchmont B&B** rents two large twin/family rooms and two small doubles in a fine old house (Db-€56–60, on N67 Galway Road near main square, just past post office, tel. 065/707-4050, Eileen Barrett). **$$ St. Enda's B&B** is an old-fashioned whitewashed place, with four modest rooms, run for the last 50 years by proper proprietress Mary Finn (Sb-€30–40, Db-€54–60, non-smoking, parking, 2-min walk north of town on N67 Galway Road, tel. 065/707-4066).

The Burren

Literally the "rocky place," the Burren is just that. The 10-square-mile limestone plateau, a ▲▲ sight, is so barren a disappointed Cromwellian surveyor of the 1650s described it as "a savage land, yielding neither water enough to drown a man, nor a tree to hang him, nor soil enough to bury him." But he wasn't much of a botanist, because the Burren is a unique ecosystem, with flora that has managed to adapt since the last Ice Age 10,000 years ago. It's also rich in prehistoric and early Christian sites. The first human inhabitants of the Burren came about 6,000 years ago, began cutting down trees, and are partially responsible for the stark landscape we see today. This limestone land is littered with more than 2,000 historic sites, including about 500 Iron Age stone forts.

Sightseeing the Burren: The drive from Kilfenora to Bally-vaughan offers the best quick swing through the historic Burren.

The Burren

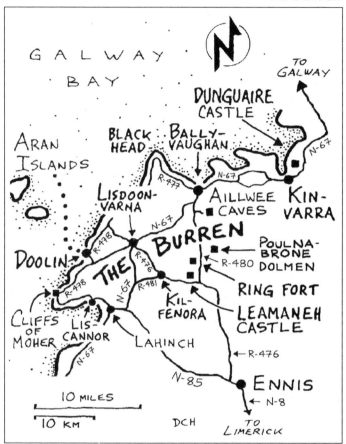

Kilfenora (5 miles southeast of Lisdoonvarna) is a good starting point. Its hardworking, community-run **Burren Centre** shows an intense 18-minute video explaining the geology and botany of the region and then ushers you into its enlightening museum exhibits (€5.75, mid-March–May and Sept–Oct daily 10:00–17:00, June–Aug daily 9:30–18:00, closed Nov–mid-March, tel. 065/708-8030, www.theburrencentre.ie). You'll see copies of a fine eighth-century golden collar and ninth-century silver brooch (now in Dublin's National Museum). The ruined church next door has a couple of 12th-century crosses, but isn't much to see. Mass is still held in the church, which claims the pope as its bishop. Kilfenora, as the smallest and poorest diocese in Ireland, was almost unable to function after the famine, so in 1866 Pope Pius the IX supported the town as best he could—by personally declaring himself its bishop.

Botany of the Burren in Brief

The Burren is a story of water, rock, geological force, and time. It supports the greatest diversity of plants in Ireland. Like nowhere else, Mediterranean and Arctic wildflowers bloom side by side in the Burren. It's an orgy of cross-pollination that attracts more insects than Doolin does music-lovers—even beetles help out. Limestone, created from layers of coral, seashells, and mud, is the basis of the Burren. (This same basic slab resurfaces 10 miles or so out to sea to form the Aran Islands.) The earth's crust heaved it up, and the glaciers swept it bare—dropping boulders as they receded. Rain, reacting naturally with the limestone to create a mild but determined acid, slowly drilled potholes into the surface. Rainwater cut through weak parts in the limestone, leaving crevices on the surface and Europe's most extensive system of caves below. These puddles grew algae, which dried into a powder. That, combined with bug parts and rabbit turds (bunnies abound in the Burren), created a very special soil. Plants and flowers fill the cracks in the limestone. Grasses and shrubs don't do well here, and wild goats eat any trees that try to grow, giving tender little flowers a chance to enjoy the sun. Different flowers appear in different months, sharing space rather than competing. The flowers are best in June and July.

For lunch in Kilfenora, consider the cheap and cheery Burren Centre Tea Room (daily 9:30–17:30) or the more atmospheric Vaughan's Pub. If you're spending the night in County Clare, make an effort to join the locals at the fun set-dancing get-togethers run by the Vaughans in the Barn Pub adjacent to their regular pub (€4, Thu and Sun at 21:30, tel. 065/708-8004, www.vaughanspub.com).

Leamaneh Castle, a ruined shell of a fortified house, is not

open to anyone these days. From the outside, you can see how the 15th-century fortified tower house (the right quarter of the remaining ruin) was expanded 150 years later (the left three-quarters of the ruin). The castle evolved from a refuge into a manor, and windows became wider to allow for better views as defense became less of a priority. From the castle, turn north on R480 (direction: Ballyvaughan). After about five miles, you'll hit the start of the real barren Burren.

The **Caherconnell (Cahercommaun) ring fort** (one of 500 or so in the area) can be seen to the left on the crest of a hill just off the road. You can park in the gravel lot and walk up to the modest visitors center for a 15-minute film (a high-tech virtual tour) followed by a quick wander through the small fort (€3 for fort only, €5 with film, Easter–June and Sept–Oct 10:00–17:00, July–Aug 9:30–18:00, closed Nov–Easter, tel. 065/708-9999, www.burrenforts.ie).

The stretch from the ring fort north to Ballyvaughan offers the

starkest scenery. Soon you'll see a 10-foot-high stone table a hundred yards off the road to the right (east, toward an ugly gray metal barn). This is the **Poulnabrone Dolmen,** a portal tomb that looks like a stone table. Two hundred years ago, locals called this a "druids' altar." Four thousand years ago, it was a grave chamber within a cairn of stacked stones that have since been eroded or carried away. Wander over for a look. (It's crowded with tour buses in midday, but it's all yours early or late.)

Be a geologist. Wander for some quiet time with the wildflowers. You're walking across a former tropical seabed, laid down at an unimaginable time when Ireland was at the equator (before continental drift nudged it north). Look for fossils: White smudges were coral. Scratches on rocks were ground by other rocks embedded in the belly of an advancing glacier. The rounded boulders came from Connemara, carried on a giant conveyor belt of ice, then left behind by the melting glaciers. As you drive away from the dolmen (continuing north), look for the 30-foot-deep sinkhole beside the road on the right (a collapsed cave chamber).

The **Aillwee Caves** are touted as "Ireland's premier showcaves." I couldn't resist a look. While fairly touristy and not worth the time or money if you've seen a lot of caves, they offer your easiest look at the massive system of caves that underlie the Burren. Your guide walks you 300 yards into the plain but impressive cave, giving a serious 40-minute geology lesson. During the Ice Age, underground rivers carved countless caves such as these. Brown bears, which became extinct in Ireland a thousand years ago, found this cave great for hibernating. But the caves are a constant 50° F, and I needed my sweater (€10, €25 family ticket, open daily at 10:00, last tour at 18:30 July–Aug, otherwise 17:30, Dec–Feb call ahead for limited tours, clearly signposted just south of Ballyvaughan, tel. 065/707-7036, www.aillweecave.ie).

Ballyvaughan

Really just a crossroads, Ballyvaughan is the closest town to the Burren and an ideal rural oasis for those intending to really explore the region.

Shane Connolly leads in-depth, three-hour guided walks through the Burren explaining the diverse flora, geology, history, and man's role in shaping this landscape. Wear comfortable shoes for wet, rocky fields and prepare to meet a proud farmer who really knows his stuff (€15, daily at 10:00, call to book and find out meeting point in Ballyvaughan, tel. 065/707-7168, http://homepage .eircom.net/~burrenhillwalks).

Sleeping in Ballyvaughan (area code: 065): Rusheen Lodge, near the fringe of the Burren, offers nine prim rooms and a great breakfast (Sb-€52–68, Db-€76–96, tel. 065/707-7092, fax 065/707-7152, www.rusheenlodge.com, rusheen@iol.ie).

Kinvarra

This tiny town, between Ballyvaughan and Galway (30 min from each), is waiting for something to happen in its minuscule harbor. It faces Dunguaire Castle, a four-story tower house from 1520 that stands a few yards out in the bay.

The **Dunguaire Castle medieval banquet** is Kinvarra's most tourist-worthy sight. The 500-year-old Dunguaire Castle hosts

a touristy but fun medieval banquet (€48, April–Oct Fri–Tue at 17:30 and 20:45, closed Nov–March, reservations tel. 061/360-788, castle tel. 091/637-108). Warning: This company also operates banquets at Bunratty Castle (30 miles south), so be sure that you've made your reservation for the correct castle.

The evening is as intimate as 55 tourists gathered under one time-stained, barrel-vaulted ceiling can be. You get a decent four-course meal with wine (or mead if you ask sweetly), served amid an entertaining evening of Irish tales and folk songs. Remember that in medieval times, it was considered polite to flirt with wenches. It's a small and multitalented cast: One harpist and three singer/actors who serve the "lords and ladies" between tunes. The highlight is the 40-minute stage show—featuring songs and poems by local writers—that comes with dessert.

Sleeping in Kinvarra (area code: 091): $$ Cois Cuain B&B is a small but stately house with a garden, overlooking the square and harbor of the most charming village setting you'll find. Mary Walsh rents three super-homey rooms for non-smokers (Db-€70, cash only, The Quay, tel. 091/637-119).

Ennis

This bustling market town (pop. 20,000), the main town of County Clare, provides those relying on public transit with a handy transportation hub (good connections to Limerick, Dublin, and Galway; see "Transportation Connections," page 241). Ennis is less than 15 miles from Shannon airport (www.shannonairport .com) and makes a good first- or last-night base in Ireland for travelers not locked into Dublin flights. It also offers a chance to wander around a workaday Irish town that is not reliant upon the tourist dollar (though not shunning it either).

Tourist Information: The TI is just off O'Connell Street Square (July–Aug daily 9:30–17:30, March–June and Sept–Dec closed Sun, Jan–Feb closed Sat–Sun, tel. 065/682-8366). Walking tours, lasting 90 minutes, depart from the TI (€8, May–Oct Wed–Mon 11:00 and 19:00, no tours Tue, mobile 087-648-3714, www .enniswalkingtours.com).

Helpful Hints

Post Office: It's on Market Place (Mon–Fri 9:00–13:00 & 14:00–17:30, Sat 9:00–13:00, closed Sun).

Laundry: Fergus launderette is opposite the Parnell Street parking lot (Mon–Sat 8:30–18:00, closed Sun, tel. 065/682-3122).

Parking: If you're not spending the night (i.e., parking at your B&B), parking is best in the pay-and-display lots (€1/hr, Mon–Sat 9:30–17:30, pay at meter in lot and display on dashboard, 3-hour maximum, free Sat–Sun).

Tours: Barratt Tours operate day tours by bus, departing the TI at 10:00 and returning by 17:00. On Monday, Wednesday, and Saturday they visit the Cliffs of Moher, Ailwee Caves, and Galway Bay. On Tuesday and Sunday they go to the Cliffs of Moher and Burren (€25, tel. 061/384-700 or mobile 087-237-5986, www.4tours.biz).

SIGHTS

Clare Museum—This worthwhile museum, housed in the large TI building, has eclectic displays on ancient ax heads, submarine development, and local boys who made good—from 10th-century High King Brian Boru to 20th-century statesman Eamon DeValera (free, June–Sept daily 9:30–17:30, Sun 9:30–13:00, Oct–May closed Mon, tel. 065/682-3382, www.clarelibrary.ie).

Ennis Friary—The Franciscan monks arrived here in the 13th century, and the town grew up around their friary (like a monastery). Today, it's still worth a look, with some fine limestone carvings in its ruined walls (€1.50, sometimes includes tour, covered by Heritage Card—see page 4, April–Oct daily 10:00–17:00, closed Nov–March, tel. 065/682-9100). Ask the guide to fully explain the crucifixion symbolism in the 15th-century *Ecce Homo* carving.

Glór Irish Music Centre—The town's modern theater center (*glór* is Irish for "sound") connects you with Irish culture. It's worth considering for traditional music, dance, or storytelling performances (€8–22, year-round usually at 20:00, 5-min walk behind TI, Friar's Walk, ticket office open Mon–Sat 10:00–17:00, closed Sun, tel. 065/684-3103, www.glor.ie).

Traditional Music—Live music begins in the pubs around 21:30. The best is **Cruise's** on Abbey Street, with music nightly year-round and good food (bar is cheaper than restaurant, tel. 065/682-8963). Other pubs offering traditional music are **Quinn's** on Lower Market Street (Sat year-round, tel. 065/682-8148); the rough-and-tumble **Kelly's** on Carmody Street at the intersection with Dumbiggle Road (Sat, tel. 065/682-8155); and the **Barge Rooms,** across the bridge from the friary, 100 yards up Newbridge Road (Sun at 18:00, tel. 065/682-4888). The **Old Ground Hotel** hosts live music year-round at its pub (Thu–Sun, open to anyone); though tour groups stay at the hotel, the pub is low-key and feels real, not staged.

SLEEPING

These are both fancy hotels that you'll share with tour groups. The stately, ivy-covered, 18th-century **$$$ Old Ground Hotel** has 114 rooms with a family feel (Sb-€80–110, Db-€105–140, suite-€130–190, rates vary with season, 2-night weekend stays include a dinner, at intersection of Station Road and O'Connell Street, a few blocks from station, tel. 065/682-8127, fax 065/682-8112, www.flynnhotels.com, oghotel@iol.ie). The **$$$ Temple Gate Hotel** is more modern and less personal (Db from €150–180, rates lower off-season, 3 non-smoking floors, O'Connell Street Square, in courtyard with TI, tel. 065/682-3300, fax 065/682-3322, www

.templegatehotel.com, info@templegatehotel.com).

B&Bs: The first two places are on Station Road, a block or two toward the town center from the train/bus station. **$$ Grey Gables B&B** is upscale and has 10 rooms (Sb-€40, Db-€65–70, cash only, parking, wheelchair access, tel. 065/682-4487, www .bed-n-breakfast-ireland.com, marykeane.ennis@eircom.net, Mary Keane). **$$ Rockfield B&B,** a little nearer to town, has four decent, simple rooms (S-€25–35, Db-€50, Tb-€75, cash only, parking, tel. 065/682-4749, Pauline O'Driscoll). **$$ Stonehaven B&B** is a kid-friendly place with three comfortable rooms (Sb-€45–50, Db-€64–70, Tb-€85–90, cash only, 10-min walk from town on N68 Kilrush road, tel. 065/684-1775, www.stonehavenclare.com, keatinge.ennis@eircom.net).

EATING

Hal Pino's is my pick for quality dinners, a cheerful atmosphere, and a central location (€15–27 dinners, 15 percent discount on à la carte menu before 19:00, daily 18:00–22:00, 7 High Street, tel. 065/684-0011). The **Old Ground Hotel** does hearty meals in its Poet's Corner pub (€9–11 lunches, €14–22 dinners, daily 12:00–21:00). Find basic **pub grub** at one of the places mentioned under "Traditional Music," above. Or, for an easy pub-free place for dinner, try the simple **Numero Uno Pizzeria** (Tue–Fri 12:00–23:30, Sun–Mon 17:00–23:30, closed Sat, tel. 065/684-1740, on Old Barrack Street off Market Place).

TRANSPORTATION CONNECTIONS

From Ennis by Train to: Limerick (6/day, 40 min), **Dublin** (2/day, 4 hrs). Train info: tel. 065/684-0444.

By Bus to: Galway (14/day, 1 hr), **Dublin** (11/day, 4.5 hrs), **Rosslare** (4/day, 5 hrs), **Limerick** (15/day, 60 min), **Doolin/Lisdoonvarna** (3/day, 60–90 min), **Tralee** (8/day, 3 hrs). Bus info: tel. 065/682-4177.

Aran Islands

The Aran Islands consist of three limestone islands: Inishmore, Inishmaan, and Inisheer. The largest, Inishmore (9 miles by 2 miles), is by far the most populated, interesting, and visited. The landscape of all three islands is harsh: steep, rugged cliffs and windswept, rocky fields divided by stone walls. During the winter, severe gales sweep the islands; because of this, most of the settlements on Inishmore are found on its more peaceful eastern side.

There's a stark beauty about these islands and the simple lives its inhabitants eke out of six inches of topsoil and a mean sea. Precious little of the land is productive. In the past, people made a precarious living from fishing and farming. The layers of limestone rock meant that there was little natural soil. Farming soil has been built up by the islanders—the result of centuries of layering seaweed with sand. The fields are small, divided by several thousand miles of drystone wall. Most of these are built in the Aran "gap" style, in which angled upright stones are filled with smaller stones. This allows a farmer who wants to move stock to dismantle and rebuild the walls easily. Nowadays, tourism boosts the local economy.

The islands are a Gaeltacht area. While the islanders speak Irish among themselves, they happily speak English for their visitors. Many of them have direct, personal connections with America and will ask you if you know their cousin Paddy in Boston.

Today, the 800 people of Inishmore (literally "the big island") greet as many as 2,000 visitors a day. The vast majority of these are day-trippers. They'll hop on a minibus at the dock for a 2.5-hour tour to Dún Aenghus, then spend an hour or two browsing through the few shops or sitting at a picnic table outside a pub with a pint of Guinness.

The other islands, Inishmaan and Inisheer, are smaller, much less populated, and less touristy. While extremely quiet, they do have B&Bs, daily flights, and ferry service. For most, the big island is quiet enough. For more information, look up an old issue of *National Geographic* on the Aran Islands (April 1981).

On Inishmore Island: Kilronan

By far the Aran Islands' largest town, Kilronan is still just a village. Groups of backpackers wash ashore with the landing of each ferry. Minibuses, bike shops, and a few men in pony carts sop up the tourists. There are around a dozen shops and B&Bs and about half as many restaurants. Most of Kilronan huddles around the pier. A few blocks inland up the high road, you'll find the Heritage Centre (primitive Internet access upstairs, €4/30 min, daily 10:00–17:00), the best folk-music pub, a post office (Mon–Fri 9:00–13:00 & 14:00–17:30, Sat 9:00–13:00, closed Sun), and a tiny bank across from the roofless Anglican church ruins (open only on Wed 10:00–12:30 & 13:30–15:00, plus Thu June–Aug). The huge SPAR supermarket, two blocks inland from the harbor, seems too big for the tiny community and has the island's only ATM (Mon–Sat 9:00–20:00, Sun 10:00–17:00). Bring cash: Some B&Bs and other

Inishmore Island

businesses don't accept credit cards. A couple of huts near the pier rent bikes (€10/day plus €10 deposit).

Tourist Information

Kilronan's TI is helpful, but don't rely on it for accommodations. The B&B owners who work with the TI are out of town and desperate (daily 10:00–17:00, July–Aug until 18:00, shorter winter hours, faces the harbor, tel. 099/61263). Ask the TI for a map of the island (if your ferry operator didn't already give you one). This map is all the average day-tripper or leisure biker will need to navigate. But serious hikers who plan on scampering out to the island's craggy fringes will want to invest in the detailed black-and-white Oileain Aran map by Tim Robinson (€8, sold in Kilronan TI and many mainland bookstores). Public WCs are 100 yards beyond the TI on the harbor road.

Getting Around Inishmore

Just about anything on wheels functions as a taxi. A trip from Kilronan to Dún Aenghus to the Seven Churches and back to Kilronan costs €10 per person in a shared minibus. Flag them down and don't hesitate to bargain. Pony carts cost about €40 for two people (€60 for 4) for a trip to the west end of the island. Biking is great, although the terrain is hilly and there are occasional headwinds (30 min to start of trailhead up to Dún Aenghus). Bikers should take the high road over and the low road back—fewer hills,

scenic shoreline, and, at low tide, 50 seals basking in the sun. Keep a sharp lookout along the roads for handy modern stone signposts (with distances in kilometers) that point the way to important sites. They're in Irish, but you'll be clued in by the small metal depictions of the site embedded within them.

TOURS

▲**Island Minibus Tours**—There can't be more than 100 vehicles on the island, and most of them seem to be minibuses. A line of buses awaits the arrival of each ferry, offering 2.5-hour, €10 island tours. Chat with a few drivers to find one who likes to talk. On my tour, I learned that 800 islanders live in 14 villages, with three elementary schools and three churches. Most islanders own a small detached field where they keep a couple of cows (sheep are

too much trouble). When pressed for more information, my guide explained that there are 400 different flowers and 19 different types of bees on the island. The tour, a convenient time-saver, zips you to the end of the island for a quick stroll in the desolate fields, gives you 10 minutes to wander through the historic but visually unimpressive "Seven Churches," and then drops you for two hours at Dún Aenghus (30 min to hike up, 30 min at the fort, 20 min hike back down, 40 min in café for lunch or shopping at drop-off point) before running you back to Kilronan. Ask your driver to take you back along the smaller coastal road (scenic beaches and sunbathing seals at low tide).

SIGHTS

▲**Aran's Heritage Centre**—This little museum, while nothing impressive, offers a worthwhile introduction to the island's traditional lifestyle, its geology, and its archaeological wonders (€3.50 for museum only, €5.50 combo-ticket includes *Man of Aran* movie, April–Oct daily 10:00–17:00, July–Aug until 19:00, closed Nov–March, tel. 099/61355).

Man of Aran: This 1934 silent movie, giving a good look

at traditional island life with an all-local cast, is shown at the Heritage Centre (included in €5.50 ticket to Heritage Centre, 1 hr, 4 shows/day in summer, 3 shows/day off-season). The movie features currachs (canoe-like boats) in a storm, shark fishing with hand-held harpoons, cultivation of the fields from bare rock, and life in the early 1900s, when you couldn't rent bikes.

▲▲▲**Dún Aenghus (Dun Aonghasa)**—This is the island's blockbuster sight. The stone fortress hangs spectacularly and precariously on the edge of a cliff 300 feet above the Atlantic. The

crashing waves seem to say, "You've come to the end of the world." Little is known about this 2,000-year-old Celtic fort. Its concentric walls are 13 feet thick and 10 feet high. As an added defense, the fort is ringed with a commotion of spiky stones, sticking up like lances, called a *chevaux-de-frise* (literally, "Frisian horses," named for the Frisian soldiers who used pikes like these to stop charging cavalry). Slowly, as the cliff erodes, hunks of the fort fall into the sea. Dún Aenghus doesn't get crowded until after 11:00. I enjoyed a half-hour completely alone at 10:00 in the tourist season. If you can, get there early or late (€2, covered by Heritage Card—see page 4, April–Oct daily 9:00–18:00, Nov–March daily 10:00–16:00, guides at fort June–Aug answer questions and can sometimes give free tours if you call ahead, 5.5 miles from Kilronan, tel. 099/61008). A small museum displays findings from recent digs and tells the story of the fort. Advice from rangers: Wear walking shoes and watch your kids closely; there's no fence between you and a 200-foot cliff overlooking the sea.

Seven Churches (Na Seacht Teampaill)—Close to the western tip of the island, this gathering of ruined chapels, monastic houses, and fragments of a high cross dates from the 8th–11th centuries. The island is dotted with reminders that Christianity was brought to the islands in the fifth century by St. Enda, who established a monastery here. Many great monks studied under Enda. Among these "Irish apostles," who started Ireland's "Age of Saints and Scholars" (A.D. 500–900), was Columba (Colmcille in Irish), the founder of a monastery on the island of Iona in Scotland.

Kilmurvey—The island's second village sits below Dún Aenghus. With a gaggle of homes, a B&B, a great sheltered beach, and a pub, this is the place for peaceful solitude (except for the folk music in the pub).

Ancient Sites near Killeany—The quiet eastern end of Inishmore offers ancient sites in evocative settings for overnight visitors with more time, or for those seeking rocky hikes devoid of crowds.

First, get a good hiking map from the Kilronan TI. Then consider a soup-and-sandwich lunch at Tigh Fitz pub to fuel up either before or after a half-day spent exploring these sights on foot. Ask the folks at the pub for directions (almost always a memorable experience in Ireland).

Closest to the road, amid the dunes one mile past Tigh Fitz pub and just south of the airport, is the eighth-century **St. Enda's Church** (Teaghlach Einne). Protected from wave erosion by a stubborn breakwater, it sits half-submerged in a sandy graveyard, surrounded by a sea of sawgrass and peppered with tombstones. St. Enda is said to be buried here, along with 125 other saints who flocked to Inishmore in the fifth century to learn from him.

St. Benen's Church (Teampall Bheanáin) perches high on a desolate ridge opposite Tigh Fitz pub. Walk up the stone-walled lane, passing a holy well and the stubby remains of a round-tower

base. Then take another visual fix on the church's silhouette on the horizon and zigzag up the stone terraces to the top. The 20-minute hike from Tigh Fitz pub pays off with a great view. Dedicated to St. Benen, a young disciple of St. Patrick himself, this tiny sixth-century oratory is aligned north-south (instead of the usual east-west) to protect the doorway from prevailing winds.

About a five-minute walk past Tigh Fitz pub (heading toward the airport) you'll notice an abandoned stone pier and adjacent modest medieval ruin. This was **Arkin Fort,** built by Cromwell's soldiers in 1652 using cut stones taken from the round tower and monastic ruins that once stood on the hill below St. Benen's Church. The fort was used as a prison camp for outlawed priests before they were sent by English authorities to the West Indies to be sold into slavery.

Hidden on a remote, ragged headland an hour's walk from Kilronan to the south side of the island, you'll find the **Black Fort** (Dún Duchathair). Next to Dún Aenghus, this is Inishmore's most dramatic fortification. Built on a promontory with cliffs on three sides, its defenders would have held out behind drystone ramparts, facing the island's interior attackers. Watch your step on the uneven ground, be ready to course-correct as you go, and chances are you'll have this windswept ruin all to yourself.

Ragus—Irish for "desire," this is a riveting hour of quality Irish song-and-dance performed in the small Halla Ronain community center in Kilronan. Ten energetic young Irish adults give you an opportunity to see Irish step dancing up close, accompanied by a small group of musicians earnestly playing traditional Irish instruments. The center is a five-minute walk from the boat dock and offers day-trippers a mid-afternoon performance you can plan as your last stop before catching the late-afternoon boat back to the mainland. Buy tickets at the door or at the Ragus office in the ferry ticket building at the Rossaveel ferry port (€15, mid-June–Aug Sun–Fri at 14:45 and 21:00, none in off-season,

tel. 099/61515, mobile 087-237-1642, www.ragustheshow.com).

Pub Music—Kilronan's four pubs sporadically offer music on summer nights. Nothing is regularly scheduled, so ask at your B&B or look for posted notices on the front of the Spar supermarket or post office. Joe Watty's Pub, on the high road 100 yards past the post office, sometimes has good Irish folk music. Tigh Fitz, one mile down the airport road, often has folk music and dancing on Fridays, Saturdays, and Sundays. The more central Joe Mac's Pub (next to the hostel) and American Bar (next to the high cross at the base of the high road) are also possibilities.

The Halla Ronain community center becomes a dance hall on some Saturday nights, when from midnight to 2:00 locals have a *ceilidh* (KAY-lee), the Irish equivalent of a hoedown. Ask at the TI to see if it's on during your stay.

SLEEPING

(€1 = about $1.20, country code: 353, area code: 099)

Remember, this is a poor island. Most rooms are plain, with sparse plumbing. Only The Pier House takes credit cards.

$$$ Ostan Arann is Inishmore's first modern hotel, with a great restaurant and 22 large, well-furnished rooms, five with grand-patio views of the harbor (Sb-€50–90, Db-€80–130, Db with patio €90–150, Tb-€150–170, Qb-€170–210, 2- and 3-night midweek deals, 10-min walk from pier, about 100 yards past Halla Ronain, tel. 099/61104, fax 099/61225, www.aranislandshotel .com).

$$$ The Pier House stands solidly a hundred yards beyond the pier, offering 12 decent rooms, a good restaurant downstairs, a dramatic setting, and sea views from most of its rooms (Sb-€45–55, Db-€70–90, tel. 099/61417, fax 099/61122, www.pierhousearan .com, pierh@iol.ie).

$$$ Man of Aran B&B, as classy as a thatched cottage can

Kilronan

TO DÚN AENGHUS
(MAIN HIGH ROAD)

ARAN'S
HERITAGE
CENTRE

TO LOW
COAST
ROAD

200 YDS.

200 M

POST

HALLA RONAIN
COMM. CTR.
(RAGUS)

TO
AIRPORT
(KILLEANY
ROAD)

BOATS TO
ROSSAVEEL,
INISHMAAN & DOOLIN

❶ The Pier House B&B/Rest.
❷ Clai Ban B&B
❸ Costello's B&B
❹ Ostan Arann Hotel/Rest.
❺ Seacrest B&B
❻ Hostel & Joe Mac's Pub
❼ Sean Cheibh Café
❽ Aran Fisherman Rest.
❾ Joe Watty's Pub
❿ American Bar
⓫ SPAR Supermarket & Lios Aengus Café

be, is in the peaceful countryside four miles outside of touristy Kilronan toward the western end of the island. Rooms are quiet and rustic, with fireplaces. The restaurant serves all-organic, home-grown vegetables and herbs (€25–30 meals) only to guests staying with them. The setting is pristine—this is where the movie was filmed over 70 years ago (S-€45, D-€74, Db-€80, cash only, reserve well in advance, bear right just 100 yards after passing Kilmurvey beach before Dún Aenghus turnoff, 4 miles from Kilronan, tel. 099/61301, fax 099/61324, manofaran@eircom.net, Maura Wolf).

$$ Clai Ban, about the only really cheery place in town, is worth the 10-minute walk from the pier. You might be lucky enough to hear the sounds of the Hernon youngsters practicing traditional music (Sb-€40–60, Db-€55–70, Tb-€80–100, cash only, walk past bank out of town and down lane on left, tel. 099/61111, fax 099/61423, Marion Hernon).

$$ Costello's B&B has four plain rooms in a plain home

in a fine garden setting (D-€53, Db-€60, cash only, with your back to the SPAR supermarket's entrance, take little alley at one o'clock—ahead slightly to right—to last house, tel. 099/61241, Sally Costello).

$$ Seacrest B&B offers six uncluttered rooms in a central location next to the Aran Fisherman restaurant. Geraldine Faherty manages the rooms while Tom Faherty keeps the ferries afloat (Sb-€38, Db-€60, Tb-€69, non-smoking, tel. 099/61292, mobile 087-617-9911).

$ Kilronan Hostel, overlooking the harbor near the TI, is cheap but noisy above Joe Mac's Pub (€15–17 beds in 4- to 6-bed rooms, cash only, includes breakfast, self-service kitchen, tel. 099/ 61255, www.kilronanhostel.com, kilronanhostel@ireland.com).

EATING

There are three restaurants in Kilronan. The best is the classy **Ostan Arann** hotel on the south fringe of town (lunch 12:00–17:00 in the Patin Jack Bar, dinner 18:00–22:00, tel. 099/61104).

Aran Fisherman serves a good dinner (daily 12:30–16:00 & 17:00–22:00, arrive before 19:00 to avoid a wait, tel. 099/61104).

The **Pier House** operates a dependable restaurant below its guest house (€10–20 lunches, €18–26 dinners, daily 11:00–22:00, tel. 099/61811).

Otherwise, Kilronan's modest cafés dish up hearty soup, soda bread, sandwiches, and tea.

Sean Cheibh ("the old pier"), which seems to slam out more meals than the rest of the town combined, is popular for its fish and chips and great clam chowder (eat in or take out, April–mid-Oct daily 12:00–20:00, closed mid-Oct–March, tel. 099/61228).

Lios Aengus, next door to the SPAR market, does simple lunches away from the crowds (daily 9:30–17:00, June–Aug until 18:00, tel. 099/61030).

The **SPAR supermarket** has all the groceries you'll need (June–Aug Mon–Sat 9:00–20:00, Sun 10:00–17:00; Sept–May Mon–Sat until 18:00).

TRANSPORTATION CONNECTIONS

By Ferry from Rossaveel: Island Ferries sells tickets from a small counter in the Galway TI and runs a shuttle bus from Galway for the 45-minute drive to the docks from Rossaveel (see below for details). They sail to Inishmore from Rossaveel, a port 20 miles west of Galway (3/day April–Oct, 2/day Nov–March, 40-min crossing; if you're coming from Galway, allow 2 hrs one-way including 45-min bus ride, €25 round-trip boat crossing plus €6 round-trip for Galway–Rossaveel shuttle bus; ask about high-season discount for pre-booking, which can drop boat trip to €15 and shuttle bus to €5). Shuttle buses depart Galway (from Merchants Road in front of Kinlay House) 60 minutes before the sailing and return to Galway immediately after each boat arrives. Ferry schedule for April–Oct: from Rossaveel at 10:30, 13:00, and 18:30; from Inishmore at 8:30, 12:00, and 17:00 (plus 19:30 June–Aug, WCs on board). Island Ferries has three offices in Galway: one at the Galway TI, another across from Kinlay House on Merchants Road, and the third on Forster Street (tel. 091/568-903, www.aranislandferries.com).

Bad Arann Teo began operating in July of 2005 with three boats sailing to all three Aran Islands from Rossaveel. Their schedule to Inishmore is similar to Island Ferries' (above). It's €25 from Rossaveel, plus a €6 shuttle ride that picks up at their three Galway offices: Merchants Road, High Street opposite Jury's Inn, and Forester Street opposite the TI (tel. 091/865-833 or 087/697-5989, www.aranislandsdirect.com, info@aranislandsdirect.com).

Drivers should go straight to the ferry landing in Rossaveel, passing several ticket agencies and pay parking lots. At the boat dock, you'll find a convenient €5-per-day lot and a small office selling tickets for Island Ferries. Check to see what's going when and for how much.

By Ferry from Doolin: This ferry is handy if you're in Doolin, but it's notorious for being canceled because of wind or tides (for specifics, see page 233).

By Plane: Aer Arann, a friendly and flexible little airline, flies three planes a day (every hour during peak season) and stops at all three islands (€44 round-trip, groups of 4 or more €37 each, 10-min flight). These flights get booked up—reserve a day or two in advance with a credit card. Their nine-seat planes take off from the Connemara Regional Airport (not the Galway airport). It's 20 slow driving miles west of Galway, so allow a solid

45 minutes to get there. A minibus shuttle—€6 round-trip—runs from Kinlay House on Merchants Road an hour before each flight. The Kilronan airport is small (baggage is transported from the plane to the "gate" in a shopping cart). A minibus shuttle between the airport and Kilronan costs €5 one-way (2 miles from the airport). For reservations and seat availability, contact the airline (tel. 091/593-034, fax 091/593-238, www.aerarannislands.ie). Ask for a 10 percent discount—they distribute lots of coupons.

Connemara and County Mayo

If you have a car, consider spending a day exploring the wild western Irish fringe known as Connemara and straying into historic County Mayo. Gaze up at the peak of Croagh Patrick, the mountain from which St. Patrick supposedly banished the snakes from Ireland. Pass through the desolate Doo Lough valley on a road stained with tragic famine history. Bounce on a springy peat bog, and drop in at a Westport pub owned by a member of the Chieftains (a well-known traditional Irish music group). This beautiful area also claims a couple of towns—Cong and Leenane—where classic Irish movies were filmed, as well as photogenic Kylemore Abbey.

Connemara makes an easy day trip by car from Galway. Without a car, you can take a tour from Galway (see "Bus Tours of the Burren and Connemara," page 228) or at least get to Westport by bus (see "Westport," page 254). Public transportation in this region is patchy, and some areas are not served at all. Trains connect Galway and Westport to Dublin but not to each other.

This is a full day of driving (about 150 miles using Galway as your base). With an early start, your day will be less rushed. Those wanting to slow down and linger can sleep in Westport. These country roads, punctuated by blind curves and surprise bumps, are shared by trucks, tractors, and sheep. Drive sanely and bring rain gear and your sense of humor. This is the real Ireland.

Take along a good map (Michelin's maps are widely sold in Ireland) and study the loop connecting these points before you start: Galway, Cong, Westport, Louisburgh, Leenane, Kylemore Abbey, and back to Galway (for specifics, see below).

Route Summary of Connemara and Mayo Loop Trip

Take N84 north out of Galway. At Cross, take R346 into Cong and R345 back out again. At Neale, go north on R334 and pick up N84 again from Ballinrobe to Partry. Take R330 from Partry to Westport. After lunch in Westport, go west on R335 through Louisburgh and south through Doo Lough Valley all the way to Leenane. Pick up N59 in Leenane and take it to Kylemore Abbey, continuing to Letterfrack and Connemara National Park. Double-back from Letterfrack and take R344 south to the junction with N59. The N59 will take you back via Maam Cross and Oughterard to Galway.

Connemara and County Mayo

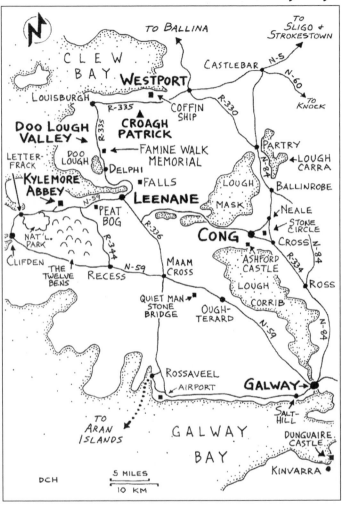

SIGHTS

From Galway's Eyre Square, drive north out of town on Prospect Hill Road. Follow the signs at each roundabout in the direction of Castlebar onto N84. You'll soon be out of Galway's suburbs and crossing miles of flat bogland laced with simple rock walls. You may notice the flags on the phone poles changing colors: from burgundy and white to green and red. These are the colors of the local hurling and football teams. You've crossed the border from County Galway into County Mayo. At Cross, take R346 into Cong. You'll pass the grand, gray gateway of Ashford Castle (on left) as you approach the town.

Cong—Plan to spend an hour in Cong. Cross the small bridge and park in front of the abbey. Drop into the **TI** across from the abbey entrance for a map (March–Nov daily 10:00–18:00, July–Aug until 19:00, closed Dec–Feb, tel. 094/954-6542). Public WCs are 50 yards down the street across from the *Quiet Man* **cottage.** That's right, pilgrim, this town is where John Wayne and Maureen O'Hara made the famous John Ford film *The Quiet Man* 50 years ago. The cottage's modest historical exhibits (upstairs) and film props (downstairs) are really only worth it for diehard fans of the Duke (€3.80, mid-March–Oct daily 10:00–17:00, closed Nov–mid-March, tel. 094/954-6089). Fuel up on a cup of coffee and homemade dessert at the **Hungry Monk Café** (July–Aug daily 10:00–18:00, mid-March–June and Sept–Oct Tue–Sun 10:00–18:00, closed Mon, closed Nov–mid-March, Internet access, on Abbey Street between WCs and TI, tel. 094/954-6866).

We're here for the ruins of **Cong Abbey** (free and always open). The abbey was built in the late 1100s, when Romanesque was going out of style and Gothic was coming in; you'll see the mixture of rounded Romanesque and pointy Gothic arch styles in the doorway. The famous Cross of Cong (an Irish art treasure now on display in Dublin's National Museum), which held a holy relic of what was supposedly a splinter of the True Cross, was held aloft at the front of processions of Augustinian monks during High Masses in this church. Rory O'Connor, the last Irish high king, died in this abbey in 1198. After O'Connor realized he could never outfight the superior Norman armies, he retreated to Cong and spent his last years here in monastic isolation.

Take a walk through the cloister and down the path behind the abbey. The forested grounds are lush, and the stream water

is incredibly clear. Cong's salmon hatchery contributes to western Ireland's reputation for great fishing. The monks fished for more than sinners. They built the modest **Monks' Fishing Hut,** just over the footbridge, right on the bank so that the river flowed underneath. They lowered a net though the floor and attached a bell to the rope; whenever a fish was netted, the bell would ring.

Next stop is **Ashford Castle.** To reach the castle from the abbey, face the Romanesque/Gothic main entrance and go left around the corner of the abbey, walking 15 minutes down the pleasant forested lane onto the grounds of the castle, which is

hidden behind the trees. Garden-lovers happily pay the stiff €5 entry fee (in effect during peak bloom June–Aug, usually free rest of year) to a kid patrolling the bridge, so they can stroll the lakeside paradise once owned by the Guinness beer family. The renovated Victorian castle rents some of the finest rooms in all of Ireland. President Reagan stayed here in 1984, and actor Pierce Brosnan chose these grounds for his wedding reception in 2001.

From Cong to Neale: Cong (from *conga,* Irish for "isthmus") lies between two large lakes. Departing Cong over the same bridge by which you entered, look down through the thick vegetation to see a dry canal. Built between 1848 and 1854, this canal was a famine work project that stoked only appetites. The canal, complete with locks, would have linked Lough Mask to the north with Lough Corrib to the south. But the limestone bedrock was too porous, and the canal wouldn't hold water.

Take R345 out of Cong (left turn opposite the main stone gateway onto the grounds of Ashford Castle). Heading north, you'll pass through the tiny hamlet of...

Neale—About 120 years ago, a retired army captain named Boycott was hired to manage the nearby estate of Lord Erne. But the strict captain harshly treated the tenants who worked his lands, so they united to ostracize him by deserting their jobs and isolating his estate. Over time, the agitation worked, and eventually "boycotting" became a popular tactic in labor conflicts.

From Neale to Westport: At Neale, go north on R334, then take N84 from Ballinrobe to Partry. At Partry, turn left off N84 onto R330 in the direction of Westport (the easy-to-miss turnoff is immediately after you pass the thatch-roofed Village Inn). Just over 200 years ago, in the countryside a few miles to your right, a French invasion force supported by locals dealt the British an embarrassing loss in the **Battle of Castlebar.** The surprised British forces were routed, and their rapid retreat is slyly remembered in Irish rebel lore as the "Castlebar races." Unfortunately for the rebels, this proved to be the last glimmer of hope for Irish victory in the uprising of 1798. The British reorganized and within weeks defeated the small force of 1,300 Frenchmen and the ill-equipped Irish rebels. The captured French soldiers were treated as prisoners of war, while the Irish rebels were executed.

Westport—On arrival in Westport, park along the Mall under the trees that line the canal-like river. This is a planned town, built

in Georgian style in the late 1700s to support the adjacent estate of Westport House (skip it for better manors at Powerscourt and Muckross). The town once thrived on the linen industry created by local Irish handlooms. But after the Act of Union with Britain in 1801, the town was unable to compete with the industrialized British linen-makers and fell into decline. The town is still pretty and a good place for a relaxed lunch and some exploration on foot.

The **TI** is on James Street (Mon–Sat 9:00–17:00, closed Sun, July–Aug daily until 18:00, tel. 098/25711). The **Westport Heritage Centre** gives a good overview of town history and the nearby Croagh Patrick pilgrimage tradition (€3, downstairs beneath the TI). On Tuesday and Thursday nights in July and August, 90-minute **town walks** depart at 20:00 from the clock tower at the top of Bridge Street (€5, tel. 098/26852). If you're not sleeping in Westport (i.e., parking at your B&B), free **parking** is allowed on the street for two hours; otherwise, use the pay-and-display lots for longer stays (€0.60/hr, pay at meter and display on dashboard). **Laundry** can be dropped off early at Gills and picked up late the same day (€8.50, Mon–Sat 9:00–18:30, closed Sun, tel. 098/25819).

Eating in Westport: Most of your best bets are clustered on Bridge Street. A good choice is **J.J. O'Malleys'** pub for lunch and upstairs restaurant for dinner (€16–24 meals, daily 12:00–22:00, Bridge Street, tel. 098/27307). For a quick and easy lunch, try **O'Cee's Coffeeshop** (cafeteria-style lunches-€8, Mon–Sat 9:00–18:30, Sun 10:00–16:00, Shop Street, tel. 098/27000) or the **Stuffed Sandwich Company** (Mon–Sat 9:30–18:00, Sun 11:00–18:00, Bridge Street, tel. 098/27611). Irish music fans seek out Matt Molloy's pub (Bridge Street, tel. 098/26655). **Matt Molloy** isn't just the owner of the pub—he's also flutist for the Chieftains, the group credited with much of the resurgence of interest in Irish music worldwide over the past 30 years. The **Super Valu** market has picnic fare (Mon–Sat 8:30–19:30, Sun 10:00–18:00, Shop Street).

Sleeping in Westport (area code: 098): For those wanting extra time to explore, Westport is the best place along this route to spend a night. All of the following listings are centrally located. Prices vary quite a bit depending on the season. **Westport Inn** has a fresh, woody feel with 34 comfortable rooms and convenient, free underground parking (Sb-€49–90, Db-€90–160, Tb-€150–230, Mill Street, tel. 098/29200, fax 098/29250, www.westportinn .ie, info@westportinn.ie). The **Clew Bay Hotel** is a couple doors down from the TI, with 50 large modern rooms with cherry-wood furniture (Sb-€60–90, Db-€80–160, Tb-€120–200, James Street, tel. 098/28088, fax 098/25783, www.clewbayhotel.com). The **Boulevard Guest House,** right on the leafy mall, has large tasteful rooms and a cushy lounge (Sb-€40–45, Db-€65–75, Tb-€90, Qb-€99, cash only, discount for multiple-night stays, tel. 098/25138 or 087/284-4018, www.boulevard-guesthouse.com, Sadie and John Moran). The homey **Teallach an Ghabha B&B** has four comfy, modest rooms (S-€45, Db-€70, cash only, Altamount Street, tel. 098/25704). A couple doors away, the **Linden Hall B&B** has four cozy, colorful rooms (Sb-€30–50, Db-€60–80, Tb-€75–90, cash only, Altamount Street, tel. 098/27005, www.lindenhallwestport .com, lindenhall@iol.ie).

Transportation Connections: If you want to visit Westport but lack wheels, here are your options. You can take a bus to/from **Galway** (7/day, 2 hrs), **Derry** (4/day, 5.5 hrs, change in Sligo), or **Dublin** (5/day, 5 hrs). You can also reach Dublin by train (3/day, 4 hrs).

From Westport to Murrisk by Car: Leave Westport heading west on R335. After about five miles, as you're driving along scenic Clew Bay, you'll reach a wide spot in the road called Murrisk. Stop here. In the field on your right (opposite Campbell's Pub) is the...

Coffin Ship—This bronze ship sculpture is one of the most powerful famine memorials you'll see in Ireland. It's a "coffin ship," like those of the 1840s that carried the sick and starving famine survivors across the ocean in hope of

a new life. Unfortunately, many of the ships contracted to take the desperate immigrants were barely seaworthy, no longer fit for dependable commerce. The poor were weak from starvation and vulnerable to "famine fever," which they then spread to others in the putrid, cramped holds of these awful ships. Many who lived through the six- to eight-week journey died shortly after reaching their new country. Pause a moment to look at the silent skeletons swirling around the ship's masts. Now contemplate the fact that famine exists today. And before judging the lack of effective relief intervention by the British government of that time, consider the rich world's ability to ignore similar suffering today.

Across the road from the coffin ship is...

Croagh Patrick—This small mountain rises 2,500 feet above the bay. In the fifth century, St. Patrick is said to have fasted on its summit for 40 days. It's from here that he supposedly rang his bell,

Ireland's Misunderstood Nomads

When you see a small cluster of trailers at the side of an Irish road, you're looking at a dying way of life. These are Travellers, a nomadic throwback to the days when wandering craftsmen, musicians, and evicted unfortunates crowded rural Ireland. Often mislabeled as Gypsies, they have no ethnic ties to those Eastern European nomads but instead have Irish heritage going back centuries.

There were once many more Travellers, living in tents and using horse-drawn carts as they wandered the countryside in search of work. Before the famine, when Irish hospitality was a given, Travellers filled a niche in Irish society. They would do odd jobs, such as repairing furniture, sweeping chimneys, and selling horses. Skilled tinsmiths, they mended pots, pans, and stills for *poitín*—Irish moonshine. (Travellers used to be called "tinkers," but they now consider this label derogatory.) Post-famine rural depopulation and the gradual urbanization of the countryside forced this nomadic group to adapt to an almost sedentary existence on the fringes of towns.

Today, the 30,000 remaining Travellers are outsiders, usually treated with suspicion by the traditionally conservative Irish. Locals often complain that petty thefts go up when Travellers set up camp in a nearby "halting site" and that they leave their refuse behind when they depart. Travellers tend to keep to themselves, marry young, have large families, and speak their own Gaelic-based language (called Shelta, Gammon, or Cant). Attempts to settle Travellers in government housing and integrate their children into schools have met with mixed success.

driving all the snakes out of Ireland. The snakes never existed, of course, but they represent the pagan beliefs that Patrick's newly arrived Christianity replaced. Every year on the last Sunday of July, "Reek Sunday" (a "reek" is a mountain peak), more than 50,000 pilgrims hike two hours up the rocky trail to the summit in honor of St. Patrick. The most penitent hike barefoot. On that Sunday, Mass is celebrated throughout the day in a modest chapel on the top.

A few years ago, valuable gold deposits were discovered within Croagh Patrick. Luckily, public sentiment has kept the sacred mountain free of any commercial mining activity.

From Croagh Patrick to Doo Lough Valley: Continue on R335. **Clew Bay** stretches out beside you, peppered with numerous humpbacked islands of glacial gravel that were left behind when the last ice age ended. A notorious 16th-century local pirate queen named Grace O'Malley once ruled this bay, earning the grudging respect of Queen Elizabeth I herself with her clever exploits. Passing through Louisburgh, you'll turn south to enter some of the most rugged and desolate country in Ireland.

Doo Lough Valley—Signs of human habitation vanish from the bogland, and ghosts begin to appear beside the road. About eight miles beyond Louisburgh, stop at the simple gray stone cross on the left. The lake ahead is Doo Lough (Irish for Black Lake), and this is the site of one of the saddest famine tales.

In the early 1800s, County Mayo's rural folk were almost exclusively dependent on the potato for food. They were the hardest-hit when the Potato Famine came in 1845. In the winter of 1849, about 600 starving Irish walked 12 miles from Louisburgh to Delphi Lodge. They hoped to get food from their landlord, but were turned away. On the walk back, almost 400 of them died along the side of this road. Today, the road still seems to echo with the despair of those hungry souls and inspires an annual walk that commemorates the tragedy. Archbishop Desmond Tutu made the walk in 1991, shortly before South Africa ended its apartheid system.

From Doo Lough Valley to Leenane: Continue south on R335. You'll get a fine view of **Aasleagh Falls** on the left. In late May, the banks below the falls explode with lush, wild rhododendron blossoms. Cross the bridge after the falls and turn right onto N59 toward Leenane. You'll drive along Killary Harbor, Ireland's version of a fjord. This long, narrow body of water was carved by an advancing glacier.

Leenane—This town is a good place for a break. The 1990 movie *The Field*, starring Limerick-born Richard Harris, was filmed here. Take a glance at the newspaper clippings about the making of the movie on the wall of Hamilton's Pub. While you're there, find the old photo of the British battleships that filled Killary Harbor when the king of England visited a century ago. Drop into the **Leenane Cultural Centre** (on the left as you enter town) to see an interesting wool-spinning and weaving demonstration (€2.50, April–Sept).

From Leenane to a Peat Bog: As you continue west on N59, notice the rows of blue floats in Killary Harbor. They're there to mark mussel farms growing in the cold seawater. Climbing out of the fjord valley about five miles past Leenane, you'll pass some good areas to get a close look at a turf cut in a peat bog.

A Slog on the Bog—Walk a few yards onto the spongy green carpet. Watch your step on wet days to avoid squishing into a couple inches of water. Find a dry spot and jump up and down to get a feel for it. Have your companion jump; you'll feel the vibrations 15 feet away.

These bogs once covered almost 20 percent of Ireland. As the climate got warmer at the end of the last ice age, plants began growing along the sides of the many shallow lakes and ponds. When the plants died in these waterlogged areas, there wasn't enough oxygen for them to fully decompose. The moss built up, layer after dead layer, over the centuries. During World War I, this sphagnum moss was collected to use in bandages to soak up blood (it absorbs many times its weight in fluids).

It's this wet, oxygen-starved ecosystem that preserved ancient artifacts so well, many of which can be seen in Dublin's National Museum. Even forgotten containers of butter, churned centuries

ago and buried to keep cool, have been discovered. Since these acidic bogs contain few nutrients, unique species of carnivorous plants have adapted themselves to life here by trapping and digesting insects. The tiny pink Sundew (about 2 inches tall) has delicate spikes glistening with insect-attracting fluid. Take a moment to find a mossy area and look closely at the variety of tiny plants. In summer, you'll see white tufts of bog cotton growing in marshy areas.

People have been cutting, drying, and burning peat as a fuel source for over a thousand years. The cutting usually begins in April or May when drier weather approaches. You'll probably see stacks of "turf" piled up to dry along recent cuts. Pick up a brick and fondle it. Dried peat is surprisingly light and stiff. In central Ireland, there are even industrial peat cuts that were begun after World War II to fuel power stations. But in the past decade, recognition of the rare habitat that the bogs provide has encouraged conservation efforts, and the smell of burning peat is becoming increasingly rare.

From Peat Bog to Kylemore Abbey: Continue west on N59 and pass the junction with R344 (direction: Recess) on the left; you'll come back to this junction on your way back to Galway. The road soon crosses a shallow lake, with a great view of Kylemore Abbey to the right. But you'll get a better photo from the parking lot a couple hundred yards ahead, so don't stop here. Pull into the lot and take a few minutes to enjoy the view.

Kylemore Abbey—This neo-Gothic country house was built by the wealthy English businessman Mitchell Henry in the 1860s,  after he and his wife had honeymooned in the area. Now they are both buried on the grounds. During World War I, refugee Benedictine nuns from Belgium took it over, and today it's an exclusive girls' boarding school. The best thing about the abbey is the view of it from the lakeshore. Tours inside are a let-down, so just enjoy its setting. WCs are in the gift shop next to the parking lot (overpriced at €11 combo-ticket for abbey and gardens, daily 9:00–17:30, tel. 095/41146, www.kylemoreabbey.com).

Connemara National Park—Less than five miles west of the abbey, just after passing through the town of Letterfrack (go left off N59), the park encompasses almost 5,000 acres of wild bog and mountain scenery. The visitors center displays worthwhile exhibits of local biology, fauna, and flora, which is well explained in the 15-minute *Man and the Landscape* film that runs every half-hour. Nature lovers may want to reverse the direction of my driving loop (and skimp on sightseeing time at other stops) in order to enjoy a two-hour walking tour with a park naturalist, departing the visitors center Monday–Friday at 10:30 in July and August. Bring rain gear and hiking shoes (visitors center-€2.75, covered by Heritage Card—see page 4, mid-March–Oct daily 10:00–17:30, June–Aug until 18:30, last admission 45 min before closing, tel. 095/41054, www.heritageireland.ie).

Returning to Galway: Drive back the way you came. Turn right on the R344 (direction: Recess). Off to the right is Connemara's Twelve Bens mountains—but it's late, and we're headed for home. At the junction with N59, turn left and follow the signs back to Galway.

Between Galway and Derry

Travelers continuing on to Northern Ireland (or County Donegal) should get an early start. Allow a long day for the drive from Galway to Derry (or Portrush) with these interesting stops along the way. Knock is right on N17 heading north out of Galway while Strokestown is further east in County Roscommon. Fill up your tank just before you leave the Republic, since unleaded is at least a dollar per gallon more expensive in Northern Ireland.

Knock—In this tiny town in 1879, locals saw the Virgin Mary and Joseph appear against the south gable of the church. Word

of miraculous healings turned the trickle of pilgrims into a flood and put Knock solidly on the pilgrimage map. Today, you can visit the shrine. At the edge of the site, a small but interesting folk museum shows "evidence" of the healings, photos of a papal visit, and interesting slices of traditional life.

▲▲**Strokestown Park National Famine Museum**—The Great Potato Famine of 1845–1849 was the bleakest period in Irish history—so traumatic that it halved the Irish population, sent desperate Irish peasants across the globe, and crystallized Irish-nationalist hatred of British rule. The National Famine Museum fills a mansion (on the former estate of the Mahon family, mentioned below) in the market town of Strokestown, 60 miles northeast of Galway. Visitors can absorb the thoughtfully done exhibits explaining how three million Irish peasants survived on a surprisingly nutritious pre-famine diet of buttermilk and potatoes (12 lbs per day per average male laborer).

Major Mahon, the ill-fated landlord during the famine, found it cheaper to fill three "coffin ships" bound for America with his evicted, starving tenants than pay the taxes for their upkeep in the local workhouse. When almost half died at sea of "famine fever," he was assassinated. After visiting the museum, take a tour of the musty "Big House" (Mon–Fri at 11:30, 14:00, 16:00, Sat–Sun additional tour at 17:00) to learn about the gulf that divided the Protestant ascendancy and their Catholic house servants. Afterward, find the servants' tunnel—connecting the kitchen to the stable—built to avoid disturbing the Mahon family's views (€12.50 for museum, house tour, and Georgian gardens, mid-March–Oct daily 10:30–17:30, tel. 071/963-3013, www .strokestownpark.ie).

Drivers connecting Westport or Galway to either Dublin or Northern Ireland can stop here en route and grab lunch in the museum café.

NORTHERN IRELAND

NORTHERN IRELAND

All of Ireland was once a colony of Great Britain. Unlike its Celtic cousins of Scotland and Wales, Ireland has always been distant from London—due more to its Catholicism than the Irish Sea.

Protestant settlers from England and Scotland were "planted" in Catholic Ireland to help assimilate the island into the British economy. These settlers established their own cultural toehold on the island, but the Catholic Irish held strong to their Gaelic culture.

Over the centuries, British rule has not been easy. By the beginning of the 20th century, the sparse Protestant population could no longer control the entire island. When Ireland won its independence in 1921 (after a bloody guerilla war against British rule), 26 of the island's 32 counties became the Irish Free State, ruled from Dublin with dominion status in the British Commonwealth—like Canada. In 1949, they left the Commonwealth and became the Republic of Ireland, removing all political ties with Britain.

Meanwhile, the six remaining northeastern counties (the only ones with a Protestant majority) had voted not to join the Irish Free State in 1922, and remained part of the U.K.

In this new political entity called Northern Ireland, the long-established Orange Order and the military muscle of the newly mobilized Ulster Volunteer Force (UVF) worked to defend the union with Britain—so their political philosophy was "Unionist." This was countered on the Catholic side by the Irish Republican Army (IRA). The IRA wanted all 32 of Ireland's counties to be united in one Irish nation—so their political goals were "Nationalist."

In World War II, the Republic stayed neutral while the North enthusiastically supported the Allied cause—winning a spot close to London's heart. After the war, the split between North and South seemed permanent, and Britain invested heavily in Northern Ireland to bring it solidly into the U.K. fold.

As 94 percent of the Republic of Ireland (the South) was Catholic and only 6 percent was Protestant, there was no question as to which group was dominant. But in the North, the Catholics,

Northern Ireland

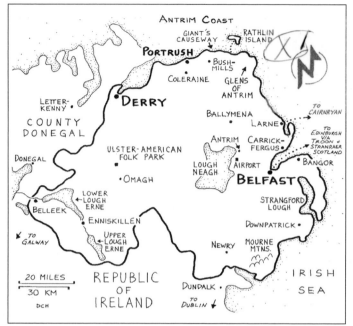

although a minority, were a sizable 35 percent and demanded attention. Discrimination was considered necessary to maintain the Protestant status quo in the North, leading to the Troubles that have filled headlines since the late 1960s.

This isn't a fight over Protestant and Catholic religious differences—it's about whether Northern Ireland will stay part of the U.K. or become part of the Republic of Ireland. The indigenous Irish of Northern Ireland, who generally want to unite with Ireland, happen to be Catholic. The descendants of Scottish and English settlers, who generally want to remain part of Britain, happen to be Protestant.

Partly inspired by the Civil Rights movement in America in the 1960s, the Catholic minority in Northern Ireland began to fight discrimination, advocating for better jobs and housing. Extremists polarized issues, and demonstrations became violent. Unionists were afraid that if the island became one nation, the relatively poor Republic of Ireland would drag down the comparatively affluent North, and the high percentage of Catholics could mean repression of the Protestants. As Protestants and Catholics clashed in 1969, the British Army entered the fray. They've been there ever since. In 1972, a watershed year, over 500 died as combatants moved from petrol bombs to guns, and a new, more violent

Northern Ireland Almanac

Official Name: Since Northern Ireland is not an independent state, there is no official country name. Some call it Ulster, while others label it The Six Counties.

Population: Northern Ireland's 1.7 million people are about 55 percent Protestant (mostly Presbyterian and Anglican) and 45 percent Catholic. English is far and away the chief language, though Gaelic is also spoken.

Despite the country's genetic homogeneity (the largest "minority" group is 8,000 Chinese), the population is highly segregated along political, religious, and cultural lines. Roughly speaking, the eastern seaboard is more Unionist, Protestant, and of English-Scottish heritage, while the south and west (bordering Ireland) is Nationalist, Catholic, and of Irish descent. Cities are often clearly divided between neighborhoods of one group or the other. Early in life, locals learn to identify the highly symbolic (and highly charged) colors, music, and language that distinguish the cultural groups.

Latitude and Longitude: 54°N and 5°W. It's a similar latitude to Alberta, Canada.

Area: 5,400 square miles (about the size of Connecticut), constituting a sixth of the island. Northern Ireland includes six of the island's traditional 32 counties.

Geography: Northern Ireland is shaped roughly like a doughnut, with the U.K.'s largest lake in the middle (Lough Neagh, 150 square miles). The terrain comprises gently rolling hills of green grass, rising to 2,800-foot Slieve Donard. The weather is temperate, cloudy, moist, windy, and hard to predict.

Biggest Cities: Belfast, the capital, has 279,000 residents. Half a million people—nearly one in three Northern Irish—inhabit the

IRA emerged. In this most-recent 35-year chapter in the struggle for an independent and united Ireland, more than 3,000 people have been killed.

A 1985 agreement granted Dublin a consulting role in the Northern Ireland government. Unionists bucked this idea, and violence escalated. That same year, Belfast City Hall draped a huge, defiant banner under its dome, proclaiming, *Belfast Says No.*

In 1994, the banner came down. In the 1990s—with Ireland's membership in the European Union, the growth of its economy, and the weakening of the Catholic Church's influence—the consequences of a united Ireland were less threatening to the Unionists. Also in 1994, the IRA declared a cease-fire, and the Protestant greater Belfast area. Derry (called Londonderry by Unionists) has 73,000 people.

Economy: Northern Ireland's economy is more closely tied to the U.K. than to the Republic of Ireland. Sectarian violence has held back growth, and the economy gets subsidies from the U.K. and the European Union. Traditional agriculture (potatoes and grain) is fading fast, though modern techniques and abundant grassland make Northern Ireland a major producer of sheep, cows, and grass seed. Modern software and communications companies are replacing traditional manufacturing.

Government: Northern Ireland is not a self-governing nation, but is part of the U.K., ruled from London by Queen Elizabeth II and Prime Minister Tony Blair, and represented in Parliament by 18 elected Members of Parliament. For 50 years (1922–1972), Northern Ireland was granted a great deal of autonomy and self-governance (known as "Home Rule"). But the national Assembly (108-seat Parliament) is currently suspended due to political strife.

Politics is dominated, of course, by the ongoing debate between Unionists (who want to preserve the union with the U.K.) and Nationalists (who want to join the Republic of Ireland). At opposite ends of this debate are two high-profile and controversial figures: the Reverend Ian Paisley, for the Unionists, and Gerry Adams of Sinn Fein, the political arm of the Irish Republican Army.

Flag: The official flag of Northern Ireland is the Union Jack of the U.K. But you'll also see the Irish tricolor (waved by Nationalists) and the Northern Irish flag (white with red cross and red hand at its center), which is used by Unionists (see "The Red Hand of Ulster" sidebar, page 280).

UVF followed suit. Talks are still underway, interrupted by sporadic hostilities.

The Nationalists want British troops out of Ireland, while the Unionists want the IRA to turn in its arms. Optimists hailed the signing of a breakthrough peace plan in 1998, called the "Good Friday Accord" by Nationalists or the "Belfast Agreement" by Unionists. This led to the emotional release of prisoners on both sides in 2000. Major hurdles to a lasting peace persist, but the downtown checkpoints are history, and "bomb damage clearance sales" are over. And today, more tourists than ever are venturing to Belfast and Derry.

Terminology

Ulster (one of Ireland's 4 ancient provinces) consists of nine counties in the northern part of the island of Ireland. Six of these make up Northern Ireland (pronounced "Norn Iron" by locals), while three counties remain part of the Republic.

Unionists—and the more hard-line **Loyalists**—want the North to remain in the U.K. The **Ulster Unionist Party (UUP),** for 10 years led by Nobel Peace Prize co-winner David Trimble (voted out in mid-2005), is the political party representing moderate Unionist views. The **Democratic Unionist Party (DUP),** led by Reverend Ian Paisley, chooses to take a harder stance in defense of Unionism. The **Ulster Volunteer Force (UVF),** the **Ulster Freedom Fighters (UFF),** and the **Ulster Defense Association (UDA)** are the Loyalist paramilitary organizations mentioned most frequently in newspapers and on spray-painted walls.

Nationalists—and the more hard-line **Republicans**—want a united and independent Ireland ruled by Dublin. The **Social Democratic Labor Party (SDLP),** founded by Nobel Peace Prize co-winner John Hume and led by Mark Durkan, is the moderate political party representing Nationalist views. **Sinn Fein** (shin fayn), led by Gerry Adams, takes a harder stance in defense of Nationalism. The **Irish Republican Army (IRA)** is the Nationalist paramilitary organization (linked with Sinn Fein) mentioned most often in the press and in graffiti.

To gain more insight into the complexity of the Troubles, see the University of Ulster's informative and evenhanded Conflict Archive at http://cain.ulst.ac.uk/index.html.

Safety

Tourists in Northern Ireland are no longer considered courageous (or reckless). A United Nations study conducted in 2003 found that Northern Ireland was statistically the second safest place in the developed world (after Japan). When a local spots you with a lost look on your face, they're likely to ask, "Wot yer lookin fer?" in their distinctive Northern accent. They're not suspicious of you, but rather trying to help you find your way. You're safer in Northern Ireland than in any other part of the U.K.—and far safer than in most major U.S. cities. You have to look for trouble to find it here. Just don't seek out spit-and-sawdust pubs in working-class Protestant neighborhoods and sing Catholic songs.

Tourists notice the tension mainly during the "marching season" (Easter–Aug, peaking in early July). July 12 is traditionally the most confrontational day of the year in the North, when proud Protestant Unionist Orangemen march to celebrate their Britishness and their separate identity from the Republic of Ireland (often through staunchly Nationalist Catholic neighborhoods). Lay low if you stumble onto any big orange parades.

Northern Ireland Is a Different Country

When you leave the Republic of Ireland and enter Northern Ireland, you are crossing an international border. Although you don't have to flash your passport, you do change stamps, phone cards, money—and your Eurailpass is no longer valid. Instead of using euros, as in the Republic of Ireland, you need to switch to the British pound sterling (£; €1 = about £0.70). Northern Ireland issues its own Ulster pound and also uses English pounds. Like the Scottish pound, Ulster pounds are interchangeable with English pounds. But if you're heading to England next, it's best to change your Ulster pounds into English ones (free at any bank in Northern Ireland, England, Wales, or Scotland).

BELFAST

Seventeenth-century Belfast was only a village. With the influx, or "plantation," of English and (more often) Scottish settlers, the character of the place changed. After the plantation—and subjugation of the native Irish—Belfast boomed, spurred by the success of the local linen, rope-making, and shipbuilding industries. The Industrial Revolution took root with a vengeance. While the rest of Ireland remained rural and agricultural, Belfast earned its nickname ("Old Smoke") during the time when many of the brick buildings you'll see today were built. The year 1888 marked the birth of modern Belfast. After Queen Victoria granted city status to this boomtown of 300,000, its citizens built the city's centerpiece, City Hall.

Belfast is the birthplace of the *Titanic* (and many ships that didn't sink). The two huge, mustard-colored cranes (the biggest in the world, nicknamed Samson and Goliath) rise like skyscrapers above the harbor. They stand idle now, but serve as a reminder of this town's former shipbuilding might.

It feels like a new morning in Belfast. It's hard to believe that the bright and bustling pedestrian zone was once a subdued, traffic-free security zone. Now there's no hint of security checks, once a tiresome daily routine. On my last visit, the children dancing in the street were both Catholics and Protestants. They were part of a community summer-camp program giving kids from both communities reasons to live together rather than apart.

Still, it's a fragile peace and a tenuous hope. Mean-spirited murals, hateful bonfires built a month before they're actually burned, and pubs with security gates are reminders that the island is split—and 800,000 Protestant Unionists prefer it that way.

Greater Belfast

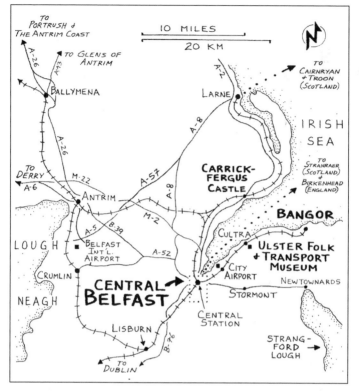

Planning Your Time

Big Belfast is thin on sights. For most, one day of sightseeing is plenty.

Day-Trip from Dublin: On the handy two-hour Dublin–Belfast train (and its cheap £25 day-return tickets, £33 on Fri or Sun), you could make Belfast a day trip: 7:35–Catch the early-morning train from Dublin; 11:00–City Hall tour (Mon–Fri), browse the pedestrian zone, lunch, ride a shared cab up the Falls Road; 15:00–Visit Ulster Museum or side-trip to the Ulster Folk and Transport Museum; evening–Return to Dublin (last train Mon–Sat at 20:10). Sunday's trains depart later and return earlier, compressing your already limited time in Belfast (1st train departs Dublin at 10:00; last train departs Belfast at 18:15). Confirm train times at local stations. Note that the TI offers Town Walks at 14:00 on Wednesday, Friday, Saturday, and Sunday. On Saturday, there's a morning market (at St. George's) and only one City Hall tour (at 14:30).

Staying Overnight: Belfast makes a pleasant overnight stop, with plenty of cheap hostels, reasonable B&Bs, hotel deals (on Fri–Sun), and a resort neighborhood full of B&Bs 30 minutes away in Bangor.

Two Days in Belfast: Splice in the Living History bus tour, Ulster Museum, and Botanic Gardens, or take a day trip to the Antrim Coast.

Two Days in Small-Town Northern Ireland: From Dublin (via Belfast), take the train to Portrush; allow two nights and a day to tour the Causeway Coast (castle, whiskey distilleries, Giant's Causeway, resort fun), then follow the Belfast-in-a-day plan above. With an extra day, add Derry.

Coming from Scotland: With good ferry connections (from Stranraer or Troon in Scotland, or Liverpool in England; see "Transportation Connections," page 289), it's easy to begin your exploration of the Emerald Isle in Belfast, then head south to Dublin and the Republic.

ORIENTATION

(area code: 028)

For the first-time visitor in town for a quick look, Belfast is pretty simple. There are three zones of interest: **central** (Donegall Square, City Hall, pedestrian shopping, TI), **southern** (Ulster Museum, Botanic Gardens, university), and **western** (working-class sectarian neighborhoods west of the freeway). Belfast's "Golden Mile"—stretching from Hotel Europa to the university district—connects the central and southern zones with many of the best dinner and entertainment spots.

Tourist Information

The modern TI (look for "Welcome Center" signs) has fine, free city maps and an enjoyable bookshop with Internet access (June–Sept Mon–Sat 9:00–19:00, Sun 12:00–17:00; Oct–May Mon–Sat 9:00–17:30, closed Sun, 47 Donegall Place, 1 block north of City Hall, tel. 028/9024-6609, www.gotobelfast.com). For the latest on evening fun, get *The List* free at the TI or *That's Entertainment* at newsstands (50p).

Arrival in Belfast

Arriving by fast train, you'll go directly to Central Station (with ATMs and free city maps at ticket counter). From the station, a free Centerlink bus loops to Donegall Square, with stops near Shaftesbury Square (recommended hostels), the bus station (some recommended hotels), and the TI (free with any train or bus ticket, 4/hr, never on Sun, during morning rush hour bus runs only between station and Donegall Square). Allow about £3 for a taxi from Central Station to Donegall Square, or £4 to my B&B listings on Eglantine Road south of Queen's University.

Slower trains arc through Belfast, stopping at several downtown stations, including Central Station, Great Victoria Station (most central, near Donegall Square and most hotels), Botanic (close to the university, Botanic Gardens, and some recommended hostels), and Adelaide (near several recommended B&Bs). It's easy and cheap to connect stations by train (75p).

Helpful Hints

Phone Tips: To call the Republic of Ireland from Northern Ireland, dial 00-353, then the area code without its initial 0, then the local number. To call Northern Ireland from the Republic of Ireland, dial 048, then the local eight-digit number.

Irish Tourist Board: Traveling on to the Republic of Ireland, are ye? If it's information you'll be wanting, pop on in (June–Sept Mon–Fri 9:00–17:00, Sat 9:00–12:30, closed Sun; Oct–May closed Sat–Sun, 53 Castle Street, off Donegall Place, tel. 028/9026-5500, www.ireland.ie).

U.S. Embassy: It's at Danesfort House (Mon–Fri 8:30–17:00, closed Sat–Sun, 233 Stranmillis Road, www.usembassy.org.uk).

Market: On Friday and Saturday mornings (roughly until 14:00), St. George's Market is a commotion of clothes, produce, and seafood (at corner of Oxford and East Bridge Streets, 5 blocks east of Donegall Square).

Internet Access: Revelations Internet Café is at 27 Shaftesbury Square, near the City Hostel (£4/hr, Mon–Fri 8:00–22:00, Sat 10:00–18:00, Sun 11:00–19:00, tel. 028/9032-0337).

Post Office: The main P.O., with lots of fun postcards, is at the intersection of High and Bridge Streets (Mon–Sat 9:00–17:30, closed Sun, 3 long blocks north of Donegall Square).

Laundry: Globe Launderers is at 37 Botanic Avenue (£5 self-serve, £7 drop-off, Mon–Fri 8:00–21:00, Sat 8:00–18:00, Sun 12:00–18:00, tel. 028/9024-3956). For the B&B neighborhood south of town, the closest is Whistle Laundry (£6 drop-off, Mon–Fri 8:00–18:00, Sat 8:30–17:30, closed Sun, 160 Lisburne Road, at intersection with Eglantine Avenue, tel. 028/9038-1297).

Bike Rental: McConvey Cycles is at 183 Ormeau Road (£10/24 hrs, Mon–Sat 9:00–18:00, Thu until 20:00, closed Sun, tel. 028/9033-0322).

Getting Around Belfast

If you line up your sightseeing logically, you can do most of the town on foot.

If you're here in July and August, you can take advantage of "Day Tracker" tickets that give individuals one day of unlimited train travel anywhere in Northern Ireland for £6.50 (making it easy to side-trip to Bangor, the Ulster Folk and Transport Museum in Cultra, or Carrickfergus Castle). Families (up to 2 adults and 2 kids under 16) visiting in July and August get an even better deal: the £15 one-day Family Pass, valid for train and bus travel. Buy your pass at any train station in the city. Outside of July and August, buy "day return" tickets to Carrickfergus, Cultra, or Bangor whenever possible (always cheaper than buying 2 one-way tickets).

For information on trains and buses in Belfast, contact Translink (tel. 028/9066-6630, www.translink.co.uk).

By Bus: Buses go from Donegall Square East to Malone Road and my recommended B&Bs (#8A or #8B, 3/hr, £1.20, all-day pass costs £3 before 10:00 and £2 after).

By Taxi: Taxis are reasonable and should be considered. Rather than use their meters, many cabs charge a flat £3 rate for any ride up to two miles. It's £1 per mile after that. Ride a shared cab if you're going up the Falls Road (explained below).

TOURS

▲**Walking Tour**—A Town Walk takes you through the historic core of town (£5, 90 min; departs from TI at 14:00 on Wed, Fri, Sat, and Sun; extra 11:00 tour added on Sat May–Oct; check all tour times with TI, tel. 028/9024-6609).

▲**Big Bus Tours**—**City Sightseeing** offers the Living History Tour, the best introduction to the city's recent and complicated political and social history. You'll cruise the Catholic and Protestant working-class neighborhoods, with a commentary explaining the political murals and places of interest—mostly dealing with the Troubles of the last 35 years. You see things from the bus and get out for photos only (£8, daily on the hour 10:00–16:30, fewer tours in winter—call first, 1.5 hours, depart from corner of Royal Avenue and Castle Place across from McDonald's, 2 blocks north of Donegall Square; pay cash at kiosk or on bus, or book by phone with credit card; tel. 028/9062-6888, www.city-sightseeing.com).

Minibus Tours—The **Mini-Coach** tour company offers a Belfast City Tour, covering the troubled areas in depth, with time for photo stops (£8, 2 hours, daily at 10:30, Mon–Fri also at 12:30, leaves from Belfast International City Hostel, book in advance, tel. 028/9031-5333, www.minicoachni.co.uk). Their Antrim Coast tour visits the Giant's Causeway, Dunluce Castle (photos only),

Belfast

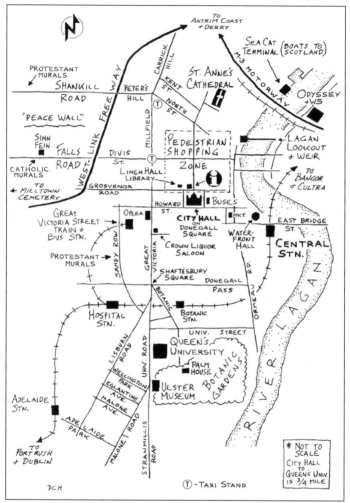

To ANTRIM COAST & DERRY

SEA CAT TERMINAL (BOATS TO SCOTLAND)

M3 MOTORWAY

ODYSSEY & W5

PROTESTANT MURALS

SHANKILL ROAD

PETER'S HILL

CARRICK HILL

KENT ST.

ST. ANNE'S CATHEDRAL

NORTH ST.

"PEACE WALL"

WEST-LINK FREE WAY

MILLFIELD

PEDESTRIAN SHOPPING ZONE

LAGAN LOOKOUT & WEIR

SINN FEIN

FALLS ROAD

DIVIS ST.

TO BANGOR & CULTRA

CATHOLIC MURALS

TO MILLTOWN CEMETERY

GROSVENOR ROAD

LINEN HALL LIBRARY

HOWARD ST.

BUSES

MKT.

EAST BRIDGE ST.

GREAT VICTORIA STREET TRAIN & BUS STN.

OPERA

CITY HALL ON DONEGALL SQUARE

WATER-FRONT HALL

CENTRAL STN.

SANDY ROW

GREAT VICTORIA

CROWN LIQUOR SALOON

PROTESTANT MURALS

SHAFTESBURY SQUARE

DONEGALL PASS

BOTANIC

ORMEAU RD.

RIVER LAGAN

HOSPITAL STN.

LISBURN ROAD

UNIV. ROAD

BOTANIC STN.

UNIV. STREET

QUEEN'S UNIVERSITY

WELLINGTON PARK

EGLANTINE AVE.

PALM HOUSE

BOTANIC GARDENS

MALONE AVE.

ULSTER MUSEUM

ADELAIDE STN.

ADELAIDE PARK

MALONE ROAD

STRANMILLIS ROAD

TO PORT RUSH & DUBLIN

DCH

Ⓣ - TAXI STAND

* NOT TO SCALE CITY HALL TO QUEENS UNIV. IS 3/4 MILE

the Carrick-a-Rede rope bridge (March–Sept), and Old Bushmills Distillery—£4 admission not included (£16, daily 9:30–17:45

depending on demand, book through and depart from hostel listed above). They also have private guides.

Boat Tours—The Lagan Boat Company shows you shipyards on a 75-minute **Titanic Tour** cruise, narrated by a member of the Belfast Titanic Society (£6, daily departures at 12:30, 14:00,

15:30 from Lagan Lookout on Donegall Quay, tel. 028/9033-0844, www.laganboatcompany.com).

Bailey's Historical Belfast Pub Walk—Mixing drinks and history, you'll start at the Crown Dining Room pub and end six pubs later (£6, drinks not included except for a free shot of Baileys at tour's end, May–Oct Thu at 19:00, Sat at 16:00, 2 hours, book in advance, pub above Crown Liquor Saloon on 46 Great Victoria Street, across from Hotel Europa, tel. 028/9268-3665, Judy Crawford).

SIGHTS

Catholic and Protestant Neighborhoods

It will be a happy day when the sectarian neighborhoods of Belfast have nothing to be sectarian about. For a look at a couple of the original home bases of the Troubles, explore the working-class neighborhoods of the Catholic Falls Road and the Protestant Shankill Road or Sandy Row.

You can get tours of Falls Road or Shankill Road (see listings below), but rarely are both combined in one tour. Ken Harper is part of a new breed of Belfast taxi drivers who will give you an insightful private tour of both. He also does tours on Titanic-related sights and on Belfast-born author C. S. Lewis (£25 minimum or £8 per person for a 75-min tour, tel. 028/9074-2711, mobile 0771-175-7178, www.harperstaxitours.co.nr).

▲▲**Falls Road**—At the intersection of Castle and King Streets, you'll find the Castle Junction Car Park. This nine-story park-ing garage's basement (entrance on King Street) is filled with old black cabs—and the only Irish-language signs in downtown Belfast. These shared black cabs efficiently shuttle residents from outlying neighbor-hoods up and down the Falls Road and to the city center. This service originated more than 30 years ago  at the beginning of the Troubles, when locals would hijack city buses and use them as barricades in the street fighting. When bus service was discontinued, local paramilitary groups established the shared taxi service. Any cab goes up the Falls Road, past Sinn Fein headquarters and lots of murals, to the Milltown Cemetery (£2, sit in front and talk to the cabbie). Hop in and out. Easy-to-flag-down cabs run every minute or so in each direction on the Falls Road. Twenty trained cabbies do one-hour tours (£22.50 for 1–3 people, £25 for 4–6 people, £10 per additional hour, cheap for a small group of up to 6 riders, tel. 028/9031-5777, www.wbta.net).

The Sinn Fein office and bookstore are near the bottom of Falls Road. The bookstore is worth a look. Page through books featuring color photos of the political murals that decorate the buildings. Money raised here supports families of imprisoned IRA members.

A sad, corrugated structure called the Peace Wall runs a block or so north of Falls Road (along Cupar Way), separating the Catholics from the Protestants in the Shankill Road area.

At the Milltown Cemetery, walk past all the Gaelic crosses down to the far right-hand corner (closest to the highway), where

the IRA Roll of Honor is set apart from the thousands of other graves by little green railings. They are treated like fallen soldiers. Notice the memorial to Bobby Sands and nine other hunger strikers. They starved themselves to death in the nearby Maze prison in 1981, protesting for political prisoner status as opposed to terrorist criminal treatment. The prison closed in the fall of 2000.

Shankill Road and Sandy Row—You can ride a shared black cab through the Protestant Shankill Road area (departing from North Street near intersection with Millfield Road, not well marked but watch where cabs circle and pick up locals on south side of street; 1-hour tour-£20 for 1–2 people, £30 for 3–6 people, tel. 028/9032-8775).

An easier (and cheaper) way to get a dose of the Unionist side is to walk Sandy Row. From Hotel Europa, walk a block down Glengall Street, then turn left for a 10-minute walk along a working-class Protestant street. A stop in the Unionist memorabilia shop, a pub, or one of the many cheap eateries here may give you an opportunity to talk to a local. You'll see murals filled with Unionist symbolism. The mural of William of Orange's victory over the Catholic King James II (Battle of the Boyne, 1690) thrills Unionist hearts. (From the south end of Sandy Row, it's a 10-min walk to the Ulster Museum, page 281.)

Central Belfast

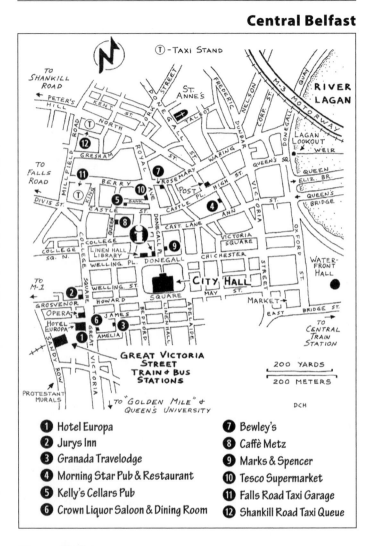

1. Hotel Europa
2. Jurys Inn
3. Granada Travelodge
4. Morning Star Pub & Restaurant
5. Kelly's Cellars Pub
6. Crown Liquor Saloon & Dining Room
7. Bewley's
8. Caffè Metz
9. Marks & Spencer
10. Tesco Supermarket
11. Falls Road Taxi Garage
12. Shankill Road Taxi Queue

More Sights

▲▲**City Hall**—This grand structure, with its 173-foot-tall copper dome, dominates the town center. Built between 1898 and 1906, with its statue of Queen Victoria scowling down Belfast's main drag and the Union Jack flapping behind her, it's a stirring sight. In the garden, you'll find memorials to the *Titanic* and the landing of the U.S. Expeditionary Force in 1942—the first stop en route to Berlin. Take the free 45-minute tour (June–Sept usually Mon–Fri at 11:00, 14:00, and 15:00, Sat only at 14:30; Oct–May Mon–Fri at 11:00 and 14:30, Sat only at 14:30; never on Sun; for Sat tours,

enter back of building—south side, otherwise enter front; call to check schedule and to reserve, tel. 028/9027-0456).
The tour gives you a rundown on city
government and an explanation of the
decor that makes this an Ulster political
hall of fame. Queen Victoria and King
Edward VII look down on city council
meetings. The 1613 original charter of
Belfast granted by James I is on display.
Its Great Hall—bombed by the Germans
in 1941—looks as great as it did the day it
was made.

If you can't manage a tour, at least step inside, admire the
marble swirl staircase, and drop into the "What's on in Belfast"
room just inside the front door.

Linen Hall Library—Across the street from City Hall, the 200-
year-old Linen Hall Library welcomes guests (notice the red
hand above the main front door facing Donegall Square North;
see sidebar on page 280). Described as "Ulster's attic," the library
takes pride in being a neutral space where anyone trying to make
sense of the sectarian conflict can view the Troubled Images, a
historical collection of engrossing political posters. It has a fine,
hardbound ambience, a coffee shop, and a royal newspaper reading
room (Mon–Fri 9:30–17:30, Sat 9:30–13:00, closed Sun, get free
visitor's pass at entrance on Fountain Street, 17 Donegall Square
North, tel. 028/9032-1707, www.linenhall.com).

Golden Mile—This is the overstated nickname of Belfast's liveliest
dining and entertainment district, which stretches from the Opera
House (Great Victoria Street) to the university (University Road).

The **Grand Opera House,** originally built in 1895, bombed
and rebuilt in 1991, and bombed and rebuilt again in 1993, is
extravagantly Victorian and *the* place to take in a concert, play, or
opera (closed to sightseers, ticket office across street on corner of

Howard Street, open Mon–Fri 8:30–21:00,
Sat 8:30–18:00, closed Sun, tel. 028/9024-
1919, www.goh.co.uk). **Hotel Europa,** next
door, while considered the most bombed
hotel in the world, feels pretty casual (listed
under "Sleeping," page 285).

Across the street is the museum-like
Crown Liquor Saloon. Built in 1849, it's
now a part of the National Trust. A wander
through its mahogany, glass, and marble
interior is a trip back into the day of Queen
Victoria (although the privacy provided by

The Red Hand of Ulster

All over Belfast you'll notice a curious symbol: a red hand facing you as if swearing a pledge or telling you to halt. You'll spot one above the Linen Hall Library door, in wrought-iron fences, on old-fashioned clothes wringers (in the Ulster Folk and Transport Museum at Cultra), in Loyalist paramilitary murals, on shield emblems in the gates of Republican memorials, and even on the flag of Northern Ireland (the white flag with the red cross of St. George). It's known as the Red Hand of Ulster and it seems to pop up everywhere. Although it's more often associated with Unionist traditions, it's one of the few emblems used by both communities in Northern Ireland.

Nationalists display the red-hand-on-a-yellow-shield as a symbol of the ancient province of Ulster. It was the official crest of the once-dominant O'Neill clan (who fought against English rule tooth and nail), and today signifies resistance to British rule in these communities.

But you'll more often see the red hand in Unionist areas. They see it as a potent symbol of the political entity of Northern Ireland. The Ulster Volunteer Force chose it for their symbol in 1913 and imbedded it in the center of the Northern Irish flag upon partition of the island in 1921. You'll often see the red hand clenched as a fist in Loyalist murals.

The origin of the red hand comes from a mythological tale of two rival clans that raced by boat to claim a far shore. The first clan leader to touch the shore would win it for his people. Everyone aboard both vessels strained mightily at their oars, near exhaustion as they approached the shore. Finally, in desperation, the chieftain leader of the slower boat whipped out his sword and lopped off his left hand...which he then flung onto the shore, thus winning the coveted land. Moral of the story? The fearless folk of Ulster will do *whatever* it takes to get the job done.

---

the snugs—booths—allows for un-Victorian behavior; Mon–Sat 11:30–24:00, Sun 12:30–23:00; consider a lunch stop, see "Eating," page 287). Upstairs, the Crown Dining Room serves pub grub, is decorated with historic photos, and is the starting point for a pub walk (see "Tours," page 276).

Lagan Lookout Visitors Centre—This center shows off the fruits of the city's £800 million investment in its harbor. The tides of the River Lagan left the town with unsightly mud flats daily. The weir, built in 1994, controls the tides, stabilizing the depth of the harbor. It also doubles as a free pedestrian bridge over the river, affording walkers a fine view of the harbor area, including the big cranes and the new convention center. The visitors center, while mildly entertaining and enthusiastically "interactive," is not worth the £1.50 entry fee (Mon–Fri 11:00–17:00, Sat 12:00–17:00, Sun 14:00–17:00, in winter shorter hours and closed Mon, 5-min walk from TI, just past tipsy 4-feet-off-center Albert Clock Tower, tel. 028/9031-5444).

▲**Ulster Museum**—While mediocre by European standards, this is Belfast's one major museum. It's free and pretty painless: Ride the elevator to the top floor and follow the spiraling exhibits downhill; there's a cheery café halfway down. You'll find an interesting *Made in Belfast* exhibit just before an arch that proclaims, "Trade is the golden girdle of the globe." The delicately worded history section is given an interesting British slant (such as the implication that the Great Famine of 1845 was caused by the Irish population doubling in 40 years—without a mention of various English contributions to the suffering). After a peek at a pretty good mummy, top things off with the *Girona* treasure. Soggy bits of gold, silver, leather, and wood were salvaged from the Spanish Armada's shipwrecked *Girona*—lost off the Antrim Coast north of Belfast in 1588 (free, Mon–Fri 10:00–17:00, Sat 13:00–17:00, Sun 14:00–17:00, in Botanic Gardens on Stranhills Road, south of downtown, tel. 028/9038-3048, www.ulstermuseum.org.uk).

▲**Botanic Gardens**—This is the backyard of Queen's University. On a sunny day, you couldn't imagine a more relaxing park setting. On a cold day, step into the Tropical Ravine for a jungle of heat and humidity. Take a quick walk through the Palm House, reminiscent of the one in London's Kew Gardens but smaller (free, Mon–Fri 10:00–17:00, Sat–Sun 13:00–17:00, less in winter, tel. 028/9032-7700). The Ulster Museum is on the grounds.

The Odyssey—This huge millennium-project complex offers a food pavilion (with a Hard Rock Café) and **W5**, a science center with stimulating, interactive exhibits for youngsters. Where else can a kid play a harp with laser-light strings? (£6, kids-£4, Mon–Thu 10:00–17:00, Fri–Sat 10:00–18:00, Sun 12:00–18:00; W5 stands for who, what, when, where, why; tel. 028/9046-7833, www.w5online.co.uk). There's also a 12-screen cinema (with IMAX) and a 10,000-seat arena where the Belfast Giants professional hockey team plays (2 Queen's Quay, 10-min walk from Central Station, tel. 028/9045-1055, www.theodyssey.co.uk).

Near Belfast

▲▲**Ulster Folk and Transport Museum**—This 180-acre, two-museum complex straddles the road and rail at Cultra, midway between Bangor and Belfast (8 miles east of town).

The Folk Museum, an open-air collection of 34 reconstructed buildings from all over the nine counties of Ulster, showcases the region's traditional lifestyles. After wandering through the old-town site (church, print shop, schoolhouse, humble Belfast row house, and so on), you'll head off into the country to nip into cottages, farmhouses, and mills. Most houses are warmed by a wonderful peat fire and a friendly attendant. It can be dull or vibrant, depending upon when you visit and your ability to chat with the attendants. Drop a peat brick on the fire.

The Transport Museum (downhill, over the road from the folk section) consists of three buildings. Start at the bottom and

trace the evolution of transportation from 7,500 years ago—when people first decided to load an ox—to modern times. The lowest building holds an intriguing section on the sinking of the Belfast-made *Titanic*. In the next two buildings, you roll through the history of bikes, cars, and trains. The car section rumbles from the first car in Ireland (an 1898 Benz) through the "Cortina Culture" of the 1960s to the local adventures of John DeLorean and a 1981 model of his car.

Cost, Hours, Location: £5 for Folk Museum, £5 for Transport Museum, £6.50 combo-ticket for both, £18 for families; July–Sept Mon–Sat 10:00–18:00, Sun 11:00–18:00; March–June Mon–Fri 10:00–18:00, Sat 10:00–18:00, Sun 11:00–18:00; Oct–Feb closes daily at 16:00. Check the schedule for special events that day (tel. 028/9042-8428, www.uftm.org.uk). Allow three hours for your visit. Expect lots of walking. Those with a car can drive from one section to the next.

From Belfast, reach **Cultra** by taxi (£10), bus #502 (2/hr, 30 min from Laganside Bus Centre), or train (£3.90 round-trip, 2/hr, 15 min, from any Belfast train station or from Bangor). Trains and buses stop right in the park, but train service is more dependable. Public-transport schedules get skimpy on Saturday and Sunday.

Carrickfergus Castle—Built during the Norman invasion of the late 1100s, this historic castle stands sentry on the shore of Belfast Lough. William of Orange landed here in 1690, when he began his Irish campaign against deposed King James

II. In 1778, the American privateer ship *Ranger* (first ever to fly the stars-and-stripes flag), under the command of John Paul Jones, defeated the more heavily armed HMS *Drake* right off shore from here. These days the castle feels a bit sanitized and geared for kids, but it's an easy excursion if you're seeking a castle experience near the city (£3; April–Sept Mon–Sat 10:00–17:30, Sun 14:00–18:00; Oct–March Mon–Sat 10:00–16:00, Sun 14:00–16:00; last entry 30-min before closing, 20-min train ride from Belfast on line to Larne costs £4.50 round-trip, tel. 028/9335-1273).

SLEEPING

South Belfast

Many of Belfast's best budget beds cluster in a comfortable area just south of the Ulster Museum and the university. Two train stations (Botanic and Adelaide) are nearby, and buses zip down Malone Road every 20 minutes. Any bus on Malone Road goes to Donegall Square East. Taxis, cheap in Belfast, take you downtown for about £3 (your host can call one).

$$$ Malone Lodge Hotel, by far the classiest listing in this neighborhood, provides slick, business-class comfort and spacious rooms in a charming environment on a quiet, leafy street (Sb-£65–95, Db-£89–109, superior Db-£109–119, weekend deals, elevator, 60 Eglantine Avenue, tel. 028/9038-8000, fax 028/9038-8088, www.malonelodgehotel.com, info@malonelodgehotel.com).

$$ Camera Guest House rents nine smoke-free rooms and comes with an airy, hardwood feeling throughout (S-£34–44, Sb-£47–50, Ds-£56, Db-£62, 44 Wellington Park, tel. 028/9066-0026, fax 028/9066-7856, malonedrumm@hotmail.com, Paul Drumm).

Sleep Code

(£1 = about $1.80; country code: 44, area code: 028)
To call Belfast from the Republic of Ireland, dial 048 before the local 8-digit number.
S = Single, **D** = Double/Twin, **T** = Triple, **Q** = Quad, **b** = bathroom, **s** = shower only). Unless otherwise noted, breakfast is included and credit cards are accepted.

To help you easily sort through these listings, I've divided the rooms into three categories, based on the price for a double room with bath:

$$$ Higher Priced—Most rooms £80 or more.
$$ Moderately Priced—Most rooms between £50–80.
$ Lower Priced—Most rooms £50 or less.

South Belfast

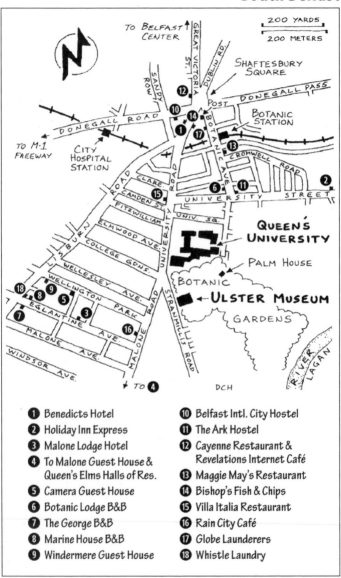

① Benedicts Hotel
② Holiday Inn Express
③ Malone Lodge Hotel
④ To Malone Guest House & Queen's Elms Halls of Res.
⑤ Camera Guest House
⑥ Botanic Lodge B&B
⑦ The George B&B
⑧ Marine House B&B
⑨ Windermere Guest House

⑩ Belfast Intl. City Hostel
⑪ The Ark Hostel
⑫ Cayenne Restaurant & Revelations Internet Café
⑬ Maggie May's Restaurant
⑭ Bishop's Fish & Chips
⑮ Villa Italia Restaurant
⑯ Rain City Café
⑰ Globe Launderers
⑱ Whistle Laundry

$$ Malone Guest House is a classy, stand-alone Victorian house fronting the busy Malone Road. It's homey and well-run by Ms. Quinn, who rents 13 prim rooms (Sb-£35, Db-£60, Tb-£70, 79 Malone Road, at intersection with Adelaide Park and bus stop, tel. 028/9066-9565, fax 028/9037-5090, maloneguesthouse @btinternet.com).

$ Windermere Guest House has 11 rooms, including several small but pleasant singles, in a large Victorian house (S-£26, Sb-£38, very small D-£38, D-£48, Db-£52, T-£56, 60 Wellington Park, tel. 028/9066-2693, fax 028/9068-2218, www.windermereguesthouse .co.uk, windermereguesthouse@ntlworld.com).

$ *Eglantine Avenue B&Bs:* On the same quiet street (Eglantine Avenue), you'll find these two budget choices: **The George B&B** (6 fine, smallish rooms, S-£25, Sb-£35, Db-£45, Tb-£65, at #9, tel. & fax 028/9068-3212), and the grand old **Marine House B&B** (10 high-ceilinged rooms, Sb-£42, Db-£55, Tb-£75, Qb-£80, at #30, tel. & fax 028/9066-2828, www .marineguesthouse3star.com, marine30@utvinternet.co.uk).

$ Botanic Lodge rents 16 decent rooms on a lively but stylish street, with lots of fun eateries nearby (S-£30, Sb-£40, D-£45, Db-£50, 87 Botanic Avenue, 10-min walk to City Hall, tel. & fax 028/9032-7682).

Hotels

Belfast is more of a business town than a tourist town, so business-class room rates are lower or soft on weekends.

$$$ Hotel Europa is Belfast's landmark hotel—fancy, comfortable, and central—with four stars and good weekend rates. Modern yet elegant, this place was Clinton's choice when he visited (Db-£100–160 plus £16 breakfast Mon–Thu, Db-£80–110 Fri–Sun—includes breakfast, President Clinton's suite-£400, 5 non-smoking floors, Great Victoria Street, tel. 028/9027-1066, fax 028/9032-7800, www.hastingshotels.com).

$$ Jurys Inn, an American-style place that rents its 190 identical modern rooms for one simple price, is perfectly located two blocks from City Hall (up to 3 adults or 2 adults and 2 kids for £78–99, breakfast-£8 extra per person, 3 non-smoking floors, Fisherwick Place, tel. 028/9053-3500, fax 028/9053-3511, U.S. tel. 800-423-6953, www.jurysdoyle.com, jurysinnbelfast@jurysdoyle .com).

$$ Granada Travelodge, quiet and extremely central, is a basic Jurys-style business hotel with 90 cookie-cutter rooms high on value, low on character (Db-£49–59, continental breakfast-£5, Irish breakfast-£7, a block from Hotel Europa and City Hall at 15 Brunswick Street, reservations tel. 08700-850-950 or 028/9033-3555, fax 028/9023-2999, www.travelodge.co.uk).

$$ Belfast Holiday Inn Express, not as central as the above hotels, offers the same basic formula (Db-£59–79, kids free, includes continental breakfast, non-smoking floors, elevator, 106A University Street, by Botanic Station, tel. 028/9031-1909, fax 028/9031-1910, www.exhi-belfast.com, mail@exhi-belfast.com).

$$ Benedicts Hotel has a local feel in a good location at the northern fringe of the Queen's University district, with a popular bar that's a maze of polished wood (Sb-£60, Db-£70, Tb-£95–100, elevator, 7–21 Bradbury Place, tel. 028/9059-1999, fax 028/9059-1990, www.benedictshotel.co.uk, info@benedictshotel.co.uk).

Hostels and Dorms

$ Belfast International City Hostel, providing the best value among Belfast's hostels, is big and creatively run, offering single and double rooms along with dorms. It's located near the Botanic train station, in the heart of the lively university district and close to the center. Features include free lockers, left luggage, Internet access in lobby, videos, kitchen, self-serve laundry (£3), cheap breakfast-only cafeteria, elevator, 24-hour reception, and no curfew (beds in 6-bed dorm-£8.50, beds in quad-£10, S-£17, D-£26, 22–32 Donegall Road, tel. 028/9031-5435, fax 028/9043-9699, www.hini.org.uk, info@hini.org.uk). Paul, the manager of the hostel, is a veritable TI, with a passion for his work. The hostel is the starting point for Mini-Coach Tours (see "Tours," page 274).

$ The Ark, a smaller, hipper, more youthful and easygoing hostel, is in the university district near the Botanic train station (38 beds in 6- to 8-bed dorms-£10.90, Db-£36, kitchen, Internet access-£1.50/30 min, 44 University Street, tel. 028/9032-9626, fax 028/9032-9647, www.arkhostel.com, info@arkhostel.com).

$ Queen's Elms Halls of Residence is a big brick Queen's University dorm renting 300 basic, institutional rooms (mainly singles) to travelers during summer break. Singles should book in advance and ask for a "self-catering room" to snare a spot in the newer building (mid-June–early-Sept only, S-£14.20, Sb-£19.40, D-£23.80, cheaper for students, coin-op laundry, self-serve kitchen; reception building is 50 yards down entry street, marked Elms Village on low brick wall, 78 Malone Road; tel. 028/9097-4525, fax 028/9097-4524, www.qub.ac.uk, qehor@qub.ac.uk).

EATING

Downtown

If it's £8 pub grub you want, consider these places. The **Morning Star** is woody and elegant (£7–11 restaurant dinners upstairs, £4 buffet Mon–Sat 12:00–15:00, open daily 12:00–21:00, down alley just off High Street at 17 Pottinger's Entry, tel. 028/9023-5986).

The very Irish **Kelly's Cellars** is 300 years old and hard to find, but worth it (Mon–Wed 11:30–20:00, Thu–Sat 11:30–24:00, closed Sun, live traditional music Fri–Sat nights and Sat at 15:30, 32 Bank Street, 50 yards behind Tesco supermarket, access via alley on left side when facing Tesco, tel. 028/9024-6058). The small, antique **Crown Liquor Saloon** (see "Sights," page 279) has a mesmerizing mishmash of mosaics and shareable snugs—booths—topped with a smoky tin ceiling (Mon–Sat lunch only 11:30–15:00, Sun 12:00–17:00, 46 Great Victoria Street, across from Hotel Europa, tel. 028/9027-9901). The **Crown Dining Room** upstairs offers dependable £7–13 meals (Mon–Sat 12:00–21:00, closed Sun, tel. 028/9027-9901, use entry on Amelia Street when the Crown is closed).

For cafés, choose among the many popular eateries in the streets north of Donegall Square. **Bewley's,** popular in Ireland, offers a good-value cafeteria with seating under a conservatory-style roof (Mon–Sat 8:00–17:30, Thu until 19:00, Sun 11:00–16:00, north end of Donegall's Arcade); there's also a take-away on the other side of the hall. **Caffè Metz** has a sleek, light-wood design and £6 meals, including salads (Mon–Sat 9:00–17:00, closed Sun, 12 Queen Street, at intersection with College Street, tel. 028/9024-9484).

Marks & Spencer has a coffee shop serving skinny lattes and a supermarket in its basement (Mon–Sat 8:30–18:00, Thu until 21:00, Sun 13:00–18:00, WCs on 2nd floor, Donegall Place, a block north of Donegall Square). **Tesco,** another supermarket, is a block north of M&S and two blocks north of Donegall Square (Mon–Sat 8:00–19:00, Thu until 21:00, Sun 13:00–17:00, Royal Avenue and Bank Street). Picnic on the City Hall green.

Near Shaftesbury Square and Botanic Station

Cayenne is a trendy-yet-friendly restaurant refuge hiding behind Belfast's most understated exterior. It's your best bet for gourmet food—innovative global cuisine—without a snobby attitude. Owner Paul Rankin stars in the *Ready Steady Cook* weekday TV show on BBC (£12–22 meals, early-bird specials before 18:45: £12 2-course menu or £15.50 3-course menu, Mon–Fri 12:00–14:30 & 18:00–22:00, Sat 18:00–23:00, Sun 17:00–21:00, reservations smart on weekends, Shaftesbury Square at 7 Ascot House, look for plain gray blocky slab front, tel. 028/9033-1532).

Maggie May's serves hearty, simple, cheap meals (£5–8, Mon–Sat 8:00–22:30, Sun 10:00–22:30, 50 Botanic Avenue, 1 block south of Botanic Station, tel. 028/9032-2662).

Bishop's is the locals' choice for fish and chips (daily 12:00–23:30, pasta and veggie options, classier side has table service, Bradbury Place, just south of Shaftesbury Square, tel. 028/9043-9070).

Villa Italia packs in crowds hungry for linguini and *bistecca*. With its checkered tablecloths and a wood-beamed ceiling draped with grape leaves, it's a little bit of Italy in Belfast (£9–15, Mon–Sat 17:00–23:00, Sun 16:00–22:30, 39 University Road, 3 long blocks south of Shaftesbury Square, at intersection with University Street, tel. 028/9032-8356).

Rain City Café is closest to my cluster of B&B listings south of Queen's University. It's a hip grill serving tasty pasta, fish, and beef dishes. While this place has the same owners as classy Cayenne (listed above), it's cheaper here, with a brighter atmosphere (£5–8 lunches, £8–15 dinners, daily 12:00–22:00, Sat–Sun brunch 10:00–16:00, 33–35 Malone Road, near corner of Eglantine Avenue, tel. 028/9068-2929).

Bangor

To stay in a laid-back seaside hometown—with more comfort per pound—sleep 30 minutes east of Belfast in Bangor (BANG-grr). Formerly a slick Belfast seaside escape, Bangor now has a sleepy and almost residential feeling. But with elegant old homes facing its newly spruced-up harbor and the lack of even a hint of big-city Belfast, Bangor has appeal. The harbor is a five-minute walk from the train station. Bangor's **TI** is at 34 Quay Street (July–Aug Mon–Fri 9:00–18:00, Sat 10:00–17:00, Sun 13:00–17:00, June and Sept closes at 17:00 Mon–Fri, Oct–May closed Sun, tel. 028/9127-0069).

Getting to Bangor

Catch the train from Belfast Central to Bangor (2/hr, 30 min, one-way-£3.50, same-day round-trip-£6.20; go to the end of the line—don't get off at Bangor West), stopping en route at Cultra (Ulster Folk and Transport Museum). The journey gives you a good close-up look at the giant Belfast harbor cranes.

If day-tripping into Belfast from Bangor, get off at Belfast Central (which has a free Rail-Link shuttle bus to the town center, 4/hr, not Sun) or stay on until the Botanic Station for the Ulster Museum, the Golden Mile, and Sandy Row.

SLEEPING AND EATING

(£1 = about $1.80, country code: 44, area code: 028)

$$ Royal Hotel is a fine old place right on the harbor with good weekend rates for its 50 rooms (Db-£75 weekdays, £65 Fri–Sun, view rooms are £10 pricier, 26 Quay Street, tel. 028/9127-1866,

fax 028/9146-7810, www.royalhotelbangor.com, royalhotelbangor
@aol.com).

For good £7–11 meals, try **Lord Nelson Bistro** (daily 12:00–
21:30, in the Marine Court Hotel facing harbor, 18–20 Quay
Street). The bar next door at the **Royal Hotel** serves £7 lunches
and £8–12 dinners (daily 12:00–14:30 & 17:00–21:00). Consider
Ganges for Indian food (daily 12:00–14:00 & 17:30–22:30, 9
Bingham Street, tel. 028/9145-3030).

TRANSPORTATION CONNECTIONS

For updated schedules and prices for both trains and buses in
Northern Ireland, check with Translink (tel. 028/9066-6630,
www.translink.co.uk).

From Belfast by Train to: Dublin (8/day, 2 hrs), **Derry**
(8/day, 2.25 hrs), **Larne** (hrly, 1 hr), **Portrush** (10/day, 1.75 hrs).
Service is less frequent on Sundays. Train info: tel. 028/9066-6630.
In July and August consider a £6.50 "Day Tracker" ticket, good for
all-day train use in Northern Ireland (see page 274, above).

By Bus to: Portrush (5/day, 2 hrs, £8), **Derry** (20/day, 1.45
hrs, £9), **Dublin** (6/day, 3 hrs), **Glasgow** (2/day, 5 hrs), **Edin-
burgh** (2/day, 6 hrs). The Europa Bus Centre is behind Hotel
Europa (Ulsterbus tel. 028/9033-7003 for destinations in Scotland
and London, tel. 028/9066-6630 for destinations in Northern
Ireland).

By Plane: Belfast has two airports. Belfast City Airport
(www.belfastcityairport.com) is a five-minute taxi ride from town
(near the docks), while Belfast International Airport (www.bial
.co.uk) is 18 miles west of town, connected by buses from the
Europa Bus Centre behind the Europa Hotel. British Airways
flies to **Glasgow** (3/day, 45 min, British Airways' Belfast office
tel. 0845-606-0747, central booking tel. 0345-222-111), and bmi
british midland flies to **London's** Heathrow Airport (12/day, tel.
0870-6070-555).

By Ferry to Scotland: There are a number of options, ports,
and companies. You can sail between Belfast and **Stranraer** on

Stena Line ferry (7/day; 5 on
fast 1.75-hr crossing, 2 on slower
3.25-hr ferry, Mon–Thu £25,
Fri–Sun £29, save £2 by booking
online, tel. 028/9074-7747, www
.stenaline.co.uk). P&O Ferry (tel.
0870-2424-777, www.poirishsea
.com) goes from **Larne** (20 miles
north of Belfast, 1 train/hr, TI

tel. 028/2826-0088) to **Cairnryan** (11/day, 1 hr, £25) or to **Troon** (2/day, 2 hrs, £28).

By Ferry to England: You can sail overnight from Belfast to **Birkenhead** (10 min from Liverpool)—with dinner and breakfast—for £35 (plus £40 for a cabin that sleeps 4) on North Merchant Ferries (8 hrs, nightly at 22:00, tel. 0870-600-4321, www.norsemerchant.com).

PORTRUSH AND THE ANTRIM COAST

 The Antrim Coast—the north of Northern Ireland—is one of the most interesting and scenic coastlines in Ireland. Within a few miles of the Portrush train terminal, you can visit some evocative castle ruins, tour the world's oldest whiskey distillery, risk your life on a bouncy rope bridge, and hike along the famous Giant's Causeway.

The homey seaside resort of Portrush used to be known as "the Brighton of the North." While it's seen its best days, it retains the atmosphere and architecture of a genteel, middle-class seaside resort. Portrush fills its peninsula with family-oriented amusements, fun eateries, and B&Bs. Summertime fun-seekers promenade along the tiny harbor and tumble down to the sandy beaches, which extend in sweeping white crescents on either side.

Superficially, Portrush has the appearance of any small British seaside resort, but its history and high population of young people (students from the University of Ulster at Coleraine) give the town a little more personality. Along with the usual arcade amusements, there are nightclubs, restaurants, summer theater in the town hall, and convivial pubs that attract customers all the way from Belfast. At the end of the train line and just a few miles from several important sights, Portrush is an ideal base for exploring the highlights of the Antrim Coast.

Planning Your Time

You need a full day to explore the Antrim Coast, so allow two nights in Portrush. An ideal day could lace together Dunluce Castle, Old Bushmills Distillery, and the Giant's Causeway, followed by nine holes on the Portrush pitch-and-putt course.

ORIENTATION

(area code: 028)

Portrush's pleasant and easily walkable town center features sea

views in every direction. On one side are the harbor and restaurants, and on the other are Victorian townhouses and vast, salty views. The tip of the peninsula is filled with tennis courts, lawn-bowling greens, putting greens, and a park.

The town is busy with students during the school year. July and August are beach-resort boom time. June and September are laid-back and lazy. Families pack Portrush on Saturdays, and revelers from Belfast crowd its hotels on Saturday nights.

Tourist Information

The TI, more generous and helpful than those in the Republic, is in the big, modern Dunluce Centre (July–Aug daily 9:00–19:00; Sept–Oct and March–June Mon–Fri 9:00–17:00, Sat–Sun 12:00–17:00; closed Nov–Feb; tel. 028/7082-3333). Get the North Ireland driving map (£4), the free *Stop & Visit* brochure, and a free Belfast map if you're Belfast-bound.

Arrival in Portrush

The train tracks stop at the base of the tiny peninsula that Portrush fills (no baggage check at station). The TI is three long blocks from the train station (follow signs down Eglinton Street and turn left at fire station). All listed B&Bs are within a 10-minute walk of the train station (see "Sleeping," page 299). The bus stop is two blocks from the train station.

Getting Around the Antrim Coast

By Bus: In July and August, a couple of all-day bus passes are available to get you around the region. The better option is the £4.20 **Bushmills Open Topper,** connecting Portrush, Old Bushmills Distillery, and the Giant's Causeway every two hours. The £3.50 **Causeway Rambler**—which links Old Bushmills Distillery, the Giant's Causeway Visitors Centre, and the Carrick-a-Rede Rope Bridge hourly—is less convenient because it doesn't include Portrush in its circuit (to get from Portrush to Bushmills, take a £7 taxi; those who want to see the Rope Bridge—along with the other sights—could consider getting both passes). For either pass, pick up a schedule at the TI and buy the ticket from the driver

Portrush

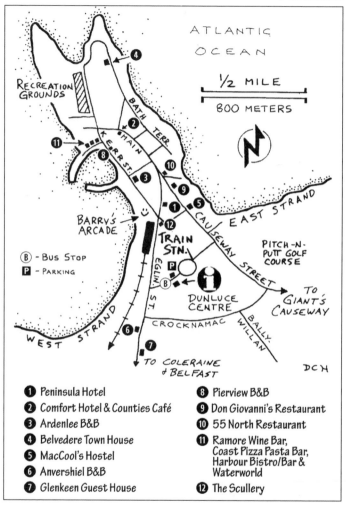

- ❶ Peninsula Hotel
- ❷ Comfort Hotel & Counties Café
- ❸ Ardenlee B&B
- ❹ Belvedere Town House
- ❺ MacCool's Hostel
- ❻ Anvershiel B&B
- ❼ Glenkeen Guest House
- ❽ Pierview B&B
- ❾ Don Giovanni's Restaurant
- ❿ 55 North Restaurant
- ⓫ Ramore Wine Bar, Coast Pizza Pasta Bar, Harbour Bistro/Bar & Waterworld
- ⓬ The Scullery

(in Portrush, the Bushmills Open Topper bus stops at Dunluce Avenue, next to public WC, a 2-min walk from TI). For more info, call Translink (tel. 028/9066-6630, www.translink.co.uk).

By Car: Distances are short and parking is easy. Don't miss the treacherous-yet-scenic coastal route down to the Glens of Antrim.

By Taxi: Groups (up to 4) go reasonably by taxi, which costs only £9 from Portrush to the Giant's Causeway. A couple companies to try are Causeway Coast Taxi (tel. 028/7082-3421) or North West Taxi (tel. 028/7082-4446).

TOURS

Awakin Causeway Quest Tour—This 90-minute bus tour takes you to viewpoints of Antrim Coast sights (Giant's Causeway, Carrick-a-Rede Rope Bridge, Dunseverick Castle, Fair Head, Whitepark Bay, and Ballycastle), but without time to get out and explore them. Interactive onboard audio-visual displays flesh out the local history, making this a quick rainy-day option for non-hikers (£15, June–Aug departs from the WWI memorial in central Bushmills once per day at 9:15; otherwise most tours depart from Giant's Causeway at 10:00, 12:00, 14:00, 16:00; to connect the dots, you can take a £9 taxi between Giant's Causeway and Portrush; book tour in advance, confirm pick-up location and schedule, tel. 028/2073-0364 or 077/9661-4844, www.causewayquest.com).

SIGHTS AND ACTIVITIES

Portrush

Barry's Old Time Amusement Arcade—This is a fine chance to see Northern Ireland at play (open weekends and summer only). Just below the train station on the harbor, it's filled with candy floss (cotton candy) and little kids learning the art of one-armed bandits, 2p at a time. Get £1 worth of 2p coins from the machine and go wild (July–Aug daily 13:00–22:30; May–June Sat–Sun 10:00–18:00, closed Mon–Fri, closed Sept–April).

Pitch-and-Putt at the Royal Portrush Golf Course—Irish courses, like those in Scotland, are highly sought after for their lush but dry greens in glorious settings. Serious golfers can get a tee time at the Royal Portrush, occasional home of the Senior British Open (greens fees Mon–Fri-£95, Sat–Sun-£110). Those on a budget can play the adjacent, slightly shorter Valley Course (greens fees Mon–Fri-£32.50, Sat–Sun-£37.50). Meanwhile, rookies can get a wee dose of this wonderful golf setting at the neighboring Skerry 9 Hole Links pitch-and-putt range. You get two clubs and balls for £4.50, and they don't care if you go around twice (daily 8:30–19:00, 10-min walk from station, tel. 028/7082-2311).

Portrush Recreation Grounds—For some easygoing exercise right in town, this well-organized park offers lawn-bowling greens (£3.40/hr with gear), putting greens, tennis courts, a great kids' play park, and a café (tennis shoes, balls, and rackets can all be rented for a low price; Easter–Sept Mon–Sat 10:00–dusk, Sun 13:00–19:00, closed Oct–Easter, tel. 028/7082-4441).

More Fun—Consider **Dunluce Centre** (kid-oriented fun zone, in same building with TI) and **Waterworld** (£4.50, pool, water-slides, bowling, Easter–Aug daily 10:00–19:00; Sept Sat–Sun

10:00–18:00, closed Mon–Fri; closed Oct–Easter, wedged between Harbor Restaurant and Ramore Wine Bar, tel. 028/7082-2001).

Antrim Coast

▲**Dunluce Castle**—These romantic ruins, perched dramatically on the edge of a rocky headland, are testimony to this region's turbulent past. During the Middle Ages, the castle resisted several sieges. But on a stormy night in 1639, dinner was interrupted as

half of the kitchen fell into the sea, taking the servants with it. That was the last straw for the lady of the castle. The countess of Antrim packed up and moved inland, and the castle "began its slow submission to the forces of nature." While it's one of the largest castles in Northern Ireland and is beautifully situated, there's precious little to see among its broken walls.

The 16th-century expansion of the castle was financed by the salvaging of a shipwreck. In 1588, the Spanish Armada's *Girona* sank on her way home after an aborted mission against England, laden with sailors and the valuables of three abandoned sister ships. More than 1,300 drowned, and only five washed ashore. (The shipwreck was excavated in 1967, and a bounty of golden odds and silver ends wound up in Belfast's Ulster Museum—see page 281.)

Castle admission includes an impromptu guided tour of the ruins. The tour is interesting for its effort to defend the notion of "Ulster, a place apart—facing Scotland, cut off from the rest of Ireland by dense forests and mountains..." Before you leave, poke your head into the building opposite the gift shop and check out the large castle model showing the joint in its fully roofed heyday (£2; April–Sept daily 10:00–18:00; off-season Mon–Sat 10:00–16:00, shorter hours Sun; last entry 30 min before closing, tel. 028/2073-1938).

▲▲**Old Bushmills Distillery**—Bushmills claims to be the world's oldest distillery. Though King James I (of Bible fame) only granted its license to distill "Aqua Vitae" in 1608, whiskey has been made here since the 13th century. Distillery tours waft you through the process, making it clear that Irish whiskey is triple distilled—and therefore smoother than Scotch whisky (distilled merely twice and minus the "e"). The 45-minute tour starts with the mash pit, which is filled with a porridge that eventually becomes whiskey. (The leftovers of that porridge are fed to the county's particularly happy cows.) You'll see thousands of oak casks—the kind used for Spanish sherry—filled with aging whiskey. The finale, of course,

Antrim Coast

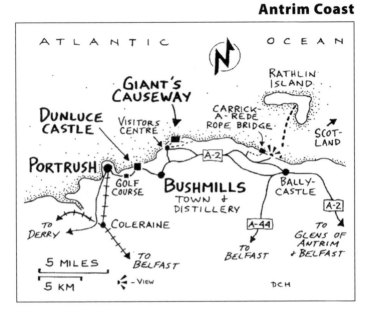

is the tasting in the 1608 Bar—the former malt barn. When your guide asks for a tasting volunteer, raise your hand quick and strong. Four volunteers per tour get to taste test eight different whiskeys (Irish versus Scotch and bourbon). Everyone else gets a single glass of his or her choice. Non–whiskey enthusiasts might enjoy a cinnamon-and-cloves hot toddy. To see the distillery at its lively best, visit when the 100 workers are manning the machinery—Monday morning through Friday noon (weekend tours see a still still). Tours are limited to 35 people and book up. In summer, call in your name to get a tour time before you arrive (£5, April–Oct daily, tours are on the half-hour from 9:30, last tour at 16:00, Sun from 12:00; Nov–March daily at 10:30, 11:30, 13:30, 14:30, and 15:30; tel. 028/2073-1521). You can get a decent lunch in the tasting room after your tour. The distillery is signposted a quarter mile from Bushmills town center.

Sleeping near Bushmills: For an overnight, consider **Valley View Farm B&B** (Sb-£25–28, Db-£40–46, 6a Ballyclough Road, 4 miles south of Bushmills, tel. 028/2074-1608, fax 028/2074-2739, www.valleyviewbushmills.com, valerie.mcfall@btinternet.com).

▲▲**Giant's Causeway**—This four-mile-long stretch of coastline is famous for its bizarre basalt columns. The shore is covered with hexagonal pillars that stick up at various heights. It's as if the earth were offering God his choice of 37,000 six-sided cigarettes.

Geologists claim the Giant's Causeway was formed by volcanic eruptions 60 million years ago. As the lava surface cooled, it contracted and cracked into hexagonal blocks. As the layer of hardened but alligatored rock settled, it broke into its many stair-like steps.

In actuality, the Giant's Causeway was made by a giant Ulster warrior named Finn MacCool who wanted to reach his love on the Scottish island of Staffa. Way back then, the causeway stretched to Scotland, connecting the two lands. Today, while the foundation has settled, the formation still extends under-sea to Staffa, just off the Scottish coast. Finn's causeway was ruined (into today's "remnant of chaos") by a rival giant. As the rival fled from ferocious Finn back to his Scottish homeland, he ripped up the causeway so Finn couldn't chase him.

For cute variations on the Finn story, as well as details on the ridiculous theories of modern geologists, start your visit in the visitors center. The real information is on the walls of the exhibition, while a video gives a worthwhile history of the Giant's Causeway, with a regional overview (£1, 4/hr, 12 min). A gift shop and cafeteria are standing by.

A minibus (80p each way, 4/hr) zips tired tourists a half-mile directly to the Grand Causeway, the highlight of the entire coast.

For a better dose of the Causeway, consider this plan: Follow the high cliff-top trail from the visitors center 10 minutes to a great viewpoint, then 10 minutes farther to reach the Shepherd's Stairway. Zigzag down to the coast; at the T junction, go 100 yards right to the towering pipes of "the Organ." Then retrace your steps and continue left to the "Giant's Boot" for some photo fun and the dramatic point where the stairs step into the sea. Just beyond that, at the asphalt turnaround, you'll see the bus stop for a lift back to the visitors center. You could walk the entire five-mile Giant's Causeway. The 75p hiking guide points out the highlights named by 18th-century guides (Camel's Back, Giant's Eye, and so on). The causeway is free and always open (visitors center open daily 10:00–17:00, July–Aug until 18:00, £5 to park, tel. 028/2073-1855).

A quaint, narrow-gauge steam locomotive connects the Causeway to Bushmills on a two-mile, 15-minute journey. Departures from the Bushmills station (on Ballaghmore Road, 15-min walk from distillery) are on the half-hour 11:30–17:30; return trips leave from the Causeway station on the hour 11:00–17:00 (£5 round-trip, £3.50 one-way, runs daily June–Sept, sporadic week-ends rest of year, tel. 028/2073-2844 or 028/2073-2594 for recorded info, www.giantscausewayrailway.org).

The Scottish Connection

The Romans called the Irish the "Scoti." When the Scoti crossed the narrow channel and invaded the land of the Picts 1500 years ago, that region became known as Scotland. Ireland and Scotland were never conquered by the Romans and retained similar clannish Celtic traits. Both share the same Gaelic branch of the linguistic tree.

On clear summer days from Carrick-a-Rede, the island of Mull in Scotland is visible only 17 miles away. Much closer on the horizon is the boomerang-shaped Rathlin Island, part of Northern Ireland. Rathlin is where the Scottish Robert the Bruce (of *Braveheart* fame) retreated in 1307 after defeat at the hands of the English. Legend has it that he hid in a cave on the island, where he observed a spider patiently rebuilding his web each time a breeze knocked it down. Inspired by the spider's perseverance, he gathered his Scottish forces once more and finally defeated the English at the decisive battle of Bannockburn.

Flush with confidence from his victory, Robert the Bruce decided to open up a second front against the English...in Ireland. In 1315, he sent his brother Edward over to enlist their Celtic Irish cousins in an effort to thwart the English. After securing Ireland, Edward hoped to move on and enlist the Welsh, thus cornering England with their pan-Celtic nation. But Edward's timing was bad—Ireland was in the midst of famine. His Scottish troops had to live off the land and began to take food and supplies from the starving Irish. He might also have been trying to destroy Ireland's crops to keep them from being used as a colonial "breadbasket" to feed English troops. The Scots quickly wore out their welcome, and Edward the Bruce was eventually killed in battle near Dundalk in 1318.

This was the first time in history that Ireland was used as a pawn by England's enemies. Ireland was seen as the English Achilles' heel by Spain and France, who later attempted Irish invasions. The English Tudor and Stewart royalty countered these threats in the 16th and 17th centuries by starting the "plantation" of loyal subjects in Ireland. The only successful long-term settlement by the English was here in Northern Ireland, which remains part of the United Kingdom today.

It's interesting to speculate how things would be different today if Ireland and Scotland had been permanently welded together as a nation 700 years ago. You'll notice the strong Scottish influence in this part of Ireland when you ask a local a question and he answers, "Aye, a wee bit." The Irish joke that the Scots are just Irish people who couldn't swim home.

▲▲**Carrick-a-Rede Rope Bridge**—For 200 years, fishermen have strung a narrow 80-foot-high bridge (planks strung between wires)

across a 65-foot-wide chasm between the mainland and a tiny island. Today the bridge (while not the original version) still gives access to the salmon nets that are set during the summer months to catch the fish turning the coast's corner. (The complicated system is described at the gateway.) A pleasant 20-minute (1-mile) walk from the parking lot takes you to the rope bridge. The island affords fine views and great seabird-watching, especially during nesting season (£2.50 trail and bridge fee, pay at hut beside parking lot, coffee shop and WCs also near parking lot, March–Sept daily 10:00–18:00, July–Aug until 19:30, closed Oct–Feb, tel. 028/2076-9839).

If you have a car and a picnic lunch, don't miss the terrific coastal viewpoint rest area one mile steeply uphill and east of Carrick-a-Rede (on B-15 road to Ballycastle). This grassy area offers one of the best picnic spots in Northern Ireland (has picnic tables, but no WCs). Feast on bird's-eye views of the rope bridge, nearby Rathlin Island, and the not-so-distant Island of Mull in Scotland.

▲**Antrim Mountains and Glens**— Not particularly high (never more than 1,500 feet), the Antrim Mountains are cut by a series of large glens running northeast to the sea. Glenariff, with its waterfalls (especially the "Mare's Tail"), is the most beautiful of the nine glens.

SLEEPING

Portrush has decent hotels, but some B&Bs seem well-worn. August and Saturday nights can be tight. Otherwise, it's a "you take half a loaf when you can get it" town. Rates vary with the view and season—probe for softness. Each listing faces the sea, though sea views are worth paying for only if you get a bay window. Ask for a big room (some doubles can be very small; twins are bigger). Lounges are invariably grand and have bay-window views. All places listed have lots of stairs, but most are perfectly central and within a few minutes' walk of the train station. Parking is easy.

Sleep Code

(£1 = about $1.80, country code: 44, area code: 028)
S = Single, **D** = Double/Twin, **T** = Triple, **Q** = Quad, **b** = bathroom, **s** = shower only. Breakfast is included and credit cards are accepted unless otherwise noted.

To help you easily sort through these listings, I've divided the rooms into three categories, based on the price for a standard double room with bath:

$$$ **Higher Priced**—Most rooms £80 or more.
$$ **Moderately Priced**—Most rooms between £50–80.
$ **Lower Priced**—Most rooms £50 or less.

$$$ Comfort Hotel, in the middle of town, is a modern, 50-room establishment with a good restaurant (Db-£75–110, elevator, limited private parking, 73 Main Street, tel. 028/7082-6100, fax 028/7082-6160, www.comforthotelportrush.com, info @comforthotelportrush.com).

$$ Peninsula Hotel is a big place right in the town center with huge (but sometimes smoky) rooms, modern decor, and all the comforts. Ask for a room far from its disco, which can be noisy on party nights (Sb-£40–50, Db-£60–80, Tb-£80–105, elevator, 15 Eglinton Street, tel. 028/7082-2293, fax 028/7082-4315, www .peninsulahotel.co.uk, reservations@peninsulahotel.co.uk).

$ Pierview B&B, close to Portrush's finest restaurants, has four comfortable, non-smoking rooms with the best breakfast atrium views in town, overlooking the quaint harbor (Sb-£25–30, Db-£45–50, Tb-£55–60, cash only, parking, 53 Kerr Street, tel. 028/7082-3234, Adeline Chambers).

$ Belvedere Town House, a stately place on the quiet side of town with 14 spacious, relatively well-appointed rooms, is the best value in town (S-£20–25, Db-£40–50, 5 percent extra if you pay with credit card, farthest from station but with easy parking—ideal for drivers, 15 Lansdowne Crescent, tel. 028/7082-2771, belvederetownhouse@hotmail.com, Thomas Burns).

$ Ardenlee B&B has six bigger-than-average rooms and a fine location near the train station (Db-£45–50, Tb-£65–80, Qb-£85–90, cash only, 10 percent discount with cash and this book in 2006, 19 Kerr Street, tel. 028/7082-2639, www.ardenleehouse .co.uk, Rosy Turnbull).

$ Anvershiel B&B, with six non-smoking rooms, is a five-minute walk from the train station. Jovial Victor Bow, who runs the show, is in the know about local golf (Sb-£30, Db-£45–50, Tb-£75, 10 percent discount on Db price only for 2-night stay with cash and this book in 2006, parking, 16 Coleraine Road, tel. 028/7082-3861, www.anvershiel.com, enquiries@anvershiel.com).

$ Glenkeen Guest House has 10 rooms down the same road, farther from town (Sb-£32, Db-£50, Tb-£57, some non-smoking rooms, parking, 59 Coleraine Road, 10-min walk from station, tel. & fax 028/7082-2279, www.glenkeenguesthouse.co.uk, glenkeen @btinternet.com, Mrs. Little).

$ MacCool's Portrush Independent Hostel is a friendly and laid-back place with 18 beds in four rooms (£10 per bed in 6- and 8-bed dorm rooms, D-£24–28, cash only, non-smoking, one all-girls room, lockers, guests' kitchen, game-stocked lounge, Internet access-£2/hr, handy laundry service-£3/load, surf lessons-£20/2 hrs, 35 Causeway Street, tel. 028/7082-4845, www.portrush-hostel .com, portrushhostel@hotmail.com, Kirsty and Gary Taylor).

EATING

Being a get-away-from-Belfast town—not to mention close to a university town (Coleraine)—Portrush has more than enough chips joints.

Eglinton Street is lined with cheap and cheery eateries. **The Scullery** makes £2 sandwiches and healthy wraps to take away and enjoy by the beach—or on an Antrim Coast picnic (July–Aug daily 8:30–20:30, Sept–June until 17:00, 4 Eglinton Lane, tel. 028/7082-1000).

Counties Café serves dependable meals at reasonable prices (daily £6–8 lunches 12:00–14:30 and £9–15 dinners 17:00–21:00, on ground floor of Comfort Hotel at 73 Main Street, tel. 028/7082-6100).

For Italian food, try candlelit **Don Giovanni's** (£7–13 pasta dishes, daily 17:30–23:00, tel. 028/7082-5516).

Dinner with Views: The best dinner sea views are found at **55 North** (named for the local longitude), with windows on all sides. Service can be slow, but the classy £8–17 pasta and fish plates are worth the wait (July–Aug daily 12:00–14:30 & 17:00–22:00, Sept–June closed Mon, 1 Causeway Street, tel. 028/7082-2811).

Harbour Road Eateries: The following four restaurants, located within 50 yards of each other (all under the same owner-ship and overlooking the harbor on Harbour Road), are just about everyone's vote for the best food values in town.

Sharing a building with the Coast Pizza Pasta Bar, the salty, modern, and much-loved **Ramore Wine Bar** is upstairs, bursting with happy eaters. They're enjoying the most inviting menu I've seen in Ireland, featuring huge £8–15 meals ranging from steaks to vegetarian food. Share a decadent Banoffee (banana toffee) pie dessert with a friend (daily 12:15–14:15 & 17:00–22:00, tel. 028/7082-4313).

Downstairs is the energetic **Coast Pizza Pasta Bar** with good red wine (from £2.50/glass) as a welcome break after all the Guinness. Come early for a table or sit at the bar (July–Aug Mon–Thu 17:00–22:00, Fri–Sat 16:00–22:30, Sun 15:00–21:30; Sept–June closed Mon–Tue, tel. 028/7082-3311).

The **Harbour Bistro** (run by the Ramore folks, with the same winning formula) offers a more subdued, darker bistro ambience than the wine bar, with meals for a few pounds more (£6 lunches July–Aug Fri–Sun 12:30–14:30, £9–16 dinners daily 17:00–22:00, £6–9 High Tea menu Mon–Fri 17:00–18:30, tel. 028/7082-2430).

The adjoining **Harbour Bar** has an old-fashioned pub downstairs and a plush, overstuffed lounge with a toasty fire and grand views upstairs—a great place to enjoy a drink.

TRANSPORTATION CONNECTIONS

From Portrush by Train to: Coleraine (2/hr, 12 min, sparse on Sun morning), **Belfast** (9/day, 4/day Sun, 2 hrs, transfer in Coleraine), **Dublin** (7/day, 2/Sun, 5 hrs, transfer in Coleraine). In July and August, consider a £6.50 "Day Tracker" ticket, good for all-day train use in Northern Ireland (see page 274).

By Bus to: Belfast (along scenic coast, 7/day, 2.5 hrs), **Dublin** (1/day, 5.5 hrs).

Useful updated schedules and prices for both trains and buses in Northern Ireland can be obtained from Translink (tel. 028/9066-6630, www.translink.co.uk).

DERRY AND COUNTY DONEGAL

The town of Derry (or Londonderry to Unionists) is the mecca of Ulster Unionism. When Ireland was being divvied up, the Foyle River was the logical border between the North and the Republic. But, for sentimental and economic reasons, the North kept Derry, which is on the Republic's side of the river. Consequently, this predominantly Catholic city has been much contested throughout the Troubles. Still, the conflict is only one dimension of Derry; this pivotal city has a more diverse history and a prettier setting than Belfast. And with a quarter of the population (73,000), it feels more manageable to visitors.

County Donegal, to the west of Derry, is about as far-flung as Ireland gets. A forgotten economic backwater (part of the Republic but riding piggyback on the North), it lacks blockbuster museums or sights. But a visit here is more about the journey, and adventurous drivers—a car is a must—will be rewarded with a time-capsule peek into old Irish ways and uncompromisingly beautiful scenery.

Planning Your Time

Travelers heading north from Westport or Galway should get an early start (the town of Donegal makes a good lunch stop), so they can spend a couple hours in Derry and see the essentials. In Derry, visit the Tower Museum and catch some views from the town wall before continuing on to Portrush for the night.

With more time, spend a night in Derry, so you can see the powerful Bogside murals and take a walking tour around the town walls—you'll appreciate this underrated city. With two nights in Derry, consider crossing the border into the Republic for a scenic driving loop through part of remote County Donegal (see page 321).

Derry

No city in Ireland connects the kaleidoscope of historical dots more colorfully than Derry. From leafy monastic hamlet, to cannon-ball-battered siege survivor, to Industrial Revolution sweatshop, to essential WWII naval base, to wrenching flashpoint of sectarian troubles...Derry has seen it all. But today you can feel comfortable wandering the streets and enjoying this unique Irish city.

ORIENTATION

(area code: 028)
The Foyle River flows north, slicing Derry into eastern and western chunks. The old town walls and worthwhile sights are all on the west side. Waterloo Place and the adjacent Guildhall Square, just outside the north corner of the old city walls, are the pedestrian hubs of city activity. The Strand Road area extending north from Waterloo Place makes a comfortable home base, with the majority of lodging and restaurant suggestions within a block or two on either side. The Diamond and its War Memorial statue mark the heart of the old city within the walls.

Tourist Information: The TI sits on the riverfront and has a room-finding service, books walking tours, and gives out free city maps (July–Sept Mon–Fri 9:00–19:00, Sat 10:00–18:00, Sun 10:00–17:00; Oct–June Mon–Fri 9:00–17:00, Sat 10:00–17:00, closed Sun; 44 Foyle Street, tel. 028/7126-7284, www.derryvisitor.com).

Arrival in Derry
Derry's little end-of-the-line train station, next to the river on the east side of town, has service to Portrush, Belfast, and Dublin. Free shuttle buses to Ulsterbus station (which is on the west side of town) await each arriving train. Otherwise, it's a 15-minute walk across Craigavon Bridge to the TI, or £3 taxi ride to Guildhall Square. The same free shuttle service leaves Ulsterbus station 15 minutes before each departing train. The Ulsterbus station is a couple minutes' walk south of Guildhall Square.

Derry is compact enough to see on foot; drivers stopping for a few hours can park at the Foyleside parking garage across from the TI (£0.80/hr, £2.20/4 hrs, Mon–Tue 8:00–19:00, Wed–Fri 8:00–22:00, Sat 8:00–20:00, Sun 12:00–19:00, tel. 028/7137-7575). Drivers staying overnight can ask about parking at their B&B, or try the Quayside parking garage behind the Travelodge (£0.60/hr, £2/4 hrs, £1/hr after first 6 hours, Mon–Fri 7:30–21:30, Sat 7:30–20:30, Sun 12:30–18:30).

Helpful Hints

Phone Tips: To call the Republic of Ireland from Northern Ireland, dial 00-353, then the area code without its initial zero, then the local number. To call Northern Ireland from the Republic of Ireland, dial 048, then the local eight-digit number.

Banking: Northern Bank, First Trust Bank, Ulster Bank, and Bank of Ireland cluster around Waterloo Place and Guildhall Square (all Mon–Fri 9:30–16:30, closed Sat–Sun).

Internet Access: Claudes Café is inside the walls, just north of the Diamond on Shipquay Street (£3/30 min, daily 9:00–17:00, tel. 028/7127-9379).

Post Office: The main post office is just off Waterloo Place (Mon 8:30–17:30, Tue–Fri 9:00–17:30, Sat 9:00–12:30, closed Sun, Custom House Street).

Laundry: City Clean can do a load of laundry for £6 (drop off in morning to pick up later that day, Mon–Sat 9:00–17:30, closed Sun, Waterloo Place, tel. 028/7136-1962).

Taxi: Try **Maiden City Taxi** (tel. 028/7126-1666) or **Sackville Taxi** (tel. 028/7135-4442).

TOURS

Walking Tours—You have several options for tours, each including a section of the Derry Walls. The TI runs solid 90-minute tours with different focuses on certain afternoons: Monday—Siege, Wednesday—Emigration, and Friday—Living History of the Troubles (£5, July–Aug Mon–Fri 11:15 and 15:15, Sept–June Mon–Fri at 14:30 only, tel. 028/7126-7284).

Martin McCrossan and his staff lead 60-minute tours of the city, departing from 11 Carlisle Road just below Ferryquay Gate (£4, Mon–Sat 10:00, 12:00, and 14:00; call to confirm schedule, tel. 028/7127-1996 or mobile 077-1293-7997, www.irishtourguides.com).

Stephen McPhilemy leads private tours of his hometown, Belfast, and the North Coast—when he's not on the road guiding tours for Rick Steves several months a year (tel. 028/7130-9051, mobile 078-0101-1027, nirelandtours@btinternet.com).

The **Bogside Artists,** famous for their dramatic wall mural painting, do informal hour-long walks in the Bogside, explaining the inspiration for their memorable works (£3, check with TI or call for current schedule, walks depart from their studio behind Bogside Inn pub, tel. 028/7137-3842, www.bogsideartists.com).

Bus Tours—City Sightseeing's double-decker bus tours are a good option on a rainy day. You'll be driven around the city in an hour-long loop that covers the Guild Hall, the city walls, the political wall murals (both Bogside and Waterside), cathedrals, and shirt factories. Your ticket is good for one lap around the loop and you stay on the bus for the duration (£6, pay driver, May–Oct daily on the hour 10:00–16:00, departs from in front of TI or beside the Guild Hall, tel. 028/7134-5335 or 028/9062-6888, www.city -sightseeing.com).

SELF-GUIDED WALKS

Though calm today, Derry is marked by years of tumultuous conflict. These two walks will increase your understanding of the town's history. The first walk, starting at the old city walls and ending at the Anglican Cathedral, focuses on Derry's early days. The second walking tour (page 311) helps you easily find the city's compelling murals, which document the time of the Troubles. These tours can be done separately or linked, depending on your time.

Walk the Walls

Squatting determinedly in the city center, the old city walls of Derry (built 1613–1618 and still intact, except for wider gates to handle modern vehicles) hold an almost mythic place in Irish history.

It was here in 1688 that a group of brave apprentice boys, many of whom had been shipped to Londonderry as orphans after the great fire of London in 1666, took their stand. They slammed the city gates shut in the face of the approaching Catholic forces of deposed King James II. With this act, the boys galvanized the

city's indecisive Protestant defenders inside the walls.

Months of negotiations and a grinding 105-day siege followed, during which a third of the 20,000 refugees and defenders crammed into the city perished. The siege was finally broken in 1689, when supply ships broke through a boom stretched across the Foyle River. The sacrifice and defiant survival of the city turned the tide in favor of newly crowned Protestant King William of Orange, who arrived in Ireland soon after and defeated James at the pivotal Battle of the Boyne.

To fully appreciate the walls, take a walk on top of them (free and open from dawn to dusk). Almost 20 feet high and at least as thick, the walls form a mile-long oval loop that you can

Derry

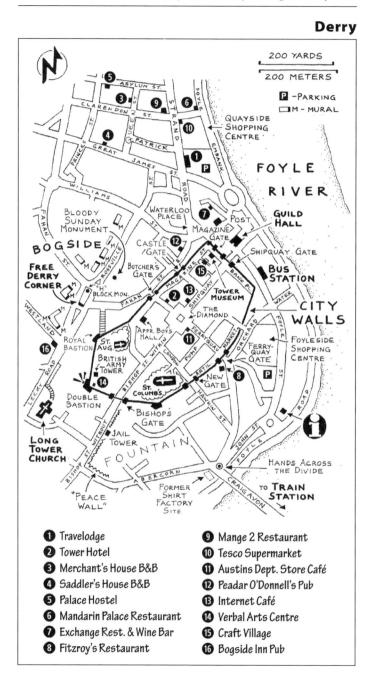

1. Travelodge
2. Tower Hotel
3. Merchant's House B&B
4. Saddler's House B&B
5. Palace Hostel
6. Mandarin Palace Restaurant
7. Exchange Rest. & Wine Bar
8. Fitzroy's Restaurant
9. Mange 2 Restaurant
10. Tesco Supermarket
11. Austins Dept. Store Café
12. Peadar O'Donnell's Pub
13. Internet Café
14. Verbal Arts Centre
15. Craft Village
16. Bogside Inn Pub

Derry's History

Once an island in the Foyle River, Derry (from *daire,* Irish for "oak grove") was chosen by St. Colmcille around A.D. 546 for a monastic settlement. He later banished himself to the island of Iona in Scotland out of remorse for sparking a bloody battle over the rights to a holy manuscript he had secretly copied.

A thousand years later, the English defeated the last Ulster-based Gaelic chieftains in the battle of Kinsale (1601). With victory at hand, the English took advantage of the power vacuum. They began the "plantation" of Ulster with loyal Protestant subjects imported from Scotland and England. The native Irish were displaced to less desirable rocky or boggy lands, sowing the seeds of resentment that fueled the modern-day Troubles.

A dozen wealthy London guilds took on Derry as an investment, and changed its name to Londonderry. They built the last great walled city in Ireland to protect their investment from the surrounding—and hostile—Irish locals. The walls proved their worth in 1688–1689, when the town's Protestant defenders, loyal to King William of Orange, withstood a prolonged siege by the forces of Catholic King James II. "No surrender" is still a passionate rallying cry among Ulster Unionists determined to remain part of the United Kingdom.

The town became a major port of emigration to the New World in the early 1800s. Then, when the Industrial Revolution provided a steam-powered sewing factory, the city developed a thriving shirt-making industry. The factories here employed mostly Catholic women who had honed their skills in rural County Donegal. Although Belfast grew larger and wealthier, Unionists cherished Londonderry and, in 1921, insisted that it be included in

cover in less than an hour. But the most interesting section is the half-circuit facing away from the river, starting at Magazine Gate (stairs face the Tower Museum inside the walls) and finishing at Bishop's Gate.

From Magazine Gate, walk the wall as it heads uphill, snaking along the earth's contours like a mini–Great Wall of China. In the row of buildings on the left (just before crossing over Castle Gate), you'll see an arch entry into the **Craft Village,** an alley lined with a cluster of cute shops that showcase the recent economic rejuvenation of Derry (Mon–Sat 9:30–17:30, closed Sun).

• *After crossing over Butcher Gate, head to the corner of Society Street (on the left) to the...*

Apprentice Boys Memorial Hall: Built in 1873, it houses the private lodge and meeting rooms of an all-male Protestant organization. The group is dedicated to the memory of the original 13 apprentice boys who saved the day during the 1688 siege. Each

Northern Ireland when it was partitioned from the new Irish Free State (later to become the Republic of Ireland). A bit of gerrymandering ensured that the Unionist Protestant minority maintained control of the city, despite the Nationalist Catholic majority.

Londonderry was a key escort base for U.S. convoys headed for Britain in World War II, and dozens of German U-boats were instructed to surrender here at the end of the war. Poor Catholics—unable to find housing—took over the abandoned military barracks, with multiple families living in each dwelling. Only homeowners were allowed to vote, and the Unionist minority, which controlled city government, was not eager to build more housing that would tip the voting balance away from them. Over the years, sectarian pressures gradually built—until they reached the boiling point. Then, the ugly events of Bloody Sunday brought worldwide attention to the Troubles (see "Touring the Murals of the Bogside," page 311).

Today, life has stabilized in Derry, and the population has increased by 25 percent in the last 30 years, to about 73,000. The modern Foyleside Shopping Centre, bankrolled by investors from Boston, was completed in 1995. The 1998 Good Friday Peace Accord has provided a two-steps-forward, one-step-back progress towards peace, and the British Army has become less visible. With a population that is 70 percent Catholic, the city has agreed to alternate Nationalist and Unionist mayors. There is a feeling of cautious optimism as Derry—the epicenter of bombs and bloody conflicts in the 1960s and 1970s—now boasts a history museum that airs all viewpoints.

year, on the Saturday closest to the August 12 anniversary date, the modern-day Apprentice Boys Society celebrates the end of the siege with a controversial march atop the walls. These walls are considered sacred ground for devout Unionists, who claim that many who died during the famous siege were buried within the battered walls because of lack of space.

Next, you'll pass a large, square pedestal on the right atop Royal Bastion. It once supported a column in honor of Governor George Walker, the commander of the defenders during the famous siege. In 1973, the IRA blew up the column, which had 105 steps to the top (one for each day of the siege). The Governor's statue survived the blast, and can be seen behind the Apprentice Boys Hall, down London Street and behind a protective fence.

• *Opposite the empty pedestal is the small Anglican...*

St. Augustine Chapel: Set in a pretty graveyard, it's where some believe the original sixth-century monastery of St. Columba

("Colmcille" in Irish) stood. This stretch of the walls was once a fashionable promenade walk in Victorian times.

As you walk ahead, it's hard to miss the British Army **surveillance tower** on the left. It's situated here for the bird's-eye view it affords of the once-turbulent Catholic Bogside district below. Stop at the Double Bastion **fortified platform** that occupies this corner of the city walls. The old cannon is nicknamed "Roaring Meg" for the fury of its firing during the siege.

From here, you can see across the Bogside to the not-so-far-away hills of county Donegal in the Republic. Derry was once an island, but as the river gradually changed its course, the area below began to drain. Over time, and especially after the Great Potato Famine (1845–1849), Catholic peasants from rural Donegal began to move into Derry to find work, and settled on this least desirable land...on the bog side of the city.

Directly below and to the right are Free Derry Corner and Rossville Street, where the tragic events of Bloody Sunday took place in 1972 (see "Touring the Murals of the Bogside," below). Down on the left is the 18th-century Long Tower Catholic church, named after the medieval round tower that once stood in the area (see "Long Tower Church," page 317).

• *Head to the building behind you, next to the army tower.*

The Verbal Arts Centre: A former Presbyterian school, the center promotes the development of local literary arts in the form of poetry, drama, writing, and storytelling. Drop in for a cup of coffee in their coffee house and see what performances might be on during your visit (Mon–Thu 9:00–17:30, Fri 9:00–16:00, closed Sat–Sun, entry next to army tower on Bishop Street, tel. 028/7126-6946, www.verbalartscentre.co.uk).

Continuing another 50 yards, left around the corner, you'll reach Bishop's Gate, from which you can look down Bishop Street Without (outside the walls) and Bishop Street Within (inside the walls), while another, shorter British Army surveillance tower peeks over your shoulder. Take a moment to look at the wall topped by a high mesh fence running along the left side of Bishop Street Without. This is a **Peace Wall,** built to ensure the security of the Protestant enclave living behind it in the Fountain neighborhood. When the Troubles reignited 30 years ago, there were 20,000 Protestants living on this side of the river. Sadly, today this small housing estate of 1,500 people is all that remains of that proud community. The rest have chosen to move across the river to the Waterside district. The old brick

tower halfway down the peace wall was part of the old jail that briefly held doomed rebel Wolfe Tone, after the 1798 revolt against the British.

• *From Bishop's Gate, those short on time can descend from the walls and walk 15 minutes directly back through the heart of the old city, along Bishop Street Within and Shipquay Street to Guildhall Square. With more time, consider visiting St. Columb's Cathedral (page 317), the Long Tower Church (page 317), and the murals of the Bogside (described below).*

Touring the Murals of the Bogside

The Catholic Bogside area was the tinderbox of the modern Troubles in Northern Ireland. A terrible confrontation 34 years ago sparked a sectarian inferno, and the ashes have not yet fully cooled. Today, the murals of the Bogside give visitors an accessible glimpse of this community's passionate perception of those events.

Inspired by civil rights marches in America in the mid-1960s and the 1968 Prague Spring uprising, civil rights groups began to protest in Northern Ireland. Initially, their goals were to gain better housing, secure fair voting rights, and end employment discrimination for Catholics in the North. Tensions mounted, and clashes with the predominantly Protestant Royal Ulster Constabulary police force became frequent. Eventually, the British Army was called in to keep the peace. On January 30, 1972, a group protesting internment without trial held an illegal march through the Bogside neighborhood. They were fired upon by members of a British regiment, who claimed that snipers had fired on them first. The tragic result of the clash, now remembered as **Bloody Sunday,** caused the death of 14 civilians and led to a flood of fresh IRA volunteers.

The events are memorialized in 10 murals painted on the ends of residential flats along a 300-yard stretch of Rossville Street and Lecky Road, where the march took place. You can reach them from Waterloo Place via William Street, from the old city walls at Butcher's Gate via the long set of stairs extending below Fahan Street on the grassy hillside, or by the stairs leading down from the Long Tower Church. These days, this neighborhood is quiet and safe.

Two brothers and their childhood friend, all of whom grew up in the Bogside during the tragic events, began painting the murals in 1994. One of the brothers, Tom Kelly, gained a reputation as a "heritage mural" painter, specializing in scenes of life in the old days. In a surprising and hopeful development, Kelly was invited into Derry's Protestant Fountain neighborhood to work with a youth club there to paint three proud heritage murals to cover over paramilitary graffiti.

The Murals of the Bogside

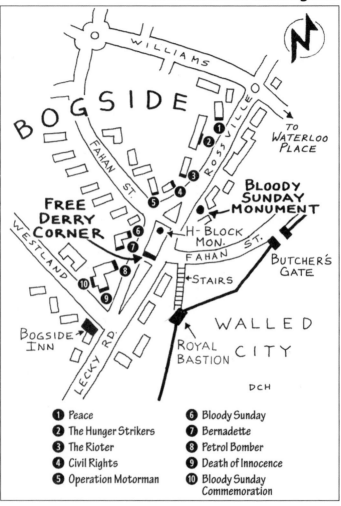

1. Peace
2. The Hunger Strikers
3. The Rioter
4. Civil Rights
5. Operation Motorman
6. Bloody Sunday
7. Bernadette
8. Petrol Bomber
9. Death of Innocence
10. Bloody Sunday Commemoration

The Bogside murals face different directions (and some are partially hidden by buildings), so they're not all visible from a single viewpoint. Plan on walking about three long blocks along Rossville Street (which becomes Lecky Road) to see them all. Locals are used to visitors and don't mind if you photograph the murals.

The best place to start is from Williams Street, walking south along the right side of Rossville Street toward Free Derry Corner (described below). The murals will all be on your right.

The first mural you'll walk past is the most recently painted

Political Murals

The dramatic and emotional murals you'll encounter in Northern Ireland will likely be one of the enduring travel memories you'll take home with you. During the 19th century, Protestant neighborhoods hung flags and streamers each July to commemorate the victory of King William III at the Battle of the Boyne. Modern murals evolved from these colorful annual displays. With the advent of industrial paints, temporary seasonal displays became permanent territorial statements.

Unionist murals were created during the extended political debate that eventually led to the partitioning of the island in 1921, and the creation of Northern Ireland. Murals expressing opposing views in Nationalist Catholic neighborhoods were outlawed. The ban remained until the eruption of the modern Troubles, when staunchly Republican Catholic communities isolated themselves behind barricades, eluding state control and gaining freedom to express their pent-up passions. In Derry, this form of symbolic, cultural, and ideological resistance first appeared in 1969 with the simple "You are now entering Free Derry" message that you'll still see painted on the surviving gable wall at Free Derry corner.

Found mostly in working-class neighborhoods of Belfast and Derry, today's political murals have become a dynamic form of popular culture. They blur the line between art and propaganda, giving visitors a striking glimpse of each community's history, identity, and values.

one. Finished in the summer of 2004, the colorful collage of *Peace* shows a silhouette of a dove in flight. It was inspired by a campaign of write-in suggestions for positive peacetime images from this generation of Derry city school children.

Next, *The Hunger Strikers* features two long-haired men wear-

ing blankets. This mural represents the IRA prisoners who refused to wear the uniforms of common criminal inmates in an attempt to force the British to treat them instead as legitimate political prisoners (who were allowed to wear their own clothes).

Now look for *The Rioter*, which depicts an outgunned but undaunted local youth behind a screen shield. He holds a stone—ready to throw—while a British armored vehicle approaches (echoing the famous Tiananmen Square photo of the lone man facing the tank).

Nearby is *Civil Rights,* showing a marching Derry crowd carrying an anti-sectarian banner. It dates from the days when Martin Luther King's successful nonviolent protest marches were having a dramatic global ripple effect. Civil rights marches—inspired into action using the same methods to combat a similar set of grievances—gave this long suffering community a powerful new voice.

Now cross over to the other side of Rossville street to see the **Bloody Sunday Monument.** This small, fenced-off stone obelisk

lists the names of those who died that day, most within 50 yards of this spot. Take a look at the map pedestal by the monument, which shows how a rubble barricade was erected to block the street. An eight-story housing project called Rossville Flats stood here in those days. When peaceful protests failed, and Republican youths became more aggressive, British troops feared being hit by Molotov cocktails thrown from the roof.

Cross again, this time over to the grassy median strip that runs down the middle of Rossville Street. At one end stands a granite letter *H* inscribed with the names of the 10 IRA hunger strikers who died in H-block of the Maze prison in 1981. From here, you get a good view of the *Operation Motorman* mural (at the corner of Fahan Street). In it, a soldier wields a sledgehammer, depicting the massive push by the British Army to open up the Bogside's barricaded "no-go" areas that the IRA had controlled for three years.

Walk down to the other end of the median strip where the white wall of **Free Derry Corner** announces "You are now entering Free Derry" (imitating a similarly defiant slogan of the time in once-isolated West Berlin). This was the gabled end of a string of houses that stood here over 30 years ago.

Cross back to the right side of the street (now Lecky Road) to see *Bloody Sunday,* in which a small group of men are carrying a body from the ill-fated march. It's based on a famous photo of Father Daly that was taken that terrible day. He waves a white handkerchief to request safe passage in order to evacuate a mortally wounded protester. The blood-stained civil rights banner was inserted under the soldier's feet for extra emphasis.

Beside it is a mural called *Bernadette.* The woman with the megaphone is Bernadette Devlin McAliskey, an outspoken civil rights leader who, at age 21, became the youngest elected member of Parliament. Behind her kneels a woman supporter, banging a trash-can lid against the street in a traditional expression of protest in Republican neighborhoods. Trash-can lids were also used to warn neighbors of the approach of British patrols.

Petrol Bomber, showing a teen wearing an army-surplus gas mask, captures the Battle of the Bogside, when locals barricaded off their community, effectively shutting out British rule. The British army attempted to use tear gas and supposedly non-lethal rubber bullets to disperse hostile crowds.

In *The Death of Innocence,* a young girl stands in front of bomb wreckage. She is Annette McGavigan, a 14-year-old who was

killed by crossfire in the Bogside in 1971. She was the 100th fatality of the Troubles, which eventually took over 3,000 lives. The gun beside her points to the ground, signifying that it's no longer being wielded. The large butterfly above her shoulder symbolizes the hope for peace. The artists have said they will return to add a rising sun within the butterfly when they feel confident that the peace process has succeeded.

Finally, around the corner, you'll see a circle of male faces. This mural, painted in 1997 to observe the 25th anniversary of the tragedy, is called *Bloody Sunday Commemoration* and shows the 14 victims. They are surrounded by a ring of 14 oak leaves—the symbol of Derry.

Take a few moments to walk into the **Bogside Inn** pub (fac-

ing this last mural across Westland Street) and order a beverage. This pub has been here through it all. Spend a little time examining the black-and-white news photos of Bloody Sunday and bomb damage around the city taken during the darkest days of Derry.

Nationalist leader John Hume (Nobel Peace Prize co-winner in 1998, along with Unionist leader David Trimble) still has a house in the Bogside. He once borrowed a quote from Gandhi to explain his nonviolent approach to the peace process when he said: "An eye for an eye leaves the whole world blind."

SIGHTS

▲▲Tower Museum Derry—Housed in a modern reconstruction of a fortified medieval tower house belonging to the local O'Doherty clan, this well-organized museum provides an excellent introduction to the city. Combining modern audiovisuals with historical artifacts, the displays tell the story of the city from a skillfully unbiased viewpoint, sorting out some of the tangled historical roots of Northern Ireland's Troubles.

The museum is divided into two sections: The Story of Derry (on the ground floor) and the Spanish Armada (on the 4 floors of the tower). Start with the Story of Derry, which explains the city's monastic origins 1,500 years ago. It moves through pivotal events, such as the 1688–1689 siege, as well as unexpected blips, including Amelia Earhart's emergency landing. Catch the thought-provoking 14-minute film in the small theater, which gives an evenhanded local perspective on the tragic events of the modern sectarian conflict, giving you a better handle on what makes this unique city tick. As you exit the small theater, scan the displays of paramilitary paraphernalia in the hallway lined with colored curb stones—red, white, and blue Union Jack colors for Loyalists; and green, white, and orange Irish tricolor for Republicans. There, you'll find tiny notes written by IRA hunger-striker Bobby Sands, which were smuggled out of the Maze prison.

The recently opened tower section holds the Spanish Armada exhibits, filled with items taken from a galleon that sank offshore in 1588 (Story of Derry-£4, Spanish Armada-£4, combo-ticket for both sections-£7, July–Aug Mon–Sat 10:00–17:00, Sun 14:00–17:00; Sept–June Tue–Sat 10:00–17:00, closed Sun–Mon; Union Hall Place, tel. 028/7137-2411).

Guild Hall—This neo-Gothic building, complete with clock tower, is the ceremonial seat of city government. It first opened in 1890 on reclaimed lands that were once the mudflats of the Foyle River.

Destroyed by fire and rebuilt in 1913, it was massively damaged by IRA bombs in 1972. In an ironic twist, Gerry Doherty, one of those convicted of the bombings, was elected as a member of the City Council a dozen years later. In November 1995, President Clinton spoke to thousands who packed into Guild Hall Square. Inside the Hall are the Council Chamber, party offices, and an assembly hall featuring stained-glass windows showing scenes from Derry history. Check to see when tours are available—usually when civic and cultural events are not taking place inside (Mon–Fri 9:00–17:00, closed Sat–Sun, tel. 028/7137-7335).

Hands across the Divide—Designed by local teacher Maurice Harron after the fall of the Iron Curtain, this powerful metal sculpture of two figures extending their hands to each other was inspired by the growing hope for peace and reconciliation in Northern Ireland (located in a roundabout at the west end of Craigavon Bridge).

Until recently, the Tillie and Henderson's shirt factory (opened in 1857 and burned down in 2003) stood on the banks of the river beside the bridge, looming over the figures. In its heyday, Derry's shirt industry employed over 15,000 workers (90 percent of whom were women) in sweathouses typical of the human toll of Industrial Revolution. Karl Marx mentioned this factory in *Das Kapital* as an example of women's transition from domestic to industrial work lives.

St. Columb's Cathedral—Marked by the tall spire inside the walls, this Anglican cathedral was built from 1628 to 1633 in a style called "Planter's Gothic." Its construction was financed by the same London companies that backed the plantation of Londonderry. It was the first Protestant cathedral built in Britain after the Reformation, and the cathedral played an important part in the defense of the city during the siege. During that time, cannons were mounted on its roof, and the original spire was scavenged for lead to melt into cannon shot. In the entryway, you'll find a hollow cannonball that was lobbed into the city, containing the besiegers' surrender terms. Inside along the nave hangs a musty collection of battle flags and Union Jacks that once inspired troops during the siege, the Crimean War, and World War II. The American flag hangs among them, from the time when the first GIs to enter the European theater in World War II were based in Northern Ireland. Check out the small chapter-house museum in the back of the church to see the original locks of the gates of Londonderry and more relics of the siege (£1 donation, Mon–Sat 9:00–17:00, closed Sun, tel. 028/7126-7313, www.stcolumbscathedral.org).

Long Tower Church—Built below the walls on the hillside above the Bogside, this modest-looking church is worth a visit for its stunning high altar. The name comes from a stone monastic round tower that stood here for centuries, but was destroyed for city building materials in the 1600s. The oldest Catholic church in Derry, it was finished in 1786, during a time of enlightened relations between the city's two religious communities. Protestant Bishop Hervey gave a generous-for-the-time £200 donation, and had the four Corinthian columns shipped in from Naples to frame the neo-Renaissance altar (free, Mon–Sat 7:30–20:30, Sun 7:30–19:00, tel. 028/7126-2301).

Hidden outside behind the church and facing the Bogside is a simple shrine beneath a hawthorn tree. It marks the spot where outlawed Masses were held secretly, before this church was built, during the infamous Penal Law period of the early 1700s. Through the Penal Laws, the English attempted to weaken Catholicism's influence by banishing priests and forbidding Catholics from buying land, attending school, voting, and holding office.

NIGHTLIFE

The **Millennium Forum** is a modern venue reflecting the city's revived investment in local culture, concerts, and plays (box office Mon–Sat 10:00–17:00, inside city walls on Newmarket Street near Ferryquay Gate, tel. 028/7126-4455, www.millenniumforum .co.uk, boxoffice@millenniumforum.co.uk).

The **Nerve Centre** shows a wide variety of art-house films (inside city walls at 7–8 Magazine Street, near Butcher Gate, tel. 028/7126-0562, www.nerve-centre.org.uk).

SLEEPING

$$$ Tower Hotel is the only hotel actually inside Derry's historic walls. It's a real splurge, with 93 modern and immaculate rooms, a classy bistro restaurant, and private basement parking (Sb-£57–99, Db-£75–110, Butcher Street, tel. 028/7137-1000, fax 028/7137-1234, www.towerhotelderry.com, reservations@thd.ie).

Sleep Code

(£1 = about $1.80, country code: 44, area code: 028)
S = Single, **D** = Double/Twin, **T** = Triple, **Q** = Quad, **b** = bathroom, **s** = shower only. Breakfast is included and credit cards are accepted unless otherwise noted.

To help you easily sort through these listings, I've divided the rooms into three categories, based on the price for a standard double room with bath:

$$$ Higher Priced—Most rooms £70 or more.
$$ Moderately Priced—Most rooms between £40–70.
$ Lower Priced—Most rooms £40 or less.

$$ Travelodge has 39 comfortable rooms, a great location, and a handy adjacent parking garage (Db-£50 Sun–Thu, Db-£55 Fri–Sat, full Irish breakfast-£6, continental breakfast-£4.50, 2 non-smoking floors, 22–24 Strand Road, tel. 028/7127-1271, fax 028/7127-1277, www.travelodge.co.uk).

$$ Merchant's House, on a quiet street a 10-minute stroll from Waterloo Place, is a fine Georgian townhouse with marble fireplaces, ornate plasterwork, and a grand, colorful drawing room (S-£25, Sb-£30, D-£45, Db-£50, 16 Queen Street, tel. 028/7126-9691, fax 028/7126-6913, www.thesaddlershouse.com, saddlershouse@btinternet.com, Joan and Peter Pyne).

$$ Saddler's House, run by the owners of Merchant's House, is a charming Victorian townhouse with seven rooms located a couple blocks closer to the old town walls (Sb-£30, Db-£45, 36 Great James Street, tel. 028/7126-9691, fax 028/7126-6913, www.thesaddlershouse.com, saddlershouse@btinternet.com).

$ The Palace Hostel Derry, located in the city center (across from a fortress-like police station), rents 40 decent beds for £10 a night with breakfast. Look for the bright yellow "Paddy's Palace" mural on the Princes Street end of the building (4–6 beds per room, family rooms with private bathroom for up to 4-£35, free Internet access in lobby, laundry facilities, kitchen, nightly movies, 1 Woodleigh Terrace, Asylum Road, tel. 028/7130-9051, www.paddyspalace.com, info@paddyspalace.com, Stephen McPhilemy).

EATING

The front window of **Mange 2** declares that "cuisine is when things taste like what they are." They deliver on that promise, serving casual £5–7 lunches and filling £11–17 dinners in a light-hearted atmosphere (daily 11:30–15:00 & 17:30–22:00, Clarendon Street, tel. 028/7136-1222).

The **Mandarin Palace** dishes up good £8–13 Chinese dinners in a crisp dining room that faces the river. Their £10 early-bird three-course deals are available from 16:30 to 19:00 (daily 16:30–23:00, buffet lunch Mon–Fri 12:00–14:00, Queens Quay at Lower Clarendon Street, tel. 028/7137-3656).

The hip, trendy **Exchange Restaurant and Wine Bar** offers £5–7 lunches and quality dinners with flair for £10–15, in a central location near the river behind Waterloo Place (Mon–Sat 12:00–22:00, Sun 17:00–21:30, Queen's Quay, tel. 028/7127-3990).

Easygoing **Fitzroy's,** tucked below Ferryquay Gate, serves good £6–10 lunches and £9–14 dinners (Mon–Tue 10:00–20:00, Wed–Sat 10:00–22:00, Sun 12:00–20:00, 2–4 Bridge Street, tel. 028/7126-6211).

Austins Department Store, right on the Diamond in the center of the old city, is Ireland's oldest department store and has a top-floor café with some nice views and £5 lunch specials (Mon–Sat 9:30–17:30, Sun 13:00–17:00, 2–6 The Diamond, tel. 028/7126-1817).

Chat with locals in pubs that rarely see a tourist. Try **Peadar O'Donnell's** pub on Waterloo Street for Derry's best nightly ballad sessions (53 Waterloo Street, tel. 028/7137-2318).

Supermarkets: **Tesco** has everything for picnics and road munchies (Mon–Thu 9:00–21:00, Fri 8:30–21:00, Sat 8:30–20:00, Sun 13:00–18:00, corner of Strand Road and Clarendon Street). **Super Valu** meets the same needs (Mon–Sat 8:30–18:30, Thu–Fri until 20:30, closed Sun, Waterloo Place).

TRANSPORTATION CONNECTIONS

From Derry, it's less than an hour's drive to Portrush.

Useful updated schedules and prices for both trains and buses in Northern Ireland can be obtained from Translink (tel. 028/9066-6630, www.translink.co.uk).

From Derry by Train to: Portrush (9/day, 1 hr, change in Coleraine), **Belfast** (8/day, 2.25 hrs), **Dublin** (7/day, 5 hrs). In July and August, consider a £6.50 "Day Tracker" ticket, good for all-day train use in Northern Ireland (see page 274).

By Bus to: Galway (4/day, 6 hrs), **Portrush** (5/day, 1.25 hrs), **Belfast** (20/day, 1.45 hrs, £9), **Dublin** (5/day, 4.5 hrs).

For Drivers: Sights Between Derry and Galway

If you're driving into Northern Ireland from Galway, Westport, or Strokestown and don't have time to explore Donegal, consider the two following interesting interior stops.

Belleek Pottery Visitors Centre—Just over the Northern Ireland border (30 miles northeast of Sligo) is the cute town of Belleek, famous for its pottery. The Belleek Parian China factory welcomes visitors with a small gallery and museum (Mon–Fri 9:00–18:00, Sat 10:00–18:00, Sun 11:00–18:00, less off-season), a 20-minute video, a cheery cafeteria, and fascinating 30-minute tours of its working factory (£4, April–June and Sept Mon–Fri 9:00–18:00, Sat 10:00–18:00, Sun 14:00–18:00; longer hours July–Aug, shorter hours Oct–March, closed Sat–Sun Nov–March, call to confirm schedule and reserve a spot, tel. 028/6865-8501, www.belleek.ie).

▲**Ulster American Folk Park**—North of Omagh (5 miles on A5), this combination museum and folk park commemorates the many Irish who left their homeland during the hard times of the 19th century. Exhibits show life before emigration, on the boat, and in America. You'll gain insight into the origins of the tough Scots-Irish stock—think Davy Crockett and Andrew Jackson—who later shaped America's westward migration (£4, April–Sept Mon–Sat 10:30–16:30, Sun 11:00–17:00; Oct–March Mon–Fri 10:30–15:30, closed Sat–Sun; tel. 028/8224-3292, www.folkpark.com).

County Donegal

Donegal is the most remote (and perhaps the most ruggedly beautiful) county in Ireland. It's not on the way to anywhere, and it wears this isolation well. With more native Irish speakers than in any other county, the old ways are better preserved here. The northernmost part of Ireland, Donegal remains connected to the Republic by a slim, five-mile-wide umbilical cord of land on its southern coast. It's also Ireland's second biggest county, with a wide-open "big sky" interior and a shattered-glass, 200-mile, jagged coastline of islands and inlets.

This is the home turf of St. Colmcille (St. Columba in English; means "dove of the church" in Irish), who was born here in 521. He's revered second only to St. Patrick in the hierarchy of Irish saints. A proud Gaelic culture held out in Donegal to the bitter end, when its two famous clans (the O'Donnells and the O'Dohertys) were finally defeated by the English in the early 1600s. After their defeat, the region became know as Dun na nGall ("the fort of the foreigner"), which was eventually anglicized to Donegal.

As the English moved in, four friars (certain that Gaelic ways would be lost forever) painstakingly wrote down Irish history from Noah's Ark to their present. This labor of love became known as the Annals of the Four Masters, and without it, much of our knowledge of early Irish history and myth would have been lost. An obelisk stands in their honor in the main square of Donegal town.

The hardy people of County Donegal were famous for their quality tweed weaving, a cottage industry that has given way to modern industrial production in far-off cities. An energetic fishing fleet still churns off shore. The traditional Irish musicians of Donegal play a driving style of music with a distinctively fast and choppy rhythm. Meanwhile, Enya (local Gweedore gal made good) has crafted languid, ethereal tunes that glide from mood to mood. Today, emigration has taken its toll, and much of the trickle of tourism comes from neighboring Northern Ireland.

County Donegal

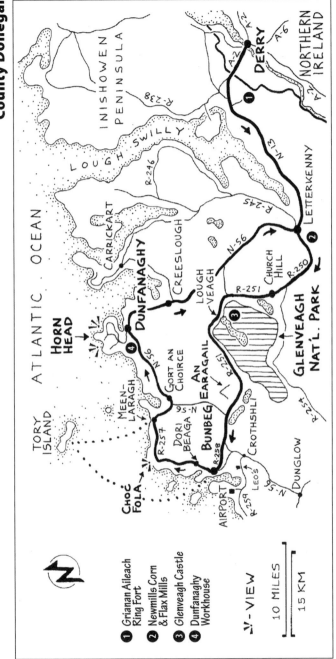

NORTHERN IRELAND

DERRY

A-2
A-6
A-2

INISHOWEN PENINSULA

R-238

LOUGH SWILLY

R-246

N-13

LETTERKENNY

R-245

ATLANTIC OCEAN

CARRICKART

CREESLOUGH

N-56

Church Hill

R-250

R-251

LOUGH VEAGH

GLENVEAGH NAT'L. PARK

DUNFANAGHY

HORN HEAD

N-56

GORT AN CHOIRCE

AN EARAGAIL

R-251

MEEN-LARAGH

N-56

DORI BEAGA

BUNBEG

R-257

R-258

CROTHSHLI

R-254

TORY ISLAND

CHOC FOLA

AIRPORT

R-259

LEO'S

N-56

DUNGLOW

① Grianan Aileach Ring Fort
② Newmills Corn & Flax Mills
③ Glenveagh Castle
④ Dunfanaghy Workhouse

N - VIEW

10 MILES

15 KM

Donegal or Bust

Part of western County Donegal is in the Gaeltacht, where locals speak the Irish (Gaelic) language. In the spring of 2005, a controversial law passed that erased all English place names from local road signs in Gaeltacht areas. Signs now only have the Irish-language equivalent, an attempt to protect the region from the further (and inevitable) encroachment by the English language.

Here's a cheat sheet to help you decipher the signs as you drive the Donegal loop (parts of which are in the Gaeltacht). There's also a complete translation of all Irish place names in the recommended Ordnance Survey road atlas, in the Gazetteer section in the back.

Gaelic Name	Pronounced	English Name
Letir Ceanainn	*LET-ir CAN-ning*	Letterkenny
Min an Labain	*MEEN on law-BAWN*	Churchill
Loch Ghleann Bheatha	*LOCKH thown eh-VEH-heh*	Lough (Lake) Veagh
An Earagail	*on AIR-i-gul*	Mt. Errigal
Gaoth Dobhair	*GWEE door*	Gweedore
Crothshli	*CROTH-lee*	Crolly
Bun Beag	*bun bee-OWG*	Bunbeg
Dori Beaga	*DOR-uh bee-OWG-uh*	Derrybeg
Cnoc Fola	*kuh-NOK FAW-luh*	Bloody Foreland
Gort an Choirce	*gurt on HER-kuh*	Gortahork
Dun Fionnachaidh	*doon on-AH-keh*	Dunfanaghy
Corran Binne	*COR-on BIN-eh*	Horn Head

SIGHTS

Donegal Loop Trip

Here's my choice for a scenic mix of Donegal highlands and coastal views, organized as a day-long circuit (150 miles) for drivers based across the border in Derry. If you're coming north from Galway or Westport, you could incorporate parts of this drive into your itinerary.

Route Summary: Drive west out of Derry (direction: Letterkenny) on Buncrana Road, which becomes A2 (and then N13 across the border in the Republic). Follow the signs into Letterkenny, and take R250 out the other (west) end of town. Veer right (north) onto R251 and stay on it through Churchill, all the way across the highlands, until you link up with N56 approaching Bunbeg. After a couple miles on N56, take R258 another four miles into Bunbeg. Depart Bunbeg going north on R257, around Bloody Foreland, and rejoin N56 near Gortahork. Take N56 through Dunfanaghy (possible Horn Head mini-loop option here), and then south, back into Letterkenny. Retrace your route from Letterkenny via N13 and A2 back into Derry.

Helpful Hints: An early start and an Ordnance Survey map are essential. It's cheapest to top off your gas tank in Letterkenny. Consider bringing along a picnic lunch to enjoy from a scenic roadside pullout along the Bloody Foreland R257 road, or out on the Horn Head loop. Bring your camera and remember—not all who wander are lost.

Once you cross into the Republic of Ireland, all currency is in euros, not pounds. For B&B rates, sight fees, and all other costs in Donegal, keep this exchange rate in mind: €1 = about $1.20.

The Tour Begins: The sights (listed below) along this route are well-marked. Don't underestimate the time it takes to get around here, as the narrow roads are full of curves and bumps. Dogs, bred to herd sheep, dart from side lanes to practice their bluffing techniques on your car. If you average 30 miles per hour over the course of the day, you've got a very good suspension system. Folks wanting to linger at more than a couple of sights will need to slow down and consider an overnight stop in Bunbeg or Dunfanaghy (accommodations listed below).

Grianan Aileach Ring Fort—This dramatic, ancient ring fort perches on an 800-foot hill just inside the Republic, a stone's throw from Derry. It's a late Iron Age fortification, built about A.D. 500, and was once the royal stronghold of the O'Neill clan, which dominated Ulster for centuries. Its stout, drystone walls (no mortar) are 12 feet thick and 18 feet high, creating an interior sanctuary 80 feet in diameter.

Once inside, you can scramble up the stairs built into the walls to enjoy panoramic views in all directions. Murtagh O'Brien, King of Desmond, destroyed the fort in 1101 (the same year he gave the Rock of Cashel to the Church). He had his soldiers carry away one stone apiece to make it tough for the O'Briens to find the raw materials to rebuild. What you see today is mostly a reconstruction from the 1870s. You'll find a sign for the fort well posted just a mile off N13, not far from the junction of R239 (entry is free and unattended). If you plan on doing the whole Donegal day loop today, skip the mediocre visitors center

(€5) in the converted church at the base of the hill, near N13.

Newmills Corn and Flax Mills—Come here for a glimpse of the 150-year-old Industrial Revolution, high-tech Ulster style. Linen,

which comes from flax, was king in this region. The 15-minute film does a nifty job of explaining the process, showing how the common flax plant ends up as cloth. Working conditions in a mill were noisy, unhealthy, and exhausting. A veteran mill worker often braved respiratory disease, deafness, lost fingers, and extreme fire danger. For his trouble, he usually got to keep about 10 percent of what he milled.

The Corn Mill is still in working condition, but takes a skilled miller to operate it. This mill ground oats—"corn" means oats in Ireland. (What we call corn, they call maize.) The huge waterwheel, powered by the River Swilly, made five revolutions per minute and generated eight horsepower.

The entire operation could be handled by one miller, who knew every cog, lever, and flume in the joint. Call ahead to see when working mill demonstrations are scheduled; otherwise, tours last 20 minutes and are available on request (€3, covered by Heritage Card—see page 4, June–Sept daily 10:00–18:30, last admission 17:45, closed off-season, 5 miles west of Letterkenny on R250, Churchill Road, tel. 074/912-5115).

Glenveagh Castle and National Park—One of Ireland's five National Parks, Glenveagh's jewel is pristine Lough Veagh (Loch Ghleann Bheatha in Gaelic). The lake is three miles long, occupying a U-shaped valley scoured out of the Derryveagh mountains by powerful glaciers during the last Ice Age.

In the 1850s, this scenic area attracted the wealthy land speculator John George Adair, who bought the valley in 1857. Right away, Adair clashed with local tenants, whom he accused of stealing his sheep. After his managing agent was found murdered, he evicted all 244 of his bitter tenants to great controversy, and set about to create a hunting estate in grand Victorian style.

His pride and joy was his country mansion, Glenveagh Castle, finished in 1873 on the shore of Lough Veagh. After his death, his widow added to the castle and introduced rhododendrons and rare red deer to the estate. After her death, Harvard art professor Kingsley Porter bought the estate, and promptly disappeared on the Donegal coast. (He's thought to have drowned.) The last owner was Philadelphia millionaire Henry McIlhenny, who filled the mansion with fine art and furniture while perfecting the lush surrounding gardens. He donated the castle to the Irish nation in 1983.

Take the 45-minute castle tour, letting your Jane Austen and Agatha Christie fantasies go wild. Antlers abound on walls, in chandeliers, and in paintings by Victorian hunting artists. A table crafted from rare bog oak (from ancient trees hundreds of years old, found buried in the muck) stands at attention in one room, while Venetian glass chandeliers illuminate a bathroom. A round pink bedroom at the top of a tower is decorated in Oriental style, with inlaid mother-of-pearl furnishings. The library displays paintings by George Russell, and has the castle's best lake views.

Afterward, stroll through the gardens and enjoy the lovely setting. A lakeside swimming pool had boilers underneath it to keep it heated. It's no wonder that Greta Garbo was an occasional guest, coming to visit whenever she "vanted" to be alone.

The castle is only accessible by 10-minute shuttle-bus rides (€2, 4/hr, depart from the park visitors center). The visitors center, located beside the parking lot and tea room, explains the region's natural history. Hiking trails in the park are tempting, but beware of tiny midges that seem to want to nest in your nostrils (€3, covered by Heritage Card—see page 4, mid-March–early-Nov daily 10:00–18:30, last admission 17:00, early-Nov–mid-March Sat–Sun only, tel. 074/37090).

Mount Errigal (An Earagail)—The mountain (2,400 feet) dominates the horizon for miles around. Rising from the relatively flat interior bog land, it looks taller from a distance than it is. Beautifully cone-shaped (but not a volcano), it offers a hearty non-technical climb with panoramic views (4 hrs round-trip, covering 5 miles). Hikers should ask for a weather report (frequent mists squat on the summit). The trail-head is southeast of the mountain, starting at the small parking lot right beside R251 on the lower slope of the mountain.

Bunbeg (Bun Beag)—This modest town lies along R257, offering a fine sandy beach. But take the trouble to seek out the quaint little hidden fishing harbor at the rocky south end of town. The harbor access road is directly in front of you as you approach the town from the east on R258 and pull up to the stop sign beside Tigh Bhreisleain B&B (on your right). At the dead end of the half-mile access road is a cute, watercolor-worthy harbor, with an old stone warehouse and a great guesthouse (see below).

There's an ATM at the AIB bank (on the left, going north on R257, 100 yards past Seaview Hotel). The post office is actually in the Spar Market in Derrybeg, a mile north of Bunbeg (Mon–Sat 9:00–17:30, Sat 9:00–13:00, closed Sun).

Turasmara operates a limited ferry service from Bunbeg harbor. It's a 90-minute voyage to the ultra-remote and rugged Tory Island (€22-round-trip, departs at 9:00 and returns at 18:00, leaves June–Sept daily—weather permitting, tel. 074/953-1340). Active travelers will enjoy the invigorating and scenic Rib Boat Excursions, which depart from Bunbeg House on the shore of cozy Bunbeg Harbor and weave among the nearby islands (€15, 45 min, daily mid-June–Aug, 8 people per boat, call for excursion schedule, tel. 074/953-1305, www.bunbeghouse.com).

Sleeping in Bunbeg: **$$ Tigh Bhreisleain B&B** surveys the crossroads where R257 and R258 meet. Georgina Breslin hosts six crisp, colorful rooms with cushy carpets (Sb-€30, Db-€60, Tb-€80, cash only, non-smoking, parking, tel. 074/953-1329, fax 074/953-2625, www.bunbeg.net, breslins@bunbeg.net).

$$ Bunbeg House overlooks the snug and charming Bunbeg fishing harbor with simple, spacious rooms and a tiny, inviting pub downstairs. Jean Carr knows about fun rib-boat sightseeing excursions, too (Sb-€35–40, Db-€60–70, Tb-€80–100, Qb-€100, parking, tel. 074/953-1305, fax 074/953-1420, www.bunbeghouse .com, bunbeghouse@eircom.net).

Eating in Bunbeg: Try the **Seaview Hotel Bistro,** which specializes in fish dishes (€24–28 meals, June–Sept daily 18:30–21:30, Oct–May Fri–Sat only 18:30–21:30, on R257, tel. 074/953-1159). You'll find a fun pub dinner, plus late-evening traditional-music sessions nightly, at **Leo's Tavern,** run by Enya's dad. To get there from Bunbeg, hop on N56 going south through the nearby hamlet of Crolly. Take a right onto R259 (sign says *Aerphort*), and go a half mile, following signs to Leo's, which will bring you to a jackknife—right turn and the pub will be 100 yards up on the left (Mon–Sat 13:00–20:30, Sun 13:00–15:30, tel. 074/954-8143). Groceries are sold at the **Spar Market** in nearby Derrybeg (Mon–Sat 9:00–19:30, Sun 9:00–13:30).

From Bunbeg to Derrybeg (Dori Beaga): The five miles of road north—as Bunbeg blends into Derrybeg (and a bit beyond)— are some of the most densely populated sections of this loop tour. Modern holiday cottages pepper the landscape in what the newly affluent Irish have come to call "Bungalow Bliss" (or "Bungalow Blight" to nature lovers).

Bloody Foreland (Cnoc Fola)—Named for the shade of red that backlit heather turns at sunset, this scenic headland is laced with rock walls and forgotten cottage ruins. Pull off at one of the road-side viewpoints and savor a picnic lunch and rugged coastal views.

Dunfanaghy Workhouse—Opened in 1845, this structure was part of an extensive workhouse compound (separating families by gender and age)—a dreaded last resort for the utterly destitute of coastal Donegal. There were once many identical compounds built across Ireland, a rigid Victorian solution to the spiraling riddle of Ireland's rapidly multiplying poor. But the system was unable to cope with the starving homeless multitudes caused by the famine.

The harsh workhouse experience is told through the true-life narrative of Wee Hannah Herrity, a wandering orphan and for-mer resident of this workhouse. She survived the famine by taking refuge here, and died at age 90 in 1926. You'll visit three upstairs rooms where hokey papier-mâché figures relate the powerful epi-sodes in her life (€4.50, April–Sept Mon–Fri 10:00–17:00, Sat–Sun 12:00–17:00; Oct–March call to confirm hours, good bookstore and coffee shop, on N56 a half mile south of Dunfanaghy town, tel. 074/913-6540).

Dunfanaghy (Dun Fionnachaidh)—This planned town, founded by the English in the early 1600s for local markets and fairs, has a prim and proper appearance. In Dunfanaghy (dun-FAN-ah-hee), you can grab a pub lunch or some picnic fixings from the town market. Enjoy them from a scenic viewpoint on the nearby Horn Head loop drive (see below).

The post office is at the southern end of town (Mon–Fri 9:00–17:30, Sat 9:00–13:00, closed Sun). Basic groceries are sold in the tiny Village Shop (daily 9:00–22:00).

Sleeping in Dunfanaghy: **$$ The Mill Restaurant and Accommodation** is a diamond in the Donegal rough. Susan Alcorn nurtures six wonderful rooms with classy decor, while her husband Derek is the chef in their fine restaurant downstairs (Sb-€55, Db-€85, Tb-€125, non-smoking, parking, tel. & fax 074/913-6985, www.themillrestaurant.com, info@themillrestaurant.com).

$$ The Whins B&B has tastefully exotic furnishings in its four prim rooms (Sb-€35–50, Db-€62–65, Tb-€90, non-smoking, parking, 10-min walk north of town, tel. 074/913-6481, www.thewhins.com, annemarie@thewhins.com).

Eating in Dunfanaghy: **The Mill Restaurant and Accommodation** is gourmet all the way, specializing in memora-ble lamb or lobster dinners worth booking days ahead of time (€37, Tue–Sun 19:00–21:00, closed Mon, tel. 074/913-6985). **Muck & Muffin** is a simple sandwich café, great for quick, cheap lunches. It's above the pottery shop in the stone warehouse on the town square (Mon–Sat 9:30–17:00, Sun 11:00–17:00).

Horn Head Loop (Corran Binne)—As you approach Dunfanaghy (if your schedule allows), take an hour and embark on a lost-world

plateau drive. This heaving headland with few trees has gripping coastal views. Consult your map and get off N56, following the Horn Head signs all the way around the eastern lobe of the peninsula. There's less than eight miles of narrow, single-lane road out here, with very little traffic. But be alert and willing to pull over at wide spots to cooperate with other cars.

This stone-studded peninsula was once an island. Then, shortly after the last Ice Age ended, ocean currents deposited a sandy spit in the calm water behind the peninsula. A hundred years ago, locals cut too much of the stabilizing grass off of the dunes, using it locally for roof thatching, and sending it abroad to Flanders for soldiers to create beds for horses during World War I. With the grass gone, the sand was free to migrate again. It promptly silted up the harbor, created a true peninsula, and ruined Dunfanaghy as a port town.

A short spur road leads to the summit of the headland, where you can park your car and walk another 50 yards up to the abandoned lookout shelter. The views from here are dramatic, looking west toward Tory Island and south to Mount Errigal. Some may choose to hike an additional 30 minutes across the heather, to the ruins of the distant signal tower (not a castle), clearly visible near the cliffs. The trails are not maintained, but it's easy bushwhacking, offering rewarding cliff views. Navigate back to your car using the lookout shelter on the summit as a landmark.

IRELAND: PAST AND PRESENT

An old Irish proverb goes, "When God made time, he made a lot of it." Ireland is rich with history, art, and language. And the country continues to transform and grow today, building on an ever-stronger economy, searching for peace, and reexamining some of its long-held social customs.

IRISH HISTORY

Hunters, Farmers, and Mysterious Mounds (Prehistory)

Ireland became an island when rising seas covered the last land bridge (7000 B.C.), a separation from Britain that the Irish would fight to maintain for the next 9,000 years. By 6000 B.C., Stone Age hunter-fishers had settled on the East Coast, followed by Neolithic farmers (from the island of Britain). These early inhabitants left behind impressive but mysterious funeral mounds (passage graves) and large Stonehenge-type **stone circles.**

The Celts: Language and Legends (500 B.C.–A.D. 500)

Perhaps more an invasion of ideas than of armies, the Celtic culture from Central Europe (particularly that of the most influential tribe, called the **Gaels**) settled in Ireland, where it would dominate for a thousand years. A warrior people with over a hundred petty kings, they feuded constantly with rival clans and gathered in ring forts for protection. The island was nominally ruled by a single high king at the **Hill of Tara** (near Dublin), though there was no centralized nation.

Druid priests conducted pagan, solar-calendar rituals among the megalithic stones erected by earlier inhabitants. The Celtic people peppered the countryside with thousands of Iron Age monuments. While most of what you'll see will be little more than rock piles that take a vigorous imagination to reconstruct (ring forts, wedge tombs, monumental stones, and so on), just standing next to a megalith that predates the pharaohs is evocative.

The Celtic world lives on today in the Gaelic language and in legends of Celtic warriors such as **Finn McCool**—the "Gaelic King Arthur"—who led a merry band of heroes in battle and in play. Tourists marvel at large ritual stones decorated with ogham (rhymes with "poem") script, the peculiar Celtic-Latin alphabet that used lines as letters. The **Tara Brooch** and elaborately inscribed, jewel-encrusted daggers attest to the sophistication of this warrior society (see the National Museum in Dublin, page 63).

In 55 B.C., the Romans conquered the Celts in Britain, but Ireland remained independent, its history forever skewed in a different direction—Gaelic, not Latin. The Romans called Ireland **Hibernia,** or Land of Winter; it was apparently too cold and bleak to merit an attempt at colonization. The biggest non-event in Irish history is that the Romans never invaded. While the mix of Celtic and Roman is part of what makes the French French and the English English, the Irish are purely Celtic. If America is bowling, France is *boules,* and England is cricket, then Ireland is hurling. This wild Irish national pastime (like airborne hockey with no injury time-outs) goes back more than 2,000 years to Celtic days, when it was played almost as a substitute for warfare.

Christianity: Monks and Scholars (A.D.500–800)

When Ancient Rome fell and took the Continent with it, Gaelic Ireland remained. There was no Dark Age here, and the island was a beacon of culture for the rest of Europe. Ireland (population c. 750,000) was still a land of many feuding kings, but the culture was stable.

Christianity and Latin culture arrived first as a trickle from trading contacts with Christian Gaul, then more emphatically in A.D. 432 with **St. Patrick,** who persuasively converted the sun-worshipping Celts. (Perhaps St. Patrick had an easy time converting the locals because they had so little sun to worship.) Patrick (c. 389–461), a Latin-speaking Christian from Roman Britain, was kidnapped as a teenager and carried off into slavery for six years in Ireland. He escaped back to Britain, then, inspired by a dream, returned to Ireland, determined to convert the pagan, often-hostile Celtic inhabitants. Legends say

Stone Circles: The Riddle of the Rocks

Ireland is home to about 250 evocative stone circles. These jaggedly sparse boulder rings are rudimentary in comparison to Britain's more famous Stonehenge. But their misty, mossy settings provide curious travelers with an intimate and accessible glimpse of the mysterious people who lived in Ireland before the arrival of the Celts.

Bronze Age Ireland (2000–600 B.C.) was populated by farming folk who had mastered the craft of smelting heated tin and copper to produce bronze, which was used to produce more durable tools and weapons. In the late Bronze Age, many of these primitive clannish communities also chose to put considerable effort into gathering huge rocks and arranging them into ceremonial circles for use in long-forgotten rituals. Many scholars believe that these circles may have been used as solar observatories, to calculate solstices and equinoxes, and to plan life-sustaining seasonal crop-planting cycles. Archaeologists have discovered a few ancient burials in the center of some circles, but their primary use seems to have been ceremonial rather than funerary. And without any written records, we can only make educated guesses as to their exact purpose.

In the Middle Ages, superstitious locals believed that the stones had been arranged by an earlier race of giants. Later Puritans thought that at least one circle was made up of petrified partiers who had dared to dance on the Sabbath. A nearby stand-

he drove Ireland's snakes (symbolic of pagan beliefs) into the sea, and explained the Trinity with a shamrock—three leaves on one stem.

Later monks (such as **St. Columba**, 521–597) continued Christianizing the island, and foreign monks flocked to isolated Ireland. They withdrew to scattered, isolated monasteries, living in Celtic-style beehive huts, translating and illustrating (illuminating) manuscripts. Perhaps the greatest works of art of Dark Age Europe are these manuscripts, including the ninth-century **Book of Kells,** which you'll see at Dublin's Trinity College (see "Irish Art," page 345, and sight listing on page 346). Irish monks—heads shaved cross-wise from ear to ear, like former Druids—were known throughout Europe as ascetic scholars.

St. Columbanus (c. 600; different from St. Columba, above) was one of several traveling missionary monks who helped to bring

ing stone was supposed to be the frozen figure of the piper who had been playing the dance tunes.

Irish stone circles are concentrated into two main regional clusters consisting of more than a hundred circles each: central Ulster in the North (radiocarbon-dated 1500–700 B.C.) and Counties Cork and Kerry in the south (radiocarbon-dated 1000–700 B.C.). The remaining two dozen circles are scattered across central Ireland. Some circles have only recently been rediscovered after having been buried by rapidly accumulating bog growth over the centuries.

Dedicated travelers seeking stone circles (while wearing shoes impervious to grass dew and sheep doo) will find them marked in the Ordnance Survey atlas, and signposted along rural Irish roads. Ask a local farmer for directions—and savor the experience.

Here are our five favorite Irish stone circles, all within a druid's dance of other destinations mentioned in this book:

Kenmare is in County Kerry, on the western fringe of Kenmare (see map on page 164).

Drombeg is in County Cork, 35 miles southwest of Kinsale, just south of the R597 coastal road.

Glebe is in County Mayo, 2 miles northeast of Cong, and 100 yards south of the R345 road to Neale.

Beltany is in County Donegal, 10 miles southeast of Letterkenny, straight south of Raphoe.

Beaghmore, pictured on the cover of this book, is in County Tyrone, 20 miles east of Omagh, north off A505 (Cookstown Road).

Christianity back to Western Europe, which had reverted to paganism and barbarism when Rome fell. The monks established monastic centers of learning that produced great Christian teachers and community builders. One of the monks, **St. Brendan,** may have even sailed to America (see page 186).

By 800, **Charlemagne** was importing Irish monks to help run his Frankish kingdom. Meanwhile, Ireland remained a relatively cohesive society based on monastic settlements rather than cities. Impressive round towers from those settlements still dot the Irish landscape—silent reminders of this glorious age.

Viking Invasion and Defeat (800–1100)

In 795, Viking pirates from Norway invaded, the first of many raids that wreaked havoc on the monasteries and shook Irish civilization. In two centuries of chaos, the Vikings raped, pillaged, and burned Christian churches. The Vikings prized monastic booty such as gold chalices, silver candlestick holders, and the jeweled book covers of sacred illuminated manuscripts. Monks stood guard from their round towers to spy approaching marauders, ring the warning bells, and protect the citizens. In 841, a conquering Viking band settled inland, building Ireland's first permanent walled cities, Dublin and Waterford. Viking raiders slowly evolved into Viking traders, who, among other things, introduced the concept of coinage to the Irish.

Finally, **High King Brian Boru** led a Gaelic revival, defeating a mercenary Viking army allied with rebellious Leinster clans at the Battle of Clontarf (1014), near Dublin. Boru died in the battle, however, and his unified kingdom quickly fell apart. Over the centuries, Viking settlers married Gaelic gals and slowly blended in.

Anglo-Norman Arrival (1100–1500)

The Normans were Ireland's next uninvited guests. In 1169, a small army of well-armed and fearless soldiers of fortune invaded Ireland under the pretense of helping a deposed Irish king regain his lands. A Welsh conquistador named **Strongbow** (c. 1130–1176) took Dublin and Waterford, married the local king's daughter, then succeeded his father-in-law as king of Leinster. This was the spearhead of a century-long invasion by the so-called Anglo-Normans—the French-speaking rulers of England, descended from William the Conqueror and his troops, who had invaded and conquered England a hundred years earlier at the Battle of Hastings (1066).

King Henry II of England soon followed (1171) to remind Strongbow who was boss, proclaiming the entire island under  English (Anglo-Norman) rule. By 1250, the Anglo-Normans occupied three-quarters of the island, clustered in walled cities surrounded by hostile Gaels. These invaders, who were big-time administrators, ushered in a new age in which society (government, cities, and religious organizations) was organized on a grander scale. They imposed feudalism and scoffed at the old Gaelic clan system that they intended to replace. Riding on the coattails of the Normans, monastic orders (Franciscans, Augustinians, and Cistercians) came over from the Continent and eclipsed Ireland's individual monastic settlements, once the foundation of Irish society in the **Age of Saints and Scholars.**

But English rule was weak and distant. Preoccupied with the Hundred Years' War with France and its own internal Wars of the Roses, England "ruled" through deputized locals such as the earls of Kildare. Many English landowners actually resided in England, a pattern of absentee-landlordism that would exist for centuries. England's laws were fully enforced only in a 50-mile foothold around Dublin (**the Pale**—from the Norman-French word for "ditch"). A couple of centuries after invading, the Anglo-Normans saw their area of control shrink to only The Pale—with the rest of the island "beyond the Pale."

Even as their power eroded, the English kings considered Ireland to be theirs. They passed the **Statutes of Kilkenny** (1366), which outlawed all things Gaelic, including intermarriage with the English settlers, the Gaelic language, and the sport of hurling. In practice, the statutes were rarely enforced.

The End of Gaelic Rule (1500s)

As European powers raced to establish profitable colonies in North and South America, Ireland's location on the eastern edge of the Atlantic became more strategic. England's naval power grew to threaten Spain's monopoly on New World riches. Meanwhile, Spain viewed Ireland as the vulnerable back door—the best place to attack England. (It was similar to the U.S.S.R. using Cuba to threaten the U.S. in the early 1960s.) Martin Luther's **Reformation** split the Christian churches into Catholic and Protestant, making Catholic Ireland an even hotter potato for newly Protestant England to handle. Catholic Spain (and later France) would use their shared Catholicism with Ireland as divine justification for alliances against heretic England.

In 1534, angered by **Henry VIII** and his break with Catholicism (and taking advantage of England's Reformation chaos), the **earls of Kildare** rebelled, led by Silken Thomas. Henry crushed the revolt, executed the earls, and confiscated their land. Henry's daughter, **Queen Elizabeth I,** gave the land to colonists ("planters"), mainly English Protestants. The next four centuries would see a series of rebellions by Catholic, Gaelic-speaking Irish farmers fighting to free themselves from rule by Protestant, English-speaking landowners.

Hugh O'Neill (1540–1616), a noble angered by planters and English abuses, led a Gaelic revolt in 1595. The rebels were joined by the Spanish, who were fellow Catholics and England's archrival on the high seas. At the Battle of Yellow Ford (1598), guerrilla tactics led to an Irish victory.

But the **Battle of Kinsale** (1601) ended the revolt. The exhausted Irish, who had marched the length of Ireland in winter, arrived to help Spanish troops, who were pinned down inside the town. But the English crushed the Irish before they could join the Spanish, who then surrendered. O'Neill knelt before the conquering general, ceding half a million acres to England. Then he and other proud, Gaelic, Ulster-based nobles unexpectedly abandoned their land and sailed to the Continent (The Flight of the Earls, 1607), an event seen as the symbolic end of Gaelic Irish rule.

English Colonization and Irish Rebellions (1600s)

King James I took advantage of the Gaelic power vacuum and sent 25,000 English and Scottish planters into the confiscated land (1610–1641), making Ulster (in the northeast) the most English area of the island. The Irish responded with two major rebellions.

In 1642, with England embroiled in civil war between a Catholic king and a Protestant Parliament, Irish rebels capitalized on the instability. Tenant farmers took up pitchforks against their English landlords, slaughtering 4,000 in the **Massacre of the Planters** (1641). Irish society was split between an English-speaking landed gentry (descendants of the first Anglo-Norman invaders, called "Old English") and the local Irish-speaking landless, or nearly landless, peasantry. But with Catholicism as their common bond, the Irish forces allied with the Old English against the Protestant Parliament of **Oliver Cromwell.**

Cromwell responded by invading Ireland (1649–1650) with 20,000 men. He conquered the country—brutally. Thousands were slaughtered, priests were tortured, villages were pillaged, and rebels were sold into slavery. Most Catholic Irish landowners, given the choice of "to hell or to Connaught," were exiled to the rocky land west of the River Shannon. Cromwell confiscated 11 million acres of Catholic land to give to English Protestants. (In 1641, Catholics owned 59 percent of Ireland—by 1714 they owned 7 percent.) Cromwell's scorched-earth invasion was so harsh (the "curse of Cromwell"), it still raises hackles in Ireland.

In 1688–1689, rebels again took advantage of England's political chaos. They rallied around Catholic **King James II,** who was deposed by Parliament in the "Glorious Revolution" of 1688, then fled to France, and wound up in Ireland where he formed an army to retake the crown. In the **Siege of Londonderry,** James' Catholic army surrounded the city but some local apprentice boys locked them out, and after months of negotiations and a 105-day standoff, James went away empty-handed.

The showdown came at the massive **Battle of the Boyne** (1690), north of Dublin. Catholic James II and his 25,000 men

were defeated by the 36,000 troops of Protestant **King William III** of Orange. From this point on, the color orange became a symbol for pro-English, pro-Protestant forces.

As the 17th century came to a close, England had successfully put down every rebellion. To counter Irish feistiness, English legislation became an out-and-out attack on the indigenous Gaelic culture. The English punished the mostly Catholic nation with the **Penal Laws.** Catholics couldn't vote, hold office, buy land, join the army, play the harp, or even own a horse worth more than £5. Catholic education was banned and priests were outlawed. But the Penal Laws were difficult to enforce, and many Catholics were taught at hidden outdoor "hedge schools" and worshipped in private or at secluded "Mass rocks" in the countryside.

Protestant Rule (1700s)

During the 18th century, Ireland thrived under the English. Dublin in the 1700s (pop. 50,000) was Britain's second city, one of Europe's wealthiest and most sophisticated. It's still decorated in Georgian (neoclassical) style, named for the English kings of the time (consecutive kings George the I, II, and III, who ruled for most of the century).

But beyond the Pale surrounding Dublin, rebellion continued to brew. Over time, greed on the top and dissent on the bottom led to more repressive colonial policies. The Enlightenment provided ideas of freedom, and the Revolutionary Age emboldened the Irish masses. Irish nationalists were inspired by budding democratic revolutions in America (1776) and France (1789). Increasingly, the issue of Irish independence was less a religious question than a political one, as poor, disenfranchised colonists demanded a political voice.

In Dublin, **Jonathan Swift** (1667–1745), the dean of St. Patrick's Cathedral, published his satirical *Gulliver's Travels* with veiled references to English colonialism. He anonymously wrote pamphlets advising, "Burn all that's British, except its coal."

The **Irish Parliament** was an exclusive club, and only Protestant, male landowners could be elected to a seat (only 1 percent of the population qualified). In 1782, led by **Henry Grattan** (1746–1820), the Parliament negotiated limited autonomy from England (while remaining loyal to the king) and fairer treatment of the Catholics. England, chastened by the American Revolution (and soon preoccupied by the French Revolution), tolerated a more-or-less independent Irish Parliament for two decades.

Then, in 1798, came the bloodiest Irish Rebellion. Inspired by the American and French revolutionary successes (with a "hey if they can do it, so can we" attitude), an idealistic band of Irish rebels rose up. The **United Irishmen** (who wanted to substitute the word "Irishman" in place of the labels Protestant or Catholic) revolted against Britain, led by **Wolfe Tone** (1763–1798), a Protestant Dublin lawyer. Tone, trained in the French Revolution, had gained French aid for the Irish cause. (Though a French naval invasion in 1796 already had failed due to a freakish "Protestant wind" that blew the ships away from Ireland's shores.) The Rebellion was marked by bitter fighting—30,000 died over six weeks—before British troops crushed the revolt.

England tried to solve the Irish problem politically by forcing Ireland into a "Union" with England as part of a "United Kingdom" (**Act of Union,** 1801). The 500-year-old Irish Parliament was dissolved, becoming part of England's Parliament in London. Catholics were not allowed in Parliament. From then on, "Unionists" have been those who oppose Irish independence, wanting to preserve the country's union with Britain.

Votes, Violence, and the Famine (1800s)

Irish politicians lobbied in the British Parliament for Catholic rights, reform of absentee-landlordism, and for **Home Rule**—i.e., independence. Meanwhile, secret societies of revolutionaries pursued justice through violence.

Daniel O'Connell (1775–1847), known as The Liberator, campaigned for Catholic equality and for repeal of the Act of Union (independence). Having personally witnessed the violence of the French Revolution in 1789 and the 1798 United Irishman Rebellion, O'Connell chose peaceful, legal means. He was a charismatic speaker, drawing half a million people to one of his "monster meeting" demonstrations at the Hill of Tara (1843). But any hope of an Irish revival was soon snuffed out by the biggest catastrophe in Irish history: the famine.

The **Great Potato Famine** (1845–1849) was caused by a fungus *(Phytophthora infestans)* that destroyed Ireland's main food crop. Roughly a million people starved to death or died of related diseases (estimates range between 500,000 and 1.1 million). Another 1–2 million emigrated—most to America, and others to Canada and Australia.

The poorest were hardest hit. Potatoes were their main food source, and any other crops were far too expensive—grown by tenant farmers on their landlords' land to pay the rent and destined for export. (If this makes you mad at the English landlords, consider American ownership of land in Central America, where the landlord takes things one step beyond by not growing the local staple at all. He devotes all the land to more profitable cash crops for export, and leaves the landless farmer no alternative but to buy his food—imported from the U.S.—at plantation wages, in the landlord's grocery store.)

Britain—then the richest nation on earth, with an empire stretching around the globe—could seemingly do nothing to help its starving citizens. A toxic combination of laissez-faire economic policies, racial bigotry, and religious self-righteousness conspired to blind the English to the plight of the Irish. While the English tend to blame the famine on overpopulation (Ireland's population doubled in the 40 years leading up to the famine), many Irish say there actually was no famine—just a calculated attempt to starve down the local population. Over the course of five long years, Ireland was ruined. (To this day, Irish weather reports include mention of potential potato-blight conditions.)

The population was cut by nearly a third (from 8.4 million to 6 million), many of their best and brightest had fled, and the island's economy—and spirit—took generations to recover. The Irish language, spoken by the majority of the population before the famine, became a badge of ignorance, and was considered useless to those hoping to emigrate. Ireland, which remained one of Europe's poorest countries for over a century, was slow to forget Britain's indifference. Ireland's population has only recently begun to grow again. Irish Nationalists point out that Britain's population, on the other hand, has grown from 12 million in 1845 to around 60 million today.

Before the famine, land was subdivided—each boy got a piece of the family estate (which grew smaller with each generation). After the famine, the oldest son got the estate and the younger siblings, with no way to stay in Ireland, emigrated to Britain, Australia, Canada, or the U.S. Because of the huge emigration to the U.S. (today there are 45 million Irish Americans), Ireland began to face west, and American influence increased. (As negotiations between Northern Ireland and the Irish Republic continue, American involvement in the talks is welcomed and considered essential by nearly all parties.)

Occasional violence demonstrated the fury of Irish nationalism, with the tragedy of the famine inflaming the movement. In 1848, the **Young Irelander** armed uprising was easily squelched. In 1858, the **Irish Republican Brotherhood** was formed (the forerunner of the IRA). Also called the **Fenians**, they launched a never-ending campaign for independence by planting terrorist bombs. Irish Americans sent money to help finance these revolutionaries. Uprising after uprising made it clear that Ireland was ready to close this thousand-year chapter of invasions and colonialism.

On the political front, Home Rule Party leader **Charles Stuart Parnell** (1846–1891), an Irishman educated in England, made "the Irish problem" the focus of London's Parliament. Parnell lobbied for independence and for the rights of poor tenant farmers living under absentee landlords, pioneering the first boycott tactics. Then, in 1890, at the peak of his power and about to achieve Home Rule for Ireland, he was drummed out of politics by a scandal involving his mistress, scuttling the Home Rule issue for another 20 years.

Culturally, the old Gaelic, rural Ireland was being swamped by the Industrial Revolution and dominated by Protestant England. The **Gaelic Athletic Association** was founded (in 1884) to resurrect pride in ancient Irish sports such as hurling. Soon after, in 1893, writers and educators formed the **Gaelic League** to preserve the traditional language, music, and poetry. Building on the tradition of old Celtic bards, Ireland produced some of the great early-modern writers: **W. B. Yeats, Oscar Wilde, G. B. Shaw,** and **James Joyce,** whose rambling, stream-of-consciousness *Ulysses* chronicles a day in the life of 1904 Dublin, and set new standards for the modern novel.

Easter Rising, War of Independence, Partition, and Civil War (1900–1950)

As the century turned, Ireland prepared for the inevitable show-down with Britain.

The **Sinn Fein** party (meaning "We, Ourselves") lobbied politically for independence. The **Irish Volunteers** were more Catholic and more militant. Also on the scene was the **Irish Citizens Army,** with a socialist agenda to clean up Dublin's hideous tenements, where infant mortality was 15 percent before children reached the age of one.

Of course, many Irish were Protestant and pro-British. The **Ulster Volunteers** (Unionists, and mostly Orangemen) feared that Home Rule would result in a Catholic-dominated state that would oppress the Protestant minority.

Meanwhile, Britain was preoccupied with World War I, where it was "fighting to protect the rights of small nations" (except Ireland's), and so delayed granting Irish independence. The increasingly militant Irish rebels, believing that England's misfortune was Ireland's opportunity, decided to rise up and take independence on their own.

On Easter Monday, April 24, 1916, 1,500 Irish "Volunteers," along with members of the Irish Citizens Army, marched on Dublin, occupied the General Post Office, and raised a green-white-and-orange flag. The teacher and poet **Patrick Pearse** stood in front of the Post Office and proclaimed Ireland an independent republic.

British troops struck back—in a week of street-fighting and intense shelling, some 300 died. By Saturday, the greatly outnumbered rebels had been killed or arrested. The small-scale uprising—which failed to go national and was never even popular in Dublin—was apparently over.

However, the British government overreacted by swiftly executing the 16 ringleaders, including Pearse. Ireland was outraged, no longer seeing the rebels as troublemakers but as martyrs. From this point on, Ireland was resolved to win its independence at all costs. A poem by W. B. Yeats, "Easter 1916," captured the struggle with his words: "All changed, changed utterly: A terrible beauty is born."

In the 1918 elections, the Sinn Fein party won big, but the new Members of Parliament refused to go to London, instead forming their own independent Irish Parliament in Dublin. The following year, Irish rebels ambushed and shot two policemen, sparking two years of confrontations called the **War of Independence.** The fledgling Irish Republican Army faced 40,000 British troops, including the notorious "Black and Tans" (named for the color of their clothes: black for police and tan for army-surplus uniforms). A thousand people died in this war of street fighting, sniper fire, jailhouse beatings, terrorist bombs, and reprisals.

Finally, Britain, tired of war after more than four years in the meat grinder of World War I, agreed to Irish independence. But Ireland itself was a divided nation—the southern three-quarters of the island was mostly Catholic, Gaelic, rural, and for Home Rule; the northern quarter was Protestant, English, industrial, and Unionist. The solution? In 1920, in the **Government of Ireland Act,** the British Parliament partitioned the island into two independent, self-governing countries within the British Commonwealth: **Northern Ireland** and the **Irish Free State.** While the northern six counties (the only ones without a Catholic majority) voted to stay with Britain as Northern Ireland, the remaining 26 counties became the Irish Free State. (For a review of the ongoing Troubles between the North and the Republic, see the Northern Ireland chapter.)

Ireland's various political factions wrestled with this compromise solution, and the island plunged into a yearlong **Civil War** (1922–1923). The hard-line IRA opposed the partition, unwilling to accept a divided island, an oath of loyalty to the queen, or the remaining British Navy bases on Irish soil. They waged a street war on the armies of the Irish  Free State, who supported the political settlement. Dublin and the southeast were ravaged in a year of bitter fighting before the Irish Free State emerged victorious. The IRA went underground, moving its fight north and trying for the rest of the century to topple the government of Northern Ireland.

In 1937, the Irish Free State severed more ties with the British Commonwealth, writing up a new national constitution and taking an old name—**Éire** (pronounced AIR-uh—a Gaelic word possibly derived from the early Greeks' name for the island, Ierne). In 1949, the separation was completed, as the country officially became the **Republic of Ireland.**

Celtic Tiger in the South, Troubles in the North (1950–2000)

Beginning in 1960, the Republic of Ireland—formerly a poor, rural region—was transformed into a modern, economic power, thanks to foreign investors and, in 1973, membership in the European Union. Through the mid-1990s, Ireland's booming, globalized economy grew a whopping 40 percent, and Dublin's property values tripled (between 1995 and 2004), earning the Republic the nickname "The Celtic Tiger."

Meanwhile, Northern Ireland—with a 55 percent Protestant majority and a large, 45 percent disaffected Catholic minority—was plagued by the Troubles. In 1967, the Northern Ireland Civil Rights Movement, inspired by America's African-American civil rights movement, organized marches and demonstrations demanding equal treatment for Catholics (better housing, job opportunities, and voting rights). Protestant **Unionist Orangemen** countered by marching through Catholic neighborhoods, flaunting their politically dominant position in the name of tradition, and thus provoking riots. In 1969, Britain sent troops to help Northern Ireland keep the peace, and met resistance from the IRA, which saw them as an occupying army supporting the Protestant pro-British majority.

From the 1970s to the 1990s, the North was a low-level battlefield, with the IRA using terrorist tactics to achieve their political ends. The **Troubles,** which claimed some 3,000 lives, continued with bombings, marches, hunger strikes, rock-throwing, and riots (notably Derry's **Bloody Sunday** in 1972), interrupted by cease-fires, broken cease-fires, and a string of peace agreements.

Then came the 1998 watershed settlement known as the **Good Friday Peace Accord** (to pro-Irish Nationalists) or the **Belfast Agreement** (to pro-British Unionists). It has proven to be a flawed breakthrough in the process of getting bitter, hard-line opponents to seek common ground. In spring of 2005, elections showed that disillusioned voters were edging away from the moderate middle ground and becoming politically polarized once again. The ranks of the ultra-Unionist DUP party—led by **Reverend Ian Paisley**—and the ultra-Nationalist Sinn Fein party—led by **Gerry Adams**—have become dominant at opposite ends of the spectrum. However, the spiraling violence of the 1970s and 80s seem to be a thing of the past. In July 2005, the IRA formally announced an end to its armed campaign, and promised that it would pursue peaceful, democratic means to achieve its goals.

Global Nations (2000 and Beyond)

Today, both Northern Ireland and the Republic of Ireland have every reason to be optimistic about the future, as their economies boom and the political and cultural Troubles lessen. The formerly isolated island is welcoming tourists with open arms, and reaching out to the rest of the globe. In 1999, the number of tourists visiting Ireland topped the six million mark, exceeding for the first time the actual native population on the island (5.7 million).

Visitors returning to Ireland are amazed at the country's transformation. Although there are still some tense areas in the North—as there are in all big cities—the peace process is grinding forward.

Now, for the first time in history, the Irish are importing labor, and they've surpassed the English in per-capita income. Since 1980, when Apple Computer set up shop here, a stream of multinational and American corporations have opened offices in Ireland. Ireland has one of the youngest populations in Europe. And those young Irish, beneficiaries of one of Europe's best educational systems, provide these corporations with a highly skilled, youthful, and educated workforce. Ireland's pharmaceutical, chemical, and software industries are booming—this little country is second only to the U.S. in the exportation of software.

Of course, with rapid growth comes problems. Urban sprawl, big-city traffic snarls, rising housing prices, water and air pollution, and the homogenous nature of globalization all left their mark. In 2003, the rising economic tide had lifted Ireland to float beside Finland as one of the two most expensive countries in the European Union. Per-capita consumption of alcohol has also tripled since 1970 (the dark side of recent prosperity). Still, the Celtic Tiger, although slightly muffled by the tech bubble bursting, continues to roar.

The challenges of immigration (new arrivals into Ireland) have replaced problems associated with the generations of emigration (young people leaving Ireland). Until recently, Ireland had the most liberal citizenship laws in the European Union, granting Irish citizenship to anyone born on Irish soil (even if neither parent had an Irish passport). This led to a flood of pregnant immigrant women arriving from Eastern Europe and Africa to give birth in Ireland for their children to gain EU citizenship. Families with a child born in an EU country face fewer border restrictions, increasing their chances of moving into one of the 25 EU nations. In 2004, the Irish people closed that legal loophole in a referendum vote.

While the Irish are embracing the new economies and industries of the 21st century, when it comes to sex and marriage, they still see their island as an oasis of morality and traditional values (homosexuality was decriminalized only a dozen years ago). The Catholic Church continues to exert a major influence on Irish society. But since the Church no longer controls the legislature, the Irish government—driven by the popular demands of the youngest population in Europe—will undoubtedly push for some changes on the following issues.

Birth Control: Americans take for granted that birth control is readily available. But Ireland only began allowing the widespread sale of condoms in 1993.

Abortion: In Ireland, women who choose to terminate their pregnancies must go to England for help. Abortion is still illegal in Ireland. And it's only been legal since 1993 to counsel Irish women to go to England for abortions. This was a big issue in 2001, when the Dutch anchored their "abortion ship" in Dublin's harbor, and again in 2002, when a referendum legalizing abortion was narrowly defeated. Watch for more referendums proposing the legalization of abortion. Locals refer to this as their next Civil War.

Divorce: Ireland voted to legalize divorce in 1995—but only on very strict conditions. After the divorce papers are signed, it takes a four-year waiting period before the divorce is considered official, and little compensation is offered to Irish women who work as homemakers.

IRISH ART

Megalithic tombs, ancient gold- and metalwork, illuminated manuscripts, high crosses carved in stone, paintings of rural Ireland, and provocative political murals—Ireland comes with some fascinating art. To best appreciate this art in your travels, kick off your tour in Ireland's two top museums (both in Dublin): the **National Museum** (see page 63) and the **National Gallery** (see page 64). Each provide a good context to help you enjoy Irish art and architecture—from ancient to modern and both rural and urban. Here's a quick survey.

Megalithic Period: During the Stone Age 5,000 years ago, farmers living in the **Valley of the Boyne,** north of Dublin, built a "cemetery" of approximately 40 **burial mounds.** The most famous of these mound tombs is the passage tomb at Newgrange (part of Brú na Bóinne). More than 300 feet in diameter and composed of 200,000 tons of loose stone, Newgrange was constructed so that the light from the winter solstice sunrise (Dec 21) would pass through the eastern entrance to the tomb, travel down a 60-foot passage, and illuminate the inner burial chamber. (Not bad engineering for Stone Age architects.) The effect is now recreated daily, so visitors can experience this ancient ritual of renewal and rebirth (see the Near Dublin chapter).

Some of Europe's best examples of megalithic (big rock) art are also at Newgrange. Carved on the tomb's stones are zigzags, chevrons, parallel arcs, and concentric spirals. Scholars think these designs symbolize a belief in the eternal cycle of life and the continuation of the life force, or that they pay homage to the elements in nature on which these ancient peoples depended for their existence.

Exploring these burial mounds (only Newgrange and Knowth

are open to the public), you begin to understand the reverence that these people had for nature, and the need they felt to bury their dead in these great mound tombs, returning their kin to the womb of Mother Earth.

Bronze Age: As ancient Irish cultures developed from 2000 B.C., so did their metalworking skills. Gold and bronze were used to create **tools, jewelry,** and **religious objects.** (The National Museum in Dublin houses the most dazzling of these works—see page 63.) Gold neck rings worn by both men and women, cufflink-like dress fasteners, bracelets, and lock rings (to hold hair in place) are just a few of the personal adornments fashioned by the ancient Irish.

Most of these objects were deliberately buried, often in bogs, as votive offerings to their gods or to prevent warring tribes from stealing them. Like the earlier megaliths, they're decorated with geometric and organic motifs.

Iron Age: The Celts, a warrior society from Central Europe, arrived in Ireland perhaps as early as the seventh century B.C. With their metalworking skills and superior iron weaponry, they soon overwhelmed the native population. And, though the Celts may have been bloodthirsty, they wreaked havoc with a flair for the aesthetic. **Shields, swords,** and **scabbards** were embellished with delicate patterns, often enhanced with vivid colors. The dynamic energy of these decorations must have reflected the ferocious power of the Celts.

The Age of Saints and Scholars: Christianity grew in Ireland from St. Patrick's first efforts in the fifth century A.D. In the sixth and seventh centuries, its many great saints (such as St. Columba) established monastic settlements throughout Ireland, Britain, and the Continent, where learning, literature, and the arts flourished. During this "Golden Age" of Irish civilization, monks, along with metalworkers and stonemasons, created imaginative designs and distinctive stylistic motifs for **manuscripts, metal objects,** and **crosses.**

Monks wrote out and richly decorated manuscripts of the Gospels. These manuscripts—which preserved the written word in Latin, Greek, and Irish—eventually had more power than the oral tales of the ancient pagan heroes.

The most beautiful and imaginative of these illuminated manuscripts is the **Book of Kells** (c. A.D. 800), on display in the Old Library at Trinity College in Dublin (see page 59). Crafted by Irish monks at a monastery on the Scottish island of Iona, the book was brought to Ireland for safekeeping from rampaging Vikings. The skins of 150 calves were used to make the vellum, which is painted with rich pigments from plants and minerals. The entire manuscript is colorfully decorated with flat, stylized human or angelic forms and intricate, interlacing animal and knot patterns. Full-page illustrations depict the life of Christ and many pages are given over to highly complex yet symmetrical designs that resemble an Eastern carpet. Many consider this book the finest piece of art from Europe's Dark Ages.

The most renowned metalwork of this period is the **Ardagh Chalice,** dating from the eighth century. Now on display at the National Museum in Dublin, the silver and bronze gilt chalice is as impressive as the Book of Kells. Ribbons of gold wrap around the chalice stem, while intricate knot patterns ring the cup. A magnificent gold ring and a large glass stone on the chalice bottom reflect the desire to please God. (He would see this side of the chalice when the priest drank during the Mass.)

The monks used Irish high crosses to celebrate the triumph of Christianity and to provide a means of educating the illiter-

ate masses through simple stone carvings. The **Cross of Murdock** (Muiredach's Cross, A.D. 923) is 18 feet tall, towering over the remains of the monastic settlement at Monasterboice (north of Dublin, see page 97). It is but one of many monumental crosses that visitors will discover throughout Ireland. Typically, stone carvers depicted Bible stories and surrounded these with the same intricate patterns seen in the Book of Kells and the Ardagh Chalice.

Early Irish art focused on organic, geometric, and linear designs. Unlike Mediterranean art, Irish art of this early period was not preoccupied with a naturalistic representation of people, animals, or the landscape. Instead, it reflects Irish society's rituals and the elements and rhythms of nature.

The Suppression of Native Irish Art: The English, after invading Ireland in 1169, suppressed Celtic Irish culture. English traditions in architecture, painting, and literature replaced native styles until the late 19th century, when revivals in Irish language, folklore, music, and art began to surface.

Painters in the late 19th and early 20th centuries went to the west of Ireland, which was untouched by English dominance and influence, in search of traditional Irish subject matter.

Jack B. Yeats (1871–1957, brother of the poet W. B. Yeats), Belfast-born painter **Paul Henry** (1876–1958), and **Sean Keating** (1889–1977) all looked to the west for inspiration. The National Gallery in Dublin holds many of these artists' greatest works, with an entire gallery dedicated to Jack Yeats. Many of his early paintings illustrate scenes of his beloved Sligo. His later paintings are more expressionistic in style and patriotic in subject matter.

Henry's paintings depict the rugged beauty of the Connemara region and its people, with scenes of rustic cottages, mountains, and boglands. Keating, the most political of the three painters, featured patriotic scenes from Ireland's struggle against the English for independence.

Contemporary Irish art is often linked to the social, political, and environmental issues facing Ireland today. Themes include the position of the Church in the daily lives of the modern Irish,

What's a Celt?

The Irish are a Celtic people. The Celts, who came from Central Europe, began migrating west around 1500 B.C. Over time, many settled in the British Isles and Western France. When the Angles and Saxons came later, grabbing the best land in the British Isles (which became Angle-land...or England), the Celts survived in Brittany, Cornwall, Wales, Scotland, and Ireland. Today, this "Celtic Crescent" still nearly encircles England. The word Celtic (pronounced with a hard C) comes from the Greek "Keltoi," meaning barbarian.

From about 700 B.C. on, various Celtic tribes mixed, mingled, and fought in Ireland. The last and most powerful of the Celtic tribes to enter the fray were the Gaels, who probably came from Scotland. The Irish language, Gaelic, is named for them. The fact that the Celts never had a written language meant that they had to pass their history, laws, and folklore down verbally from generation to generation. This may well account for the "gift of gab" attributed to today's Irish.

Celtic society revolved around warrior kings who gathered groups of families into regional kingdoms. These small kingdoms combined to make the five large provincial kingdoms of ancient Ireland (whose names survive on maps today): Leinster, Munster, Connacht, Ulster, and the Middle Kingdom (now County Meath).

For defensive purposes, these early Irish lived in small thatched huts built on manmade islands or on high ground

the effects of development on the countryside, the changing roles of women in Ireland, and the Troubles. Look for this provocative art at the Irish Museum of Modern Art in Dublin (on Military Road, www.imma.ie) and at city galleries.

In Northern Ireland, murals in sectarian neighborhoods (such as Shankill and Falls Roads in Belfast) are stirring public testaments to the martyrs and to the heroes, to resistance and to confrontation, and to the reconciliation that continues to elude the people of Northern Ireland. (For more on these murals, see the Derry and County Donegal chapter).

surrounded by ditches and a stone or earthen wall. A strictly observed hierarchy governed Celtic societies: the king on top, followed by poets, Druid priests, doctors, legal men, skilled craftsmen, freemen, and slaves. Rarely did a high king rule the entire island. Loyalty to one's clan came first, and alliances between clans were often temporary until a more advantageous alliance could be struck with a rival clan. This fluid system of alliances ebbing and flowing across the Celtic-warrior cultural landscape meant that the Celts would never unite as a single nation.

Unlike the Celtic tribes living in Western Europe and Britain, the Celts in Ireland were never conquered by the Romans. This gives Ireland a cultural continuity and uniqueness rare in Europe. Their culture—which evolved apart from Europe—remained strong and independent for centuries. Then, in the 12th century, English dominance began leading to suppression of Gaelic language and Celtic traditions. With Irish independence—won only in the 20th century—Irish ways are no longer threatened. The most traditional areas (generally along the West Coast, such as the Dingle Peninsula) are protected as Gaeltachts. Gaeltachts (literally, places where the Gaelic language is spoken) are a kind of national park for the traditional culture. If much of Ireland's charm can be credited to its Celtic roots, you'll find that charm most vivid in a Gaeltacht.

IRISH LITERATURE

Since the Book of Kells, Ireland's greatest contributions to the world of art have been through words. As there was no Irish Gaelic written language, the inhabitants of Ireland were illiterate until Christianity came in the fourth century. Far from ignorant, Celtic society maintained a complex set of laws and historical records and legends...verbally. The druidic priests and bards who passed this rich oral tradition down from generation to generation were the most respected members of the clan, next to the king. After Christianity transformed Ireland into a refuge of literacy (while the rest of Europe crumbled into the Dark Ages), Charlemagne's imported Irish monks invented "minuscule," which became the basis of the lowercase letters we use in our alphabet today. The cultural importance placed on the word (spoken, and for the past 1,500 years, written) is today reflected in the rich output of modern Irish writers.

Three hundred years ago, **Jonathan Swift** created his masterpiece, *Gulliver's Travels*, as an acidic satire of British colonialism, which has ironically survived as a children's classic. **William Butler Yeats** dedicated his early writings in the 1880s to the "Celtic Twilight" rebirth of pride in mythic Irish heroes and heroines. His early poems and plays were filled with fairies and idyllic rural innocence. His later poems reflected Ireland's painful transition to independence as "a terrible beauty" was born. His Nobel Prize for literature (1923) was eventually followed by three more prize-winning Irish authors: **George Bernard Shaw** (1925), **Samuel Beckett** (1969), and **Seamus Heaney** (1995).

Oscar Wilde wrote the darkly fascinating novel *The Picture of Dorian Gray* and the witty play *The Importance of Being Earnest,*

making him the toast of London in the 1890s—before the scandal of his homosexuality turned Victorian society against him. Meanwhile, **Bram Stoker** was conjuring up a Gothic thriller called *Dracula*. Most inventive of all, perhaps, was **James Joyce**, who broke new ground and captured literary lightning in a bottle when he developed his complex stream-of-consciousness style in his masterpiece novel, *Ulysses*.

The **Abbey Theatre** (championed by Yeats) was the world's first national theater, built to house plays intended to give a voice to Ireland's flowering playwrights. When **J. M. Synge** staged *The Playboy of the Western World* there in 1907, his unflattering comic portrayal of Irish peasant life (and mention of women's underwear) caused riots. Twenty years later, **Sean O'Casey** provoked more riots at the Abbey when his *Plough and the Stars* production depicted the 1916 Uprising in a way that was at odds with the audience's cherished views of their heroes.

In recent decades, the bittersweet Irish literary parade has been inhabited by tragically volcanic characters like **Brendan Behan,** who exclaimed, "I'm not a writer with a drinking problem...I'm a drinker with a writing problem." Bleak poverty experienced in childhood was the catalyst for **Frank McCourt**'s memorable *Angela's Ashes*. Among the most celebrated of today's Irish writers is **Roddy Doyle,** whose feel for working-class Dublin resonates in his novels of contemporary life, like *The Commitments*, as well as in historical slices of life, like a *Star Called Henry*.

IRISH LANGUAGE

The Irish have a rich oral tradition that goes back to their ancient fireside storytelling days. Part of the fun of traveling here is getting an ear for the way locals express themselves. Ask an Irish person for directions and you'll more often than not have an interesting, memorable experience. Being excessively verbal seems to be a fundamental part of being Irish: "How do I know what I think until I hear what I say?"

Gaeltacht Regions

AREAS SHOWN IN BLACK
ARE GAELTACHTS

Irish Gaelic is one of four surviving Celtic languages, along with Scottish Gaelic, Welsh, and Breton (spoken in parts of French Brittany). A couple of centuries ago, there were seven surviving Celtic languages. But three have died out: Manx (the Isle of Man), Cornish (spoken in Cornwall), and Galician (spoken in Northern Spain). Some proud Irish choose to call their native tongue "Irish" instead of "Gaelic" to ensure that there is no confusion with what is spoken in parts of Scotland.

Only 150 years ago, the majority of the Irish population spoke Irish Gaelic. But most of the speakers were of the poor laborer class that, during the famine, either died or emigrated. After the famine, Irish Gaelic was seen as a badge of backwardness. Parents and teachers understood that English was the language that would serve children best when they emigrated to better lives in America, Canada, Australia,

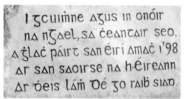

or England. Children in schools wore a tally stick around their necks, and a notch was cut by teachers each time a child was caught speaking Irish. At the end of the day, the child received a whack for each notch in the stick. It wasn't until the resurgence of cultural pride, brought on by the Gaelic League in 1884, that an attempt was made to promote use of the language.

These days, less than 5 percent of the Irish population is fluent in their native tongue. However, it's taken seriously enough that all national laws passed must first be written in Irish, then translated into English. Irish Gaelic can be heard most often in the western counties of Kerry, Galway, and Donegal. Each of these three counties has a slightly different dialect. You'll know you're entering an Irish Gaelic-speaking area when you see a sign saying Gaeltacht (GAIL-tekt).

In Irish Gaelic, there is no "th" sound—which you can hear today when an Irish person says something like "turdy tree" (33). There is also no equivalent of the simple words "yes" or "no." Instead, answers are given in the affirmative or negative rephrasing of the question. For example, a question like "Did you mail the letter today?" would be answered with "I did (mail the letter)," rather than a simple "yes." Or "It's a nice day today, isn't it?" would be answered with "It is," or "'Tis."

Irish Place Names

Here are a few words that appear in Irish place names. You'll see these on road signs or at tourist sights.

Irish	Phonetics	English
Alt	ahlt	cliff
An Lar	ahn lar	city center
Ard	ard	high, height, hillock
Baile	BALL-yah	town, town land
Bally	BAH-lee	town, town land
Beag	beg	little
Bearna	bar-na	gap
Boireann	burr-en	large rock, rocky area
Bothar	boh-er	road
Bun	bun	end, bottom
Caiseal	CASH-el	castle, circular stone fort
Caislean	cash-LOIN	castle
Cathair	caht-HAR	circular stone fort, city
Cill	kill	church
Cloch	clockh	stone
Doire	DER-ry	wooded area
Droichead	DROH-ed	bridge
Drumlin	DRUM-lin	small hill
Dun	doon	fort
Fionn	fin	white, fair-haired person
Gaeltacht	gayl-tek	Irish language district
Gall	gaul	foreigner
Gaol	jail	jail
Garda	gar-dah	police
Gort	gort	field
Innis	in-ish	island
Kil	kil	church; monk's cell
Mileac	mee-luch	low marshy ground
Mor	mor	large

Muck	muck	pig
Oifig an Phoist	UFF-ig un fwisht	post office
Poll	poll	hole, cave
Rath	rath	ancient earthen fort
Ross	ross	peninsula
Si	shee	fairy mound, bewitching
Sli	slee	route, way
Sliabh	sleeve	mountain
Sraid	shrawd	street
Teach	tagh	house
Trá	thraw	beach, strand
Tur	toor	tower

Irish Pleasantries

When you reach the more remote western fringe of Ireland, you're likely to hear folks speaking Irish. Although locals in these areas can readily converse with you in English, it's fascinating to hear their ancient Celtic language spoken. Here are some basic Irish phrases:

Irish	Phonetics	English
Dia dhuit	JEE-a dich	Good day, hello
Dia's muire dhuit	JEE-as MWUR-a dich	response to dia dhuit
Fáilte	FAHLT-shuh	Welcome
Conas ta tu?	CUNN-us thaw too	How are you?
Go raibh maith agat	guh roh moh UG-ut	Thank you
Slán	slawn	Bye

Irish Pub and Music Words

The Irish love to socialize. Pubs are like public living rooms, where friends gather in a corner to play tunes and anyone is a welcome guest. Here are some useful pub and music words:

Irish	Phonetics	English
Poitín	po-CHEEN	moonshine, homemade liquor
Craic	crack	fun atmosphere, good conversation
Bodhrán	BO-run	traditional drum
Uilleann	ILL-in	elbow (uilleann pipes are elbow bagpipes)
Trad	trad	traditional Irish music
Ceilidh	KAY-lee	Irish dance gathering

Fleadh	flah	music festival
Slainte	SLAWN-chuh	cheers, to your health
Táim súgach!	thaw im SOO-gakh	I'm tipsy!
Lei thras	LEH-hrass	toilets
Mná	min-AW	women's room
Fir	fear	men's room

Irish Politics

Politics is a popular topic of conversation in Ireland. Whether you pick up a local newspaper or turn on your car radio, you'll often encounter these Irish political terms in the media:

Irish	Phonetics	English
Taoiseach	TEE-shock	Prime Minister of Irish Republic
Seanad	SHAN-ud	Irish Senate
Dáil	DOY-ill	Irish House of Representatives
TD, Teachta Dála	TALK-ta DOLL-a	Member of Irish Parliament

IRISH-YANKEE VOCABULARY

If some of these words seem more British than Irish, those are ones you're likely to hear more often in Northern Ireland (part of the UK).

advert—advertisement
afters—dessert
anticlockwise—counterclockwise
aubergine—eggplant
banger—sausage
bang on—correct
bank holiday—legal holiday
bap—hamburger-type bun
beer mat—coaster
bespoke—custom
billion—a thousand of our billions (a trillion)
biro—ballpoint pen
biscuit—cookie
black pudding—sausage made from dried blood
blather—rambling, empty talk
bloody—damn
blow off—fart
boffin—nerd
bog—slang for toilet
bolshy—argumentative

bonnet—car hood

boot—car trunk

braces—suspenders

bridle way—path for walkers, bikers, and horse riders

brilliant—cool

bum—bottom or "backside"

busker—street musician

candy floss—cotton candy

car boot sale—temporary flea market with car trunk displays (a good place to buy back your stolen goods)

caravan—trailer

cat's eyes—road reflectors

champ—mashed potatoes and onions

cheap and nasty—cheap and bad quality

chemist—pharmacist

chicory—endive

chips—french fries

chipper—fish and chips shop

chockablock—jam-packed

chuffed—pleased

cider—alcoholic apple cider

clearway—road where you can't stop

coach—long-distance bus

concession—discounted admission

cotton buds—cotton swabs

courgette—zucchini

cos—romaine lettuce

crisps—potato chips

crusties—New Age hippies

cuppa—cup of tea

dear—expensive

deadly—really good

dodgy—iffy, risky

digestives—round graham crackers

dinner—lunch or dinner

diversion—detour

done and dusted—completed

donkey's years—until the cows come home

draughts—checkers

draw—marijuana

dual carriageway—divided highway (four lanes)

Dubs—people from Dublin

eejit—moron

en suite—bathroom attached to room

face flannel—washcloth

fanny—vagina

fell—hill or high plain
first floor—second floor
fluthered—drunk
flutter—a bet
football—Gaelic football
fortnight—two weeks
full monty—The whole shebang. Everything.
GAA—Gaelic Athletic Association
gallery—balcony
gammon—ham
gangway—aisle
gargle—to have an alcoholic drink
give way—yield
giving off—complaining
glen—narrow valley
gobsmacked—astounded
goods wagon—freight truck
grand—good, well ("How are you?", "I'm grand, thanks")
gurrier—hooligan
half eight—8:30 (not 7:30)
heath—open treeless land
holiday—vacation
homely—likable or cozy
hoover—vacuum cleaner
hurling—Irish field hockey/rugby
ice lolly—popsicle
interval—intermission
ironmonger—hardware store
jacket potato—baked potato
jars—drinks (alcohol)
jelly—Jell-O
jumble—sale, rummage sale
jumper—sweater
just a tick—just a second
keep your pecker up—be brave
kipper—smoked herring
knackered—exhausted
knickers—ladies' panties
knocking shop—brothel
knock up—wake up or visit
ladybird—ladybug
left luggage—baggage check
let—rent
listed—protected historic building
lorry—truck
mac—mackintosh (trench) coat

mangetout—snow peas
mate—buddy (boy or girl)
mean—stingy
mews—courtyard stables, often used as cottages
minced meat—hamburger
mobile (MOH-bile)—cell phone
Mod cons—modern conveniences
naff—dorky
nappy—diaper
natter—talk and talk
norn iron—Northern Ireland
nought—zero
noughts & crosses—tic-tac-toe
off license—store selling take-away liquor
on offer—on sale
paddywhackery—exagerated Irish accent
paralytic—passed out drunk
pasty—crusted savory (usually meat) pie
pavement—sidewalk
pear-shaped—messed up, gone wrong
petrol—gas
**pissed (rude), paralytic, bevvied,
   wellied, popped up, ratted,
   pissed as a newt**—drunk
pitch—playing field
plaster—Band-Aid
publican—pub manager
pull—to attract romantic attention
punter—partygoer
punter—customer
put a sock in it—shut up
quay—waterside street, ship offloading area
queue—line
queue up—line up
quid—pound (money in Northern Ireland, worth about $1.80)
RTE—Irish Republic's broadcast network
ramps—speed bumps
randy—horny
redundant, made—fired
return ticket—round-trip
ring up—call (telephone)
roundabout—traffic circle
rubber—eraser
sanitary towel—sanitary pad
sausage roll—sausage wrapped in a flaky pastry
Scotch egg—hard-boiled egg wrapped in sausage meat

self-catering—apartment with kitchen
sellotape—Scotch tape
serviette—napkin
shag—intercourse
single ticket—one-way ticket
skip—Dumpster
slag—to ridicule, tease
smalls—underwear
snogging—kissing, cuddling
solicitor—lawyer
spanner—wrench
spend a penny—urinate
starkers—buck naked
starters—appetizers
stick—criticism
stone—14 pounds (weight)
strand—beach
stroppy—bad-tempered
subway—underground pedestrian passageway
sultanas—golden raisins
surgical spirit—rubbing alcohol
sort out—figure out
swede—rutabaga
take the mickey—tease
tatty—worn out or tacky
taxi rank—taxi stand
theatre—live stage
tick—a check mark
tight as a Scotsman—cheapskate (water-tight)
tights—panty hose
tip—public dump
tipper lorry—dump truck
tin—can
to let—for rent
top up—refill a drink
torch—flashlight
towpath—path along a river
Travellers—itinerants, once known as Tinkers
turf accountant—bookie
twitcher—bird watcher
underground—subway
verge—grassy edge of road
victualler—butcher
wain—small child
way out—exit
Wellingtons, wellies—rubber boots

wee—urinate
whacked—exhausted
whinge (rhymes with hinge)—whine
witter on—gab and gab
your man—that guy, this guy
zebra crossing—crosswalk
zed—the letter z

APPENDIX

Let's Talk Telephones

Here's a primer on making phone calls. For information specific to Ireland, see "Telephones" in the Introduction.

Making Calls within a European Country: About half of all European countries use area codes (like we do); the other half uses a direct-dial system without area codes.

To make calls within a country that uses a direct-dial system (Belgium, the Czech Republic, Denmark, France, Italy, Portugal, Norway, Spain, and Switzerland), dial the same number whether you're calling across the country or across the street.

In countries that use area codes (such as Austria, Britain, —the Republic of Ireland, Finland, Germany, the Netherlands, and Sweden), dial the local number when calling within a city, and add the area code if calling long-distance within the country.

Making International Calls: Always start with the international access code (011 if you're calling from the U.S. or Canada, 00 from Europe), then dial the country code of the country you're calling (see chart below).

What you dial next depends on the phone system of the country you're calling. If the country uses area codes, drop the initial 0 of the area code, then dial the rest of the number.

Countries that use direct-dial systems (no area codes) vary in how they're accessed internationally by phone. For instance, if you're making an international call to the Czech Republic, Denmark, Italy, Norway, Portugal, or Spain, simply dial the international access code, country code, and the local phone number. But if you're calling Belgium, France, or Switzerland, drop the initial zero of the phone number. Example: To call a Paris hotel (tel. 01 47 05 49 15) from Dublin, dial 00, 33 (France's country code), then 1 47 05 49 15 (phone number without the initial zero).

European Calling Chart

Just smile and dial, using this key:
AC = Area Code, LN = Local Number.

European Country	Calling long distance within ...	Calling from the U.S.A./ Canada to ...	Calling from a European country to ...
Austria	AC + LN	011 + 43 + AC (without the initial zero) + LN	00 + 43 + AC (without the initial zero) + LN
Belgium	LN	011 + 32 + LN (without initial zero)	00 + 32 + LN (without initial zero)
Britain	AC + LN	011 + 44 + AC (without initial zero) + LN	00 + 44 + AC (without initial zero) + LN
Croatia	AC + LN	011 + 385 + AC (without initial zero) + LN	00 + 385 + AC (without initial zero) + LN
Czech Republic	LN	011 + 420 + LN	00 + 420 + LN
Denmark	LN	011 + 45 + LN	00 + 45 + LN
Finland	AC + LN	011 + 358 + AC (without initial zero) + LN	00 + 358 + AC (without initial zero) + LN
France	LN	011 + 33 + LN (without initial zero)	00 + 33 + LN (without initial zero)
Germany	AC + LN	011 + 49 + AC (without initial zero) + LN	00 + 49 + AC (without initial zero) + LN
Greece	LN	011 + 30 + LN	00 + 30 + LN
Hungary	06 + AC + LN	011 + 36 + AC + LN	00 + 36 + AC + LN
Ireland	AC + LN	011 + 353 + AC (without initial zero) + LN	00 + 353 + AC (without initial zero) + LN
Italy	LN	011 + 39 + LN	00 + 39 + LN

European Country	Calling long distance within ...	Calling from the U.S.A./ Canada to ...	Calling from a European country to ...
Netherlands	AC + LN	011 + 31 + AC (without initial zero) + LN	00 + 31 + AC (without initial zero) + LN
Norway	LN	011 + 47 + LN	00 + 47 + LN
Poland	AC + LN	011 + 48 + AC (without initial zero) + LN	00 + 48 + AC (without initial zero) + LN
Portugal	LN	011 + 351 + LN	00 + 351 + LN
Slovakia	AC + LN	011 + 421 + AC (without initial zero) + LN	00 + 421 + AC (without initial zero) + LN
Slovenia	AC + LN	011 + 386 + AC (without initial zero) + LN	00 + 386 + AC (without initial zero) + LN
Spain	LN	011 + 34 + LN	00 + 34 + LN
Sweden	AC + LN	011 + 46 + AC (without initial zero) + LN	00 + 46 + AC (without initial zero) + LN
Switzerland	LN	011 + 41 + LN (without initial zero)	00 + 41 + LN (without initial zero)
Turkey	AC (if no initial zero is included, add one) + LN	011 + 90 + AC (without initial zero) + LN	00 + 90 + AC (without initial zero) + LN

- The instructions above apply whether you're calling a fixed phone or mobile phone.
- The international access codes (the first numbers you dial when making an international call) are 011 if you're calling from the U.S.A./Canada, or 00 if you're calling from anywhere in Europe.
- To call the U.S.A. or Canada from Europe, dial 00, then 1 (the country code for the U.S.A. and Canada), then the area code and number. In short, 00 + 1 + AC + LN = Hi, Mom!

Country Codes

After you've dialed the international access code (00 if you're calling from Europe, 011 if calling from the U.S. or Canada), dial the code of the country you're calling.

Austria—43	Italy—39
Belgium—32	Morocco—212
Britain—44	Netherlands—31
Canada—1	Norway—47
Croatia—385	Poland—48
Czech Rep.—420	Portugal—351
Denmark—45	Slovakia—421
Estonia—372	Slovenia—386
Finland—358	Spain—34
France—33	Sweden—46
Germany—49	Switzerland—41
Gibraltar—350	Turkey—90
Greece—30	U.S.A.—1
Ireland—353	

Dial Away...

Note that the Republic of Ireland (country code: 353) has a different country code than Northern Ireland, which is part of Britain (country code: 44). The Republic of Ireland has a special way to call Northern Ireland: dial 048, then the local number without the area code.

From the U.S./Canada to the Republic of Ireland: Dial 011-353, then the area code without its initial 0, then the local number.

From European countries (including Northern Ireland) to the Republic of Ireland: Dial 00-353, then the area code without its initial 0, then the local number.

From the U.S./Canada to Northern Ireland: Dial 011-44-28 (28 is Northern Ireland's area code without its initial 0), then the local number.

From the Republic of Ireland to Northern Ireland: Dial 048, then the local number. (In this case, Northern Ireland's area code, 028, is omitted entirely.)

From any European Country (except the Republic of Ireland) to Northern Ireland: Dial 00-44-28 (Northern Ireland's area code without its initial 0), then the local number.

From Anywhere in Ireland (north or south) to the U.S or Canada: 00-1, then the area code and local number.

Useful Numbers in the Republic of Ireland

Emergency: tel. 999

Operator Assistance: tel. 10 for Ireland, tel. 114 to call outside Ireland
Directory Assistance within Ireland: tel. 11811 (free from phone booth, or 34p from anywhere else)
International Info: tel. 11818 (free from phone booth)
    Note that calls beginning with 1-800 are free throughout Ireland, but 1-850 calls cost the same as local calls.

Useful Numbers in Northern Ireland
Emergency (police and ambulance): tel. 999
Operator Assistance: tel. 100 for Britain, tel. 155 to call outside Britain
Directory Assistance within Britain: tel. 192 (20p from phone booth, otherwise £1.50)
International Info: tel. 153 (20p from phone booth, otherwise £1.50)

U.S. Embassies
In the Republic of Ireland: 42 Elgin Road, Dublin, tel. 01/668-7122 or 01/668-8777, www.usembassy.ie
In Northern Ireland: Danesfort House, 223 Stranmillis Road, tel. 028/9038-6100, www.usembassy.org.uk

Airlines
These are phone numbers for the Republic of Ireland. (To call the special 1-800 numbers from the U.S., dial 011-353, then the 800 number without the initial 1).
Aer Arann: tel. 01/814-1058 (www.aerarann.com)
Aer Lingus: tel. 01/886-8888 (www.aerlingus.com)
American: tel. 01/602-0550 (www.aa.com)
British Airways: tel. 1-800-626-747 (www.ba.com)
bmi british midland: tel. 01/407-3036 (www.flybmi.com)
Continental Airlines: tel. 1-890-925-252 (www.continental.com)
Delta: tel. 1-800-768-080 (www.delta.com)
Lufthansa: tel. 01/844-5544 (www.lufthansa.ie)
Ryanair (cheap fares): tel. 01/609-7878 (www.ryanair.com)
Scandinavian Airlines System (SAS): tel. 01/844-5888 (www.scandinavian.net)
United Airlines: tel. 01/819-1760 (www.united.com)
Virgin Atlantic: tel. 01/500-5500 (www.virginatlantic.com)

Dublin Car-Rental Agencies
Avis: 35-39 Old Kilmainham Road, tel. 01/605-7502, airport tel. 01/605-7500, www.avis.ie
Hertz: 151 South Circular Road, tel. 01/660-2255, airport tel. 01/844-5466, www.hertz.com

Budget: 151 Lower Drumcondra Road, tel. 01/837-9611, airport tel. 01/844-5150, www.budget.com

Europcar: 2 Haddington Road, tel. 01/614-2840, airport tel. 01/812-0410, www.europcar.ie

Public Holidays and Festivals in 2006

This is a partial list of holidays and festivals. Some dates have yet to be set. For more information, contact **Tourism Ireland** in New York (tel. 800-223-6470 or 212/418-0800, www.tourismireland.com, info.us@tourismireland.com) and check out these Web sites: www.whatsonwhen.com, www.whatsgoingon.com, and www.festivals.com.

Jan 1–2	New Year's weekend (banks closed on Mon)
March 15–19	St. Patrick's Day celebration throughout Ireland (parades, drunkenness, 5-day festival in Dublin, www.stpatricksday.ie)
April 14	Good Friday (banks closed)
April 16–17	Easter Sunday and Monday
April 18–23	Pan Celtic International Festival, Tralee, Kerry (festival rotates locations every year, www.panceltic.com)
May 1	May Day (some closures), Ireland and U.K.
June 5	June Holiday (banks closed), Ireland and U.K.
June 16	Bloomsday (James Joyce festival, www.jamesjoyce.ie), Dublin
July 12	Battle of the Boyne anniversary (Protestant marches, protests), Northern Ireland
July 17–30	Galway Arts Festival, Galway (www.galwayartsfestival.com)
Aug 7	August Holiday (banks closed), Ireland
Aug 8–15	Féile an Phobail, West Belfast Irish cultural festival, Northern Ireland (www.feilebelfast.com)
Aug 28	Late Summer Holiday (banks closed), U.K. only
2nd weekend in Aug	Dingle Races (boat races), Dingle
2nd weekend in Aug	Puck Fair, Killorglin, Kerry ("Ireland's Oldest Fair" and drink-fest, www.puckfair.ie)
3rd weekend in Aug	Dingle Regatta, Dingle
mid–Aug	Rose of Tralee International Festival, Tralee

2006

		JANUARY				
S	**M**	**T**	**W**	**T**	**F**	**S**
1	2	3	4	5	6	7
8	9	10	11	12	13	14
15	16	17	18	19	20	21
22	23	24	25	26	27	28
29	30	31				

		FEBRUARY				
S	**M**	**T**	**W**	**T**	**F**	**S**
			1	2	3	4
5	6	7	8	9	10	11
12	13	14	15	16	17	18
19	20	21	22	23	24	25
26	27	28				

		MARCH				
S	**M**	**T**	**W**	**T**	**F**	**S**
			1	2	3	4
5	6	7	8	9	10	11
12	13	14	15	16	17	18
19	20	21	22	23	24	25
26	27	28	29	30	31	

		APRIL				
S	**M**	**T**	**W**	**T**	**F**	**S**
						1
2	3	4	5	6	7	8
9	10	11	12	13	14	15
16	17	18	19	20	21	22
23/30	24	25	26	27	28	29

		MAY				
S	**M**	**T**	**W**	**T**	**F**	**S**
	1	2	3	4	5	6
7	8	9	10	11	12	13
14	15	16	17	18	19	20
21	22	23	24	25	26	27
28	29	30	31			

		JUNE				
S	**M**	**T**	**W**	**T**	**F**	**S**
				1	2	3
4	5	6	7	8	9	10
11	12	13	14	15	16	17
18	19	20	21	22	23	24
25	26	27	28	29	30	

		JULY				
S	**M**	**T**	**W**	**T**	**F**	**S**
						1
2	3	4	5	6	7	8
9	10	11	12	13	14	15
16	17	18	19	20	21	22
23/30	24/31	25	26	27	28	29

		AUGUST				
S	**M**	**T**	**W**	**T**	**F**	**S**
		1	2	3	4	5
6	7	8	9	10	11	12
13	14	15	16	17	18	19
20	21	22	23	24	25	26
27	28	29	30	31		

		SEPTEMBER				
S	**M**	**T**	**W**	**T**	**F**	**S**
					1	2
3	4	5	6	7	8	9
10	11	12	13	14	15	16
17	18	19	20	21	22	23
24	25	26	27	28	29	30

		OCTOBER				
S	**M**	**T**	**W**	**T**	**F**	**S**
1	2	3	4	5	6	7
8	9	10	11	12	13	14
15	16	17	18	19	20	21
22	23	24	25	26	27	28
29	30	31				

		NOVEMBER				
S	**M**	**T**	**W**	**T**	**F**	**S**
			1	2	3	4
5	6	7	8	9	10	11
12	13	14	15	16	17	18
19	20	21	22	23	24	25
26	27	28	29	30		

		DECEMBER				
S	**M**	**T**	**W**	**T**	**F**	**S**
					1	2
3	4	5	6	7	8	9
10	11	12	13	14	15	16
17	18	19	20	21	22	23
24/31	25	26	27	28	29	30

Late Aug–early Sept	Blessing of the Boats (maritime festival), Dingle
Sept 28–Oct 1	Galway Oyster Festival (4 days), Galway (www.galwayoysterfest.com)
Oct 30	October Holiday (banks closed), Ireland
Late Oct	Belfast Queens Festival (music, 12 days), Belfast (www.belfastfestival.com)
Dec 25	Christmas holiday, Ireland and U.K.
Dec 26	St. Stephen's Day (religious festival), Ireland; Boxing Day, U.K.

Dublin Climate

The first line is the average low, the second line is the average high, and the third line is the number of days with no rain. Note that temperatures are moderate throughout the country, so use the Dublin temperatures listed below as a model. For more detailed weather statistics for destinations throughout Ireland (as well as the rest of the world), check www.worldclimate.com.

J	F	M	A	M	J	J	A	S	O	N	D
34°	35°	37°	39°	43°	48°	52°	51°	48°	43°	39°	37°
46°	47°	51°	55°	60°	65°	67°	67°	63°	57°	51°	47°
18	18	21	19	21	19	18	19	18	20	18	17

Numbers and Stumblers

- Europeans write a few of their numbers differently than we do. 1 = 1, 4 = 4, 7 = 7. Learn the difference or miss your train.
- In Europe, dates appear as day/month/year, so Christmas is 25/12/06.
- Commas are decimal points and decimals commas. A dollar and a half is $1,50, and there are 5.280 feet in a mile.
- When pointing, use your whole hand, palm down.
- When counting with fingers, start with your thumb. If you hold up your first finger to request one item, you'll probably get two.
- What Americans call the second floor of a building is the first floor in Europe.
- Europeans keep the left "lane" open for passing on escalators and moving sidewalks. Keep to the right.

Metric Conversion (approximate)

1 inch = 25 millimeters	32°F = 0°C
1 foot = 0.3 meter	82°F = about 28°C
1 yard = 0.9 meter	1 ounce = 28 grams
1 mile = 1.6 kilometers	1 kilogram = 2.2 pounds
1 centimeter = 0.4 inch	1 quart = 0.95 liter
1 meter = 39.4 inches	1 square yard = 0.8 square meter
1 kilometer = .62 mile	1 acre = 0.4 hectare

Converting Temperatures: Fahrenheit and Celsius

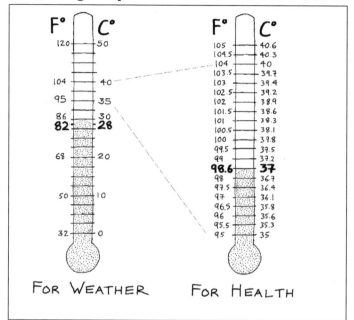

Europe takes its temperature using the Celsius scale, while we opt for Fahrenheit. For weather, remember that 28°C is 82°F—perfect. For health, 37°C is just right.

Making Your Hotel Reservation

Most hotel managers know basic "hotel English." Faxing or e-mailing are the preferred methods for reserving a room. They're more accurate than telephoning and much faster than writing a letter. Use this handy form for your fax or find it online at www.ricksteves.com/reservation. Photocopy and fax away.

One-Page Fax

To: _____ @ _____
              hotel   *fax*

From: _____ @ _____
              name   *fax*

Today's date: _____/_____/_____
                day   *month*   *year*

Dear Hotel _____ ,
Please make this reservation for me:

Name: _____

Total # of people: _____ # of rooms: _____ # of nights: _____

Arriving: _____/_____/_____ My time of arrival (24-hr clock): _____
          day month year   (I will telephone if I will be late)

Departing: ____/____/____
           day month year

Room(s): Single _____ Double ____ Twin _____ Triple ____ Quad_____

With: Toilet _____ Shower _____ Bath _____ Sink only _____

Special needs: View____ Quiet____ Cheapest ____ Ground Floor ____

Please fax, mail, or e-mail confirmation of my reservation, along with the type of room reserved and the price. Please also inform me of your cancellation policy. After I hear from you, I will quickly send my credit-card information as a deposit to hold the room. Thank you.

_____
Signature

_____
Name

_____
Address

_____
City   *State*   *Zip Code*   *Country*

_____
E-mail Address

INDEX

CREDITS

Contributor

Gene Openshaw

Gene is the co-author of eight Rick Steves books. For this book, he wrote material on Europe's art, history, and contemporary culture. When not traveling, Gene enjoys composing music, recovering from his 1973 trip to Europe with Rick, and living everyday life with his wife and daughter.

Images

Location	Photographer
Republic of Ireland (full-page): Cliffs of Moher, near Galway	Rick Steves
Dublin: Dublin's Ha' Penny Bridge	Pat O'Connor
Near Dublin: Newgrange, in Valley of the Boyne	Pat O'Connor
Kilkenny and Cashel: Rock of Cashel	Pat O'Connor
Waterford and County Wexford: Waterford's Waterfront	Pat O'Connor
Kinsale and Cobh: Kinsale's Summer Cove Area	Pat O'Connor
Kenmare and Ring of Kerry: Ring of Kerry	Pat O'Connor
Dingle Peninsula: An Blascoad Mór (Great Blasket Island)	Pat O'Connor
Galway: Galway's High Street	Pat O'Connor
Near Galway: Lough Corrib, Connemara	Pat O'Connor
Northern Ireland (full-page): Giant's Causeway, Antrim Coast	Pat O'Connor
Belfast: Belfast's Donegall Square and City Hall	Pat O'Connor
Portrush and Antrim Coast: Portrush Harbor	Pat O'Connor
Derry and County Donegal: Derry's Bogside Neighborhood	Pat O'Connor

Start your trip at
www.ricksteves.com

Rick Steves' website is packed with over 3,000 pages of timely travel information. It's also your gateway to getting FREE monthly travel news from Rick—and more!

Free Monthly European Travel News

Fresh articles on Europe's most interesting destinations and happenings. Rick will even send you an e-mail every month (often direct from Europe) with his latest discoveries!

Timely Travel Tips

Rick Steves' best money-and-stress-saving tips on trip planning, packing, transportation, hotels, health, safety, finances, hurdling the language barrier...and more.

Travelers' Graffiti Wall

Candid advice and opinions from thousands of travelers on everything listed above, plus whatever topics are hot at the moment (discount flights, packing tips, scams...you name it).

Rick's Annual Guide to European Railpasses

The clearest, most comprehensive guide to the confusing array of railpass options out there, and how to choo-choose the railpass that best fits your itinerary and budget. Then you can order your railpass (and get a bunch of great freebies) online from us!

Great Gear at the Rick Steves Travel Store

Enjoy bargains on Rick's guidebooks, planning maps and TV series DVDs—and on his custom-designed carry-on bags, wheeled bags, day bags and light-packing accessories.

Rick Steves Tours

Every year more than 6,000 lucky travelers explore Europe on a Rick Steves tour. Learn more about our 30 different one-to-three-week itineraries, read uncensored feedback from our tour alums, and sign up for your dream trip online!

Rick on Radio and TV

Read the scripts and run clips from public television's "Rick Steves' Europe" and public radio's "Travel with Rick Steves."

Respect for Your Privacy

Ordering online from us is secure. When you buy something from us, join a tour, or subscribe to Rick's free monthly travel news e-mails, we promise to never share your name, information, or e-mail address with anyone else. You won't be spammed!

Have fun raising your Travel I.Q. at
www.ricksteves.com

Travel smart...carry on!

The latest generation of Rick Steves' carry-on travel bags is easily the best—benefiting from two decades of on-the-road attention to what really matters: maximum quality and strength; practical, flexible features; and no unnecessary frills. You won't find a better value anywhere!

Convertible, expandable, and carry-on-size:
Rick Steves' Back Door Bag $99

This is the same bag that Rick Steves lives out of for three months every summer. It's made of rugged water-resistant 1000 denier Cordura nylon, and best of all, it converts easily from a smart-looking suitcase to a handy backpack with comfortably-curved shoulder straps and a padded waistbelt.

This roomy, versatile 9" x 21" x 14" bag has a large 2600 cubic-inch main compartment, plus three outside pockets (small, medium and huge) that are perfect for often-used items. And the cinch-tight compression straps will keep your load compact and close to your back—not sagging like a sack of potatoes.

Wishing you had even more room to bring home souvenirs? Pull open the full-perimeter expando-zipper and its capacity jumps from 2600 to 3000 cubic inches. When you want to use it as a suitcase or check it as luggage (required when "expanded"), the straps and belt hide away in a zippered compartment in the back.

Attention travelers under 5'4" tall: This bag also comes in an inch-shorter version, for a compact-friendlier fit between the waistbelt and shoulder straps.

Convenient, expandable, and carry-on-size:
Rick Steves' Wheeled Bag $129

At 9" x 21" x 14" our sturdy Rick Steves' Wheeled Bag is rucksack-soft in front, but the rest is lined with a hard ABS-lexan shell to give maximum protection to your belongings. We've spared no expense on moving parts, splurging on an extra-long button-release handle and big, tough inline skate wheels for easy rolling on rough surfaces.

Wishing you had even more room to bring home souvenirs? Pull open the full-perimeter expando-zipper and its capacity jumps from 2600 to 3000 cubic inches.

Rick Steves' Wheeled Bag has exactly the same three-outside-pocket configuration as our Back Door Bag, plus a handy "add-a-bag" strap and full lining.

Our Back Door Bags and Wheeled Bags come in black, navy, blue spruce, evergreen and merlot.

For great deals on a wide selection of travel goodies, begin your next trip at the Rick Steves Travel Store!

Visit the Rick Steves Travel Store at
www.ricksteves.com

FREE-SPIRITED TOURS FROM

Rick Steves

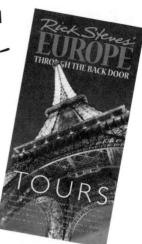

Small Groups
Great Guides
No Grumps

Best of Europe ▪ **Eastern Europe**
Italy ▪ **Village Italy** ▪ **South Italy**
France ▪ **Britain** ▪ **Ireland**
Heart of France ▪ **South of France**
Turkey ▪ **Spain/Portugal**
Germany/Austria/Switzerland
Scandinavia ▪ **London** ▪ **Paris** ▪ **Rome**
Venice ▪ **Florence…and much more!**

Looking for a one, two, or three-week tour that's run in the Rick Steves style? Check out Rick Steves' educational, experiential tours of Europe.

Rick's tours are an excellent value compared to "mainstream" tours. Here's a taste of what you'll get…

- **Small groups:** With just 24-28 travelers, you'll go where typical groups of 40-50 can only dream.

- **Big buses:** You'll travel in a full-size 40-50 seat bus, with plenty of empty seats for you to spread out and be comfortable.

- **Great guides:** Our guides are hand-picked by Rick Steves for their wealth of knowledge and giddy enthusiasm for Europe.

- **No tips or kickbacks:** To keep your guide and driver 100% focused on giving you the best travel experience, we pay them well—and prohibit them from accepting tips and merchant kickbacks.

- **All sightseeing:** Your tour price includes all group sightseeing, with no hidden extra charges.

- **Central hotels:** You'll stay in Rick's favorite small, characteristic, locally-run hotels in the center of each city, within walking distance of the sights you came to see.

- **Visit www.ricksteves.com:** You'll find all our latest itineraries, dates and prices, be able to reserve online, and request a free copy of our "Rick Steves Tour Experience" DVD!

Rick Steves' Europe Through the Back Door, Inc.
130 Fourth Avenue North, PO Box 2009, Edmonds, WA 98020 USA
Phone: (425) 771-8303 ▪ Fax: (425) 771-0833 ▪ www.ricksteves.com

Rick Steves

More *Savvy*. More *Surprising*. More *Fun*.

COUNTRY GUIDES 2006

England
France
Germany & Austria
Great Britain
Ireland
Italy
Portugal
Scandinavia
Spain
Switzerland

CITY GUIDES 2006

Amsterdam, Bruges & Brussels
Florence & Tuscany
London
Paris
Prague & The Czech Republic
Provence & The French Riviera
Rome
Venice

BEST OF GUIDES

Best of Eastern Europe
Best of Europe

As the #1 authority on European travel, Rick gives you inside information on what to visit, where to stay, and how to get there—economically and hassle-free.

www.ricksteves.com

PHRASE BOOKS
& DICTIONARIES

French
French, Italian & German
German
Italian
Portuguese
Spanish

MORE EUROPE FROM RICK STEVES

Easy Access Europe
Europe 101
Europe Through the Back Door
Postcards from Europe

RICK STEVES' EUROPE DVDs

All 43 Shows 2000-2005
Britain
Eastern Europe
France & Benelux
Germany, The Swiss Alps & Travel Skills
Ireland
Italy
Spain & Portugal

PLANNING MAPS

Britain & Ireland
Europe
France
Germany, Austria & Switzerland
Italy
Spain & Portugal

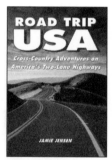

For a complete list of Rick Steves' guidebooks, see page 10.

Avalon Travel Publishing
1400 65th Street, Suite 250
Emeryville, CA 94608

AVALON
publishing group incorporated

Avalon Travel Publishing is a division of Avalon Publishing Group

Text © 2006 by Rick Steves.
Maps © 2006 by Europe Through the Back Door.

Printed in the United States of America by Worzalla.
First printing January 2006.

Thanks to Rozanne Stringer for her writing on the Celts, Celtic Tiger, St. Brendan, and Irish art. Thanks also to Gene Openshaw and Mike Kelly for their help.

For the latest on Rick's lectures, guidebooks, tours, public radio show, and public television series, contact Europe Through the Back Door, Box 2009, Edmonds, WA 98020, tel. 425/771-8303, fax 425/771-0833, www.ricksteves.com, rick@ricksteves.com.

ISBN(10) 1-56691-726-3
ISBN(13) 978-1-56691-726-1
ISSN 1538-1587

Europe Through the Back Door Managing Editor: Risa Laib
ETBD Editors: Kevin Yip, Jennifer Hauseman, Cameron Hewitt
Avalon Travel Publishing Editor and Series Manager: Patrick Collins
Avalon Travel Publishing Project Editor: Madhu Prasher
Copy Editor: Chris Hayhurst
Indexer: Stephen Callahan
Production & Typesetting: Patrick David Barber, Holly McGuire
Interior Design: Jane Musser, Laura Mazer, Amber Pirker
Cover Design: Kari Gim, Laura Mazer
Maps & Graphics: David C. Hoerlein, Laura VanDeventer, Lauren Mills, Mike Morgenfeld
Front Matter Color Photos: p. i and p. iv, © Pat O'Connor
Cover Photos: front image, Newman's Mall. © Richard Cummins McCormack / Lonely Planet Images; back image: Beaghmore Stone Circles © Gareth McCormack / Lonely Planet Images